Valerie Wilson's World

Valerie Wilson's World

The Top Hotels & Resorts
Second Edition

Valerie Ann Wilson

*Dear Daisy —
With best wishes,
Valerie*

Publisher and Editor-in-Chief
Valerie Ann Wilson

Editor
Nancy DePalma

Authors
Valerie Ann Wilson & Nancy DePalma

Author's Acknowledgements

Valerie Wilson's World…The Top Hotels & Resorts could not have been possible without the dedication and enthusiasm of many talented individuals. I am extremely grateful to all of the hotel general managers, senior executives at hotel companies, and the numerous management teams for encouraging me to issue a second edition and for wholeheartedly supporting the project. With the exception of the cover and the photo collage pages, all of the photography was graciously provided by the featured properties. Special thanks go to Kurt Wallace of KW Graphics, who brought the photography and text together with his imaginative designs. Most importantly, I offer my sincere gratitude to Nancy DePalma for her collaboration. She has literally been my right hand. This book would not have been possible without her keen editorial sense, invaluable insight, tireless energy, and commitment to perfection. Together, she and I crafted a lyrical writing style that indeed brings the story alive on each page.

The pictures on the jacket cover and the photo collage pages at the beginning and end of the book are personal photographs taken by me highlighting some of my favorite places around the world, with a couple of photographs taken by my daughters, Jennifer Wilson-Buttigieg and Kimberly Wilson Wetty.

All photographs are described clockwise from left:

Jacket cover: African Elephant • San Giorgio Maggiore, Venice • Beach in French Polynesia, Bora Bora • Taj Mahal, Agra

Jacket back: Ancient Library of Celsus, Ephesus, Turkey • Sunset on Zambezi River, Zambia • Beach in the Maldives by Jennifer Wilson-Buttigieg • Sahara Desert, Morocco

Page 1: Sailing into New York Harbor • Houses of Parliament, London • Eiffel Tower, Paris • Gondola, Venice

Page 2: Parthenon at the Acropolis, Athens • Statue of Liberty, New York by Kimberly Wilson Wetty • Caribbean Beach by Jennifer Wilson-Buttigieg • Hong Kong Harbour

Page 400: Blue Mosque, Istanbul • Orca Whale, Alaska • A Pyramid of Giza, Egypt • Sunset, New Zealand • Red Square, Moscow • Caribbean Beach

First published in the United States in 2001
Second edition published in the United States in 2012
Copyright 2012 by Valerie Ann Wilson and Nancy DePalma
All rights reserved. No part of this publication may be reproduced, stored in a retrieval system, or transmitted by any means, electronic or mechanical, photocopying, recording or otherwise, without prior permission in writing from the publisher.

Published by Valerie Wilson Publications
475 Park Avenue South, New York, New York 10016

ISBN: 978-0-615-51032-3
Printed in China by Toppan

INTRODUCTION

Is there anything as innocent and pure as young love? I was only 16 when it first struck me, though it wasn't a boy who stole my heart - it was the allure of travel. I boarded a train from Waterloo, Iowa for a trip to the United States Naval Academy in Annapolis, Maryland, but I might as well have been visiting the moon with the excitement and anticipation I felt that day. In the many years that have followed, I have been everywhere from Agra to Zambia, and many places in between, but my love affair with the world and my passion for travel has never waned. For me, nothing quite replicates the feeling of boarding a plane, embarking on a cruise, or stepping inside a hotel.

The very best hotels are rather like heaven. Blessedly free of mundane concerns, hotels envelop you in their luxurious environs. Suddenly, it seems rather normal to take a bath while wild game graze outside your window or dine on Michelin-starred cuisine for breakfast. She may have been a child, but Eloise certainly had it right by living in a hotel!

Whether you gaze upon the sparkling sea from your terrace or enjoy postcard-perfect views of ancient ruins or iconic landmarks, truly great hotels and resorts bring you the world. Some have long, fascinating histories filled with stories of glittering balls and scandalous affairs. Others, long on style, are just beginning to share their stories, so go ahead and be a main character.

What makes a great hotel? Yes, distinctive destinations, superior locations, sensational style, and extraordinary service are all definitions of luxury, but to me, it is not complete without a certain "joie de vivre."

Within these pages you will find my tribute to 400 of the world's finest hotels and resorts. You might not think that contemporary towers and country estates have much in common, but for me, these properties represent the best of their countries, cities, and towns.

Join me on this journey as we skip across the globe visiting my favorite spots and let me tell you my stories.

Welcome to my world – again!

Valerie

With grateful appreciation, I dedicate this second edition to my daughters, Jennifer and Kimberly.
They share my passion for travel and commitment to excellence.

About Valerie Wilson Travel

It is often said that "necessity is the mother of invention," and that adage certainly holds true when it comes to Valerie Wilson Travel, Inc. As an American living in London and an avid traveler, Valerie Ann Wilson had difficulty finding a travel advisor who had the breadth of knowledge and delivered the high level of personalized service she expected. She returned to New York in the summer of 1980 and on September 8, 1981 opened the doors of Valerie Wilson Travel in the former Pan Am Building. While there were only three people and a part-time bookkeeper in the beginning, today Valerie Wilson Travel employs nearly 300 travel consultants and associate agents with approximately $300 million in annual sales. Thirty years later, the company is now one of the largest privately owned and family managed travel consulting firms in the United States. Travel Weekly ranked VWT as the 29th largest U.S. agency in 2011.

Headquartered in New York City on Park Avenue South, Valerie Wilson Travel now has 15 locations running from Maine to Florida and reaching across the country to Chicago and California. The team consists of a diverse and highly specialized network of "lifestyle consultants." Each advisor brings a wealth of knowledge and depth of experience to the company.

Dedication to the founding principles of integrity, honesty, and customer service has made Valerie Wilson Travel an industry leader. The Power of Access™ guarantees clients value added amenities, exclusive rates, VIP treatment, exceptional service, and memorable experiences. Valerie Wilson Travel is a proud and active contributing member of Virtuoso, the leading luxury travel organization networking with nearly 300 agencies and 1,200 preferred suppliers worldwide.

Valerie Wilson Travel services a global clientele for both their personal travel and business needs. VWT handles companies and organizations and the travel management requirements of industries as diverse as fashion, publishing, finance, media, pharmaceuticals, and not-for-profits.

Valerie Wilson Travel has a strong second generation management in place, as Jennifer Wilson-Buttigieg has been with the company over 20 years and Kimberly Wilson Wetty over 16 years. Today, as Co-Owners and Co-Presidents, they jointly manage Valerie Wilson Travel with Founder and Chairman Valerie Ann Wilson.

Valerie Wilson Travel, Inc.
475 Park Avenue South
New York, New York 10016
Telephone: 212-532-3400
www.valeriewilsontravel.com

CONTENTS

EUROPE

AUSTRIA
Fuschl
Schloss Fuschl Resort & Spa — 17
Salzburg
Hotel Goldener Hirsch — 18
Hotel Sacher Salzburg — 19
Vienna
Hotel Imperial — 20
Hotel Sacher Wien — 21

BELGIUM
Brussels
Rocco Forte Hotel Amigo — 22

CZECH REPUBLIC
Prague
Four Seasons Hotel Prague — 23
Mandarin Oriental, Prague — 24
Rocco Forte The Augustine — 25

ENGLAND
Ascot
Coworth Park — 26
Chester
The Chester Grosvenor and Spa — 27
Hampshire
Four Seasons Hotel Hampshire — 28
London
Berkeley — 29
Claridge's — 30
The Connaught — 31
The Dorchester — 32
45 Park Lane — 33
Four Seasons Hotel London at Park Lane — 34
The Lanesborough — 35
Mandarin Oriental Hyde Park, London — 36
The Milestone Hotel — 37
The Ritz London — 38
Rocco Forte Brown's Hotel — 39
The Savoy — 40
New Milton
Chewton Glen — 41

FRANCE
Les Baux de Provence
Oustau de Baumanière — 42
Biarritz
Hotel du Palais — 43
Bordeaux
Grand Hôtel de Bordeaux & Spa — 44
Cannes
InterContinental Carlton Cannes — 45
Cap d'Antibes
Hôtel du Cap-Eden-Roc — 46
Éze
Château de la Chèvre d'Or — 47
Paris
Hotel Le Bristol — 48
Four Seasons Hotel George V, Paris — 49
Mandarin Oriental, Paris — 50
Le Meurice — 51
Park Hyatt Paris-Vendome — 52
Hôtel Plaza Athénée — 53
Ritz Paris — 54
Le Royal Monceau-Raffles Paris — 55
Shangri-La Hotel, Paris — 56
Saint-Tropez
Byblos — 57
Vence
Château Saint-Martin & Spa — 58

GERMANY
Baden-Baden
Brenners Park-Hotel & Spa — 59
Berlin
Hotel Adlon Kempinski Berlin — 60
The Regent Berlin — 61
The Ritz-Carlton, Berlin — 62
Rocco Forte Hotel de Rome — 63
Dresden
Hotel Taschenbergpalais Kempinski Dresden — 64
Düsseldorf
Breidenbacher Hof — 65
Frankfurt
Rocco Forte Villa Kennedy — 66
Munich
Mandarin Oriental, Munich — 67
Rocco Forte The Charles Hotel — 68

GREECE
Athens
Hotel Grande Bretagne — 69
Costa Navarino
The Romanos — 70
Crete
Blue Palace — 71

CONTENTS

Mykonos
  Mykonos Blu — 72
Santorini
  Mystique — 73
  Vedema — 74

HUNGARY
Budapest
  Four Seasons Hotel Gresham Palace Budapest — 75

IRELAND
Cong
  Ashford Castle — 76
Dublin
  Four Seasons Hotel Dublin — 77
  The Merrion Hotel — 78
Enniskerry
  The Ritz-Carlton Powerscourt — 79

ITALY
Capri
  Hotel Caesar Augustus — 80
  Capri Palace Hotel & Spa — 81
Fiesole
  Villa San Michele — 82
Florence
  Four Seasons Hotel Firenze — 83
  Rocco Forte Hotel Savoy — 84
  The St. Regis Florence — 85
  The Westin Excelsior, Florence — 86
Lake Como
  Villa d'Este — 87
Milan
  The Bulgari Hotel Milan — 88
  Four Seasons Hotel Milan — 89
  Park Hyatt Milan — 90
  Hotel Principe di Savoia — 91
Portofino
  Hotel Splendido — 92
Positano
  Le Sirenuse — 93
Ravello
  Hotel Caruso — 94
  Palazzo Sasso — 95
Rome
  Hotel Hassler — 96
  Rocco Forte Hotel de Russie — 97
  The St. Regis Rome — 98
  The Westin Excelsior, Rome — 99

Sardinia
  Cala di Volpe, Hotel Pitrizza & Hotel Romazzino — 100
Sciacca, Sicily
  Rocco Forte Verdura Golf & Spa Resort — 101
Taormina, Sicily
  Grand Hotel Timeo & Villa Sant'Andrea — 102
Venice
  Bauer Il Palazzo — 103
  Hotel Cipriani — 104
  Hotel Danieli — 105
  Hotel Gritti Palace — 106
  Luna Hotel Baglioni — 107

MONACO
Monte Carlo
  Hôtel Metropole — 108
  Hôtel de Paris — 109

THE NETHERLANDS
Amsterdam
  InterContinental Amstel Amsterdam — 110
  Hotel Pulitzer — 111
  Sofitel Legend The Grand — 112

PORTUGAL
Lisbon
  Four Seasons Hotel Ritz Lisbon — 113
Madeira
  Reid's Palace — 114
Sintra
  Penha Longa Hotel Spa & Golf Resort — 115

RUSSIA
Moscow
  Hotel Baltschug Kempinski — 116
  The Ritz-Carlton, Moscow — 117
St. Petersburg
  Grand Hotel Europe — 118
  Rocco Forte Hotel Astoria — 119

SCOTLAND
Auchterarder
  The Gleneagles Hotel — 120
Edinburgh
  Rocco Forte The Balmoral — 121
Turnberry
  Turnberry Resort — 122

CONTENTS

SPAIN
Barcelona
    Hotel Arts Barcelona   123
    Mandarin Oriental, Barcelona   124
    El Palace   125
Madrid
    Hotel Ritz Madrid   126
    Hotel Villa Magna   127
Mallorca
    La Residencia   128
Marbella
    Marbella Club Hotel, Golf Resort & Spa   129

SWEDEN
Stockholm
    Grand Hotel Stockholm   130

SWITZERLAND
Geneva
    Mandarin Oriental, Geneva   131
    Le Richemond   132
Interlaken
    Victoria-Jungfrau Grand Hotel & Spa   133
Lausanne
    Beau-Rivage Palace   134
Lucerne
    Palace Luzern   135
St. Moritz
    Badrutt's Palace Hotel   136
Zurich
    Baur au Lac   137
    The Dolder Grand   138
    Park Hyatt Zurich   139

TURKEY
Istanbul
    Cirağan Palace Hotel Kempinski   140
    Four Seasons Hotel Istanbul,
    Sultanahmet and Bosphorus   141

AFRICA · INDIA
INDIAN OCEAN · MIDDLE EAST

AFRICA

BOTSWANA
Chobe · Moremi Game Reserve · Okavango Delta
    Savute Elephant Camp · Khwai River Lodge ·
    Eagle Island Camp   143
Chobe, Okavango Delta
    Sanctuary Chobe Chilwero & Sanctuary Chief's Camp   144

EAST AFRICA
Kenya
    Fairmont Mount Kenya Safari Club   145
Kenya & Tanzania
Masai Mara & Tarangire National Park
    Sanctuary Olonana & Sanctuary Swala   146
Tanzania
Serengeti
    Singita Grumeti Reserves   147

EGYPT
Cairo
    Four Seasons Hotel Cairo at The First Residence   148
    Mena House Oberoi, Cairo   149

MOROCCO
Fez
    Sofitel Palais Jamaï   150
Marrakech
    Amanjena   151
    Four Seasons Hotel Marrakech   152
    Royal Mansour Marrakech   153
Rabat
    Sofitel Rabat Jardin des Roses   154

SOUTH AFRICA
Cape Town
    Mount Nelson Hotel   155
    One&Only Cape Town   156
Franschhoek
    La Residence   157
Hoedspruit
    Royal Malewane   158
Johannesburg
    The Saxon Boutique Hotel, Villas and Spa   159
Kruger National Park
    Singita Lebombo & Singita Sweni   160
Sabi Sand Game Reserv
    Singita Ebony and Singita Boulders   161

INDIA
Agra
    The Oberoi Amarvilas   162
Gurgaon – New Delhi Capital Region
    The Oberoi, Gurgaon   163
Hyderabad
    Taj Falaknuma Palace   164

CONTENTS

Jaipur
    The Oberoi Rajvilas   165
    Rambagh Palace   166
Jodhpur
    Umaid Bhawan Palace   167
Mumbai
    The Oberoi, Mumbai   168
    The Taj Mahal Palace   169
Ranthambore
    The Oberoi Vanyavilās   170
Udaipur
    The Oberoi Udaivilās   171
    Taj Lake Palace   172

INDIAN OCEAN

MALDIVES
    Four Seasons Resort Maldives, Kuda Huraa and
    Landaa Giraavaru   173
    One&Only Reethi Rah, Maldives   174
    Soneva Fushi   175
    Soneva Gili   176

MAURITIUS
    Four Seasons Resort Mauritius   177
    The Oberoi, Mauritius   178
    One&Only Le Saint Géran, Mauritius   179

SEYCHELLES
Four Seasons Resort Seychelles   180

MIDDLE EAST

LEBANON
Beirut
    Four Seasons Hotel Beirut   181

OMAN
Zighy Bay, Dibba
    Six Senses Zighy Bay   182

SYRIA
Damascus
    Four Seasons Hotel Damascus   183

UNITED ARAB EMIRATES
Dubai
    Al Maha Desert Resort   184
    Armani Hotel Dubai   185
    Burj al Arab   186
    Raffles Dubai   187
    The Ritz-Carlton Dubai, International Financial Centre   188

ASIA & PACIFIC

AUSTRALIA
Great Barrier Reef
    Qualia   190
Sydney
    Park Hyatt Sydney   191

BHUTAN
    Amankora   192

BORA BORA
    Four Seasons Resort Bora Bora   193
    The St. Regis Bora Bora   194

CAMBODIA
Phnom Penh
    Raffles Hotel Le Royal   195
Siem Reap
    Raffles Grand Hotel d'Angkor   196
    La Résidence d'Angkor   197

CHINA
Beijing
    The Peninsula Beijing   198
    Raffles Beijing   199
    The Ritz-Carlton Beijing, Financial Street   200
    The St. Regis Beijing   201
Beijing • Guilin • Xian
    Shangri-La China World Summit Wing •
    Shangri-La Hotel, Guilin • Shangri-La Hotel, Xian   202
Hong Kong
    Four Seasons Hotel Hong Kong   203
    Mandarin Oriental, Hong Kong   204
    The Peninsula Hong Kong   205
    The Ritz-Carlton, Hong Kong   206
Shanghai
    Four Seasons Hotel Shanghai   207
    Grand Hyatt Shanghai   208
    Park Hyatt Shanghai   209
    The Peninsula Shanghai   210
    The Ritz-Carlton Shanghai, Pudong   211
Tibet
    The St. Regis Lhasa Resort   212

FIJI
    InterContinental Fiji Golf Resort & Spa   213

CONTENTS

Laucala Island	214
The Wakaya Club & Spa	215

INDONESIA
Bali
Amandari	216
Bulgari Hotels & Resorts, Bali	217
Four Seasons Resort Bali, Jimbaran Bay and Sayan	218
The Oberoi, Bali	219
The St. Regis Resort Bali	220

Lombok
The Oberoi, Lombok	221

JAPAN
Tokyo
Mandarin Oriental, Tokyo	222
Park Hyatt Tokyo	223
The Peninsula Tokyo	224
The Ritz-Carlton, Tokyo	225

LAOS
Luang Prabang
La Résidence Phou Vao	226

MALAYSIA
Langkawi
Four Seasons Resort Langkawi	227

MYANMAR
Yangon
The Governor's Residence	228

NEW ZEALAND
Featherston
Wharekauhau Country Estate	229

Glenorchy
Blanket Bay	230

Hawke's Bay & Matauri Bay
The Farm at Cape Kidnappers & Kauri Cliffs	231

Taupo
Huka Lodge	232

SINGAPORE
The Fullerton Hotel and The Fullerton Bay Hotel	233
Mandarin Oriental, Singapore	234
Raffles Hotel Singapore	235
The Ritz-Carlton Millenia, Singapore	236

THAILAND
Bangkok
Four Seasons Hotel Bangkok	237
Mandarin Oriental, Bangkok	238
The Peninsula Bangkok	239
The St. Regis Bangkok	240

Chiang Mai
Four Seasons Resort Chiang Mai	241
Mandarin Oriental Dhara Dhevi, Chiang Mai	242

Chiang Rai
Four Seasons Tented Camp Golden Triangle	243

Koh Koo
Soneva Kiri	244

Koh Samui
Four Seasons Resort Koh Samui	245

Krabi
Phulay Bay, A Ritz-Carlton Reserve	256

Phuket
Amanpuri	247

VIETNAM
Con Dao & Ninh Van Bay
Six Senses Con Dao and Six Senses Hideaway Ninh Van Bay	248

Hanoi
Sofitel Legend Metropole Hanoi	249

Hoi An
The Nam Hai	250

Saigon (Ho Chi Minh City)
Park Hyatt Saigon	251

NORTH AMERICA
CENTRAL AMERICA
SOUTH AMERICA

CANADA
Banff
The Fairmont Banff Springs	253

Jasper
The Fairmont Jasper Park Lodge	254

Lake Louise
The Fairmont Chateau Lake Louise	255

Toronto
Four Seasons Hotel Toronto	256
The Ritz-Carlton, Toronto	257

Vancouver
Shangri-La Hotel, Vancouver	258

Whistler
Four Seasons Resort Whistler	259

CONTENTS

UNITED STATES

ARIZONA
Scottsdale
The Phoenician — 260
Tucson
Canyon Ranch — 261
The Ritz-Carlton, Dove Mountain — 262

CALIFORNIA
Laguna Beach
Montage Laguna Beach — 263
Laguna Niguel
The Ritz-Carlton, Laguna Niguel — 264
Lake Tahoe
The Ritz-Carlton, Lake Tahoe — 265
Los Angeles & Beverly Hills
The Beverly Hills Hotel — 266
Beverly Wilshire, A Four Seasons Hotel — 267
Montage Beverly Hills — 268
The Peninsula Beverly Hills — 269
Hotel Bel-Air — 270
Four Seasons Hotel Los Angeles at Beverly Hills — 271
The Ritz-Carlton, Los Angeles — 272
SLS Beverly Hills Hotel — 273
Menlo Park
Rosewood Sand Hill — 274
Napa
Auberge du Soleil — 275
Newport Beach
Pelican Hill Resort — 276
San Diego
The Grand Del Mar — 277
The Lodge at Torrey Pines — 278
San Francisco
Mandarin Oriental, San Francisco — 279
The Ritz-Carlton, San Francisco — 280
The St. Regis San Francisco — 281
Santa Barbara
Four Seasons Resort Santa Barbara — 282

COLORADO
Aspen
The St. Regis Aspen Resort — 283
Avon
The Ritz-Carlton, Bachelor Gulch — 284
Vail
Four Seasons Resort Vail — 285

DISTRICT OF COLUMBIA
Four Seasons Hotel Washington, D.C. — 286
The Jefferson — 287
Mandarin Oriental, Washington, D.C. — 288
The St. Regis Washington, D.C. — 289

FLORIDA
Amelia Island
The Ritz-Carlton, Amelia Island — 290
Key Biscayne
The Ritz-Carlton, Key Biscayne — 291
Miami
Canyon Ranch Hotel & Spa — 292
Mandarin Oriental, Miami — 293
The Ritz-Carlton, South Beach — 294
Orlando
The Ritz-Carlton Orlando, Grande Lakes — 295
Palm Beach
The Breakers — 296
Four Seasons Resort Palm Beach — 297
The Ritz-Carlton, Palm Beach — 298

GEORGIA
Atlanta
The Ritz-Carlton, Buckhead — 299
The St. Regis Atlanta — 300

HAWAII
Honolulu
Halekulani — 301
The Royal Hawaiian — 302
Kauai
The St. Regis Princeville Resort — 303
Kona
Four Seasons Resort Hualalai — 304
Lana'i
Four Seasons Resort Lanai at Manele Bay — 305
Maui
Four Seasons Resort Maui at Wailea — 306
The Ritz-Carlton, Kapalua — 307

ILLINOIS
Chicago
Four Seasons Hotel Chicago — 308
Park Hyatt Chicago — 309
The Peninsula Chicago — 310
The Ritz-Carlton, Chicago, A Four Seasons Hotel — 311

CONTENTS

MARYLAND
St. Michaels
    The Inn at Perry Cabin   312

MASSACHUSETTS
Boston
    Four Seasons Hotel Boston   313
    The Liberty   314
    Mandarin Oriental, Boston   315
    The Ritz-Carlton, Boston Common   316
    Taj Boston   317
Lenox
    Blantyre   318
    Canyon Ranch Hotel & Spa   319

NEVADA
Las Vegas
    Four Seasons Hotel Las Vegas   320
    Mandarin Oriental, Las Vegas   321

NEW MEXICO
Santa Fe
    Encantado   322

NEW YORK
New York
    The Carlyle, A Rosewood Hotel   323
    Four Seasons Hotel New York   324
    Mandarin Oriental, New York   325
    The Peninsula New York   326
    The Pierre   327
    The Plaza   328
    Hôtel Plaza Athénée, New York   329
    The Ritz-Carlton, New York, Battery Park   330
    The Ritz-Carlton, New York, Central Park   331
    The Setai Fifth Avenue   332
    The St. Regis New York   333
Saranac Lake
    The Point   334

PENNSYLVANIA
Philadelphia
    Four Seasons Hotel Philadelphia   335

RHODE ISLAND
Watch Hill
    Ocean House   336

SOUTH CAROLINA
Bluffton
    The Inn at Palmetto Bluff   337

TEXAS
Dallas
    The Joule   338
    The Ritz-Carlton, Dallas   339
    Rosewood Mansion on Turtle Creek   340

UTAH
Canyon Point
    Amangiri   341
Park City
    Montage Deer Valley   342
    The St. Regis Deer Valley   343

VERMONT
Barnard
    Twin Farms   344

WASHINGTON
Seattle
    Four Seasons Hotel Seattle   345

WYOMING
Jackson Hole
    Amangani   346
    Four Seasons Resort Jackson Hole   347

MEXICO
Cabo San Lucas
    Capella Pedregal   348
    Esperanza   349
    Las Ventanas al Paraíso, A Rosewood Resort   350
    One&Only Palmilla   351
Ixtapa
    Capella Ixtapa, Resort & Spa   352
Mexico City
    Four Seasons Hotel México City   353
    The St. Regis Mexico City   354
Punta Mita
    Four Seasons Resort Punta Mita   355
    The St. Regis Punta Mita   356
Riviera Maya
    Maroma Resort and Spa   357
    Rosewood Mayakobá   358
San Miguel de Allende
    Casa de Sierra Nevada   359
    Rosewood San Miguel de Allende   360

CONTENTS

CENTRAL AMERICA

COSTA RICA
Four Seasons Resort Costa Rica — 361

SOUTH AMERICA

ARGENTINA
Buenos Aires
Alvear Palace Hotel — 362
Four Seasons Hotel Buenos Aires — 363
Palacio Duhau, Park Hyatt Buenos Aires — 364
Bariloche
Llao Llao Hotel and Resort, Golf-Spa — 365

BRAZIL
Iguassu Falls
Hotel das Cataratas — 366
Rio de Janeiro
Copacabana Palace — 367

COLOMBIA
Cartagena
Sofitel Legend Cartagena Santa Clara — 368

PERU
Colca Canyon
Las Casitas del Colca — 369
Cusco
Hotel Monasterio — 370
Lima
Miraflores Park Hotel — 371
Machu Picchu
Machu Picchu Sanctuary Lodge — 372
Sacred Valley
Hotel Rio Sagrado — 373

BAHAMAS BERMUDA CARIBBEAN

ANGUILLA
Cap Juluca — 375
CuisinArt Resort & Spa — 376
Viceroy Anguilla Resort & Residences — 377

ANTIGUA
Curtain Bluff Resort — 378
Jumby Bay, A Rosewood Resort — 379

BAHAMAS
The Cove Atlantis — 380
One&Only Ocean Club, Bahamas — 381

BARBADOS
Sandy Lane — 382

BERMUDA
Cambridge Beaches Resort & Spa — 383

CAYMAN ISLANDS
The Ritz-Carlton, Grand Cayman — 384

JAMAICA
Jamaica Inn — 385
Round Hill Hotel and Villas — 386

NEVIS
Four Seasons Resort Nevis — 387

PUERTO RICO
The Ritz-Carlton, San Juan Hotel, Spa & Casino — 388
The St. Regis Bahia Beach Resort — 389

SAINT-BARTHÉLEMY
Eden Rock — 390
Hotel Guanahani & Spa — 391

ST. JOHN
Caneel Bay, A Rosewood Resort — 392

ST. MARTIN
La Samanna — 393

ST. THOMAS
The Ritz-Carlton, St. Thomas — 394

TURKS & CAICOS
Amanyara — 395
Gansevoort Turks + Caicos — 396
Grace Bay Club — 397
Parrot Cay — 398

VIRGIN GORDA
Rosewood Little Dix Bay — 399

AUSTRIA

BELGIUM

CZECH REPUBLIC

ENGLAND

FRANCE

GERMANY

GREECE

HUNGARY

IRELAND

Europe

ITALY

MONACO

THE NETHERLANDS

PORTUGAL

RUSSIA

SCOTLAND

SPAIN

SWEDEN

SWITZERLAND

TURKEY

AUSTRIA
FUSCHL

Schloss Fuschl Resort & Spa

Imagine your own fairytale castle nestled in the verdant hills outside Salzburg. Are you dreaming? Not if you're staying at the incomparable Luxury Collection Schloss Fuschl Resort & Spa. This unique hideaway, set in an 85 acre wooded park on Lake Fuschl, looks like a stage set, but is a fairytale castle come to life. Dating from the 15th century, it was built as a hunting lodge and summer residence for Salzburg archbishops and has been welcoming guests ever since.

"On my first visit in the late 1970s, I was told the story how secretly Mussolini and Hitler met at Schloss Fuschl. Just imagine if the walls could talk and tell us their conversation. Thankfully, we are free to enjoy this idyllic setting today."

Boasting an impressive Old Masters art collection, the Schloss Fuschl is a veritable museum, but this legendary hotel feels warm and welcoming. No detail is overlooked in its 66 rooms, 40 suites, and 4 lakeside cottages. While some accommodations sport a traditional Austrian country charm, others are defined by a traditional elegance. Of course, it is the views of the spectacular Fuschlsee and the rolling hills that make this place truly memorable

Alpine adventures abound: choose from hiking, fishing, or golfing. If the fresh Austrian air hasn't soothed your nerves, an appointment at the spectacular Schloss Fuschl Spa certainly will.

"My favorite part of a stay at Schloss Fuschl is dining like a queen. The elegant setting and traditional Austrian dishes complete the unrivaled experience which includes tasting fish caught in the lake that day, but save room for decadent desserts."

Feel like a fairytale prince at Schloss Fuschl.

SCHLOSS FUSCHL RESORT & SPA, A LUXURY COLLECTION RESORT
Schloss Strasse 19
5322 Fuschlsee-Salzburg, Austria
luxurycollection.com/schlossfuschl

AUSTRIA
SALZBURG

Hotel Goldener Hirsch

Seeking authentic Salzburg charm? Look no further than the Hotel Goldener Hirsch, a Luxury Collection property. In the heart of winsome Old Town, a UNESCO world heritage site, and on the famed Getreidegasse, this landmark has welcomed visitors since 1407. The golden stag marks the entrance and this iconic image is a theme throughout. Only minutes from Mozart's house and near Festival Hall, home of the annual Salzburg Festival, the Goldener Hirsch makes everyone feel like a virtuoso with its warm welcome.

Beat the Austrian chill or simply relax by settling into a cozy nook or comfortable chair in one of the 65 rooms and 4 suites. Many of the handmade local country-style furnishings and antiques were selected by Countess Harriet Walderdorff in the late 1940s and give the accommodations a unique flavor and honor the hotel's 600 years of hospitality.

"The Goldener Hirsch isn't just a favorite of tourists; this hotel is beloved by locals for its sense of history and its fine dining. You'll find local politicians and theater-goers feasting on fine cuisine at the Restaurant." For a true taste of old world charm, take a seat inside The Herzl, where dirndl-clad waitresses serve hearty Austrian classics. Sit beneath the stags at the Bar – certainly appropriate given the inner courtyard's history as a spot where horses waited for their owners.

The Walderdorff family was responsible for reviving the hotel and the incomparable Count Johannes Walderdorff reigned over this hotel's heritage for more than 40 years. "My fondest memory of the Goldener Hirsch is waltzing with Count Johannes Walderdorff at a Virtuoso Symposium as he regaled me with twists and turns."

**HOTEL GOLDENER HIRSCH,
A LUXURY COLLECTION HOTEL**
Getreidegasse 37
5020 Salzburg, Austria
luxurycollection.com/goldenerhirsch

AUSTRIA
SALZBURG

Hotel Sacher Salzburg

It's no surprise that visitors find themselves humming a tune while walking the streets of Salzburg. After all, it is the birthplace of Mozart, the site of the renowned musical festival, and of course, the setting of that world-famous Rodgers and Hammerstein classic movie, *The Sound of Music*.

Step inside the traditional Hotel Sacher Salzburg and you'll soon be singing its praises. This elegant hotel, set on the banks of the Salzach River, has a revered 135-year history. Originally known as the Österreichischer Hof, the Sacher Salzburg has been owned by the Gürtler family since 1988 and is the sister property to the Hotel Sacher Wien. The Sacher Salzburg has enjoyed an illustrious history of hosting luminaries from all over the world.

Individually designed by owner Elisabeth Gürtler, the 84 rooms and 29 suites reflect tradition with antique carpets, furnishings, and artwork. The rooms facing the river frame the magnificent and unforgettable views of Salzburg's Old Town and the Fortress Hohensalzburg, and gracious service completes the memorable experience. Whether you are retracing the steps of Maria and the von Trapp family or exploring the charms of Salzburg, Hotel Sacher is a picture-perfect home.

From the traditional dishes of the Roter Salon to gourmet dining in the wood-paneled Zirbelzimmer to the grilled offerings at the Salzach Grill, there are a variety of dining opportunities at the Sacher.

"When I first visited Salzburg, *The Sound of Music* was not widely celebrated, however, today take advantage of one of the tours and you will discover that the hills are alive with sound. One of 'my favorite things' is certainly the Hotel Sacher Salzburg."

HOTEL SACHER SALZBURG
Schwarzstrasse 5-7
5020 Salzburg, Austria
sacher.com

AUSTRIA
VIENNA

Hotel Imperial

From its confections to its culture, Vienna is a glorious European city that retains a strong link to its imperial past.

The regal Hotel Imperial, a Luxury Collection hotel, shares the grandeur of a bygone era. Built on the site of Vienna's old city walls, it was originally the private palace of the Duke of Wurttemberg. Since 1873, the Hotel Imperial has been the preferred choice for state visits; however, all guests are treated to white-glove service.

The hotel's entrance, originally designed to allow carriages, was lined with horses and feedbags for years. Today, this magnificent lobby leads to the glorious foyer, known as the Yellow Room because of its yellow Giallo di Siena marble walls.

The 76 glorious guest rooms and 62 sumptuous suites echo the hotel's stately décor with antiques and artwork that honor Vienna's past. A visit to the Hotel Imperial instills reverence; even Russian troops who occupied after World War II covered the precious wood floors to protect them from harm!

Dining at the Restaurant Imperial is a refined experience in an elegant setting with haute cuisine, but don't miss coffee and a sweet at Café Imperial, long thought to have inspired the coffeehouse tradition in Vienna.

If you have ever wanted to make a grand entrance, the Hotel Imperial's resplendent staircase is surely the spot. You will never want to take the elevator again after one glance at this awe-inspiring setting capped off with gleaming marble, ornate ceiling, and glittering chandelier. "I savor the memories of my many visits to the Hotel Imperial and treasure a photograph taken on the Belle Etage of the grand staircase."

**HOTEL IMPERIAL,
A LUXURY
COLLECTION HOTEL**
Kärntner Ring 16
1015 Vienna, Austria
luxurycollection.com/imperial

AUSTRIA
VIENNA

Hotel Sacher Wien

You can have your cake - as long as it is Sacher-torte - and eat it too at the lovely Hotel Sacher.

This Viennese institution has a sweet history. In 1832, a young apprentice, Franz Sacher, created a delectable chocolate cake filled with apricot jam for Prince Metternich. It soon became Austria's most desired dessert and remains a well-guarded secret. Sacher's son opened the Hotel Sacher in 1876. Now owned by the Gürtler family, who also own the Sacher Salzburg, it has a distinct personality – pure Viennese.

Opposite the Vienna State Opera, the hotel is a favorite stop for music lovers. In fact, Beethoven's Ninth Symphony was played here for the first time. Culture buffs can take their pick from a variety of Vienna's sights, all within walking distance.

The 119 rooms and 14 suites are a delightful blend of traditional design with all the modern amenities. An extensive art collection of more than 1,000 original oil paintings and engravings, rare antique furnishings, and tapestries are enjoyed in every room and in all reception areas.

In a city synonymous with sweets, even the Spa at the Hotel Sacher indulges guests with chocolate wraps and masks. Hotel Sacher also spoils diners with its plentiful dining choices.

Relive the turn of the century at the traditional Anna Sacher Restaurant, experience exquisite dining at Restaurant Rote Bar, or sip coffee and snack on treats at the famous Café Sacher Wien.

"Over 30 years ago, I tasted the delicious Sacher-torte after a Nureyev ballet performance at the State Opera. I have been going back to the Hotel Sacher Wien for a stay and a slice ever since."

HOTEL SACHER WIEN
Philharmonikerstrasse 4
1010 Vienna, Austria
sacher.com

BELGIUM
BRUSSELS

Rocco Forte Hotel Amigo

Everything is coming up roses at Rocco Forte Hotel Amigo. This style-savvy hotel is quite simply the best in Brussels. From its prime location (adjacent to the cobblestoned streets of Grand Place – site of that famous Flower Carpet) to its fresh interiors, the Amigo offers a perfect home base in this amiable European capital.

Everything old will be new again to you as you wander through the antiques district known as Le Sablon, reachable by foot from the hotel, or peruse the area's many flea markets. Brussels is renowned for its chocolate, lace, and tapestries, as well as many interesting boutiques.

Windows frame picture-perfect views of the city's charm, but there's nothing old-world about these accommodations since the hotel's restoration by Sir Rocco Forte. Instead, the 154 rooms and 19 suites share a lively spirit with guests. His sister, Olga Polizzi, has turned this former prison on its head with her flair for modern styling. Cool contemporary furnishings, Magritte prints, and bright bursts of color create a sense of harmony in this well-appointed city hotel. There is even a bit of whimsy reflected in the accommodations, where figures of Hergé's characters Tintin, Snowy the dog, and Captain Haddock enliven the walls.

One of Italy's most beloved chefs, Fulvio Pierangelini, has shared his expertise at the Amigo's signature Ristorante Bocconi, making it one of the hottest tables in town.

Belgians are famous for beer, so stop by the Bar Amigo for a pint. You will likely feel inspired…the walls are decorated with pictures and quotes from many of the famous scribes who have stayed in the hotel over the last 50 years.

ROCCO FORTE HOTEL AMIGO
Rue de l'Amigo
Brussels 1000, Belgium
roccofortehotels.com

CZECH REPUBLIC
PRAGUE

Four Seasons Hotel Prague

Few places capture the magic of Old-World Europe like Prague. This so-called "city of a hundred spires" is rich with treasures. From cobblestone streets to sidewalk cafés, this city enchants visitors around every corner with its harmonious mix of Gothic, Renaissance, Romanesque, Baroque, and Art Nouveau architecture.

Set on the banks of the Vltava River in the heart of Old Town, the Four Seasons Hotel is the perfect complement to this architecturally rich city. Comprised of four buildings blending styles ranging from Baroque to neo-Renaissance to modern, the hotel seamlessly blends past and present.

The hotel is just steps from the 600-year-old Charles Bridge and showcases spectacular views of Prague Castle, the city's leading landmark. Hunt for fine Bohemian crystal in nearby Wenceslas Square or simply stroll the streets of Old Town. The stunning 141 rooms and 20 suites, among Prague's largest, patiently await your return. The décor is sophisticated contemporary with a nod to the past, and the top-notch comforts even include in-room spa services.

Dine indoors or outside on the terrace during the summer at Allegro Restaurant, the only Michelin-starred restaurant in the Czech Republic. No matter the seat, the view looking over Vltava River, Malá Strana, and Prague Castle is matched only by the award-winning cuisine. Dine on classic Continental, Italian, and Mediterranean dishes or for a taste of the old world, enjoy a few traditional bohemian specialties.

"I adore sightseeing in Prague, a UNESCO World Heritage Site, and wandering the cobblestone streets or admiring the fascinating periods of architecture, but it's wonderful to come home and be pampered at the Four Seasons Hotel Prague."

FOUR SEASONS HOTEL PRAGUE
Veleslavínova 2a/1098
110 00 Prague, Czech Republic
fourseasons.com

CZECH REPUBLIC
PRAGUE

Mandarin Oriental, Prague

Tucked amidst the cobblestone streets of Malá Strana – Old Town, the Mandarin Oriental, set beneath Prague Castle, shares a unique vantage point in this historic city. Looking for a little peace and quiet? You have found your place of serenity at this restored monastery with roots dating back to the 14th century.

The Mandarin Oriental juxtaposes old and new in its 77 rooms and 22 suites. Choose from rooms in the sleek new Garden Wing, with floor-to-ceiling windows and views out to the garden, cobbled streets, and Prague Castle, or in the former monastery, where suites feature vaulted ceilings, wooden beams, and parquet flooring. Expect to be dazzled by the striking Asian-influenced décor complete with contemporary furnishings and bold splashes of royal blues and cherry reds.

Say ahhh-men to the Spa at Mandarin Oriental, Prague. This spa, widely considered to be one of Europe's best, is tucked inside a Renaissance chapel. The design is extraordinary - think elegant ecclesiastic. Walk in the path of history as you step on the glass-blocked walkway that offers a view of the ancient ruins below. All treatments, including Asian and Thai massages and hydrotherapy, are heavenly.

Each of the Mandarin Oriental's dining outlets takes full advantage of the historic setting. Gaze at the imposing Baroque columns of the former cloisters as you sip tea in the Monastery Lounge, or enjoy the ultra-modern ambience and mood elevating cocktails of the sizzling Barego. "Essensia restaurant's stunning ecclesiastical vaulted design sets the stage for the modern Asian accented cuisine peppered with Czech classics. It best captures the essence of this luxurious hotel – bridging old and new with spectacular results."

MANDARIN ORIENTAL, PRAGUE
Nebovidska 459/1
118 00 Prague, Czech Republic
mandarinoriental.com

CZECH REPUBLIC
PRAGUE

Rocco Forte The Augustine

What's in a name? At The Augustine, it is a hint of its former incarnation. The Augustine, which strings together seven different buildings of historic importance, occupies the former Augustinian St. Thomas Monastery. It retains direct access to St. Thomas Church, making it a favorite venue for brides and grooms, but you don't need to say your prayers to gain access to this exceptional hideaway.

It may be steeped in history, but The Augustine bears that inimitable Rocco Forte stamp. Olga Polizzi's modern sensibility has pumped up the volume. From the public spaces to the 85 rooms and 16 suites inspired by the 1930s Czech cubism movement, the look is modern monastic. Don't worry, you won't live like a monk, though you may run across one – practicing friars still live adjacent to the hotel grounds. Modern amenities and creature comforts abound at this property, as do charming views of the courtyard, monastery, and Prague castle.

One of the most unique experiences of a stay at The Augustine is a stop in the Brewery Bar. Everything from the vaulted stone ceiling to the artwork shows off its former existence as the cellar of the St. Thomas Brewery. Other enjoyable spots include the barrel vaulted hall of Tom's Bar with its adjacent cloister terrace for al fresco seating during warmer months. The brasserie menu of Monastery Restaurant is a hit with visitors and locals alike.

"I did a hard hat tour in the winter of 2007 when the buildings were in a rough state; however, I could easily see the vision of this spectacular site, and knew The Augustine would become an instant success."

ROCCO FORTE THE AUGUSTINE
Letenská 12/33
118 00 Prague, Czech Republic
roccofortecollection.com

ENGLAND
ASCOT

Coworth Park

A country getaway unlike anything you've ever experienced before. That's the promise of Coworth Park. Minutes from Ascot, in 240 acres of lush parkland surrounding Windsor Great Park, this Dorchester Collection resort occupies a stunning Georgian manor estate.

Coworth Park has crafted an exceptional new way to look at the English countryside. It glows with a bit of whimsy and a thoroughly modern take on country living. Farmers cottages have been transformed into 11 spacious guest quarters, while the former stables have taken on a new life as 28 rooms and suites with a fresh and playful take on rustic design. Those who prefer to be in the heart of it should opt for one of the 30 accommodations in the Mansion House, also home to the Summer and Drawing Rooms ideal for taking tea or chatting by the fire.

Fancy a polo match or a ride through the rolling meadows? Coworth Park is an equestrian Eden with a variety of magnificent horses ranging from ponies for child riders to dressage horses.

With lime hemp walls and an herb garden roof, to the organic products, to the holistic treatments, it is easy and wonderfully luxurious – being green at the Spa.

Delight in the haute cuisine of Michelin-starred chef John Campbell in the Mansion House, or the comfort food of the informal Barn, or the light meals of the Spatisserie.

"I will never forget my inaugural trip to Coworth Park. As one of their guests, I attended a gala benefit at Windsor Castle where I was presented to Prince William. Little did I know he would announce his engagement the next morning!"

COWORTH PARK
Blacknest Road
Ascot, Berkshire SL5 7SE, England
coworthpark.com or
dorchestercollection.com

ENGLAND
CHESTER

The Chester Grosvenor and Spa

Escape the everyday with a memorable trip to Chester. One of Great Britain's oldest towns, this 2000-year-old walled city has a unique charm and has long been a tourist's treasure – its first guidebook was published in 1781! In the center of it all is the lovely Chester Grosvenor. Owned by and named after The Duke of Westminster (surname Grosvenor), this black-and-white-timbered mansion in the heart of the city center blends the ambience of a country house with the services of a luxury hotel.

Enjoy a chauffeur driven sightseeing tour of the beautiful gardens of Cheshire or take a two-hour boat ride on the River Dee for a relaxing sightseeing trip. Roam the streets of this fascinating Roman city or browse through some of the interesting shops.

The Grosvenor Spa is a destination unto itself with five treatment rooms, a salt grotto, ice fountain, herb sauna, and themed shower. Book a half-day and enjoy the beautifying rituals.

The Chester Grosvenor's 68 rooms and 12 suites have been updated with a twist on traditional design. Leather furnishings, striped walls, and contemporary artwork lend a stylish flair, while the watchful eye of a highly trained staff ensures that no detail goes overlooked.

The attention to detail continues at The Chester Grosvenor's famed restaurant Simon Radley. With one of the largest wine cellars in England and meals expertly prepared by Michelin starred chef Radley, this is certainly a memorable dining experience. The Arkle Bar and Lounge hits the spot with its cozy atmosphere perfect for drinks or afternoon tea. The casual dining at La Brasserie, with its French flair and food, is a must.

Experience English charm at the Chester Grosvenor.

THE CHESTER GROSVENOR
Eastgate
Chester CH1 1LT, England
chestergrosvenor.com

ENGLAND
HAMPSHIRE

Four Seasons Hotel Hampshire

Drive just an hour from London and you will find yourself firmly planted in the English countryside. Don your Wellies (don't worry if you forgot yours as the hotel has them on hand) and prepare yourself for something off the beaten path of the typical country getaway. This is the English countryside Four Seasons style.

Straight out of the pages of a Jane Austen novel, The Four Seasons Hotel Hampshire is nestled on acres of rolling hills and historic gardens. Once a private estate, the Georgian manor house is splendid. Whether staying in one of the 111 rooms or 22 suites in the period building or in the newer wings, you will awaken to the sounds of chirping birds. From your window, watch sheep grazing or simply take in the relaxing Hampshire countryside.

Three restaurants and two bars provide a flurry of activity, but this hotel is especially well known for its hunger inducing outdoor activities. Swim in the glass-enclosed, greenhouse-style indoor pool or soak in the outdoor vitality pool. Work out in the well-equipped fitness center, hit the tennis courts, or bike along the paths of this 500-acre estate. Sporting activities like clay pigeon shooting, falconry, and horseback riding can also be arranged.

The pièce de résistance at the Four Seasons Hotel Hampshire is its terrific Spa, tucked inside the former stables. The original arched gateway, gabled roofs and bell turret capture the essence of the past while the 15 treatment rooms and ESPA treatments are thoroughly modern. "I look forward to returning to the luxuries of the Four Seasons Hotel Hampshire and spending the day being pampered at the spa!"

FOUR SEASONS HOTEL HAMPSHIRE
Dogmersfield Park, Chalky Lane,
Dogmersfield, Hook,
Hampshire RG27 8TD, England
fourseasons.com

ENGLAND
LONDON

Berkeley

Enjoy the civilized lifestyle of the Berkeley. "When my family moved to London in 1977, The Berkeley was our temporary home as we awaited the arrival of our belongings. From the residential area of Belgravia, with its tree-lined streets and gracious townhouses, to the bustling areas of the Knightsbridge neighborhood, my daughters and I explored our new London surroundings. The Berkeley always brings back cherished memories."

In the early 1970s, the Berkeley moved to its current location in an enticing modern building opposite Hyde Park. The sophisticated accommodations are as natty as a Savile Row suit. Graciously styled with gray overtones, the 149 rooms and 65 suites are incredibly spacious and welcoming. Italian marble bathrooms and luxurious fabrics are just two of the "standard" offerings in these timeless accommodations. Three suites have private conservatories, lending an air of the countryside to this city hotel.

A celebrity-studded crowd frequents the Berkeley's Blue Bar, while the hotel's two restaurants shine on their own accord. Marcus Wareing at the Berkeley is the highly acclaimed Michelin 2 star restaurant. Legendary Pierre Koffmann showcases his classic provincial French cuisine in the informal restaurant called Koffmann's.

BERKELEY
Wilton Place
London SW1X 7RL, England
the-berkeley.co.uk

Feel in top form at the rooftop health club and spa, which allows you to escape the city without ever leaving the hotel. The swimming pool is a monument to tranquility with its soothing ambience and views of Hyde Park and central London, and its roof retracts on nice days to let the golden sunshine blanket you with its warmth. A full-fledged fitness center and spa are on hand to make you feel fit from head to toe.

ENGLAND
LONDON

Claridge's

Claridge's has been at the top of its game for over a century. This London red brick Victorian landmark building in posh Mayfair masterfully blends elegant British tradition with the drama of Art Deco design. One step inside its gleaming black and white lobby and you'll be immediately swept up by its magic spell.

Even the spacious hallways share a part of the Claridge's legend, as they were designed so that crinolined Victorian ladies could pass each other. It has long been a favorite haunt of A-listers and royals, due in large part to the discreet service and the high levels of personalized attention. One favorite anecdote from its storied past has a caller asking to speak to the King. "Certainly, sir," said the operator, "but which one?"

The 136 rooms and 67 suites are the picture of elegance, offering a collection of accommodations designed by fashion designer Diane von Furstenberg and David Linley, the renowned furniture designer and son of Princess Margaret.

"Whether staying in an Art Deco accommodation or going all the way to the top and staying in the Davies Penthouse with its marvelous collection of English antiques, sumptuous silks, and views overlooking London, Claridge's is a grand lady that knows how to entertain her guests."

The Reading Room, with its roaring marble fireplaces, suede walls, and leather columns, feels every bit the club and is just the spot for afternoon tea, while The Fumoir has the seductive feel of the 1930s down pat. Of course, Claridge's is perhaps best known as the home of restaurant Gordon Ramsay, where reservations are among London's most coveted.

CLARIDGE'S
Brook Street, Mayfair
London W1K 4HR, England
claridges.co.uk

ENGLAND
LONDON

The Connaught

Located in the heart of fashionable Mayfair, The Connaught is one of London's most distinguished addresses. It was originally created as a place for landed gentry during their visits to London. Built in 1897, the hotel's name was changed to honor Queen Victoria's son, the Duke of Connaught.

Almost like an exclusive men's club, the Connaught is a British institution. Travelers from around the world choose the highly regarded Connaught and its prestigious address. French general Charles De Gaulle resided in a suite here during World War II.

Having just undergone a restoration and addition of a new wing, the 87 rooms and 34 suites have been freshened up by renowned designer Guy Oliver. The accommodations are sleek with a classic contemporary look, but the Connaught's Edwardian features are not left behind.

Retreat to the new fitness center, indoor pool, or Aman Spa, a luxurious day spa from Aman Resorts.

"While living in London, the Connaught Restaurant was a place of gastronomic delights, particularly classic English presentations such as pheasant or grouse with all the accoutrements. We were fond of entertaining here since it was such a traditional English experience. Now, the wood paneling is all that remains, but it still remains a favorite dining venue of mine."

Where does a French chef who has garnered top awards for her Left Bank restaurant go? The Connaught, of course! Hélène Darroze at the Connaught is reason alone to stay here. The new design is a perfect setting for this Michelin-starred cuisine. If that's not enough, the Connaught also boasts two buzzing bars and the light-filled Espelette.

THE CONNAUGHT
Carlos Place, Mayfair
London W1K 2AL, England
the-connaught.co.uk

ENGLAND
LONDON

The Dorchester

There's reason to celebrate at The Dorchester, as it marked its 80th birthday in 2011. "For me, the celebration was a few years ago when I was a guest of the hotel and the Dorchester Collection at a benefit honoring the 50th anniversary of Opera Australia and Dame Joan Sutherland with a performance and gala in Buckingham Palace. If that wasn't enough to entice, being presented to Prince Charles certainly was!"

Built on a site where nobles lived during the 18th and 19th centuries, The Dorchester has been a favorite of England's royalty since its opening in 1931. Prince Philip celebrated his bachelor party in the Park Suite, while the royal guests attending the wedding of HRH Queen Elizabeth primped at The Dorchester before proceeding to Westminster Abbey.

Overlooking Hyde Park, The Dorchester's 195 rooms and 55 suites bring the English countryside in to London. No two rooms are alike, but many include romantic floral fabrics. Perhaps one of the most treasured suites is the unique Oliver Messel Suite, designed by the famed theater designer of the 1950s. The three roof suites capture the Hollywood glamour with a dazzling décor.

The Dorchester Spa exudes 1930s Art Deco glamour combined with a contemporary edge. From its chandelier crafted of South Sea pearls to its top-notch treatments, this spa features refined relaxation.

There is truly something to suit every palate at The Dorchester, where a host of restaurants and bars await your arrival. Choose from British favorites at The Grill, have a drink or take tea in the Promenade, opt for scrumptious Asian cuisine at China Tang, or indulge at Alain Ducasse.

THE DORCHESTER
Park Lane, Mayfair
London W1K 1QA, England
thedorchester.com or
dorchestercollection.com

ENGLAND
LONDON

45 Park Lane

45 might just be the luckiest number that you have ever seen - at least if you're staying at 45 Park Lane, one of London's newest hotels. Opened in late 2011, this über-chic hotel not only shares its address in its name, but it also shares its number of rooms and suites. With just 45 rooms and suites, this luxury lodging feels every bit the exclusive club.

Part of The Dorchester Collection, 45 Park Lane has been fashioned by leading designer Thierry Despont who has paid homage to the sleek styling of the 1930s while incorporating modern elements.

The 45 rooms and suites reflect Despont's desire to create the ambience of a private residence. Of course, the views of Hyde Park and the charming environs of Mayfair aren't bad either! Expect to be wowed by everything from state-of-the-art technology to over-the-top details.

Another boon for this intimate hotel? CUT at 45 Park Lane, the first European restaurant of leading restaurateur Wolfgang Puck. As its name suggests, this innovative American style restaurant specializes in prime aged beef.

Meet in Bar 45 for cocktails or enjoy a bottle of wine in the cozy Library, where you can also check in with the office if need be. Skip across to the sister Dorchester, whether for a spa treatment or multiple dining choices.

"While doing a hard hat tour, I could not forget that the new 45 Park Lane was once the infamous London Playboy Club. During its heyday, I was certainly unlucky at the gaming tables, but I am not gambling when I say this latest incarnation will surely be a winner."

45 PARK LANE
45 Park Lane, Mayfair
London W1K 1PN, England
45parklane.com or
dorchestercollection.com

ENGLAND
LONDON

Four Seasons Hotel London at Park Lane

How does a legend begin? If you are the standard setting Four Seasons brand of world-renowned hotels and resorts, that defining moment began in London in 1970. Isadore Sharp's first luxury hotel opened in London and was originally known as The Inn on the Park and later renamed the Four Seasons.

This hotel set the standards for all future Four Seasons properties, but it definitely does not rest on any laurels. The Four Seasons London was literally rebuilt from the inside out over 16 months, reopening in January 2011 – the plans even included moving the lobby staircase and adding a floor for a stunning rooftop spa. The expansive first floor encompasses the lobby and flows through to multiple areas for every guest's pleasure. The dramatic look is punctuated with bright red pops of color, setting the tone and adding contemporary flair.

In the fully transformed building, the 141 luxury guest rooms and 45 one, two and three bedroom suites are infused with glamour, and a select few have fireplaces and private terraces. Bright, airy views range from charming streetscapes to Hyde Park treetops. The contemporary décor in either blonde sycamore or walnut woods sets a high style.

Elevate your senses at the spa on the tenth-floor, where panoramic city views meet sleek urban design. Watch the world go by as you unwind in the Sky Suite.

Choose the setting that fits your mood at Italian-inspired Amaranto, where three different areas – restaurant, bar, and lounge – beckon.

"Here are a few of my favorite things…the ideal location…the lovely Conservatory rooms… all the exceptional people who deliver extraordinary service. I even celebrated my recent birthday at the Four Seasons Hotel London to experience the rebirth of this legend!"

FOUR SEASONS HOTEL LONDON AT PARK LANE
Hamilton Place, Park Lane
London W1J 7DR, England
fourseasons.com

ENGLAND
LONDON

The Lanesborough

Facing "Number One London" or Apsley House, home of the first Duke of Wellington, and adjacent to Buckingham Palace, The Lanesborough is one of London's most coveted addresses.

First developed as a private residence by James Lane, Viscount Lanesborough, and later rebuilt in 1844 as St. George's Hospital, it opened as a hotel twenty years ago on New Year's Eve.

The richly decorated style of this hotel is reminiscent of a London mansion. Indeed, with just 50 guest rooms and 43 suites, The Lanesborough, a St. Regis Hotel, exudes privacy and intimacy. The jewel-toned accommodations are sumptuously defined by reproduction furnishings of the period and accented with antique furniture and accessories. 24-hour butler service, from the country that perfected the art of service, pampers you in style. The five-room Royal Suite, with its views of Constitution Arch and Buckingham Palace, just might convince you that you are the newest member of the Royal Family.

Michelin-starred chef Heinz Beck runs the delicious show at Apsleys, his first restaurant outside of Rome. There are plenty of places to sip a drink, including the Regency-style Withdrawing Room, the elegant wood-paneled Library, and the Garden Room, where it is de rigueur to smoke a cigar. Afternoon tea at The Lanesborough is even an award-winning affair – the UK Tea Council has granted its excellence award since 2008.

"Just a couple weeks after its opening, I took my mother to London to celebrate her 75th birthday at The Lanesborough. Having driven past this building thousands of times while living in London, it was wonderful to see the revival of this English Regency landmark. For me, The Lanesborough still defines world-class style."

THE LANESBOROUGH, A ST. REGIS HOTEL
Hyde Park Corner
London SW1X 7TA, England
stregis.com/lanesborough.com

ENGLAND
LONDON

Mandarin Oriental Hyde Park, London

Commanding a premier location in London for more than a century, the Mandarin Oriental Hyde Park is one of the city's most distinguished hotels.

The Mandarin Oriental has always welcomed prominent members of society, including many members of the Royal Family. Here, Princess Elizabeth and Princess Margaret learned to dance, and Prince Philip often held his cocktail and polo parties. While tradition holds that no entrances open out to Hyde Park, this hotel is the one exception. Added in 1926, it was used during George VI's coronation in 1937, while today it is used for both royals and dignitaries.

The 173 guest rooms and 25 suites are characterized by Thai silks, fine furnishings, English antiques, and exquisite art objects. Views look out over the shops of Knightsbridge or the expanse of Hyde Park.

"What a treat it is to occupy a suite looking out over the park and watch the Royal Horse Guards in parade formation head to Buckingham Palace. I felt like a queen!"

The spa's sleek design makes it one of the hippest places to unwind. Rather than choosing from a treatment menu, clients can book Time Rituals, where therapists design programs based on individual needs. An indoor pool is slated to open in the near future.

Fine dining is a hallmark of the Mandarin Oriental, where two of the world's leading chefs are stars of the show. Bar Boulud, by New York's legendary Daniel Boulud, shows off his signature French bistro cooking. Heston Blumenthal's unmatched "historic" cooking reaches into the past for ideas while being thoroughly modern. "I can honestly say this unique menu was a delicious experience."

MANDARIN ORIENTAL HYDE PARK, LONDON
66 Knightsbridge
London SW1X 7LA, England
mandarinoriental.com

ENGLAND
LONDON

The Milestone

There is no mistaking where you are once you step into The Milestone. This hotel is unmistakably English. From its charming exterior to its traditional décor, The Milestone sums up the best of Britain. In fact, *Condé Nast Traveler* Readers' Choice Awards selected it as the top hotel in the British Isles in 2010.

This boutique hotel, the flagship of the Red Carnation Hotel Collection, is tucked inside a 19th century Victorian architectural gem. Overlooking Kensington Palace and Hyde Park in the royal borough of Kensington and Chelsea, all of London is within reach from this mansion.

Bring along the entire family, including small children and pets, since this welcoming hotel will indulge all. This hotel employs two staff members, including 24-hour butlers, for each guest to ensure ultimate service. The 44 rooms, 12 suites, and 6 long-term apartments are each individually designed creating unique personalities, but all are richly decorated with original artwork, antiques, and custom-made fabrics.

Each of the three dining establishments showcases a different style and mood. There is the tartan fabric and leather furnishings of the clubby Stables Bar, the black-and-white beauty of the airy Conservatory, and the elegant Victorian arches and ornate windows of Cheneston's.

"I enjoy popping in for a taste of the contemporary British cuisine. Try one of the regional dishes; Orkney scallops, Cornish red mullet, Scottish smoked salmon, Angus beef, Gloucester pork, or Dover sole." Top it off with a bottle of fine wine from the hotel's cellar with more than 400 vintages. Of course, you could always have the butler prepare a picnic basket for an impromptu afternoon in the park across the street.

THE MILESTONE
1 Kensington Court
London W8 5DL, England
milestonehotel.com

ENGLAND
LONDON

The Ritz London

The Ritz is so much more than just a hotel. It is a landmark, an icon, and an institution. These words immediately conjure up images of grandeur and glamour. How many hotels can claim to have added a word to the English language - ritzy - simply by being their best-dressed selves?

Of course, The Ritz is in a class of its own. Just four hotels in the world are members of this elite family of hotels designed by legendary hotelier César Ritz. Stunning the world with his first hotel in Paris, he set his sights on London and opened The Ritz in 1906. He succeeded in creating a magical world where the upper crust of society played and stayed.

From its expertly crafted exterior to its luscious Louis XVI interiors, the Ritz exudes the elegance of a French chateau on Piccadilly overlooking Green Park. The 112 rooms and 25 suites are exquisitely decorated with luxuriant fabrics and dignified furnishings.

Taking tea at The Ritz is a rite of passage for every Londoner and visitor to London. Everyone from Evelyn Waugh and Sir Winston Churchill to King Edward VII has nibbled scones in the venerable Palm Court. The Ritz's Restaurant, capped off with a gorgeous trompe l'oeil ceiling, is largely considered one of the most beautiful dining rooms in the world.

"If the 'corner table' could only talk...I would love the tidbits it would share. Known as the Queen Mother's table, and frequented by Maggie Thatcher, can you imagine the conversations it was privy to? Dining at this table was certainly a memorable event with its sumptuous setting and delicious haute cuisine."

THE RITZ LONDON
150 Piccadilly
London W1J 9BR, England
theritzlondon.com

ENGLAND
LONDON

Rocco Forte Brown's Hotel

Rocco Forte Brown's Hotel is one of London's greatest treasures.

This prestigious hotel is situated in the heart of Mayfair, placing it within walking distance of shopping, major theaters, and museums, but Brown's offers so much more than just a fantastic address. This hotel has a fascinating history – it was London's first hotel! Brown's opened in 1837 and has been charming guests ever since.

Rocco Forte and designer Olga Polizzi carefully updated the accommodations while preserving the special charm that makes Brown's so unique. Warm and welcoming with soft color tones and light fabrics, the 88 rooms and 29 suites are quintessentially English with a contemporary twist. Thoughtful touches are abundant…just glance at the selection of books. Frequent visitor Winston Churchill's *The Wicked Wit* is one…another is Rudyard Kipling's *Jungle Book*, as he penned this classic while staying right here in the hotel.

The superior staff attends to every wish, from spa treatments to fine dining. HIX at The Albemarle offers a fresh take on classic Britain. From its walls hung with a large, diverse collection of contemporary British artwork to its plates bursting with contemporary cuisine, HIX is a breath of fresh air. Donovan Bar is just right for cocktails, but you simply cannot visit Brown's, or even London for that matter, without a proper cup of tea from the award-winning afternoon tea celebration.

"Just a few blocks for a stroll through Green Park, around the corner from shopping on Bond Street and Burlington Arcade, London is at your fingertips…or should I say footsteps…when you make Brown's your home away from home."

ROCCO FORTE BROWN'S HOTEL
Albemarle Street, Mayfair
London W1S 4BP, England
roccofortecollection.com

ENGLAND
LONDON

The Savoy

Founded in 1889 by Richard D'Oyly Carte, the producer of Gilbert & Sullivan operas, The Savoy shares a dramatic history in the heart of London's West End. This historic hotel has more than just a passing interest in the arts – it has been privy to many premieres and private performances by some of the world's biggest stars. Prima ballerina Anna Pavlova first danced in the cabaret here, Strauss conducted in the Thames Foyer, and Claude Monet painted scenes of the Thames from his fifth-floor room.

Guests again meet at The Savoy thanks to Fairmont's three-year top-to-bottom restoration. The Savoy has a grand tradition – it was the first London hotel to have a lift (elevator). All 210 rooms and 58 suites have individual English detailing. Decked out in Edwardian or Art Deco décor, the accommodations sparkle with the finest touches, including Murano glass chandeliers and marble bathrooms with giant rain showers.

The Art Deco-styled River Restaurant and smashing Savoy Grill have reclaimed their place among London's finest. Sir Winston Churchill favored the Grill and his table remained unoccupied in his memory for one year following his death. Toast at the time-honored favorite American Bar or bring on the drama at the new Beaufort Bar, built on the original cabaret stage.

"I have a long history with The Savoy. From honeymooning in a room overlooking the river, to dining on smoked salmon and Dover sole in the River Restaurant, to countless tea times in the Thames Foyer, to dancing with George Balanchine of the New York City Ballet at a private party here, The Savoy continues to have a special place in my heart."

**THE SAVOY,
A FAIRMONT
MANAGED HOTEL**
Strand
London WC2R OEU, England
fairmont.com/savoy

ENGLAND
NEW MILTON

Chewton Glen

Once you enter the magical world of Chewton Glen, you may never want to leave.

Only a short distance from Southampton, enjoy the south coast of England at the enchanting Chewton Glen. Set on 130 acres nestled between the sea and the ancient New Forest; its history is captivating. Smugglers traveling inland once used the path that runs along the house down to the sea. Today, though you may not be running from the law, it is an excellent path for jogging.

Chewton Glen's 33 rooms and 25 suites are done up in English country style with fresh, contemporary fabrics and colors, plus many feature terraces or balconies for further enjoyment of the lovely setting.

The activities for adults and children are boundless. The property offers a 9-hole par 3 golf course, plus 12 of the most spectacular British courses are within 20 miles. Play tennis indoors and outside or have a croquet match on the lawn, but don't be surprised if you have a small gallery because of the guests who linger on the garden's patio. Horseback riding in the New Forest, known as William the Conqueror's hunting ground, is sure to be memorable.

Enjoy downtime by hitting the luxurious spa, which garners top awards for its superior facilities and treatments.

The Corinthian-columned indoor pool is a marvel, relax in the hydrotherapy pool, or swim in the heated outdoor pool.

The Chewton Glen restaurant, Vetiver, is spread across five rooms, including a Conservatory and Wine Room, and is perfect for any occasion.

"Chewton Glen, with its incredible style and gracious manners, will always be one of my favorites."

CHEWTON GLEN HOTEL & SPA
New Milton, New Forest
Hampshire BH25 6QS, England
chewtonglen.com

FRANCE
LES BAUX DE PROVENCE

Oustau de Baumanière

Provence has been delighting visitors for centuries. Its natural beauty, light, and laid-back lifestyle have inspired countless artists, including Cezanne and Van Gogh, who painted many of their masterpieces here.

If you have ever had the French farmhouse fantasy, Oustau de Baumanière is the answer to your dreams. This delightful country estate echoes the essence of Provence. Built in the hollow of the Vallon de La Fontaine, it is shaded by mulberry and olive trees; quite a contrast to the imposing rock formation of Les Baux in the distance. Founded over 60 years ago, its gentle manner, soft sophistication, and tranquil setting have become synonymous with the best of Provence.

Gourmet cuisine is an integral part of the Oustau de Baumanière experience – in fact, it was the guiding principle of founder Raymond Thuilier and continued with his grandson, Jean-Andrè Charial. The food is delicately prepared with the finest and freshest ingredients, many of which are grown on the property. "Although Mr. Charial is no longer cooking full time, for a real treat, take a private cooking class with him."

The casual elegance of Oustau de Baumanière extends to the 19 rooms and 11 suites spread throughout three centuries-old stone buildings. The décor offers a modern take on country living interspersed with unexpected touches (a tree is planted smack dab in the middle of Suite 63!).

The family-owned Oustau de Baumanière continues the grand tradition of fine dining and warm hospitality while keeping up with the times – the spa is a popular new feature.

"While I certainly can't spend a year in Provence, I'll take a week at Oustau de Baumanière anytime!"

OUSTAU DE BAUMANIÈRE
Les Baux de Provence
13520 France
oustaudebaumaniere.com

FRANCE
BIARRITZ

Hotel du Palais, Imperial Resort & Spa

The arrival of Eugenie and Napoleon III transformed the Basque village of Biarritz, where the waters of France and Spain meet, from a sleepy fishing village to the playground of royalty almost overnight. The cavalcade of nobility helped Biarritz earn its nickname as "the Queen of Resorts and the Resort of Kings." After the imperial villa became the Hotel du Palais in 1883, the grand fetes and balls continued, prompting Sacha Guitry to write in the hotel's guest book, "Whenever one hesitates between two resorts, one of them is always Biarritz."

The Hotel's romantic history is as enchanting as its clifftop views of the crashing sea. The palace was built by Napoleon III for his wife Eugenie, who spent her summers here as a child. Though the famously rough waters - now popular with surfers – almost claimed her life, Eugenie was forever captivated by the stunning coastline. Today's visitors will find the superb oceanfront pool a restful alternative to the unpredictable surf.

The majestic Hotel du Palais is one of the world's grandest palace hotels where guests are made to feel like royalty. Opulent, yet refined, the Hotel's 120 rooms and 30 suites are lavishly decorated with fine French antiques, all with views of the wild sea or manicured gardens.

You have many dining options; grand views from La Rotonde, elegant cuisine at Villa Eugénie, and casual outdoor dining at Hippocampe during the summer.

From the regal indoor swimming pool complete with counter-current swimming to the tempting 30,000 square foot Guerlain spa, everything here speaks to its noble past.

The Hotel du Palais is a romantic seaside and spa resort.

HOTEL DU PALAIS, IMPERIAL RESORT & SPA
1, avenue de l'Impératrice
64200 Biarritz, France
hotel-du-palais.com

FRANCE
BORDEAUX

Grand Hôtel de Bordeaux & Spa

Some things do get better with age – certainly fine wines from the Medoc or St. Emilion – as does the Grand Hôtel de Bordeaux & Spa. This landmark building, the Palais Bordelais, has over 200 years of history and was lovingly transformed into a luxury hotel.

Commanding a stately presence from the grand square and across from the Grand Theatre in the pedestrian Golden Triangle, the hotel's neo-classical façade belies its chic and stylish interiors. Internationally renowned designer Jacques Garcia's unique style – a dazzling and revved-up version of classic French décor – is found throughout the rooms and public spaces.

The 128 rooms and 22 suites are luxuriously appointed with fine fabrics, elegant furnishings, and top amenities. Marble bathrooms and enchanting views of the city center complete the refined experience.

The Grand Hôtel's Les Bain de Lea Spa is a two-floor monument to serenity and its heated rooftop pool is a highlight of any visit to this hotel.

Two bars and two restaurants both honor and make history at The Grand. Victor Bar is named for native son Victor Hugo, who played a part in the hotel's history, while the refined cooking of Le Pressoir d'Argent has earned it a Michelin star. Other venues include the lovely L'Orangerie and the stylish Brasserie l'Europe.

"True to the 18th century, the historic section of Bordeaux (a UNESCO World Heritage Site- called urban architectural ensemble) and the magnificent riverfront have been restored and revitalized. I recommend several days at The Grand Hôtel so you have plenty of time to explore the city and the legendary wine regions of Medoc, Graves, and St. Emilion. Together - truly an oenophile's delight."

GRAND HÔTEL DE BORDEAUX & SPA
2-5 Place de la Comédie
33000 Bordeaux, France
ghbordeaux.com

FRANCE
CANNES

InterContinental Carlton Cannes

Nothing captures the glamour and glitz of the French Riviera quite like Cannes. This capital of chic on the Mediterranean is perhaps best known for its annual film festival, where the flash of cameras is upstaged only by the glittering jewels worn by the movie stars. Though the stars converge on Cannes just once a year, they leave an indelible mark on the city.

Whether you are a star of the silver screen or simply the main character in your life story, you will be enveloped by the sheer sophistication of it all while staying at the InterContinental Carlton Cannes, a legendary hotel that has been welcoming guests for over a century. "This Belle Epoque palace has an enviable address on the world-famous Croisette, the palm-lined boulevard dotted with renowned boutiques (where I have certainly overshopped!), and has a front row seat to the Mediterranean. While at the InterContinental, you get the best of both worlds – city chic with a private stretch of Cote d'Azur beach."

The InterContinental cossets guests with a variety of superb amenities. From fine French dining in the Restaurant to cocktails at the bars to casual fare served beachside, the hotel tempts and delights. Of course, the best part of any stay is access to its prestigious private beach. Sun on a chaise and gaze at the blue sea or hop a boat from the hotel's private pier.

INTERCONTINENTAL CARLTON CANNES
58, Boulevard La Croisette BP155
06414 Cannes, France
intercontinental.com/cannes

The hotel's 304 rooms and 39 suites share a decidedly French décor populated with soft creams, yellows, and blues. The accommodations tastefully blend a touch of formality with a breezy elegance. Large windows showcasing stunning views are surely a highlight.

FRANCE
CAP D'ANTIBES

Hôtel du Cap-Eden-Roc

Perhaps it should come as no surprise that Hôtel du Cap-Eden-Roc has made news since opening its doors to guests in 1870. After all, this exclusive hideaway on the Cote d'Azur was built by the one-time owner of *Le Figaro* newspaper, Auguste de Villemess. This jewel of the Riviera underwent a recent four year restoration and the results? C'est magnifique!

Dramatically positioned on the southernmost tip of the Cap d'Antibes in a verdant private park, the Napoleon III-style Hôtel du Cap is a beacon of elegance. It enjoys a polished reputation as a preferred retreat for celebrities and movie stars who want to get away from the flashbulbs of the paparazzi without forsaking their A-list comforts.

The 56 rooms, 52 junior suites, and 7 suites are a breath of fresh air and share a quiet luxury with lovely pastel colors or floral prints and stunning sea views. The accommodations entice with refined comforts, but with stunning gardens and the azure sea just outside, you will certainly want to spend much of your time enjoying the spectacular setting. The ultimate hideaway within this secluded retreat is the Villa Eleana, a three-bedroom private villa.

In a 100-year-old pine preserve, 33 sea cabins, including a well-being Cabin featuring La Prairie treatments, provide sanctuary from the world's stresses. Enjoy a competitive round of tennis on one of five courts. "But the place to be and be seen is the lovely seafront Eden-Roc Pavilion. I can still taste the zucchini flowers and fresh seafood while lunching on the terrace. The views of the infinity pool and seemingly endless sea are truly unforgettable."

HÔTEL DU CAP-EDEN-ROC
Boulevard JF Kennedy - BP 29
06601 Antibes, France
hotel-du-cap-eden-roc.com

FRANCE
EZE

Château de la Chèvre d'Or

The enchanting Château de la Chèvre d'Or is tucked away in the tiny Côte d'Azur hamlet of Eze.

Le Château de la Chèvre d'Or invites you to experience a different side of the French Riviera. Its location perched on a clifftop affords panoramic views of the seaside, while the ambience of the heated swimming pool and flowering gardens is pure bliss.

Though relatively small with only 30 rooms and 7 suites, the intimacy at Château de la Chèvre d'Or is part of its charm. The accommodations are comfortably elegant, and most have amazing panoramic sea views. Whether dining

at one of four restaurants, including the two Michelin starred gourmet restaurant, relaxing poolside, or enjoying the view from the terrace, it's easy to see why this hotel is consistently honored with awards.

The namesake of the hotel, "the golden goat," is a wonderful tale. Many years ago, an elderly woman carefully hid gold coins among the stones in her modest house. When she died, so did her secret. Years later, a peasant was led by a goat with a golden fleece to the abandoned house and discovered the secret. He was overjoyed that he was able to fulfill his dream of building a new, magnificent house at the top of the village, but he disappeared soon after. Another owner acquired the chateau and while reading one summer evening, a golden goat appeared before him. When he went to touch it, the goat disappeared.

"For me, time stands still in the magical village of Eze… perhaps you will catch a glimpse of "the golden goat" at the unique Château de la Chèvre d'Or."

CHÂTEAU DE LA CHÈVRE D'OR
Rue du Barri
06360 Eze Village, France
chevredor.com

GERMANY
MUNICH

Mandarin Oriental, Munich

The Mandarin Oriental, Munich is a haven from the pace of urban life yet enjoys a prime location in the center of the city. Walk in one direction and you have the legendary Hofbrauhaus and Maximiianstrasse, known for Munich's best art galleries, boutiques, and restaurants. Five minutes is all you need to arrive at Marienplatz, the central square with its gothic Town Hall and glockenspiel clock. Walk in the other direction and you have Viktualienmarkt, a cobblestone market that sells regional wares and gourmet food. The Mandarin Oriental puts Munich at your feet, but its location on a side street helps it maintain an unmatched intimacy.

The Neo-Renaissance hotel feels like a private residence with just 73 rooms and suites. Special furnishings and beautiful fabrics enhance the exclusivity of these accommodations, while wonderful views over Munich's red roofs and spires are charming reminders of the locale.

Swim while you sightsee at the heated rooftop pool (open seasonally), or if you prefer to stay dry, enjoy the panoramic views from the China Moon Roof Terrace. The Mandarin Oriental has six distinct settings to wine and dine you. Smoke a cigar at the Rum Club, sip a cappuccino at Le Café, or let the day's worries dissipate in the Lobby Lounge, with its piano and people watching. BistroMO is a casual spot for a meal, while Restaurant Mark's demands more of your attention with its superb setting and elegant French cuisine.

Mandarin Oriental, Munich places the city at your fingertips!

MANADARIN ORIENTAL MUNICH
Neuturmstrasse 1
80331 Munich, Germany
mandarinoriental.com

GERMANY
MUNICH

Rocco Forte The Charles Hotel

Close to the historic square of Königsplatz, the old town, and the shopping area, the custom built Rocco Forte The Charles Hotel serves up the best of this beautiful Bavarian city from its stylish perch. Situated in the Old Botanical Gardens, The Charles has an unmatched tranquility in the city center.

Wake up to magical views over the Old Botanical Gardens or the historical buildings of Munich from one of the exceedingly comfortable 132 rooms and 28 suites. From the classic and deluxe king rooms to junior suites, all of the accommodations are spacious and airy. Sporting a fresh, contemporary look and feel, the rooms and suites are decked out with the latest creature comforts.

Expect to be wowed at every turn, since this Rocco Forte hotel has been designed with the company's commitment to excellence and dedication to details. Custom built for this site, the hotel has quite literally thought of everything, so guests will want for nothing. Nods to history include the collection of original paintings by Munich's celebrated 19th century artist Franz von Lenbach in the public spaces as well as the Presidential Monforte Suite.

Feast on fantastic fare at Restaurant Davvero, where the food is matched only by the beautiful views of the Max Palais and the Gardens. Visit the Bar for live music and libations.

The Spa & Wellness Club is reason alone to stay at this posh property. From Ayurvedic treatments to Asian massages, the treatment menu presents a panoply of options. Enjoy a particularly striking swim in the indoor pool, where murals of coral will soothe the body and mind.

**ROCCO FORTE
THE CHARLES HOTEL**
Sophienstrasse 28
80333 Munich, Germany
roccofortehotels.com

GREECE
ATHENS

Hotel Grande Bretagne

Ancient Greece is quite literally at your doorstep when you are a guest of the legendary Hotel Grande Bretagne. You can leave the pocket change at home…you won't be buying any postcards after marveling at the jaw-dropping views of the Acropolis from this Luxury Collection hotel.

The Hotel Grande Bretagne commands an impressive location across from the Acropolis and overlooking Constitution Square and Parliament. Elegant and historic, the hotel has 140 years of welcoming guests under its belt, so you will be well taken care of from the moment you arrive to the time of your departure.

The interiors of the hotel are a study in the classics, with traditional design, intricate moldings, and old-world appeal. An 18th century tapestry is a focal point in Alexander's Bar, while distinguished antiques and fine furnishings define the elegance of the 264 guest rooms and 56 suites.

From fine dining at one of many glamorous venues to posh pampering at the GB Spa to escaping the heat at the rooftop pool, the first-class amenities are anything but ancient at the Hotel Grande Bretagne. You certainly won't forget meals at the Roof Garden Restaurant - it seems as if you could reach out and touch the Acropolis.

"The best place to stay in Athens is, without a doubt, the Grande Bretagne. Whether you are on your honeymoon or doing a family celebration like I have done more than once, it is the perfect location for exploring ancient Greek history. Where else can you walk in almost any direction and find ancient artifacts at your feet? Take home special memories from the Grande Bretagne."

**HOTEL GRANDE BRETAGNE,
A LUXURY COLLECTION HOTEL**
Constitution Square
10564 Athens, Greece
luxurycollection.com/grandebretagne

GREECE
COSTA NAVARINO

The Romanos

Over 4,500 years of history have shaped this pristine coastline, but it is the history it is about to make that sets Costa Navarino apart. Located in the southwest Pelopennese, it is a place of great beauty and unspoiled nature. Byzantine churches dot the landscape which snakes its way along the sparkling blue Ionian Sea.

Never heard of Costa Navarino? "Well, you've heard it from me; this is the next "it" spot in the Mediterranean and its jewel-in-the-crown is The Romanos."

The Romanos, A Luxury Collection Resort, takes full advantage of its spectacular setting overlooking Dunes Beach. The sparkle of the bluer-than-blue Ionian Sea makes a perfect backdrop for this glorious resort. An entire world of ancient sites and charming villages awaits, but you could easily find yourself swept up in the beauty and majesty of this sensationally stylish resort.

Stay in one of the 289 mod guest rooms and 32 suites, where dark woods and white-on-white palettes envelop you in a world of contemporary luxury. The views of the landscaped gardens, olive groves, or shimmering sea will delight you morning, noon, and night. Villas, complete with private infinity pools, offer the ultimate exclusivity.

Play a challenging round of golf on the Bernhard Langer designed Dunes Golf Course, lounge at the Beach Club, or bliss out at the terrific Anazoe Thalassotherapy Spa. Swim in the indoor-outdoor pools while the kids splash in their own heated pool – little ones are coddled at Cocoon while Sand Castle entertains older kids. Enjoy the fresh air while climbing, biking, or hiking. Afterwards, fresh Greek cooking at the restaurants will hit the spot.

**THE ROMANOS,
A LUXURY COLLECTION RESORT**
Navarino Dunes, Costa Navarino
24001 Messinia, Greece
luxurycollection.com/romanos

GREECE
CRETE

Blue Palace Resort & Spa

Where in the world can you travel to discover rich history, crystal-clear waters, golden beaches, and traditional villages all in one enchanting place? Why, Crete, of course! This southernmost island in the Mediterranean offers a Greek island experience unlike any other.

For the crème de la crème of Crete, visit Elounda, a breathtaking landscape of coastline in the northeast. Explore ancient Minoan ruins like Knossos, visit the sites attributed as the birthplace to Zeus, the greatest god of ancient Greece, or simply dig your toes in the sand. However you spend your time in this magical spot, be sure it is at the unmatched Blue Palace Resort & Spa.

From a luxury spa and five restaurants to cocoon-like accommodations, Blue Palace welcomes you to a privileged world of restrained elegance with a modern and hip vibe.

Blue Palace romances its guests with 195 rooms plus 56 suites and villas bungalows, suites, and villas decorated with a cool, clean, and simple look. After all, it is the views of the Aegean Sea that are the focus. This resort wows with 142 private pools, so everything is centered around the blues of the sea and pools.

Indeed, from the thalassotherapy treatments of the spa to the three outdoor swimming pools, two outdoor children's pools, and a heated indoor pool at award-winning Elounda Spa, Blue Palace is truly all about water. Daydream on the private beach under the shade of a thatched umbrella, take a cruise aboard a caique (traditional wooden boat), dive in with an extensive array of available watersports, or dine on fresh seafood with a view of the azure Aegean.

It's all here waiting for you.

**BLUE PALACE
A LUXURY COLLECTION
RESORT & SPA**
72053, Elounda, Crete, Greece
luxurycollection.com/bluepalace

71

GREECE
MYKONOS

Mykonos Blu

Oh my, Mykonos! A bit of a party girl, Mykonos is a gorgeous Greek island in the Cyclades. It is where fashionistas and fishermen converge, and the world comes to celebrate. With its sun-kissed beaches and whitewashed villages, it's easy to see why this stunner enjoys the good life - there is perhaps no better way to enjoy the good life than at the Mykonos Blu, a Grecotel Exclusive Resort. Nothing sums up the cool quotient of Mykonos better than this hip hideaway.

Set on a bluff overlooking famed Psarou Beach, the resort is awash in a world of blue and white. Blending Cubism with traditional Cycladic architecture, the architecture is nothing less than striking. The 111 bungalows, suites, and villas are dreamy private hideaways scattered among the gentle slope of the gardens and along the beach. The ultimate extravagance is a junior suite with infinity pool or unique indoor pool. From blue-roofed terraces overlooking the sun-splashed sea to the stunning bathrooms that coax every last tension out of your body, these accommodations are the antithesis of the thumping beat in the nearby night clubs.

Not to be outdone is the fabulous Elixir Fitness Gallery, where azure-washed walls lend a feeling of the nearby grottoes at Psarou Beach. Whether you had a bit too much ouzo or simply want to further relax, this spa is non-pareil.

Sipping drinks at Delos Lounge, snacking poolside at L'Archipel, or enjoying the bounty of Greek cuisine at Aegean Poets, the experience is exceptional. Arrange for a private dinner on the beach or in your private retreat for an extra touch of romance at Mykonos Blu.

**MYKONOS BLU,
A GRECOTEL
EXCLUSIVE RESORT**
Psarou 84600 Mykonos, Greece
mykonosblu.com

GREECE
SANTORINI

Mystique

How do you describe a place of majestic beauty, unforgettable views, and one-of-a-kind design? There's just one word for it… Mystique.

Carved into the cliffside of the charming village of Oia on the island of Santorini, Mystique casts a spell over its guests from the moment they arrive. Its undulating terraces mimic the craggy cliffs while the views extending over the Caldera are enough to make a poet out of a plebeian. From its blindingly white exteriors to its seductive interiors, this resort is the embodiment of crisp white simplicity. Nothing distracts you from the view. Take one look… you'll never look back.

The 22 suites and villas have an inimitable artistic flair. Largely white, these chic cave-like dwellings are enhanced with unique driftwood-inspired objects and artwork. Simplistic, yet fitted with every conceivable amenity, the suites and villas evoke an instant sense of calm. Private terraces are one of the many ways to soak up the scenery. Succumb to a massage in the privacy of your own room.

Mystique invites you to dine and drink al fresco at Aura Bar and Charisma Restaurant, where unending views of the infinity pool create a romantic setting. Secret yourself away to the Wine Cellar, where 150 years of history and an impressive collection are just two of the reasons to visit this enchanting cave-like hideaway.

"The infinity pool with its staggering views is the centerpiece of this resort. Like me, spend your days sunning by its edge or your nights sipping and sampling under the stars. It's all part of the magical intimacy of Mystique, a place that exudes romance."

**MYSTIQUE,
A LUXURY COLLECTION HOTEL**
Oia 847 02, Santorini, Greece
luxurycollection.com/mystique

GREECE
SANTORINI

Vedema

Leave the tourists and tee-shirt shops of Fira and retreat to the blissfully quiet village Megalohori on Santorini's southwestern Caldera side. It is a picture-perfect place of ancient vineyards and historic mansions once belonging to wealthy wine merchants. A place of unmatched beauty, it is also home to the luxurious Vedema resort.

Beauty spills forth from Vedema, and it is no wonder, since this resort is built around a 400-year-old winery. Comprised of 45 pastel-hued townhouses (11 with private pools) set on the grounds of this lovely vineyard and surrounded by a wall, Vedema is truly a world of its own – in fact, it is a village within the village. The stylish accommodations showcase traditional island elements with graceful arches and shuttered windows alongside shocks of brightly colored furnishings and accents. It's a delightfully modern take on Greek island living.

"Vedema, A Luxury Collection Resort, knows how to spoil its guests and their children with a bevy of top tier amenities. From shuttle service to their private beach to a full-service holistic-minded spa to creative cuisine at two restaurants, Vedema enchants at every turn. Take in the views at a variety of open-air dining venues - Pergola Pool for casual fare, Vinsanto's rooftop for more elegant dining - but don't miss dinner in the one of a kind 400-year-old winery."

Hop on one of the hotel's mountain bikes for a ride around the island, enjoy a cruise and volcanic sightseeing tour, play tennis, or enjoy watersports. Enjoy your downtime and the picturesque setting at the lovely pool set within the village and overlooking the rolling vineyards.

**VEDEMA
A LUXURY COLLECTION RESORT**
Megalohori, Santorini 84700, Greece
luxurycollection.com/vedema

HUNGARY
BUDAPEST

Four Seasons Hotel Gresham Palace Budapest

The River Danube cuts an impressive swath through the combined regions of Buda and Pest, which merged in 1873. Historic Buda, set high on the river's west bank, is defined by its charming cobblestoned streets, medieval castles and churches, while the east bank of Pest is home to the city's commercial center and a rich blend of architectural styles ranging from Renaissance to modern.

Just as the Danube bridges the two regions, the Four Seasons Hotel Gresham Palace also bridges two worlds, the old and the new, of this dynamic Eastern European city. Set within an Art Nouveau landmark at the foot of the historic Chain Bridge, the Four Seasons Hotel Gresham Palace celebrates the culture and history of this city while infusing it with a contemporary verve.

Vaulted ceilings and little private balconies are just some of the details that reflect the architectural heritage of Gresham Palace in the 162 striking guest rooms and 17 suites. The accommodations, enhanced with soothing earth tones, share vistas over the courtyard, Old City, or the Danube.

The hotel's signature restaurant, with the ambience of a famous coffeehouse culture, specializes in new interpretations of traditional Hungarian cuisine. Enjoy the Bar's lovely setting beneath the glass cupola of the historic Páva Udvar (Peacock Passage). Even the Spa honors Hungary in its style and treatments.

"From incredible Gothic architecture, former Royal Palaces housing world-class museums, stately churches, and shops filled with collectibles, I found Budapest a feast. For me, I'll only stay at the Four Seasons Hotel Gresham Palace, particularly in one of the suites with panoramic views of the Danube and the hills of Buda."

FOUR SEASONS HOTEL GRESHAM PALACE BUDAPEST
Széchenyi István Tér 5-6
1051 Budapest, Hungary
fourseasons.com

IRELAND
CONG

Ashford Castle

Not far from Galway, Ashford Castle is on the shores of Lough Corrib in western Ireland. A visit to this magical castle is an experience to cherish. Dating back to 1228 and rebuilt as a hunting and fishing lodge in the 1800s, the castle was once the private estate of the Guinness ale family. First opened as a hotel in 1939, Ashford Castle is full of tradition.

From four-poster beds and old-fashioned claw-foot bathtubs in the staterooms to charming prints in the sun-filled deluxe rooms, the 83 accommodations are delightfully appointed. Warm and inviting, you could find yourself spending entire days in these cozy guest rooms, but with a wondrous array of outdoor activities at this spectacular resort, it would be a shame to spend your time closeted away.

Golf and fishing are two of Ashford Castle's biggest draws. The Castle's location on the banks of the River Cong and Lough Corrib make it one of the country's top spots for anglers seeking trout and salmon. Not a seasoned fisherman? Take one of the Orvis endorsed fly fishing lessons.

Enjoy the challenge and the sheer beauty of the Eddie Hackett designed golf course. The grounds, comprised of 300 acres dotted with plants and trees, are perfect for hand-in-hand walks or quiet exploration. Join the resident historian, a ship captain, aboard a lake cruise to the island of St. Patrick, or spa-goers will enjoy the peaceful relaxation and treatments of the spa.

It is a good thing that you've worked up an appetite while exploring the grounds, since fine dining at four unique restaurants is part and parcel of the superb experience here.

ASHFORD CASTLE
Cong
County Mayo, Ireland
ashfordcastle.ie

IRELAND
DUBLIN

Four Seasons Hotel Dublin

Looking for a sophisticated choice in Dublin? Step right up to the exclusive Four Seasons Hotel. Set just outside the city center in the historic and prestigious Ballsbridge neighborhood, the Four Seasons occupies several acres of the Royal Dublin Society's 42-acre showgrounds, site of the annual Dublin Horse Show. Dublin's bustling pubs and thriving scene are just a short walk away, but here, life is quiet and restful.

The six-level Georgian-inspired red brick building fits right in with this pastoral setting, while the 183 rooms and 14 suites are among the most spacious in Dublin. The views, extending out over the hotel's landscaped gardens and the stately homes of Ballsbridge, are a highlight of any visit. The lush setting is brought indoors through the use of floral fabrics and pastel-hued furnishings and accents in the accommodations, while the public rooms have a grand design complete with details like Brazilian granite, polished Italian marble, inlaid woods, and handwoven carpets.

Enjoy Dublin's nightlife until the wee hours but come home to the sophisticated countryside quiet at the Four Seasons, which is also home to an airy spa. It is one of Dublin's finest and features a complete treatment menu, as well as a fitness center and indoor swimming pool. Golf, horseback riding, and trout and salmon fishing are all easily arranged nearby.

The Four Seasons upholds Ireland's tradition of friendly hospitality in its two restaurants and three bars. The Lobby Lounge and Bar are both styled with an eye for tradition, but Ice breaks the mold with its striking décor showcasing the works of contemporary Irish artists.

FOUR SEASONS HOTEL DUBLIN
Simmonscourt Road
Dublin 4, Ireland
fourseasons.com

IRELAND
DUBLIN

The Merrion

Tradition reigns at The Merrion. This elegant hotel meticulously converted from four Georgian townhouses feels like a classic because it is. Lord Monck, Lord Mornington, and the Duke of Wellington, the former owners of the private residences, could walk right in and feel at home at this gracious hotel with impeccable standards.

Located in the heart of Dublin, across from the Irish Parliament and Government Buildings, The Merrion is just a stone's throw from esteemed Trinity College and the city's best museums are down the street.

The 123 rooms and 19 suites in the main hotel and the specially commissioned garden wing are decorated with Irish fabrics, reproduction furnishings, and antiques indicative of the original townhomes. Refined and formal, the accommodations are a lovely step back in time. Enjoy views of the surrounding neighborhood and its two glorious period gardens – even dine outdoors amid the fresh air and flowers on the Garden Terrace.

The Merrion isn't just a work of art itself… it houses one of the most impressive private collections in Ireland. Arrange a tour for a first-hand look at the hotel's astonishing collection of 19th and 20th century artwork.

Tethra Spa draws on Ireland's literary history for its name. Tethra, or "land of the young and living," comes from a collection of stories and is an appropriate name for this revitalizing retreat.

No. 23 has a classic Irish pub look of leather chairs and emerald green walls. The Drawing Rooms with roaring fires are just right for afternoon tea. Simple Irish cuisine headlines at The Cellar Restaurant, while the renowned Restaurant Patrick Guilbaud features Michelin starred gourmet dining.

THE MERRION
Upper Merrion Street
Dublin 2, Ireland
merrionhotel.com

IRELAND
ENNISKERRY

The Ritz-Carlton Powerscourt, County Wicklow

Visiting Ireland and unsure whether to spend your time touring Dublin or enjoying the lush countryside? Stay at The Ritz-Carlton Powerscourt, County Wicklow and you won't need to choose. This spectacular resort is set on one of Ireland's most scenic and historic estates, yet it is just a short drive from the sights and attractions of Dublin.

This stunning resort will take your breath away. It is the countryside as only the luscious green of Ireland can promise. Whether you are enjoying the grounds of the 12th century Powerscourt House or wandering the private pathways along the River Walk, take in the beauty of the outdoors at this majestic Estate. The resort is a showpiece of Palladian style architecture, while its 107 rooms and 93 suites are elegantly appointed with striped wallpaper and wing chairs, dark wood furnishings, and green, blue, or gold color tones.

It is the superior facilities at this resort that will have you and your children's eyes smiling - regardless of your heritage. Ireland is celebrated for its challenging and scenic golf courses, and the Estate's two championship level courses are no exception.

The Ritz-Carlton's Spa is a sybarite's paradise. Topping out at 30,000 square feet, this luxurious ESPA Spa truly has it all. Twenty treatment rooms…a Swarovski crystal-lit pool…views of The Sugar Loaf Mountain - stress has certainly met its match here.

But wait, it doesn't end there. Fine dining is available at five spots, including the renowned Gordon Ramsay restaurant. If you've always wanted to take a peek behind the scenes but can't quite stand the heat, book the Gordon Ramsay Chef's Table for a special memory.

THE RITZ-CARLTON POWERSCOURT, COUNTY WICKLOW
Powerscourt Estate
Enniskerry, Ireland
ritzcarlton.com

ITALY
CAPRI

Hotel Caesar Augustus

Ah, Capri. If there is any better representation of *la dolce vita*, I do not know it. This magical island has captivated everyone from ancient Roman emperors to Jackie O, who famously walked its streets in her 'capri pants' and handmade sandals. You can still pick up a pair today.

There is perhaps no better way to enjoy the unique spirit of this atmospheric island than by staying in a private villa, but don't worry if you don't have a key. Check in at the Caesar Augustus instead. This hilltop mansion is quite literally the height of luxury – located nearly 1,000 feet above the sea in the quiet town of Anacapri. The views are just breathtaking, but it is the intimacy and gentle spirit that make this hotel a stand-out.

The mansion's 13 rooms and 42 suites are styled to look like guest rooms in a private home. Traditional Italian details and accessories, including terracotta-tiled floors and handpainted ceramics, give the rooms a comfortable elegance. Of course, it is the views, best enjoyed from the private balconies, that will have you forfeiting any thought of returning to your home.

"The infinity edge pool is the meeting place for all of the guests of the Caesar Augustus and its poolside restaurant is just the spot for an al fresco plate of pasta. By day or night, marvel at the expanse of sea views overlooking the islands of Capri and Ischia to the Bay of Naples from this elevation. Lucullo Terrace marries the flavors and culinary traditions of Capri and Naples in its elegant and romantic candlelit setting."

HOTEL CAESAR AUGUSTUS
Via G. Orlandi, 4
80071 Anacapri, Capri, Italy
caesar-augustus.com

ITALY
CAPRI

Capri Palace Hotel & Spa

While the island has always been a playground for the rich and famous, where do they stay when they want to get away from it all? The impossibly ultra-chic Capri Palace Hotel & Spa!

The 67 luxurious rooms are sun-filled aeries with soothing palettes and handmade terracotta tile floors, along with inspiring views of the sea or the hillside gardens. While their flavor is cosmopolitan sophistication, what really sets the Capri Palace Hotel apart are its five Art and four Star suites. Contemporary in feel and furnishings, each pays homage to a different artist or celebrity. From the bright splashes of Miro and the orderly geometric Mondrian designs to the glamorous Monroe Suite, each has its own personality and panache.

The artistic flair of this one-of-a-kind hotel is everywhere. The Art Gallery showcases contemporary pieces, while the Artist's Bar shows off an impressive collection of artwork. Even dining is a work of art, especially at L'Olivo, where its cuisine has earned a Michelin star (the only one on Capri). Feeling more casual? Visit Bistrot Ragu or the Wine Cellar, with its 10,000-bottle wine list.

Capri Palace Hotel elevates health and beauty to an art form in its award-winning Spa. Treatments are more than skin deep; there is a medical health club too. Il Riccio Beach Club, next to the famous Blue Grotto, is just a short ride away for sun seekers.

"Ever since *Breakfast at Tiffany's*, Audrey Hepburn has been a favorite of mine, thus it's no wonder that I'm partial to the Hepburn Suite. However, I'd settle for a sea view room during my Italian holiday anytime."

CAPRI PALACE HOTEL & SPA
Via Capodimonte, 14
80071 Anacapri, Capri, Italy
capripalace.com

ITALY
FIESOLE

Villa San Michele

Many people can say they have seen Michelangelo's handiwork, but how many have stayed in it? Welcome to the world of Villa San Michele.

Tucked in the hills of Fiesole, overlooking Florence, Villa San Michele allows you to live and breathe Renaissance history. It is said that Michelangelo designed the façade of his 15th century monastery, an Orient-Express hotel, and its vantage point allows you to admire Florence's glory in its entirety.

Travelers flock to Florence for its renowned culture, but only a privileged few stay in one of Villa San Michele's 21 rooms or 25 suites. The rooms and suites are handsomely appointed with a classic Renaissance decor. The headboards, either handpainted wood or intricate wrought iron, are delightfully unique. The Limonaia, where the monks in the 17th century stored their lemon trees during the winter, has been beautifully converted into a spacious "villa within the Villa" with one to three bedrooms and access to a private garden with a secluded plunge pool. All guests, including children, will no doubt feel the magic of this special place.

The stunning views of Florence and the Arno Valley make for a particularly spectacular backdrop, whether you are feasting on Italian dishes at the Loggia Restaurant or taking a break from sightseeing and splashing in the cool waters of the hilltop swimming pool.

"I left the Uffizi for another day and took an afternoon cooking class with the hotel's well-respected chef Attilio di Fabrizi where I learned how to bring back a taste of Tuscany from salad to dessert. It's worth adding an extra day to your visit for this delightful experience."

VILLA SAN MICHELE
Via di Doccia 4
50014 Fiesole, Florence, Italy
villasanmichele.com or
orient-express.com

ITALY
FLORENCE

Four Seasons Hotel Firenze

The Four Seasons Hotel Firenze is an enchanted sanctuary in the heart of Florence. This art-filled Renaissance palazzo and convent frame a centuries-old private park.

Reflecting Florence's rich architectural and art history, the 92 sun-filled rooms and 24 suites showcase many original frescoes, friezes, and hand-painted sculptured reliefs. The accommodations are artfully appointed, and are blessed with an inviting residential comfort. Located in both the Palazzo della Gherardesca and the Conventino, they are designed to feel welcoming with picturesque views of the area streets, surrounding palazzos and gardens, and the Hotel's own central Giardino della Gherardesca.

Relax amidst original frescoes and sculptured reliefs, graced by sunlight

and airy garden vistas. Sip cappuccino under majestic trees, or lounge by the open-air pool. Bask in Italian beauty secrets at the Spa, the only facility in the world to use products from Officina Profumo – Farmaceutica di Santa Maria Novella. One of the world's oldest pharmacies, it continues to use natural ingredients and follow the traditional recipes of monks from the 13th century.

The centuries-old large private garden creates a park-like feeling, yet this hotel is centrally located near all of the major museums, landmarks, and cafés. Listen to the birdsong as they flit from flower to tree in this serene resort within a city. Do not miss an elegant occasion and exquisite Italian cuisine crafted by chef Vito Mollica at Il Palagio.

"From its frescoes to its gardens, The Four Seasons Hotel Firenze is sure to make you feel as if you are a Renaissance aristocrat living in your own palazzo but pampered the Four Seasons way. I certainly felt like Catherine de Medici!"

FOUR SEASONS HOTEL FIRENZE
Borgo Pinti, 99
50121 Florence, Italy
fourseasons.com

ITALY
FLORENCE

Rocco Forte Hotel Savoy

Looking for a bit more modern than Michelangelo while exploring the charms of Florence? Head for Rocco Forte Hotel Savoy, where historic Florence is given a chic, contemporary slant.

Located on the Piazza della Repubblica, travelers will delight in the convenience of the hotel's central location. Midway between the Duomo and the Ponte Vecchio, Florence's sights and sounds are within a short walk, and many can be viewed from the windows of the hotel.

Rocco Forte Hotel Savoy breathes fresh air into the city with its sleek design and clean, simple décor. Olga Polizzi, designer of all Rocco Forte hotels, has worked her magic again in the 88 rooms and 14 suites. The interiors are largely contemporary and far from stuffy or serious – look for the quirky prints of shoes found throughout the hotel which pay humorous homage to the city's many craftsmen. The large windows allow for unobstructed views of the Piazza and the Duomo. Sleek without being stark and cool without being impersonal, the service is always first rate and friendly.

Chef Fulvio Pierangelini's collaboration has skyrocketed L'Incontro Restaurant and Bar into the stratosphere with his award-winning cooking and stylish setting. Opening onto the Piazza from spring through fall, this modern Italian restaurant is one of the top people-watching spots in town.

"Invariably on my walk to the Ponte Vecchio, I stop at Salvatore Ferragamo, another Florentine legend. If you're like me, you'll want the shopping bags delivered to your home away from home. Sleep in style at Rocco Forte Hotel Savoy; the Renaissance is a walk away and the contemporary is just inside your door."

ROCCO FORTE HOTEL SAVOY
Piazza della Repubblica 7
50123 Florence, Italy
roccofortehotels.com

ITALY
FLORENCE

The St. Regis Florence

Some things in life do live up to their expectations, and the new St. Regis Florence, formerly known as the Grand, is one of them. It was closed in August 2010 for nearly one year to create the St. Regis.

The building was designed by Renaissance architect Filippo Brunelleschi, the architect of the city's famed, and instantly recognizable, Duomo. Originally a private palace, it has been a hotel since the 18th century. From society balls to royal marriages, this hotel has always hosted and feted the most distinguished guests in the resplendent ballroom.

Located in a glittering palace in the heart of the city, the hotel immerses you in Florence's timeless attractions. Stroll over to the Uffizi, Duomo, or Ponte Vecchio - it's all within this walking pedestrian zone.

The St. Regis Florence's 81 guestrooms and 19 suites celebrate the artistic heritage of Florence and are decorated with one of three exquisite Medici, Florentine, and Renaissance styles. Enhanced with antique artworks, brilliant crystal chandeliers, and custom frescoes, the accommodations are the very definition of sumptuous.

The Wintergarden is the architectural center and spiritual heart of the hotel.

Its stained glass roof is breathtaking and it is again a fashionable meeting place to socialize over coffee, cocktails, and cuisine.

"This grand lady has always been a favorite of mine and I had even suggested it become a St. Regis. Needless to say, I was delighted when this became a reality and even had a sneak preview. Having just returned from the debut of The St. Regis Florence, I can tell you that it is absolutely fabulous!"

THE ST. REGIS FLORENCE
Piazza Ognissanti 1
50123 Florence, Italy
stregis.com/florence

ITALY
FLORENCE

The Westin Excelsior, Florence

The Westin Excelsior occupies a prime city center location on the Arno River and dominates Piazza Ognissanti, where shops dating back to the Renaissance rest alongside modern luxury boutiques. Though the hotel opened in 1927, this site has seen more than 700 years of Florentine history. In the 13th century, this area was marshland and was first settled by a religious order. Eventually, religion gave way to nobility and this area was home to grand private residences.

The Westin Excelsior Florence offers an enchanted stage set where every step reveals a new and astonishing interpretation of 15th century elegance but this palatial hotel offers a host of up-to-the-minute amenities, such as a fitness center and a variety of top-notch restaurants.

Traditional Florentine grace and beauty are reflected in the 159 rooms and junior suites plus 12 suites. Breathtaking views stretch from the Arno, over the winding medieval streets, and as far as the rolling hills in the distance.

From the Duomo and the Pitti Palace to the Uffizi Gallery and Santa Maria Novella, all of Florence's storied landmarks are within blocks of the Excelsior. Browse the glittering jewelry stores of the Ponte Vecchio and peruse the boutiques, but come home to a world of easy elegance at The Westin Excelsior.

"Orvm Restaurant on the ground floor features a fun 1920s feel and serves Italian fare; however the hot spot to be is Se-Sto on Arno. Twenty years of perseverance has brought The Excelsior its dream of a rooftop setting. Hands down the best views of Florence are showcased from this 1960s-style bar and restaurant serving up contemporary Mediterranean cuisine."

THE WESTIN EXCELSIOR
Piazza Ognissanti 3
50123 Florence, Italy
westin.com/excelsiorflorence

ITALY
LAKE COMO

Villa d'Este

Overlooking majestic Lake Como, Villa d'Este has been attracting visitors for over 500 years. Nuns were the first ones to make their presence and the gardens contain columns that are attributed to their convent.

The palatial villa was constructed in 1568 as the elegant summer residence of Cardinal Tolomeo Gallio. The exquisite villa and 25 acres of stunning gardens have been home to many, including aristocrats, an empress, and an English queen.

Since opening as a luxury hotel in 1873, Villa d'Este has inspired passion in its guests. Both Puccini and Verdi visited, and it is said that Verdi composed his *Traviata* at Villa d'Este.

The rarefied world of Villa d'Este is shared in its regal rooms and suites, 125 in the Cardinal's residence and 27 in the Queen's Pavilion. Fabulous Como silks create an added element of luxury.

From its riveting lakefront setting to its incomparable Renaissance period gardens to its legendary hospitality, there is nothing quite like Villa d'Este. Marvel at the 16th century Mosaic with its Nympheum.

Relax at the floating pool that stretches into the lake or be active with a variety of water sports. Luciano Parolari's delectable Italian haute cuisine has earned him worldwide recognition, so dining is always a tantalizing event.

"Villa d'Este holds a special place in my heart. Whether dating back to when we as a family vacationed here in the late 1970s to my son-in-law's romantic proposal to my daughter Jennifer twenty years ago to anticipating taking my three grandchildren to share the Lake Como experience, I could tell you so many stories about living la dolce vita at Villa d'Este."

VILLA D'ESTE
Via Regina, 40
22012 Cernobbio, Italy
villadeste.com

ITALY
MILAN

Bulgari Hotel Milan

On a private street between Via Montenapoleone, Via della Spiga, La Scala and the Accademia di Brera, The Bulgari Hotel Milan sets the stage as one of this style setting city's best.

This posh hotel is located in a tastefully renovated 18th century Milanese palazzo. The exterior, characterized by its white marmorino stucco, may seem simple, but like a pearl inside an oyster, this hotel surprises with hidden jewels. One of these surprises is the blissfully peaceful private garden. It is an absolute oasis of serenity and relaxation in the heart of busy Milan, as well as a natural extension of the nearby Botanical Garden.

High fashion is synonymous with Milan, so it should come as no surprise that the sun-filled 47 rooms and 11 suites have been designed to look like they stepped right off a catwalk. Fashion editors and trendsetters will appreciate the attention to detail, while the warm earth tones have that unmistakable Milanese flair for the contemporary. Windows look out onto the beautiful garden or courtyard, thus offering guests an unexpected sense of tranquility in the center of the city.

Il Bar and Il Ristorante have both become a meeting place for hotel guests and those locals who want to sip and socialize with the sophisticated set. Set against a spectacular glass wall that opens onto the private garden, both spaces are light. Sample the contemporary creations of Italian cuisine in the convivial bar or in the chic restaurant – it's up to you. Or, if the weather permits, take any of your meals in the tranquil garden. It's modern Milan at its most magical.

BULGARI HOTEL MILAN
Via Privata Fratelli Gabba 7B
20121 Milan, Italy
bulgarihotels.com

ITALY
MILAN

Four Seasons Hotel Milan

Just off the via Montenapoleone in the heart of Milan's shopping district, the Four Seasons Hotel Milan sets a style of its own in one of the world's most famous fashion capitals.

This hotel has an intimate character with just 67 welcoming rooms and 51 soothing suites. Take a look at the Neoclassical façade and the cloistered courtyard; they are both hints of the hotel's former incarnation. This 15th century monastery retains other nods to its history, such as vaulted ceilings and bits of frescoes, but this plush hotel is far from monastic.

Clean lines and casual elegance define the classic Italian design in the rooms and suites, while Cassina furniture, Frette linens, and Fortuny fabrics up the luxe factor. Unwind at the new large spa.

It is a mark of success when a hotel is enjoyed by its guests, but when it is also beloved by locals, you know it's a winner. Even the hard-to-please Milanese adore the Four Seasons and have adopted its two restaurants and lounge as their own. Il Teatro has a stylish ambience, complete with French walnut woodwork and leather upholstered walls, while La Veranda has a view of the garden and terrace for a more airy feel. The lounge is fashionable for cocktails… sip an Amaretto while admiring the fragments of original frescoes and the rare Peroni stage set drawings for La Scala.

"My favorite rooms overlook the tranquil cloistered courtyard, while others have views over Via Gesù and the city. Leave Milan's bustle at the door and enjoy the peaceful setting of the Four Seasons Hotel Milan. Service always shines here."

FOUR SEASONS HOTEL MILAN
Via Gesù, 8
20121 Milan, Italy

ITALY
MILAN

Park Hyatt Milan

From its location to its look, the Park Hyatt Milan is a perfect representation of this oh-so-sleek city. This contemporary luxury hotel is ideally situated in the heart of the historic center and is just steps from Piazza Duomo and Teatro alla Scala, and within walking distance of the renowned fashion houses of Via Montenapoleone and Via della Spiga. "Of course, its claim to fame is its location overlooking the magnificent Galleria Vittorio Emanuele II, home to chic boutiques and cafés which I always visit."

The Park and La Cupola. Warm colors create a calming atmosphere in The Park, where Italian culinary traditions are updated with modern twists. La Cupola Lobby Lounge is marked by its glass dome and bewitching "Medusa's Head" masterpiece by Lucio Fontana. "Cozy, yet refined, La Cupola is the heart of this hotel and invites patrons to enjoy everything from breakfast and afternoon tea to cocktails, even pre or post opera meals."

Set in a palatial classical building dating back to 1870, the Park Hyatt's look is completely of-the-moment. The earth-toned palette is at once soothing and slick. The 108 rooms and 30 suites echo the restrained elegance found throughout the hotel's lobby, restaurants, and spa and incorporate high-tech amenities to suit the many business travelers who make this their home-away-from-home.

PARK HYATT MILAN
Via Tommaso Grossi, 1
20121 Milan, Italy
parkhyatt.com

The Spa, decorated with pastel Venetian stucco finishes, is a world of chic serenity spotlighting Italian artistry. The magical whirlpool wall, made of smooth glass and composed of 250,000 tiny pieces of mosaic, each with 24 carat gold leaf, explodes with shimmering gold light.

The Park Hyatt Milan hotel is home to two restaurants,

ITALY
MILAN

Hotel Principe di Savoia

Need a stylish base in the heart of Milan's business district? Principe di Savoia, a Dorchester Collection hotel, is at your service from its commanding presence on Piazza della Repubblica.

"If you think Milan is synonymous with cream and beige palettes and simple furnishings, head straight for the Principe di Savoia for a lesson in elegant turn-of-the-century grandeur. This Neo-classical grande dame is a former palazzo, so expect a glittering celebration of old-world tradition."

Since the 1920s, this hotel has hosted the well-heeled and well-known in the heart of the financial district. The 269 rooms and 132 suites are a testament to luxury. Hand-painted frescoes and gorgeous jewel tones reflect the glamour of the Principe Suites. The Deluxe Mosaic Rooms, all overlooking Piazza della Repubblica, feature three different styles. Venetian-style rooms are done in gold and turquoise fabrics with Murano glass mirrors, Florentine style rooms feature azure-grey shades and mosaics, and Neoclassical style rooms highlight ruby and amethyst tones with exquisite bathroom glass mosaics.

The pièce de résistance is certainly the sumptuous Presidential Suite. One of the largest hotel suites in Europe, this three bedroom accommodation even features a private pool decorated with Pompeii-style frescoed walls.

Club 10 Fitness & Beauty Center deserves a perfect 10 for its appealing ambience and top-notch amenities, including an indoor pool.

Renowned designer Thierry Despont has infused the Hotel Principe di Savoia lobby's Il Salotto with a luxurious blend of Italian furnishings and a custom-made Murano glass chandelier, while the magical setting of Acanto restaurant is a city favorite. Tables overlook the grand Italian garden with an 18th century fountain for a particularly enchanting setting.

HOTEL PRINCIPE DI SAVOIA
Piazza della Repubblica, 17
20124 Milan, Italy
hotelprincipedisavoia.com or
dorchestercollection.com

ITALY
PORTOFINO

Hotel Splendido

Life is indeed splendid at Portofino's Hotel Splendido, an Orient-Express Hotel.

Once a simple fishing village, tiny Portofino with only 500 residents is considered the jewel of the Italian Riviera. Resting high above the bay in this glamorous seaside village, Hotel Splendido rests on four acres of semi-tropical, terraced gardens…dotted with palm trees and olive groves. This hotel appeals to your senses with its heady fragrances and views of the azure Mediterranean Sea. Exceptionally private and tucked away from it all, this hideaway has long been a favorite haunt of film stars seeking a retreat from their public personas. Greta Garbo, Humphrey Bogart, Lauren Bacall, and Elizabeth Taylor all sought refuge here.

Breathe in the relaxed elegance of the Italian Riviera in the pastel-hued 29 rooms and 35 suites. The resort's hilltop perch allows for spectacular panoramic views of the harbor filled with luxury yachts and the vistas are best enjoyed from the private terraces or balconies.

"I've spent many a day basking in the glorious golden sunshine by the pool or unwinding with an al fresco massage set within the bountiful gardens. No matter where you choose to rest, soaking up the view of this harborfront village is de rigueur."

Typical Ligurian cuisine, emphasizing local seafood, is served at Hotel Splendido's La Terrazza. Dine indoors in the elegant setting or enjoy the salt air and the scene outdoors on the terrace overlooking the sea. "I have been known to select a cruise because it includes Portofino – all for the pure pleasure of having a scrumptious lunch at Splendido!"

"Morning, noon, and night, I never tire of Hotel Splendido's sophisticated and peaceful pace."

HOTEL SPLENDIDO
Salita Baratta, 16
16034 Portofino, Italy
hotelsplendido.com or
orient-express.com

ITALY
POSITANO

Le Sirenuse

Nothing captures the heart of romantics quite like the Amalfi Coast. This serpentine stretch of coastline is a place of great beauty – a spot that enchants visitors at every twist and turn.

Tucked amidst the baroque houses of the hillside village of Positano, Le Sirenuse is a one-of-a-kind hideaway. This 18th century summer house was transformed into a luxurious hotel in 1951 and has been captivating chic travelers ever since. Owned and managed by the Neapolitan noble Sersale family, Le Sirenuse welcomes guests as if they are members of the family.

Le Sirenuse will sweep you up in its magic. Don't be surprised…after all it does take its name from the islands it faces that were the mythical home of the sirens that once seduced Odysseus.

58 rooms and 2 suites face the water and all are beautifully decorated with period furnishings, handmade Vietri tile floors, and unique artwork. Its well-collected look is no accident – many of the items that enhance the accommodations have been in the Sersale family for generations. In contrast, go modern at the hip spa.

"Nearly 25 years ago, I fell in love with the Amalfi Coast because of Le Sirenuse. Whether daydreaming by the pool or sampling Neapolitan delicacies, relaxing on the terrace is my favorite activity. The terrace, filled with flowers and lemon trees, is absolutely stunning and the panoramic views from this vantage point are unforgettable."

Sample the creations of the acclaimed chef amid the bougainvillea-covered archways on the terrace at La Sponda, where many dishes are Sersale family recipes, but it is the 400 hundred glowing candles at night that are unbelievably romantic.

LE SIRENUSE
Via Cristoforo Colombo, 30
84017 Positano, Italy
lesirenuse.com

ITALY
RAVELLO

Hotel Caruso

The spellbinding ancient ruins of Pompeii, the bustling streets of Naples, and the island of Capri are all nearby, but once you are ensconced in the wonderful world of Hotel Caruso, it is unlikely you will ever want to leave.

This Orient-Express hotel is terraced into the hills of Ravello. A former 11th century palace, this unique sanctuary offers insight into a grander time. Its ancient walls and fresco covered ceilings have been restored with painstaking detail. Enjoy a gentler pace from one of the gloriously decorated 48 rooms or suites.

Spend your days unwinding by the infinity pool, where the jaw-dropping views will mystify you. On a clear day, you can see all the way to the Bay of Salerno.

Walk through the fragrant centuries-old gardens to the Caruso Wellness Centre and indulge your senses with an aromatherapy treatment. You can even enjoy the healing effects of massage in the tranquil gardens.

"Dining in the Belvedere gardens for my 65th birthday with my family was beyond memorable."

Choose between three restaurants, all with breathtaking Amalfi Coast backdrops. The Belvedere Restaurant is perfect for al fresco dining, while the Caruso Restaurant has an elegant indoor dining room and a beautiful outdoor terrace. A poolside restaurant provides lighter meals during the day.

"I often say that I am a frustrated hotelier and I must admit that when I think back, I wish I had purchased the Caruso Belvedere in 1990 as the first in a collection of hotels that I would own. Orient-Express more than fulfilled my vision for the property, though selfishly I wish I could call it my own!"

HOTEL CARUSO
Piazza San Giovanni del Toro 2
84010 Ravello, Italy
hotelcaruso.com or
orient-express.com

ITALY
RAVELLO

Palazzo Sasso

Enjoy the exotic flavor of Palazzo Sasso.

This stunning 12th century villa is set high above the cliffs in the charming medieval village of Ravello. Its Moorish influences and staggering views combine to offer an unforgettable Amalfi Coast experience.

Named for the original owners, the noble "Sasso" family, the Palazzo has a fascinating history. More than a century ago, Richard Wagner wrote part of the Parsifal in this palace, Roberto Rossellini and Ingrid Bergmann stayed several times during the 1950s, and General Eisenhower planned a liberation operation during World War II here. Unoccupied for almost 20 years, it opened as a luxury hotel in 1997.

From its Moorish architectural influences to its staggering views, Palazzo Sasso seduces guests with its signature style. Reproduction Italian furniture and antique pieces complete the historic look in the 43 rooms and suites at this romantic retreat. The grounds, filled with flowering shrubs, palm trees, and trickling fountains, are majestic. Enjoy the view with a swim or soak in the pool set within the gardens. The Carita Spa offers a comprehensive array of beauty and wellness therapies.

Caffé dell'Arte, with its trendy setting of arched windows and a dazzling black-and-white patterned floor, and the Terrazza Belvedere are both ideal for casual dining. The magical mood continues at Rossellinis, named in honor of Roberto and Ingrid, where the Italian haute cuisine has earned two Michelin stars. "Its flavorful food served by a superb staff is enough to capture your heart, but combine it with swoon-worthy views of the fishing boats in the water nearly 1,000 feet below, and you will be head-over-heels in love with this award-winning spot."

PALAZZO SASSO
Via San Giovanni del Toro, 28
84010 Ravello, Italy
palazzosasso.com

ITALY
ROME

Hotel Hassler

Plenty of hotels can say they are within walking distance of major attractions, but how many can say they rest at the top of one of Rome's most camera worthy spots? Only one – the Hotel Hassler. This hotel has an enviable location atop the Spanish Steps, adjacent to the Church of Trinita dei Monti and just a short walk to the Via Condotti. Hotel Hassler has long been considered one of the world's best.

Marble columns, Oriental carpets, and Murano chandeliers set a stately tone in this former palazzo. The 85 rooms, 10 suites, and 3 Presidential suites are defiantly decadent…original paintings and even Louis XV furnishings enhance some rooms. Bathrooms are grand with 23kt gold-plated faucets!

Hotel Hassler may be named for its founder, but its regal spirit is upheld by the reputable Wirth family, who has owned and managed the hotel for almost a century. The Hassler has hosted many celebrities and dignitaries, giving it a mythical feel. Prince Rainier and Grace Kelly honeymooned here, and Princess Diana used to visit often for a taste of their special Bellinis.

Dining at the Hassler is a magnificent memory. From the Michelin-starred rooftop Imàgo to the Salone Eva, Palm Court Restaurants, and Hassler Bar, it is an experience to cherish.

"There are too many times to count when I have wined, dined, and stayed at the Hassler over the last 35 years, but each is a fond memory. One of the most memorable was a dinner I hosted nearly 20 years ago at the rooftop restaurant for forty Valerie Wilson Travel agents. What a special treat for all!"

HOTEL HASSLER
Trinita dei Monti 6
00187 Rome, Italy
hotelhasslerroma.com

ITALY
ROME

Rocco Forte Hotel de Russie

Rome may be known for its ancient ruins, but the Eternal City is constantly reinventing itself. Case in point? The Rocco Forte Hotel de Russie. This recreated hotel shows the mid-century mod side of Rome.

Just because Hotel de Russie has a fresh look doesn't mean this hotel lacks history (it is Rome, after all). This hotel was a favorite of the Russian Imperial House, Stravinsky, and even Picasso in the 19th century. Its venerable exterior belies the interiors with its striking juxtaposition of classical and contemporary styles.

The 89 rooms and 33 suites are done in restful hues and spotlight an eclectic mix of furnishings. Views over the Piazza del Popolo are intriguing, but the views over

the garden make you think you're in the countryside rather than the city.

Book the signature treatment, the ancient Roman ritual, at the De Russie Wellness Zone, which is complete with a full-service spa, Finnish sauna, and fully equipped gym.

Hotel de Russie's best surprise is its terraced "Secret Garden." Once a modest vineyard, the garden filled with ancient trees, fruit trees, and flowering shrubs

is legendary. It is said that Picasso and Cocteau picked the oranges from the garden's trees while staying here. Hidden behind the building which overlooks Via del Babuino, it is a tranquil oasis amidst the bustle of Rome and serves as the delightful setting for dining al fresco on the Michelin-starred cuisine at Le Jardin de Russie.

"Recently, I dined with Sir Rocco Forte in the magnificent gardens and while the pasta was the best I have ever tasted, sharing stories with Sir Rocco was even better!"

ROCCO FORTE HOTEL DE RUSSIE
Via del Babuino 9
00187 Rome, Italy
roccofortehotels.com

ITALY
ROME

The St. Regis Rome

Via Veneto…the Spanish Steps…and a taxi ride away from the Coliseum, Piazza Navona, Trevi Fountain, and Roman ruins. Are you in heaven? No, you're at The St. Regis Rome, but it is easy to confuse the two.

It originally opened its doors in 1894 and was founded by successful hotelier Cesar Ritz. Formerly known as The Grand, Ritz demanded the same superb standards for hospitality as in his other European hotels. It recently underwent a meticulous $35 million restoration.

The 138 guest rooms and 23 suites at The St. Regis Rome are refined and resplendent. Lavish appointments include Empire, Regency, and Louis XV decorative styles. The glorious history of Rome plays out on the walls with hand-painted fresco-type decoration. Each represents a significant ruin, villa, or area of Rome.

The Bottega Veneta Suite, designed by Tomas Maier, is one-of-a-kind. Unlike the hotel's other accommodations, the Bottega Veneta Suite has a serene palette and is adorned with contemporary items from the Bottega Veneta furniture collection.

The St. Regis strays from its Italian roots in its innovative Asian influenced kamiSpa. Suffering from jet lag? Find a cure with the energy-boosting St. Regis Rome signature massage.

The superlative service at The St. Regis can also be found in its award-winning Vivendo Restaurant and Le Grand Bar. *Zagat* named the restaurant the "best in Europe," while *Newsweek* tapped Le Grand Bar as Rome's best. Rome's first ballroom, the Salone Ritz, is simply astounding with rich details, magnificent marble columns, sparkling chandeliers, and frescoed ceilings.

"This iconic hotel is another favorite of mine. I only wish I had given a grand ball at The St. Regis Rome!"

THE ST. REGIS ROME
Via Vittorio E. Orlando, 3
00185 Rome, Italy
stregis.com/rome

ITALY
ROME

The Westin Excelsior, Rome

The Westin Excelsior has a prime location on Rome's fashionable Via Veneto, across the street from the American Embassy, and only steps away from the Borghese Gardens. In a city that exudes history and culture, this hotel stands out for its unique ability to blend the past with the present. For almost a century, this hotel has been the meeting place for Romans and visitors alike.

Pass through the glass doors to the graceful world of the Excelsior. The entry hall is full of sparkling chandeliers, gilded mirrors, breathtaking Oriental rugs, tapestries, and paintings. All 281 rooms and 35 suites are magnificent with walls and ceilings hand-decorated by artisans, furnished in Empire or Biedermeier styles with white-and-gold ceilings, Bohemian crystal chandeliers, and modern amenities.

Without a doubt, the hotel's crowning achievement is the Villa Cupola. The largest suite in Europe and recipient of a $7 million renovation, this one-of-a-kind suite simply sparkles. Located on the fifth and sixth floors of the building and under the signature cupola, this suite is beyond your wildest dreams with almost 11,700 square feet! It tastefully showcases marbles, frescoes, and elegant furnishings inspired by Roman villas and palaces.

In keeping with The Westin's commitment to wellness, the fitness center and indoor pool are thoroughly modern and make fitting in a work out convenient and pleasant.

The hotel's lobby and accommodations reflect an old-world style, but the restaurants are very chic and contemporary. ORVM has a modern and elegant Art Deco flair, while the Restaurant Doney is a people-watcher's paradise.

"After spending my Roman holiday at The Westin Excelsior, I always have a hard time saying Arrivederci Roma!"

THE WESTIN EXCELSIOR, ROME
Via Veneto, 125
00187 Rome, Italy
westin.com/excelsiorrome

ITALY
SARDINIA

Cala di Volpe • Hotel Pitrizza • Hotel Romazzino

Off the coast of Italy, Sardinia is a wondrous island comprised of golden beaches and glorious sunshine. The Costa Smeralda, or "emerald coast," is a stretch of beautiful coastline in the northeast corner. "Named for its stunning water, this playground of the rich and famous celebrates 50 years as the embodiment of the ideal European island holiday."

The Luxury Collection's three properties spotlight different slants on Sardinia.

Cala di Volpe, nestled on a scenic bay, resembles an ancient fishing village. The resort's 105 rooms and 19 suites share a rustic ambience, but the big-time amenities include a large pool, five restaurants and bars, and a spa. Take a boat ride to the private beach or sharpen your skills on the 9-hole putting green.

Hotel Pitrizza is for romantics. Set on a rugged stretch of coastline jutting into the bay, it is an intimate hideaway where beaches beg for attention. Privacy is paramount at Pitrizza, where 45 rooms and 10 suites and 3 new villas beckon. The accommodations are fitted with handcrafted Sardinian furnishings. Enjoy the unspoiled Costa Smeralda here, where guests dock their yachts and frolic on the beach, the saltwater pool, the bar, and restaurant.

Set atop a hillside of lush gardens, the whitewashed architecture of Hotel Romazzino looks every bit the part of the Mediterranean resort, but with its pristine beaches and watersports, it acts it too. Romazzino's 78 guest rooms and 16 suites share the spirit of Sardinia with breezy interiors and glorious sea or garden views. From the saltwater swimming pool to a Wellness Centre with a private beach gazebo, tennis courts, and boutiques, Romazzino is a delight.

CALA DI VOLPE
HOTEL PITRIZZA
HOTEL ROMAZZINO
LUXURY COLLECTION RESORTS
Costa Smeralda, Porto Cervo, 07020 Italy
luxurycollection.com/caladivolpe
luxurycollection.com/hotelpitrizza
luxurycollection.com/romazzino

ITALY
SCIACCA, SICILY

Rocco Forte Verdura Golf & Spa Resort

It's time to give any preconceived notions about Sicily the boot. Rocco Forte Verdura Golf & Spa Resort is going to knock your socks off. Set within 570 acres on a perfect slice of southern Sicilian coastline, Verdura is perfect for getting away from it all.

This sleek, contemporary playground has it all. There is golf – in particular two 18-hole championship golf courses and a 9-hole course designed by leading architect Kyle Phillips. Swim in the infinity pool, kick around on the full-size soccer field, or play a set of tennis on one of six courts. Exercise enthusiasts will appreciate the fully-equipped gym, the running trails that meander through the olive and lemon groves, and the beachfront water sports activities. Verdura Spa, with four thalassotherapy pools both indoors and out, is a sybarite's delight.

All 203 spacious sea view accommodations have private terraces or balconies. Designed to blend with the natural setting, the Olga Polizzi interiors have a simple and striking look with polished concrete floors and earth tones reflecting a contemporary sensibility, while bright fabrics and local pottery show off Sicilian roots.

Expect terrific dining… you are in Italy, after all. The resort's four restaurants specialize in Sicilian cuisine with fresh organic ingredients. From beachside barbeques to romantic clifftop settings, there is something to match any mood.

"From acquiring small pieces of land, to piecing together this resort, to replanting 2,000 orange trees on the edge of the golf course, Verdura is a labor of love. It's obviously true – all good things come to those who wait - but don't wait too long to visit this golf and spa retreat!"

ROCCO FORTE VERDURA GOLF & SPA RESORT
S.S. 115 Km 131
92019 Sciacca, Sicily, Italy
roccofortehotels.com

ITALY
TAORMINA, SICILY

Grand Hotel Timeo & Villa Sant'Andrea

Don't know much about Sicily? Experience its serious and its softer sides at Grand Hotel Timeo and Villa Sant'Andrea. These two Orient-Express resorts are a perfect match.

Enjoy the historic sights of Taormina at Grand Hotel Timeo. Set high in the rocky hills of eastern Sicily, this retreat was the first to be built here. Its location does not get any better, from sweeping views of the bay and majestic coastline, Mount Etna, and front and center, the ancient Greek amphitheater. "It is perfect for exploring the area's treasures, plus wonderful boutiques, and fun dining." The 43 rooms and 27 suites share an Italian flair. Relax in the terraced gardens, take a dip in the pool, or soothe yourself with a spa treatment. Romantics will fall in love with the stunning panorama at The Restaurant, while gastronomes will appreciate the haute cuisine.

Prefer to be on the beach? Head straight for Villa Sant'Andrea, nestled on its own private beach overlooking a secluded bay. Glorious golden sunshine blankets this former private residence, built by an aristocratic family in 1830. Quiet and luxurious, you can be as relaxed as you like at the sandy beach or shimmering infinity-edge pool. "This is Sicily's undiscovered St. Tropez." You can always hop aboard a cable car up to Taormina's center. The 37 rooms and 23 suites are the picture of breezy elegance, while the picture-perfect views from the terraces are par excellence. Take a seat at Restaurant Oliviero, with its unmatched views of the bay and the Calabrian coastline. "Whichever azure bay you prefer, both Timeo and Sant'Andrea will match your Sicilian pleasures…why not do both? Que bella!"

GRAND HOTEL TIMEO
Via Teatro Greco 59
98039 Taormina, Italy
grandhoteltimeo.com or
orient-express.com

VILLA SANT'ANDREA
Via Nazionale 137
98039 Taormina Mare, Italy
hotelvillasantandrea.com or
orient-express.com

ITALY
VENICE

Bauer Il Palazzo

Ah, Venice. Few places in the world cause your heart to skip a beat, but this alluring city of canals and palazzos is certainly one. It will take your breath away from the first moment you see its inimitable architecture and it will stay in your heart forever.

Set along the Grand Canal is the glorious Bauer Il Palazzo. Originally an 18th century nobleman's private residence, this Venetian palace is just the place to live out your fantasies. Decorative ceilings…inlaid woods…priceless antiques…museum-quality tapestries crafted by masters like Bevilacqua and Rubelli…it's just so opulent and sumptuous in that wonderful Venetian way.

Il Palazzo is a cherished family heirloom that first opened in 1949. Francesca Bortolotto Possati, granddaughter of the founder, shows off her fabulous taste in the 38 guest rooms and 34 suites. It is all about the details here, where period furnishings and art fill every corner with grand Venetian style, complete with Murano glass chandeliers, Italian marble, sumptuous fabrics, and exclusive toiletries of Santa Maria degli Angeli. "All this and storybook views of the Grand Canal, Giudecca Canal, and St. Mark's Basin!"

You will not want to miss crossing to Giudecca Island for a visit to the Bauer Palladio Hotel & Spa. This former convent houses an elegant European spa within the sister property.

Settimo Cielo on the seventh floor is a casual lounge for breakfast, or jazz up your night at the B-Bar. "De Chisis is quite literally a 'room with a view.' This stunning restaurant has a grand old-world glory indoors, but take a seat on the terrace for a front row view of the Grand Canal."

BAUER IL PALAZZO
San Marco 1459
Campo San Moise
Venice 30124 Italy
Ilpalazzovenezia.com

ITALY
VENICE

Hotel Cipriani

One word says it all. Cipriani. "An icon, a landmark, a legend…Cipriani needs no introduction."

Situated on the lagoon side of Venice on Giudecca Island, the first Orient-Express hotel is away from the bustling crowds, yet close enough to enjoy the splendors of Venice. Step aboard the hotel's boat for a five-minute ride to Piazza San Marco. "However, here tranquility reigns. Set within lush gardens and with the largest swimming pool in all of Venice, Cipriani is truly a world unto itself."

As if the views of the lagoon, San Giorgio Maggiore, the gardens, or the pool are not enough, the breathtakingly beautiful redecorated 48 rooms and 47 suites are elegantly appointed with traditional furniture, luscious fabrics, Murano glass, and antique accents.

Named for the legendary romantic who once held trysts in the gardens here, the Casanova Wellness Centre primps and pampers in regal style. Snag a seat alongside Venetians at Cip's, set on a dock looking across to St. Mark's.

Cipriani's see-and-be-seen bars and restaurants are always packed with a stylish crowd. The hotel has a proud culinary tradition and sterling reputation for superb Italian cuisine. The Fortuny is the hotel's shining star, adorned with delicately blown glass and amber-colored mirrors and boasting magnificent views of the lagoon. Whether dining inside or out on the garden terrace, its candlelit setting is unmatched. "For more than 30 years, I have savored the taste of Cipriani's carpaccio and tagliorini verde, even trying to master these delicacies at home. Of course, nothing compares to the original. Oh, if I could only have regular Saturday night reservations, I'd be in heaven."

HOTEL CIPRIANI
Giudecca 10
30133 Venice, Italy
hotelcipriani.com or
orient-express.com

ITALY
VENICE

Hotel Danieli

From its location on the lagoon across from Palladio's San Giorgio Maggiore to its style, the Danieli is a Venetian landmark.

Built for the noble Dandolo family who conquered Constantinople and brought back the four horses that stand sentry at the Basilica, this 14th century palace occupies a prime location adjacent to the Doge's Palace on St. Mark's Square. You are part of the postcard when staying at this palatial hotel. An opulent staircase transports you to a refined world.

Converted into a hotel in 1822, it was christened as the Danieli after owner Giuseppe Dal Niel's nickname. Now part of the prestigious Luxury Collection, the hotel is comprised of three buildings. There is the original Dandolo building, which is linked by a flying bridge to the adjacent palace Casa Nuova, and the Danielino, constructed in 1948. In total, 206 rooms and 19 suites await your arrival. Rich silk damasks grace the walls, while Venetian-style furnishings, Oriental rugs, antiques, and Murano glass reflect the hotel's Byzantine and Venetian charm.

The lobby lounge is a marvel to behold with six huge sparkling chandeliers crafted on Murano exclusively for the hotel's opening. Pop in for drinks or head upstairs to the rooftop Bar Terrazza Danieli for jaw-dropping views.

"No stay in Venice is complete without a visit to the stunning Terrazza Restaurant. The Hotel Danieli terrace has the best panoramic views and splendors of Venice…a perfect place for breakfast, lunch, or dinner. Sample a plate of yummy pasta and my favorite - grilled scampi. Venice is one of my two favorite cities in the world… and a summer sunset at the Danieli is unbeatable."

**HOTEL DANIELI,
A LUXURY COLLECTION HOTEL**
Castello 4196
30122 Venice, Italy
luxurycollection.com/danieli

ITALY
VENICE

Hotel Gritti Palace

Live like a Doge at Hotel Gritti Palace. Home to the 77th Doge of Venice, Andrea Gritti, this prestigious hotel feels every bit the former palace. Everywhere has an old-world and traditional elegance with modern amenities.

The 82 rooms and 9 suites are luxuriously decorated with splendid furnishings and sparkling Venetian glamour. Located right on the Grand Canal and facing the Santa Maria della Salute Church, the Gritti Palace allows for terrific views.

One of the best ways to soak up the atmosphere in Venice is by spending time lingering over drinks in cafés and bars, and the Gritti's Bar Longhi is a perfect spot. Named for the 18th century Venetian painter, this bar is truly a work of art with hand-sculptured mirrors, Murano glass appliqués, and a carved marble bar. "There are few things in life more pleasant than to sit on the terrace of the Gritti," said frequent hotel guest Somerset Maugham.

"Indeed, the Gritti is one of my favorite spots. Take a table and dine superbly as you listen to the serenading of the passing gondoliers. Indoors, it is an elegant affair. How could I not adore a place that features peach-colored marble?! After all, it is my company's calling card! Outside on the terrace, you may need to pinch yourself – you are not dreaming – this view is straight out of a romantic movie."

You will need to contain your excitement… Hotel Gritti Palace has recently closed for a complete restoration and is scheduled to reopen in spring 2013…but expect this grand Venetian palace to be decked out in all of its glory. "I can't wait to return!"

HOTEL GRITTI PALACE, A LUXURY COLLECTION HOTEL
Campo Santa Maria del Giglio
Venice 30124 Italy
luxurycollection.com/grittipalace

ITALY
VENICE

Luna Hotel Baglioni

How do you blend a sense of history with the 21st century? Luna Hotel Baglioni is a shining star.

Housed within an aristocratic Venetian palace, this hotel has a prime position just a one-minute walk to St. Mark's Square. The property faces the San Marco Basin and Dogana da Mar, Venice's original customs house, topped by the Atlantis statue of Fortune and its golden sphere, it still marks the entrance to the Grand Canal. "With excellent views and open arms, the Luna Hotel Baglioni welcomes world travelers with its intimate character and inviting atmosphere."

History abounds in this 12th century building, where records show that the Knights of Templar were given shelter here in 1118. Known as the Locanda della Luna, the building was decorated with frescoes by students of Tiepolo during the 18th century. Today's guests can still admire the artwork in the Marco Polo Ballroom.

Arrive by gondola or water taxi to the Luna Hotel Baglioni, where a small private canal and jetty ensures a magical first impression. The 67 rooms and 37 suites also make a lasting impression with sensational style. Beige and pastel hues are enhanced with rich brocades and period furnishings. Art and antiques give the accommodations a well-collected look, while modern amenities make modern travelers feel right at home.

Savor Venetian culinary traditions at the lovely Canova restaurant, recipient of both the Fogher d'Oro and Gambero Rosso awards, or enjoy the relaxed elegance of Caffè Baglioni, which faces a small canal running alongside the hotel with charming views of the famous Giardini Reali of Piazza San Marco.

Luna Hotel Baglioni gives you the moon.

LUNA HOTEL BAGLIONI
San Marco, 1243
30124 Venice, Italy
baglionihotels.com

MONACO
MONTE CARLO

Hôtel Metropole

It is hard to believe that Monte Carlo was once a deserted plateau with little more than lemon trees and olive groves. This jewel of the French Riviera symbolizes the gilded life better than any other spot. It is where millionaires mingle and celebrities canoodle. It may be a tiny principality with a prince and princess, but it packs a glamorous punch and one of the best places to experience that l'art de vivre is the Hôtel Metropole.

This Belle Epoque beauty is set within blooming and fragrant gardens just steps from the Place du Casino with its splendiferous L'Opéra de Monte-Carlo Salle Garnier and the infamous Casino.

Don't be fooled by the hotel's seemingly traditional exterior. It may have first welcomed guests in 1886, but after a recent artful reinvention by renowned designer Jacques Garcia, the 77 guest rooms and 64 suites are the cat's meow.

Soak up the sun and the French Riviera vibe at the seawater swimming pool and teak sun deck, indulge at the ESPA Spa where Asia meets French elegance with a comprehensive treatment menu, or sip cocktails with celebrities in the cozy bar before dinner.

From its style to its service, Hôtel Metropole seems to outdo itself, but wait, there's more! French master chef Joël Robuchon is behind the scenes…both at Yoshi, the one-Michelin-starred Japanese restaurant and at Restaurant Joël Robuchon Monte-Carlo, where bejeweled beauties banter over imaginative cuisine.

"Whether you are touring the Prince's Palace, the Oceanographic Museum, smelling the nearly 4,000 roses at The Princess Grace Rose Garden, or disco dancing into the early hours at Jimmy'z, the Metropole awaits your return."

HÔTEL METROPOLE
4, avenue de la Madone
98007 Monte Carlo, Monaco
metropole.com

MONACO
MONTE CARLO

Hôtel de Paris

The truly glorious Hôtel de Paris is synonymous with Monte Carlo.

Hôtel de Paris opened in 1864 and put Monte Carlo on the map. Dazzling visitors with its opulence and glamour, this renowned palace hotel emanates the refinement of a bygone era.

"If Monte Carlo is the playground of the rich and famous, then the Hôtel de Paris is its clubhouse." Situated adjacent to the world-famous Monte Carlo Casino, this hotel provides royal box seats to all of the action. Watch the parade of high fashion enter the Casino or gaze out at the yachts dotting the coast and harbor from one of the 99 rooms and 83 suites, set largely with a dressed up French country style.

Leave it to the Société des Bains de Mer to use the most expensive harbor-front real estate for its five-star spa. The Thermes Marins Monte-Carlo features four floors dedicated to well-being and beauty with a spectacular swimming pool and terrace.

Speaking of over the top, take the elevator up to the Hôtel's eighth floor to Le Grill for delectable modern Mediterranean dishes. Le Bar Américain entertains nightly with live music from Doctor Gabs's piano, but the crown jewel at Hôtel de Paris is certainly Le Louis XV by Alain Ducasse. The dining room pulls out all the stops with its majestic design, while the kitchen is a gastronomic glory deserving of every international award it has garnered.

"Whenever I am in Monte Carlo, I pretend I am starring in *'To Catch a Thief,'* and as Grace Kelly, I always fall in love with Cary Grant and the good life at the Hôtel de Paris."

HÔTEL DE PARIS
Place du Casino
98000 Monte Carlo, Monaco
hoteldeparismontecarlo.com

THE NETHERLANDS
AMSTERDAM

InterContinental Amstel Amsterdam

Set along the Amstel River, the InterContinental Amstel Amsterdam has been a part of this historic city since 1867. Located where the financial, cultural, and shopping districts converge, the hotel is in the heart of the action in a storybook setting. It is close to the Rijksmuseum, Van Gogh Museum, Spiegelkwartier, and the Royal Carré Theatre.

Stately, yet welcoming, the Amstel enjoys a riverside location. Hop aboard one of the hotel's three authentic canal boats and ply the renowned canals of Amsterdam, stop for coffee, or visit the Anne Frank House. After a busy day, retire to one of the 79 guest rooms and 24 suites, where classic design effortlessly blends with of-the-moment amenities.

The Health & Fitness Club, situated at the river level, boasts beautiful views of the historic bridges and will likely inspire you. The indoor pool, Turkish bath, and sauna are on hand to melt away any stresses of the day.

Relax in the refined atmosphere of The Amstel Lounge, where crystal chandeliers, Persian carpets, and Dutch Delft lamps set a dignified tone for dining and high tea. In contrast, lighten the mood at The Amstel Bar. This classic bar paneled in wood has the friendly neighborhood pub feel down pat. No visit to this hotel is complete without a window seat at La Rive. Facing the river, this Michelin-starred restaurant tantalizes with its gourmet cuisine and its spectacular setting.

"Here's one day of my Amsterdam spring itinerary: marvel at the Van Goghs, snap photos of the tulips, and then come back to the InterContinental Amstel. Before dinner at La Rive, sneak a peek at the magnificent Mirror Room."

INTERCONTINENTAL AMSTEL AMSTERDAM
Professor Tulpplein 1
1018 Amsterdam, The Netherlands
ichotelsgroup.com

THE NETHERLANDS
AMSTERDAM

Hotel Pulitzer

What do you get when you take 25 classic 17th and 18th century canalside houses and add a sleek verve? The unique and eye-catching Hotel Pulitzer!

Set on the picturesque Keizersgracht and Prinsengracht canals, this amalgam of buildings known as the Hotel Pulitzer is ideally located in the middle of the old city center of Amsterdam. Whether you want to explore the Anne Frank House, the Royal Palace, Dam Square, or the Rijkmuseum, these are within walking distance. Of course, the best way to see this city is by boat, and the hotel provides its own, moored directly in front and available for private tours.

Sprinkled among the 25 buildings are the delightfully Dutch 223 guest rooms and 7 suites. From wooden beams and split-level rooms to oak floors and handpainted tiles, the accommodations reflect an unmistakable pride of place. Not everything is historic, though, as evident in the contemporary Dutch artwork found on the walls of every room. See more of the hotel's commitment to the arts and local artists at the impressive art gallery, located in the gardens.

Restaurant Keizersgracht 238, a grill restaurant with stunning views over the canals of Amsterdam, has a chic and trendy atmosphere, while its private dining room, De Apotheek, is a former pharmacy that still boasts original details. During the summer months, meals and the renowned afternoon tea are enjoyed in the lovely courtyard garden terrace.

"Hotel Pulitzer feels like my Amsterdam residence and I treasure my welcoming experiences. I love flowers, so I wander to the famed flower market by a nearby canal and handpick bunches of flowers to decorate my room."

**HOTEL PULITZER,
A LUXURY COLLECTION HOTEL**
Prinsengracht 315-331
1016 Amsterdam, The Netherlands
luxurycollection.com/pulitzer

THE NETHERLANDS
AMSTERDAM

Sofitel Legend The Grand

Leave the Old World behind as you enter the Sofitel Legend The Grand Amsterdam. This is where cutting edge meets the canals.

Sofitel takes a landmark building and turns it on its head. Set between two quiet canals in the heart of the city, this building has seen many lives – from a 15th century convent to the City Hall – and is now living the dream as Amsterdam's trendiest spot. From the sleek entrance to the cinnamon and chartreuse accented lobby lounge, the Sofitel surprises you at every turn.

The 125 rooms and 52 suites are at once splashy and serene. Contemporary artwork lends a decidedly hip flair, while muted tones instill a sense of serenity. Beautiful views over the quiet canals, inner garden, or courtyard are an added bonus in these cocoon-like accommodations.

SO Spa and SO Fit brings an element of high-tech to healthy living with its fully equipped fitness center, 2 hammams, and indoor heated pool.

"The Sofitel doesn't just deliver style; this hotel offers terrific services. From butlers who attend to every whim, to horse-drawn carriage tours of the city, to a historic marriage chamber with Art Nouveau glass murals for exchanging vows, Sofitel Legend The Grand delivers it all."

Cutting-edge doesn't end at design…it continues to cuisine. Home to the Netherlands' first raw bar, Bridges Raw Bar celebrates the bounty of the sea. From the Flying Dutchman Bar to the Vinothèque and Garden Terrace, sample a beer and snack on Dutch treats in several spots. Trend-setting continues at Bridges Restaurant, once the cafeteria for the City Hall workers and now home to a white-hot scene.

SOFITEL LEGEND THE GRAND
Oudezijds Voorburgwal 197
1012 Amsterdam, The Netherlands
sofitel-legend-thegrand.com

PORTUGAL
LISBON

Four Seasons Hotel Ritz Lisbon

Lisbon has many charms. From its castles and churches to monuments and museums, this capital city of Portugal offers many delights for the traveler. Spread across the slopes of seven hills, Lisbon enjoys a fascinating multi-layered history.

Prince Henry the Navigator, Ferdinand Magellan, and Vasco de Gama all explored the world in Portugal's name, but if they were alive today, they would look no further than the Four Seasons Hotel Ritz for treasures. This hotel has its own impressive collection of artwork, carpets, and tapestries. Among the highlights is surely Pablo Picasso's Girl with a Guitar.

Facing the Parque Eduardo VII, the hotel is just a short distance from Lisbon's major attractions and sights, but from this perch you can see it all. Gaze out at St. George's Castle, the Old Town, the Tagus River, and the 25th of April Bridge from one of the 241 guest rooms and 44 suites. The accommodations share an updated and elegant sense on tradition, plus exceedingly comfortable in pastel and gentle tones.

With floor-to-ceiling windows overlooking the hotel garden and with a Zen-like design and spirit, the Spa and indoor pool evoke a sense of calm immediately upon entrance.

Enjoy afternoon tea at Almada Negreiros Lounge or duck into the dramatic red-and-black setting of the Ritz Bar. French chef Pascal Meynard leads a team of chefs who serve delicious Continental cuisine at the highly regarded Varanda.

"Recently, I pampered myself with two days at the Four Seasons Hotel Ritz Lisbon. What a treat! We selected 'the chef's menu' at Varanda and it was the most innovative and delicious dinner we experienced in all of Lisbon."

**FOUR SEASONS
HOTEL RITZ LISBON**
Rua Rodrigo da Fonseca, 88
1099-039 Lisbon, Portugal
fourseasons.com

PORTUGAL
MADEIRA

Reid's Palace

Looking for a bit of the exotic without straying too far from the Continent? Madeira marks the spot. This sub-tropical Portuguese island sits 400 miles off the western coast of Africa, but has an unmistakable European sophistication. Sharing its name with the island's most famous export, Madeira wine, it has a unique flavor and just so happens to be home to Reid's Palace, a wonderful Orient-Express property.

This world-famous resort was founded in 1891 by William Reid. Its stunning clifftop setting amidst luscious gardens has long attracted travelers seeking a respite from the world. Winston Churchill spent time here working on his memoirs. Its afternoon tea was legendary, especially on Sundays when it was enhanced by tango lessons on the lawn. Irish playwright and Nobel Prize winner George Bernard Shaw learned to tango while visiting Reid's for two months. Today, you will find everyone from children to grandparents romping in this sunny playground, where three pools, tennis courts, and a top-notch spa are just some of the ways to fill your days.

The 128 rooms and 35 suites echo the hotel's commitment to upholding tradition with classic tradition with light and airy Madeira touches. Views looking out over the gardens or the Atlantic are mesmerizing, especially when enjoyed from the privacy of your own balcony.

Edwardian traditions continue at the Dining Room, where dressing for dinner is de rigueur. The proper English afternoon tea remains, but with a bevy of casual spots ranging from Villa Ristorante Cipriani and Les Faunes to Brisa do Mar, The Garden Room, and Pool Terrace, there are plenty of ways to create your own traditions, too.

REID'S PALACE
Estrada Monumental 139
9000-098 Funchal, Madeira, Portugal
reidspalace.com or orient-express.com

PORTUGAL
SINTRA

Penha Longa Hotel, Spa & Golf Resort

Penha Longa, which translates to "long rock," is long on history…first chosen by Friar Vasco Martins in 1355 as a site to build his monastery, the palace at Penha Longa became a favorite retreat for the Portuguese royal family in the 16th and 17th centuries. Many of the fountains, gardens, and water mills were established during that time.

Set in the rolling hills of the southern Sintra mountains, only 20 minutes from Lisbon, Penha Longa is a grand European resort with a palazzo-style estate, two championship golf courses, great spa, and five restaurants managed by Ritz-Carlton.

The 150 rooms and 44 suites are exceptionally comfortable and soothing. Mood-brightening red and orange accents enhance the beige contemporary styling of these inviting accommodations.

"Featuring some of the best golf in Europe, Penha Longa lures lovers of the game from around the world with its award-winning Atlantic Course, designed by Robert Trent Jones, Jr." The equally stunning nine-hole Monastery course owes its name to the unique hermitage built into the resort´s rockspace by 14th century Franciscan friars.

Utter relaxation is paramount at Penha Longa, where the Six Senses Spa is reason alone to visit. The Spa is located within Penha Longa's historic complex, a few minutes from the Hotel's main building, and boasts beautiful gardens with a pool and waterfall. Practice yoga on the pool platform or retreat to one of two gazebos for meditation and Shiatsu massage.

Five restaurants deliver the world on a silver platter. Choose from Japanese at Midori, Portuguese cuisine at assaMassa, or fusion cuisine at Arola.

"Having just been there, I found it peaceful and perfect, whether you play golf or explore Sintra, Penha Longa is a Portuguese paradise."

PENHA LONGA HOTEL, SPA & GOLF RESORT
Estrada da Lagoa Azul, Linhó 2714
511 Sintra, Portugal
penhalonga.com or ritzcarlton.com

RUSSIA
MOSCOW

Hotel Baltschug Kempinski

Rising on the banks of the Moskva River, the Hotel Baltschug Kempinski is situated in the heart of Moscow's historic center with views across to Red Square, the Kremlin, and St. Basil's Cathedral. Minutes from everything, yet nestled in the relatively quiet Zamoskvorechye district, this hotel puts visitors close to the action but away from the jostling crowds.

Hotel Baltschug Kempinski is much like Moscow itself…its historical façade belies its strikingly modern interiors. This building once housed studios for 19th century artists like Kramskoi and Vasnetsov, so don't be surprised if you feel an artistic urge. After all, those same views that were captured by these famous artists are framed for your personal enjoyment in the luxurious 190 rooms and 40 suites. For a truly unique spirit, book one of four design suites. From the sultry Art Deco of the Living Design Suite and the delightfully feminine designs of the Princess Suite to the inimitable upper-class pedigree of the Linley Suite, these one-of-a-kind accommodations are sure to surprise.

The Baltschug Health Club and Beauty Center cover all of the bases from primping to pampering. Take a swim in the indoor pool, work out in the gym, or have your hair and nails done for a night out on the town.

Restaurant Baltschug is a feast for the eyes and the palate. "Its dramatic views of the Kremlin are unmatched, but this signature restaurant outdoes itself with an over-the-top celebration of European classics and the Russian table. Feast on my favorites – caviar and beef Stroganoff, among other traditional dishes. Sunday Brunch is a favorite of Muscovites, so plan ahead!"

HOTEL BALTSCHUG KEMPINSKI
Ulitsa Balchug 1
115035 Moscow, Russia
kempinski.com

RUSSIA
MOSCOW

The Ritz-Carlton, Moscow

Why travel somewhere and not be in the heart of it all? The Ritz-Carlton, Moscow places you quite literally steps from Red Square and the Kremlin, the nerve center of the intriguing Russian capital city.

Spend the day traveling back in time to the days of the Czars or enjoying the modern delights of the world-class shopping, but then return to the splendors of The Ritz-Carlton. This regal hotel pampers guests from check-in to check-out.

Baby, it's cold outside, but inside this hotel, warmth pervades. The 311 rooms and 23 suites reflect the classic lines and traditional furnishings of a Ritz-Carlton hotel. Rich colored tones and brocaded fabrics peppered with Russian accents and interesting city views enhance the picture.

If the temperatures have wreaked havoc on your skin, visit the ESPA Spa. Stunningly designed, this superior facility with indoor pool, crystal steam room, and ice fountain caters to time-starved and stressed travelers.

Expect nothing less than the best in the wide array of restaurants and bars. Celebrate the flavors of Thailand, Vietnam, China, and Japan at the sleek Gingko restaurant, or head up to the spectacular rooftop 02 Lounge. This hot spot dazzles with its incomparable Red Square views, plus its sushi-sashimi bar, steak and seafood grill, and DJ dance floor.

"Naturally, you cannot visit Moscow without a taste of caviar and a shot of iced vodka, so be sure to head straight for Caviarterra. With its traditional setting, this is where you come for borscht, chicken Kiev, and other Russian favorites. Complete with a Russian folklore band, it's not a state secret this place is on the mark."

THE RITZ-CARLTON, MOSCOW
Tverskaya Street 3
125009 Moscow, Russia
ritzcarlton.com

RUSSIA
ST. PETERSBURG

Grand Hotel Europe

Brimming with history and culture, St. Petersburg is a place of magic and mystery.

Grand Hotel Europe, St. Petersburg's oldest hotel, is a landmark in its own right for more than 130 years. It has faced revolution, war, and changes in political ideology. It has also seen its share of high culture. Anna Pavlova danced, Tchaikovsky composed, and Shostakovitch played the piano for Prokofiev here.

This historic Orient-Express property enjoys a prime location off Nevsky Prospekt in the heart of the historic district. Near the Church of the Spilled Blood, where Czar Alexander II was assassinated, and within walking distance of the Hermitage and the Mariinsky Theatre, this hotel is a dream for culture and history buffs.

menu is inspired by traditional Russian recipes and ingredients.

"I have visited magnificent St. Petersburg in summer and winter and its seasonal personalities are uniquely different. In summer, spend time outdoors at the marvelous palaces like Peterhof, but in winter do not miss a ballet. Whether the sun is shining or the grounds are blanketed in snow, it's always warm inside Grand Hotel Europe."

GRAND HOTEL EUROPE
Nevsky Prospekt,
Mikhailovskaya Ulitsa 1/7
191186 St. Petersburg, Russia
grandhoteleurope.com or
orient-express.com

The hotel's rich history is best seen in its 110 rooms and 91 suites, where 19th century charm, traditional design, and magnificent views blend for a memorable experience.

Ten historic suites have a particularly Russian ambience with lavish antiques.

Five international restaurants, two elegant cafés, and a bar are the center of attention. Sip champagne or vodka while sampling the best caviar at the Caviar Bar. L'Europe is a glory to behold with stained glass ceilings and windows plus five balconies. Relive the grandeur of the Czars here, where the

RUSSIA
ST. PETERSBURG

Rocco Forte Hotel Astoria

With its many islands linked by canals resembling Venice and its confectionary architecture resembling Paris, St. Petersburg is a many splendored place. Of course, it is the Russian aristocratic roots that make it so architecturally and culturally unique. The Winter Palace and Hermitage are simply beyond compare.

The stylish Rocco Forte Hotel Astoria mirrors this city's world-class sophistication. Its exclusive address in St. Isaac's Square places the hotel just minutes from Peter the Great's Winter Palace, and its location opposite one of the city's most famous landmarks, St. Isaac's Cathedral, makes this hotel truly stand out.

Rocco Forte Hotel Astoria blends contemporary sensibility. The 168 rooms and 42 suites have an uncluttered, modern décor with Russian touches, yet the fascinating history of the city is never forgotten thanks to the terrific views of St. Isaac's Square and the monument of Nicholas I.

The La Maison de Beauté Carita Astoria is designed with the same elegant styling as the Paris flagship. Need to beautify in a flash? Book the express treatment room, where guests can enjoy four services simultaneously. Spa Decleor, on the seventh floor, is a temple of wellness, complete with a hammam.

Come inside to the delightfully inviting Kandinsky Bar, Rotonda Lounge, or Davidov's Restaurant, which offers everything from contemporary European delicacies to traditional Russian caviar and blinis.

"I can still taste the sublime caviar devoured with Sir Rocco Forte while he entertained a group of Virtuoso leaders. Like St. Petersburg itself, it was a feast for the senses! With his taste for modernity, there is no doubt that Peter the Great himself would adore the Rocco Forte Hotel Astoria."

ROCCO FORTE HOTEL ASTORIA
39 Bolshaya Morskaya
190000 St. Petersburg, Russia
roccofortehotels.com

SCOTLAND
AUCHTERARDER

The Gleneagles Hotel

Head for the Scottish Highlands…and to the incomparable Gleneagles Hotel.

This palatial resort rests within 850 acres of Perthshire countryside just one hour northwest of Edinburgh. Opened in 1924, Gleneagles was built by the Caledonian Railway Company and had its own railway station. With its grand tradition, Gleneagles indeed feels like a private club. Every bit a Scottish estate, the resort's 206 rooms and 26 suites are spacious and relaxing, while traditional tartans add local flair.

is an extravagant event. "To me, Gleneagles sets the Scottish gold standard. I've been coming back for nearly 35 years and I don't even play golf! Whether one is engrossed in the rich area history - visit Sterling and Scone Castles like me - playing several rounds of golf, or taking in the resort's pastoral pleasures, you will always come home to warm Scottish hospitality at Gleneagles."

Gleneagles is a world-class golf destination. Three renowned championship courses, The Queen's Course, The King's Course, and The PGA Centenary Course, have all hosted prestigious tournaments throughout the years. In 2014, the Ryder Cup will be held on the Centenary Course. Practice your swing at the 9-hole PGA National Academy Course or with a pro from the state-of-the-art PGA National Golf Academy.

There's so much more than golf at Gleneagles. From off-road driving, falconry, equestrian activities, fishing, shooting, and the Gundog School to unwinding at the ESPA Spa, Gleneagles has country estate activities down pat.

From the hearty dishes of The Dormy Clubhouse and the Mediterranean fare at Deseo to the fine Scottish food at Strathearn and the two-Michelin-starred French cuisine at Andrew Fairlie, dining at Gleneagles

THE GLENEAGLES HOTEL
Auchterarder, Perthshire
PH3 1NF, Scotland
gleneagles.com

SCOTLAND
EDINBURGH

Rocco Forte The Balmoral

Scotland's capital city of Edinburgh is home to the winsome Rocco Forte Balmoral. This regal Edwardian-style hotel opened in 1902 at the top of Princes Street, the main shopping promenade. Though Edinburgh's most famous landmark is the imposing castle, The Balmoral's clock tower is a close second. Don't set your watch to it, as it runs two minutes ahead to ensure catching your train on time!

In the center of it all, The Balmoral is a stylish base for exploring this culturally rich city. From the latest West End productions to the famous Military Tattoo held annually each August, entertainment is abundant. History lovers will delight in the many sights, including the Castle, Hopetoun House, and the Palace of Holyrood House, a royal residence and one-time home to Mary, Queen of Scots.

The clock tower may be a landmark, but there's nothing old-fashioned about the hotel's 168 guest rooms and 20 suites, where a soft, muted palette creates a haven of serenity. Don't expect blackwatch plaids and other Scottish clichés, since this décor is contemporary and slightly idiosyncratic. The views of Edinburgh Castle, the gardens, and the rolling hills are proof that you are in Scotland. Break away from it all at the Spa, an award-winning urban oasis, and then delight in the hotel's culinary wonders. Hadrian's Brasserie is a casual place for a bite, while Number One demands your attention with its sophisticated Michelin starred cuisine.

"Whether you are coming or going on the Royal Mile, your trip is not complete without spending time at Rocco Forte The Balmoral. Great Scott, this hotel is Edinburgh at its best!"

ROCCO FORTE THE BALMORAL
1 Princes Street
Edinburgh EH2 2EQ, Scotland
roccofortehotels.com

SCOTLAND
TURNBERRY

Turnberry Resort

Close your eyes and dream of Scotland. What do you see? Windswept grasses and craggy cliffs, perhaps? How about traditional links golf courses? Open your eyes. You are at Turnberry Resort.

This exceptional resort is tucked away in the wild and untamed southwest coast of Scotland. It is a place of great beauty, fables, and folklore – a spot that has long inspired poets and artists. Play a few rounds of legendary golf, bliss out at the spa, or live like a country lady or gentleman. It's all totally Turnberry.

The 114 rooms and 4 suites have a refreshing Edwardian-meets-edgy style. Inviting and spacious, the rooms take advantage of enchanting ocean and golf views. You could easily hole up in these delightful havens…but that would be a crime given the plethora of world-class amenities.

The only mulligan you won't take is booking the tee time on the majestic and iconic Ailsa Golf Course. Play in the footsteps of giants like Palmer, Nicklaus, Watson and Norman. Enjoy the challenges and natural beauty of the Kintyre Course. From the TaylorMade custom fittings to the professional golf school, even if your name doesn't show up on the leader board, you can play like it does. Surprise you or your favorite golfer with a trip to the Colin Montgomerie summer golf school.

Turnberry is not just a paradise for golfers. A spectacular spa, a working farm, horseback riding… the opportunities for family bonding are endless. And don't forget fine dining! From French Escoffier and haute cuisine to casual family-friendly fare, Turnberry Resort has it all.

**TURNBERRY RESORT,
A LUXURY COLLECTION RESORT**
Ayrshire KA26 9LT Scotland
luxurycollection/turnberryscotland

SPAIN
BARCELONA

Hotel Arts Barcelona

Barcelona is a cultural mecca and a feast for the eyes and the soul. Perhaps best known for Gaudi's fanciful, and often outrageous buildings, one of the city's finest hotels is also one of its architectural landmarks.

The 44 stories of exposed glass and steel make Hotel Arts Barcelona stand apart. This striking, contemporary building sits on the waterfront in the Olympic Village area, with astounding views of the port and the Mediterranean. Minutes away from the wide boulevards and busy social scene of Las Ramblas and the medieval intimacy of the Gothic Quarter, the Hotel Arts managed by Ritz-Carlton is an exciting locale of its own with five restaurants and a fantastic pool with sun deck. All this and an impressive collection of art to boot!

Like the eye-catching exterior, the interiors of the Hotel Arts are also sleek and contemporary. The 396 spacious guestrooms, 59 stylish Barcelona suites, and 28 sophisticated apartments are flooded with light and feature panoramic city or Mediterranean views.

Elevate your senses at the Six Senses Spa. Located on the 42nd and 43rd floors of the hotel, this sky-reaching spa might just convince you that you're in a hip heaven.

Choose from one of five chic, Mediterranean inspired restaurants with everything from tapas on the terrace, poolside snacks and sips, and lavish buffets and brunches to Michelin-starred dining.

"After a busy day of seeing the city's sights from the Gaudi Catholic Church to the Joan Miró Museum, the best way to spend a beautiful Barcelona afternoon is by stretching out in the Spanish sun by the pool and gazing at the glittering Peix d'Or sculpture by Frank Gehry."

HOTEL ARTS BARCELONA
Marina 19-21
8005 Barcelona, Spain
ritzcarlton.com

SPAIN
BARCELONA

Mandarin Oriental, Barcelona

Feel the exciting pulse of this vibrant, creative, and exciting city while staying at Mandarin Oriental, Barcelona. This of-the-moment hotel is in the heart of it all opposite Casa Batlló. Stroll over to La Pedrera or peruse the chic boutiques and retailers that share the Passeig de Gràcia with the hotel. Don't miss Gaudi's astonishing Sagrada Familia church, not far from the hotel. Still unfinished, this work of art will inspire you.

Even in a city well known for its architectural masterpieces, the Mandarin Oriental is no wallflower. Never blending in with any background, this eye-catching hotel enraptures you with its creative design. The 88 rooms and 10 suites are designed by one of Spain's leading designers, Patricia Urquiola, who has imparted a subtle sophistication with her largely white designs punctuated by a few well-placed shocks of electric hues. Large windows focusing views on the bustling boulevard or landscaped interior garden give the rooms and suites a studio-like ambience.

Mandarin Oriental's Asian roots really come alive at the spa where everything from the minimalist design to the therapies hints of the Orient. Dark and sultry, the look may be nightclub hot as is the rooftop pool, but the mood is defiantly serene.

The Mandarin Oriental's restaurants and bars are right on the money. See the artistic transformation of this former bank at the Banker's Bar, where the ceiling's art installation is comprised of security boxes. Upstairs at Blanc, the white-on-white brasserie, the focus is on modern Mediterranean, while Mimosa Garden and Terrat are both lovely al fresco alternatives. Moments is the hotel's winning spot with Michelin-starred cuisine and trailblazing female chef, Carme Ruscalleda.

MANDARIN ORIENTAL, BARCELONA
Passeig de Gràcia, 38-40
08007 Barcelona, Spain
mandarinoriental.com

SPAIN
BARCELONA

El Palace

Not many places can say that they are as elegant today as they were when they opened in 1919, but El Palace certainly can.

Located in the heart of Barcelona not far from Las Ramblas, El Palace charms visitors with its distinguished elegance. It may be historic, but you won't be dusting off any cobwebs at this polished palace after its two-year modernization. This hotel will dazzle you with its new take on the old world.

El Palace's lobby is a grand affair that begs guests to take a seat in one of its plush chairs and watch the world go by.

The 83 guest rooms and 42 suites have plenty of personality. At first glance, it may seem traditional – think historic decorative fireplaces and silk-covered walls – but look again and you'll find a trace of the quirky throughout these accommodations. From velvet chairs in unusually alluring burnt sienna hues to interesting contemporary artwork, these accommodations take the historic and add pizazz.

The Spa celebrates the unique traditions and heritage of Mayan culture.

Romain Fornell, the youngest French chef to be awarded a Michelin star, oversees the restaurants here.

From the French brasserie style of AE to the city's favorite Sunday Brunch at El Jardin to the gourmet cuisine at Caelis, dining at El Palace is a joy.

"In 1965, I had the pleasure of spending some of my honeymoon in Barcelona at The Ritz, today called El Palace. What a wonderful way to begin my passion for travel by staying in a legendary hotel created by Cesar Ritz. He would still be proud of this classic showpiece."

EL PALACE
Gran Via de les Corts Catalanes 668
08010 Barcelona, Spain
hotelpalacebarcelona.com

SPAIN
MADRID

Hotel Ritz Madrid

Madrid is a thriving city with a regal past. Once the center of a far-reaching global empire, Madrid has a grand history and its Golden Age splendors can be enjoyed in its many museums. In fact, there are more masterpieces per square mile in Madrid than anywhere else in the world.

Where do you begin to explore the city's rich cultural heritage? The Prado, of course, and privileged guests at the prestigious Hotel Ritz are right across from this world-famous treasury of art.

This Orient-Express hotel's regal bearing is no coincidence. When King Alfonso XIII realized that no hotel was worthy of hosting his distinguished guests for his daughter's wedding, he set about constructing a grand hotel himself. The King hired legendary hotelier César Ritz to design, build, and personally supervise construction of this exquisite Belle Epoque beauty opened in 1910.

The 137 rooms and 30 suites are richly appointed with period furnishings, antique art objects and paintings, luxurious handmade carpets, and lustrous fabrics. These lavish accommodations are truly fit for royalty.

Afternoon tea at the Ritz is upheld with great pride. The Goya Restaurant continues to be one of Madrid's institutions, and the delightful Terrace lures many locals.

"I love the grand traditions at Hotel Ritz Madrid. I plan my sightseeing to the Royal Tapestry Factory or the Royal Palace around mealtime to avoid missing lunch on the Terrace or teatime. However, you can't visit Madrid without having a delicious dinner served formally with china, silver, crystal, and all. If you're really lucky, you might catch the swing band for a dance around the floor of the grand lobby."

HOTEL RITZ MADRID
Plaza de la Lealtad 5
28014 Madrid, Spain
ritzmadrid.com or
orient-express.com

SPAIN
MADRID

Hotel Villa Magna

What comes to mind when you think of Madrid – a world-class capital city? Royalty and royal palaces? Famous art collections? Fabulous shopping? Flamenco? When you stay at Villa Magna, you're surrounded by all of these features that make Madrid one of the world's most alluring cities.

Nestled in the sophisticated Salamanca neighborhood on a beautiful boulevard, Villa Magna offers a taste of modern Madrid. The hotel's creative expression will impress and intrigue you at every turn. Take the lobby and adjoining areas, for instance. With huge paintings, sculptures, decorative pottery, and even its geometrically-designed carpets, it could easily double as a gallery in a museum.

The 100 rooms and 50 suites are equally dramatic in soothing shades of mocha, cappuccino, and cream with an Art Deco verve. Gorgeous wood paneling is a nod to the historic, while graphic patterns and quilted headboards are so…chic and current.

If we could all look as good as these interiors…but wait, with a fully equipped fitness center and Club Wellness by Kiara Kare on hand, Villa Magna makes looking and feeling good a bit easier.

From Magnum Bar's sultry nightlife to the golden sunshine blessing the terrace at Magna 22, the dining and entertainment choices are larger than life. Tse Yang Cantonese delights the senses with its dressed up design and delicious food. Villa Magna Restaurant is a temple of modern cooking.

"On a recent visit, I strolled over to the many fashionable boutiques of Ortega y Gasset, Madrid's most famous shopping street, but I was so happy to return to the calming influence of Hotel Villa Magna after the hustle and bustle."

HOTEL VILLA MAGNA
Paseo de la Castellana 22
28046 Madrid, Spain
villamagna.es

SPAIN
MALLORCA

La Residencia

Where do you go when you truly want to get away from it all? Do as the Spaniards and others in-the-know do and head for Mallorca. This enchanting island in the Mediterranean Sea is just off the coast of Spain but feels worlds away from the everyday.

It is so easy to be swept up in the romance of it all at La Residencia. This Orient-Express resort, comprised of 16th and 17th century manor houses, occupies a piece of sun-kissed land that poets could only dream of imagining. Surrounded by orange groves and ancient olive trees, it has that country charm that only the Mediterranean can supply.

Crisp white walls are offset by vibrant artwork, reflective of the hotel's location in the artist's village of Deià. Rich wooden beams, antique Mallorquin furniture, and charming nooks and crannies make the 36 rooms and 23 suites particularly endearing. A sense of history pervades – the Tower Suite was thought to be built by Templar Knights – but there's nothing stuffy or serious about these fresh and inviting accommodations.

Choose to be as active or restful as you like at La Residencia. Explore the local art galleries or play a set of tennis. Of course, you could while away the day at The Spa, voted one of the best in Europe. "I prefer lounging poolside, where you are surrounded by the spectacular Tramuntana Mountains overlooking the endless Mediterranean."

"It is difficult to say which is better – the gourmet cuisine or the stunning setting at El Olivo Restaurant. It is arguably Mallorca's top spot and after a meal in this lovely setting, you will certainly agree with me."

LA RESIDENCIA
Son Canals s/n
07179 Deià, Mallorca, Spain
hotel-laresidencia.com or
orient-express.com

SPAIN
MARBELLA

Marbella Club Hotel, Golf Resort & Spa

Not many resorts can claim royal roots, but Marbella Club Hotel, Golf Resort & Spa surely can. This pedigreed resort on the shores of the Mediterranean was the brainchild of Prince Alfonso von Hohenlohe. The prince's family residence, the Finca Santa Margarita, grew in popularity and sparked an idea…why not turn it into a private club? Voilá! The Marbella Club was born, and it has been luring jetsetters ever since.

Surrounded by lush gardens and kissed by golden sunshine, the Marbella Club is a posh playground and tranquil getaway. Dig your toes in the sand at the beach club or take a massage at the Thalasso Spa. Drive 20 minutes and get your heart racing at the expertly equipped Riding Stables or private 18-hole Dave Thomas-designed golf course with spectacular views of the Sierra, Gibraltar, the North African coastline, and the Mediterranean.

This beachfront resort has 84 rooms and 37 elegant suites nestled amongst lush gardens designed by the Prince himself. The interiors are a blend of seaside elegance and Spanish tradition. Or, steal away to one of 14 Andalucían-style villas, with their own gardens and pools. These accommodations show off a stylish and modern take on the classic whitewashed village of Andalucía.

There are so many options for dining at Marbella Club, from the famous Beach Club buffet, the Grill, MC Café, MC Beach, Pool Bar, to the Golf Resort.

"Seeking the ultimate hideaway? Come to the Marbella Club where even the sun loves the intimate, clubby atmosphere. Succumb to the peaceful setting, mingle with the jet set crowd in Europe's best climate, but always unwind in sophisticated style."

MARBELLA CLUB HOTEL, GOLF RESORT & SPA
Bulevar Principe Alfonso von Hohenlohe
29600 Marbella, Spain
marbellaclub.com

SWEDEN
STOCKHOLM

Grand Hôtel Stockholm

Often referred to as the "Venice of the North," Stockholm is a stunningly beautiful city with a rich history, abundant culture, and a glorious waterfront setting. "Of course, my Swedish roots sway my opinion just a bit!"

Grand Hôtel Stockholm truly lives up to its name. This elegant hotel has graciously welcomed guests since 1874. Opposite the Royal Palace, the Grand exudes prestige from its waterfront setting. Step inside the palatial lobby, with its warm sophistication, then retreat to one of the luxurious 331 guest rooms and 37 suites. The accommodations are done in pastel colors and classic furnishings, and have charming views of the city streets, waterfront, or quiet courtyard.

The Raison d'Etre Spa also lives up to its name…you won't want to miss a minute of life's little luxuries at this palatial spa.

Dining at the Grand is one of Stockholm's greatest pleasures. The Veranda is a popular meeting place with a wonderful view over the water, Old Town, and the Royal Palace. "Don't miss the smorgasbord. I am particularly partial to the herrings and gravlax with honey mustard sauce, so much so that I always bring back several jars of Slotts Swedish mustard to make the sauce."

Mathias Dahlgren has a bit of a split personality with a dining room and food bar to match your moods. Named after the hotel's founder Regis Cadier, the Cadier Bar has a wonderful ambience complete with rich dark wood paneling and lively bartenders who shake and stir with precision. "Maybe it's not surprising that I ran smack into James Bond - Roger Moore, that is, here!"

GRAND HÔTEL STOCKHOLM
Södra Blasieholmshamnen 8
103 27 Stockholm, Sweden
grandhotel.se

SWITZERLAND
GENEVA

Mandarin Oriental, Geneva

With its cobblestone streets, breathtaking mountain backdrop, and crystal-clear lake, Geneva is indeed a one of a kind city. Brimming with business, culture, and energy, it is a delight to visit – either on business or pleasure.

On the right bank of the Rhône River, Mandarin Oriental is a fashionable selection in the heart of Geneva's flourishing businesses, exclusive boutiques, and cultural attractions.

Its early Modernist architecture reflects its history as the first hotel built in Europe following World War II. However, this hotel has been totally revamped inside to reflect a contemporary, Art Deco design, with a slightly Asian ambience. Expect Swiss attention to every service detail throughout the hotel, especially in the 180 luxurious rooms and 20 suites. Their look is contemporary European with a few Asian accents – a Buddha here, a silk shantung pillow there. It's all very subtle, serene, and sophisticated.

"What better way to enjoy the spectacular setting than by sipping a hot chocolate on your terrace, but with the great outdoors at your fingertips, you might prefer active pursuits like boat rides on Lake Geneva or skiing in a nearby village."

It's nothing but the best when it comes to dining, too. Dance to the beat and snack on tapas at MO Bar. Award winning chefs run the show at two of the three venues. Put a little spice in your life at Rasoi by Vineet. This Michelin starred contemporary Indian restaurant is the brainchild of Chef Vineet Bhatia and Anupam Banerjee. As if that isn't enough, legendary Paul Bocuse is behind Le Sud, the brasserie on the banks of the Rhône.

"Dare we say, it runs like clockwork…"

MANDARIN ORIENTAL, GENEVA
Quai Turrettini 1
1201 Geneva, Switzerland
mandarinoriental.com

SWITZERLAND
GENEVA

Le Richemond

All world-class cities must have one. A grand dame, of course!

In Geneva, that is Le Richemond. Now a member of the Dorchester Collection, this historic hotel has attracted guests with its sumptuous interiors and club-like atmosphere for over 135 years. Founded by the Armleder family, Le Richemond has been home to many artists, including Charlie Chaplin, Marc Chagall, and Colette, who lovingly wrote about the hotel.

Gracing the shores of Lake Geneva, Le Richemond overlooks the Lake's geyser and the greenery of Jardin Brunswick - all within a short distance from the international business district. You won't have trouble finding this impressive hotel - simply look for its crimson red awnings. Its signature color (and mine also!) is used throughout the hotel.

Le Richemond does not rely on its rich history to dazzle today's travelers. The 88 rooms and 21 suites play out a relaxed contemporary design with soothing colors and simple furnishings. Beautiful views are part of the lovely picture.

This hotel is not just a city landmark, it is also where all of Geneva comes to dine, drink, and even dance. Le Jardin impresses with its modern Italian cooking and sleek setting, while Le Bar dazzles with its eye-catching and splashy red décor and live music. Of course, you can't beat a seat on the terrace overlooking the lake as the Jet d'Eau sprays upwards!

"Le Richemond marked the first stop on my honeymoon in the spring of 1965. It was the first time I traveled abroad and what an introduction it was! Since then, I have returned numerous times and Le Richemond continues to welcome me with open arms."

LE RICHEMOND
Jardin Brunswick
1201 Geneva, Switzerland
lerichemond.com or
dorchestercollection.com

SWITZERLAND
INTERLAKEN

Victoria-Jungfrau Grand Hotel & Spa

Nestled between Lake Thun and Lake Brienz in the scenic Bernese Oberland, Interlaken is the Swiss capital of year-round sports and adventure. Its mountainous setting makes for terrific hiking and paragliding in summer, while winters months are a powdery paradise for skiers and snowboarders.

For over 145 years, Victoria-Jungfrau Grand Hotel & Spa has welcomed guests to this gorgeous natural setting with an elegant, ever-changing design. Keeping up with the trends while honoring rich traditions is this hotel's mantra...just look at the exterior. From its cathedral-like Renaissance style architecture to its Zen modern spa, this resort is an amalgam of unique styles blended into one spectacular resort.

You can definitely play hard here, but sleep will come oh so easily once you enter your private domain in the 117 rooms and 95 suites. Reflecting a Swiss contemporary décor, the accommodations are livened up with colors and patterns. Superb views of the snow-capped or green mountains top off the pleasant surroundings.

If you are a spa devotee, Victoria-Jungfrau is your end-all and be-all. This 59,000-square-foot temple of serenity and wellness is begging for your overworked and overwrought soul. Spend a few days here and you'll truly feel reinvigorated and recharged.

The ESPA Spa may be the crown jewel of Victoria-Jungfrau, but when it comes to dining, this is not your carrot sticks-and-celery kind of resort. Instead, there are six restaurants and bars with a variety of offerings, including Italian and gourmet French. So go ahead and enjoy that fresh alpine air on an adventure...a good meal is waiting back here for you.

VICTORIA-JUNGFRAU HOTEL & SPA
Höheweg 41
3800 Interlaken, Switzerland
victoria-jungfrau.ch

SWITZERLAND
LAUSANNE

Beau-Rivage Palace

Have you ever walked in the steps of Russian archdukes, English lords, and other notables? Well, at Beau-Rivage Palace, you will. This esteemed hotel opened in 1861 and its tradition of grand excellence has made it a legend ever since.

Beau-Rivage Palace occupies an idyllic spot on the shores of Lac Leman (French for Lake Geneva) in Lausanne's residential area. Surrounded by ten acres of greenery and private gardens, the hotel affords picturesque views of the Alps and the lake. It makes a wonderful place for a relaxing holiday. Head to the hills to cycle the countryside or ski the slopes in wintertime.

All 137 guest rooms and 31 suites have been individually decorated; each has its own formal ambience and personality with traditional décor. The accommodations blend French and European influences for a distinctive look.

While staying at Beau-Rivage Palace, take advantage of its many amenities, which include indoor and outdoor pools and a large Cinq Mondes Spa. Translating to "five worlds," this spa's philosophy and design incorporate ancient health and beauty rituals from Japan, India, North Africa, China, and Bali.

Live music entertains nightly at the Bar. Enjoy sushi in a sophisticated setting at Miyako or take a seat inside the airy brasserie of Café Beau-Rivage. For a gastronomic delight, book a table at Anne-Sophie Pic at Beau-Rivage Palace. Her talented and artful cuisine has earned two Michelin stars here.

"For me, Beau-Rivage Palace is one of the prettiest places in the world. I always get swept up in its majesty, whether I am riding the antique steamer boat, relaxing at the spa, or savoring haute cuisine."

BEAU-RIVAGE PALACE
Place du Port
1010 Lausanne, Switzerland
brp.ch

SWITZERLAND
LUCERNE

Palace Luzern

Covered bridges, medieval chapels, and narrow streets make Lucerne a storybook setting, but add breathtaking Alpine views and you have an out-of-this-world enchanting destination. Located in central Switzerland, Lucerne is blissfully quiet…the perfect place to relax and take a deep breath. Palace Luzern, set on the banks of Lake Lucerne and nestled within private gardens, is the place to be in this ultimate resort town.

The distinguished Palace Luzern has elegantly greeted guests since 1906. It was the first hotel in Switzerland to offer en suite bathrooms. During World War II, it was used as a military ambulance station and commissariat. After a top-to-bottom renovation, it reopened in 1946. Modernized many times since, Palace Luzern never shakes its esteemed Swiss traditions.

The spacious 79 guest rooms and 57 suites feature a trendy mix of classic and contemporary design. Let your creative juices flow in the Art Suites, where the interiors are inspired by Kandinsky, Miró, and Chagall.

Explore the surroundings by jogging along the lake, playing at one of nine area golf courses, or climbing aboard a boat for an excursion. In addition, hiking, mountain biking, and skiing are all favored ways to take in the splendid setting. Or, do nothing but admire the beauty of the lake and mountain panorama from your private spa suite in between treatments at the Palace Spa by ESPA.

With its prestigious tradition, perhaps it comes as no surprise that Palace Luzern is home to two fine dining establishments. Enjoy the playful ambience and internationally inspired regional specialties at Restaurant Les Artistes or let yourself be mesmerized by Restaurant Jasper's Mediterranean-influenced Michelin-starred menu.

PALACE LUZERN
Haldenstrasse 10
6002 Lucerne, Switzerland
palace-luzern.ch

SWITZERLAND
ST. MORITZ

Badrutt's Palace Hotel

The Badrutt family pioneered winter tourism in St. Moritz. Five generations later, Badrutt's Palace, which opened in 1896, remains a winter wonderland and summer paradise. Set on private grounds, it has unmatched views of the mountains and lake.

Badrutt's Palace operates a top ski school and the ice rink even boasts its own resident pro. Polo matches are held year-round, but imagine it on the frozen lake! During warmer months, guests take lessons with the tennis pro, hike the great outdoors, or swim in the indoor or outdoor pools. Prefer perusing to perspiring? Take a soothing spa treatment or walk through the exclusive shopping gallery.

The 121 rooms and 38 suites are tastefully enhanced with an elegant country appeal. If the Alpine air hasn't increased your endorphins, the floral fabrics and bright colors certainly will. Overlooking the lake, mountains, or the resort's grounds, the views are equally delightful.

Badrutt's Palace is a hot spot - numerous restaurants from Japanese to French cuisine will entice you. Spend a romantic evening at Chesa Veglia, just a few minutes away. One of the oldest houses in St. Moritz, this spot lures diners with its Swiss specialties and unique charm. In contrast, dance until dawn and watch the sun rise over the Engadin Alpine mountains at the King's Club, where DJs spin tunes for the beautiful people.

"I was brand new to the travel business when I first stayed at Badrutt's Palace Hotel, so what a surprise to be greeted in Le Grand Hall by a dapper gentleman. Mr. Badrutt introduced himself and welcomed me to his home as if I were a celebrity."

BADRUTT'S PALACE HOTEL
Via Serlas 27
7500 St. Moritz, Switzerland
badruttspalace.com

SWITZERLAND
ZURICH

Baur au Lac

Zurich is a beautiful, walkable city with a wonderful combination of the old and new. Charming cobblestone streets and Alpine clocktowers in Old Town seamlessly coexist with the exclusive boutiques of the modern Bahnhofstrasse. In the center is the lovely Baur au Lac.

The Baur au Lac is snuggled on private landscaped grounds overlooking the lake. Resembling a large villa, this aristocratic hotel was founded in 1844 by Johannes Baur. Six generations later, it remains in the Baur-Kracht family. It has always been a favorite of a powerful, international set. It hosted the world premiere of Wagner's Die Walküre with Wagner himself performing and the idea for the Nobel Prize was hatched here! Everyone from Hitchcock to Hepburn hid here.

The Baur au Lac's style is influenced by its worldly clientele. The 93 rooms and 27 suites are individually decorated in everything from Louis XVI, Directoire, and Chippendale to contemporary. Elegant, but very livable, too!

From the relaxed elegance of the Rive Gauche and the Rive Gauche Terrasse to the fabulously French Pavillon, dining at Baur au Lac is a joy. More than fine food, it is sparkling service and ambient settings that make for memories.

Many hotels may leave a piece of chocolate on your pillow, but how many have their own signature flavor? The 1844 Chocolate, named for the hotel's birth year, is a sultry dark chocolate with the full-bodied flavor of the Marona almond.

"The Baur au Lac exudes peace and privacy and I always feel like I'm coming home. Everything from dining al fresco on the Terrasse to the squares of 1844 chocolate is absolute perfection."

BAUR AU LAC
Talstrasse 1
8001 Zurich, Switzerland
bauraulac.ch

SWITZERLAND
ZURICH

The Dolder Grand

For more than a century, The Dolder Grand has stood watch overlooking the city of Zurich from its wooded hillside locale.

This landmark hotel brings together the best of both worlds in Zurich. Corporate offices and attractions are just a funicular ride away, but this natural setting and resort-within-a-city is a tranquil alternative to the bustling city. "The original castle-like building housed a health and wellness center in the late 19th century, and while its turrets and gables are among the romantic features seen today, inside, the 114 rooms and 59 suites blend crisp contemporary interiors with Swiss heritage. Rooms in the main building are particularly inviting with their Juliet balconies, while the modern wings have an über-chic vibe."

A 9-hole golf course sits just outside the hotel's entrance, and clay tennis courts are nearby. Enjoy the city's only miniature golf course with your little ones, rent skates at the ice skating rink during the winter, or enjoy the warmth of the sun with a swim in the shimmering pool. The forests that shade this exclusive residential neighborhood are also perfect for exploration, whether you choose to don your running shoes or simply want to amble.

The Dolder Grand has a palpable cool factor, especially at the enormous, sleek spa, where a Euro-Japanese sensibility dominates.

The restaurants and bars continue the theme with cutting-edge culinary styles and minimalist interior design. Enjoy the Garden Restaurant and terrace, where views of the lake and distant Alps are uplifting, or visit The Restaurant for a taste of award-winning cuisine.

"High above Zurich, The Dolder Grand effortlessly integrates traditional Swiss service with avant-garde art and innovations."

THE DOLDER GRAND
Kurhausstrasse 65
8032 Zurich, Switzerland
thedoldergrand.com

SWITZERLAND
ZURICH

Park Hyatt Zurich

Home to one of the world's largest stock exchanges, Zurich is the powerhouse of Switzerland, but it's not all just business in this Swiss capital.

Park Hyatt Zurich is surrounded by the major financial houses around Paradeplatz square, while the boutiques of Bahnhofstrasse are just steps away. "Whether you are traveling to Zurich for strategy sessions, shopping, or sightseeing, it makes a convenient and cosmopolitan home-away-from-home."

The Park Hyatt isn't a former residence, converted factory, or restored bank. Instead, this building was built for the sole purpose of housing the sophisticated traveler.

The result is a luxury hotel with abundant creature comforts and sharp modern design.

This hotel's 130 rooms and 12 suites are exceptionally welcoming. Padded cream colored headboards, gleaming walnut furnishings, touches of chocolate brown…these interiors are as comforting as a hot cup of coffee topped with whipped cream and chocolate shavings!

Wellness is a big part of the Park Hyatt experience, whether sampling nutritious food or practicing yoga, exercising in the fitness center, or relaxing with a natural-based treatment at Club Olympus Spa.

Warm up by the fire in the Lounge, where light meals, hot drinks, and cocktails are served throughout the day. Drop by Café Z, with its selection of sandwiches and snacks. The Onyx Bar is ideal for a gathering and draws local businesspeople for after-work cocktails. The unique Parkhuus restaurant is Park Hyatt's stand-out, though. With three sides constructed completely of floor-to-ceiling glass on the corner of Beethoven-Strasse and Dreikönig-Strasse, Parkhuus is a bold setting with an open kitchen. From the passersby to the kitchen staff hard at work, it is a perpetual show.

PARK HYATT ZURICH
Beethoven-Strasse 21
8002 Zurich, Switzerland
parkhyatt.com

TURKEY
ISTANBUL

Ciragan Palace Hotel Kempinski

Straddling the Asian and European continents, Istanbul offers an intoxicating blend of cultures. The city, founded in 330 AD as Constantinople, has a dizzying pace and its sounds and sights intensify your experience. Whether you are haggling in its Grand Bazaar or listening to the muezzin's call to prayer, it is a place that will mystify you.

Byzantines and Romans conquered Istanbul, but it was the Ottomans that we have to thank for the glorious Cirağan Palace Hotel Kempinski. This former palace of an Ottoman sultan is one-of-a-kind. Rebuilt several times over the last centuries, it sits right on the European side of the Bosphorus. Like a phoenix, the Cirağan rose from the ashes of a devastating fire in 1910 and was carefully restored to its original splendor.

This hotel is the very definition of opulence. Ottoman fabrics and furnishings, sunny oranges, and jewel tones dominate the 280 rooms and 31 suites with views over the Bosphorus or Yıldız Park, once the hunting grounds of the Sultans.

Sanitas Spa is both traditional and trendsetting, while Asian-accented treatments are a surefire way to soothe tired souls. The infinity pool, which might just convince you that you are floating in the timeless Bosphorus, is truly a sight for sore eyes.

From lobster lunches by the pool to bountiful buffets, Cirağan Palace Hotel Kempinski spoils its guests. "I suggest dining like a Sultan at Tuğra Restaurant, where traditional Ottoman cuisine recreated from genuine Palace recipes will enthrall you."

"From its historical palace wing with its splurge-worthy suites to its glittering pool to its gourmet cuisine, Cirağan Palace Hotel Kempinski is a Turkish delight."

CIRAĞAN PALACE HOTEL KEMPINSKI
Cirağan Caddesi 32
Besiktas, 34349, Istanbul, Turkey
kempinski.com

TURKEY
ISTANBUL

Four Seasons Hotel Istanbul at The Bosphorus
Four Seasons Hotel Istanbul at Sultanahmet

The Four Seasons Hotel at The Bosphorus is a lovingly transformed 19th century palace with modern wings set on the Bosphorus. Classic exteriors meet chic interiors here in the delightful 145 rooms and 25 suites. Highlights include the Bosphorus-facing pool and spa inspired by the enduring mystique of the hammam (Turkish bath). Enjoy the cool breezes at the water's edge whether sunning or dining at the Poolside Grill or Aqua. Wherever you are, the Bosphorus is the focus and blissful is the mood.

"Take in the sights, munch on mezes, sit at the pool, or unwind at the spa. Only the Four Seasons brings you Istanbul quite like this…go ahead and stay at both…be held captive by their exotic mix in a destination that I truly love."

Look closely to discover its past at the Four Seasons Hotel at Sultanahmet. A few tiles here, and some marble columns there, but it is the enclosed courtyard that is the largest clue to its former life as the Sultanahmet prison. Built eighty years ago to house Turkey's dissident writers and politicians, today it houses dignitaries and tourists. Located in the historic quarter, with views of the Blue Mosque and the Hagia Sofia, nothing gets you as close to the action as this Four Seasons. Just outside the door is Istanbul, in all of its heady and dizzying glory, but inside, it is peaceful and uncluttered. The 54 rooms and 11 suites have an unmatched intimacy. Fine dining at two restaurants ensures you won't be living on bread and water!

FOUR SEASONS HOTEL ISTANBUL AT THE BOSPHORUS
Çırağan Cad. No. 28
Besiktas, 34349,
Istanbul, Turkey
fourseasons.com

FOUR SEASONS HOTEL ISTANBUL AT SULTANAHMET
Tevkifhane Sokak No. 1
Sultanahmet-Eminönü, 34110, Istanbul, Turkey
fourseasons.com

BOTSWANA

EGYPT

KENYA

MOROCCO

SOUTH AFRICA

TANZANIA

INDIA

Africa • India • Indian Ocean • Middle East

MALDIVES

MAURITIUS

SEYCHELLES

LEBANON

OMAN

SYRIA

UNITED ARAB EMIRATES

BOTSWANA
CHOBE • MOREMI GAME RESERVE • OKAVANGO DELTA

Savute Elephant Camp • Khwai River Lodge • Eagle Island Camp

Botswana is wild Africa at its best. From its green wetlands and forested islands to its rivers and desert sands, Botswana has a diverse landscape. Stunning scenery and abundant wildlife make it an ideal safari destination at these 3 Orient-Express camps.

Chobe National Park is blessed with one of Africa's largest elephant populations. Safari doesn't mean you should forsake luxury. Savute Elephant Camp takes comfort very seriously. Home to 12 permanent tents housed on raised wooden platforms, Savute lets you have your *Out of Africa* fantasy with a side of sophistication. "Spot elephants from your bed…this isn't camping like you remembered."

Moremi Game Reserve tucked within the Okavango Delta, is a special spot. The Okavango Delta is the only inland delta of its kind and a unique oasis of life in the heart of the Kalahari and it is all yours while staying at Khwai River Lodge. Spot hippos from the raised deck of the 15 tents. "Game drives looking for cheetah and lion, star gazing, moonlight safaris, even hippos under your deck…it's all part of the magic at Khwai River Lodge."

Eagle Island Camp is a secluded retreat on remote Xaxaba Island in the Okavango Delta. Here, you will explore the waterways by dugout canoe, walk the paths, enjoy a game drive, or even swim laps in the pool. The 11 raised tents and 1 suite are your home in this pristine wilderness, where 400 different species of birds are known to fly. "The bar, on its own island away from the camp, has to be one of the most romantic spots in the world, but do not miss a helicopter safari for a bird's eye view of the Delta's wildlife."

SAVUTE ELEPHANT CAMP
savutelephantcamp.com or orient-express.com
KHWAI RIVER LODGE
khwairiverlodge.com or orient-express.com
EAGLE ISLAND CAMP
eagleislandcamp.com or orient-express.com

BOTSWANA
CHOBE & OKAVANGO DELTA

Sanctuary Chobe Chilwero & Sanctuary Chief's Camp

Sanctuary Retreats, a collection of luxurious safari camps, by esteemed Abercrombie & Kent, will bushwhack any preconceived notions of what it's like to be on an African safari.

Have you ever had a massage in the treetops of the African bush? If not, head straight for Sanctuary Chobe Chilwero! Nestled on the edge of Chobe National Park with the world's largest elephant population, Sanctuary Chobe Chilwero ups the ante in the African wild. Intimate, with just 15 guest cottages and each with private gardens, it has the only spa in Botswana. What a spa it is…all the niceties of a resort spa with the unique element of a treatment room elevated in the treetops. Jump on the 4x4 for a game drive to get up close and personal with hippos, buffalos, lions, leopards, and of course - elephants! For a classic African adventure, take a sundowner cruise on the river for a dramatic end to a life-changing day.

No man is an island, but Sanctuary Chief's Camp is… at least it is nestled on one. It rests on Chief's Island in Moremi Game Reserve in the Okavango Delta. This area is teeming with wildlife from antelope to zebra and is one of the best places for spotting the impressive Big 5 creatures (can you name them?). The 12 luxury bush pavilions look straight out of a Hemingway novel; think four poster-style beds swathed in mosquito netting and director's chairs. The dining area set around a firepit is a romantic and inspiring location where you are never far from game viewing.

"Vast and untamed, this exquisite wilderness should not be missed."

SANCTUARY CHOBE CHILWERO
SANCTUARY CHIEF'S CAMP
sanctuaryretreats.com

EAST AFRICA
KENYA

Fairmont Mount Kenya Safari Club

Kenya is a place of many stories, but perhaps one of its most fabled locations is the Fairmont Mount Kenya Safari Club. It became the private retreat of silver screen legend William Holden in 1959. He and friends created the Club, added cottages, tennis courts, and a pool. His most significant contribution was the addition of a 1000 acre wildlife reserve with more than 800 animals. During that heyday, the Club counted dignitaries and movie stars as members, Winston Churchill, Lord Mountbatten, Bob Hope, and Bing Crosby, to name a few.

Visit Fairmont Mount Kenya Safari Club to experience a bygone era. Set on over 100 landscaped acres, this bush resort is close to Mount Kenya National Park, part of a UNESCO World Heritage Site, and close to Aberdare National Park.

The resort's 120 guest rooms, suites, and cottages are spread across the manicured grounds. The accommodations feature a sophisticated British Colonial style with views of Mount Kenya.

For all generations, there are so many ways to enjoy this setting high on the slopes of Africa's second highest mountain. Horseback riding, golf, croquet, tennis, and bicycle riding are just some of the available outdoor activities. Sit by the pool with its views of Mount Kenya, but be sure to visit the animal orphanage managed by the William Holden Wildlife Foundation.

The clubby Zebar is fun and lively, while Tusks Restaurant and Terrace shows off local cooking traditions and dishes.

"Over 22 years ago at the Fairmont Mount Kenya Safari Club, while sipping a martini and smoking a cigarette in the bar, I felt like a star on a movie set."

FAIRMONT MOUNT KENYA SAFARI CLUB
Mount Kenya, Nanyuki, Kenya
fairmont.com

EAST AFRICA
KENYA & TANZANIA

Sanctuary Olonana & Sanctuary Swala

When you think of the classic African safari, chances are you are thinking of indescribable Kenya. The Masai Mara is home to the Big Five, and between summer and early fall, it welcomes the greatest show on Earth – the annual wildebeest migration.

Olonana was the first in the collection of Sanctuary Retreats' luxury safari properties created by Abercrombie & Kent. There are just 14 private canvas tents decked out with parquet floors, four-poster beds, en suite bathrooms and private verandas. Eco-conscious designs and practices make this award-winning camp an industry leader. Indulge in a treatment at the mini-spa, where traditional African remedies blend with French marine-based therapies. And then there are the animals. It's why you've come and you'll be rewarded with a front-row seat to the action. From grunting herds of wildebeest and zebra to noisy hippos who lounge on the banks below the camp, Sanctuary Olonana delivers a once-in-a-lifetime experience.

Kenya might be the most recognized African destination, but Tanzania is for those in-the-know. From the snow-capped peak of Mount Kilimanjaro, to the game-rich Ngorongoro Crater, to the vast Serengeti, Tanzania is paradise on Earth. Tucked away in an exceptionally private section of Tarangire National Park, Sanctuary Swala welcomes guests to retreat with an intimate character. There are just 12 tented canvas pavilions here, but all are in sight of the water hole, which lures lions and leopards, among others. Swala is famous for its resident bull elephants…watch them from the comfort of your own private world.

"I think a safari is a life-changing experience, so enjoy the splendors of East Africa at both Sanctuary Olonana and Sanctuary Swala."

SANCTUARY OLONANA
Masai Mara, Kenya
SANCTUARY SWALA
Tarangire National Park, Tanzania
sanctuaryretreats.com

TANZANIA
SERENGETI

Singita Grumeti Reserves
Sasakwa Lodge • Sabora Tented Camp • Faru Faru Lodge

It turns out that good things do come in threes. Singita Grumeti Reserves is a trio of lodges and camps placed within a massive 340,000 acre private concession. These properties are carefully placed along the migratory route of the wildebeest… more than a million traverse this route annually, along with the predators that lie in wait. It's a good thing they can't stay in one of the cottages or tents at Singita, since they'd never leave!

Singita Grumeti Reserves is comprised of three distinct properties: Sasakwa Lodge, Sabora Tented Camp and Faru Faru Lodge. Each has its own signature personality and flavor.

Sasakwa Lodge embodies the best of the British Colonial design with an Edwardian style manor house and 9 guest cottages – all complete with private infinity pools. Decorated with a proper European feeling that meets the African bush, it is laid-back luxury for the whole family.

Sabora Tented Camp brings out the dashing adventurer in all of us with its rich sense of romance and elegance of a gentler time. Each of the 9 canvas tents has an unbelievably enchanting interior set with antique mahogany travel chests, Persian rugs, and silk curtains. Rekindle your romance at the sensational Sabora Tented Camp (children over 10 only).

Faru Faru Lodge is the ultimate rustic family getaway resting on a gentle slope overlooking a water hole. With just 8 suites, Faru Faru Lodge pours on the privacy, but this spot also spoils with amenities, like two pools designed to echo the shape of the water hole below and even a private "beach" for some R&R.

Who said you can't have it all on safari?

SINGITA GRUMETI RESERVES
Serengeti, Tanzania
singita.com

SOUTH AFRICA
SABI SAND GAME RESERVE

Singita Ebony Lodge & Singita Boulders Lodge

Don't worry if you feel like you might be seeing spots – at least if you are at Sabi Sand Game Reserve and the lodges of Singita Ebony and Singita Boulders. That's because this area is home to the world's largest number of leopards.

Stretch out on the timber deck of Singita Ebony Lodge with its views over the Sand River. Elephant, buffalo, and antelope graze just steps away, but here you will be cocooned in luxury. You are welcome to make this 12 suite property your own – the feel here is one of great comfort and warmth. Each suite is like its own private world, complete with en suite bathrooms, outside showers, two-sided fireplaces, and heated private swimming pools. Whether you are dining in the traditional boma or admiring the regional throws and accents decorating the suites, Africa's heritage is on display here.

Singita chose not to move mountains, or even boulders, when it came to constructing Boulders Lodge. Named for the giant boulder that sat where the wine cellar was intended, this Lodge decided to build around it. It's just part of the principle of avoiding the disruption of nature, and Boulders rewards its guests with an authentic African experience with serious creature comforts thrown in for good measure. Enjoy panoramic views from the stone lounge or the 12 suites packed with all of the necessities. Guided game drives are included here, as with all Singita properties, but you might just find yourself whiling away your time in the wild right here. With spa services and fine dining, why not?

Exotic destination…wild animals to see…luxury lodges… Singita has it all.

SINGITA EBONY LODGE
SINGITA BOULDERS LODGE
Sabi Sand Game Reserve, South Africa
singita.com

INDIA
AGRA

The Oberoi Amarvilās

Few things in this world can compare to the Taj Mahal. It is the most romantic symbol of eternal love – a monumental tribute by Shah Jehan to his beloved wife, Empress Mumtaz Mahal.

The Oberoi Amarvilās brings you the Taj Mahal like no one else can. This hotel is a marvel to behold within nine acres of landscaped gardens, terraced lawns, geometric pools, fountains, and pavilions, yet it is steps away from this iconic temple. Amarvilās stands out with its stately five-story Indian palace defined by graceful arches and domes. Enter through its courtyard of 64 fountains and arched colonnade decorated with Mughal murals. The domed lobby is decorated with cobalt blue and gold leaf, reviving the ancient traditions of local craftsmen.

Amarvilās bears the distinction of having unobstructed views of the Taj Mahal from all 95 rooms and 7 suites, the restaurants, and the lobby. Most of the accommodations have private terraces and all have exquisite bathrooms. Polished Burmese teak floors, inlaid furniture, and rich fabrics reflect the region's history and heritage.

Unwind in the splendid surroundings of the swimming pool or partake in a treatment at The Oberoi Spa by Banyan Tree, where three of the seven treatment rooms have Taj Mahal views and ancient Ayurvedic principles are incorporated into the holistic therapies.

Whether you dine at Esphahan, with its indescribably tasty Indian food, or Continental and fusion cuisine at Bellevue, the resort's two restaurants are scrumptious.

"Visit the Taj Mahal at sunrise and sunset, but save time to enjoy the romance of Amarvilās. The view is not a mirage and it is not something you will easily forget."

THE OBEROI AMARVILĀS
Taj East Gate Road
Agra 282001, India
oberoihotels.com

INDIA
GURGAON
NEW DELHI CAPITAL REGION

The Oberoi, Gurgaon

All work and no play? Not at The Oberoi, Gurgaon. This sleek new hotel knows that down time is just as important as meeting time.

Gurgaon is India's most exciting new development. This burgeoning area just outside of Delhi is home to a large number of corporate headquarters, but what really takes center stage is the cutting-edge Oberoi hotel.

Set in the heart of Gurgaon's business and shopping district, you can get anywhere from here but what makes this modern masterpiece special is its many reasons to never leave.

The 187 rooms and 15 suites are the most spacious accommodations of any business hotel in the capital region. Massive windows let the sun shine in and focus views on the serene reflection pools and landscaped gardens.

We now live in a world where business never stops (is that your Blackberry buzzing?) and The Oberoi, Gurgaon has been designed to keep up with its hard-charging clientele. There is simply no quitting time at this hotel. Massage at 2 am? No problem…this spa is open 24 hours a day. Need your shirt pressed for tomorrow's early morning meeting? Just ring the butler at any time – they are on call.

The five restaurants of The Oberoi, Gurgaon will let you eat your way across the globe in enticing venues. Whether you're up for a lively show at the all-day spot with five interactive show kitchens or want to ease down your day on the teak deck stretching out into the reflection pool, there's a seat waiting for you.

THE OBEROI, GURGAON
443 Udyog Vihar, Phase V
Gurgaon, Haryana 122 016, India
oberoihotels.com

INDIA
HYDERABAD

Taj Falaknuma Palace

Relive India's royal past at the Taj Faluknuma Palace. The Royal Family of Hyderabad leased this palace to Taj Hotels to create this regal hotel. The grand former residence of the Nizam will open your eyes to a world of opulence.

You could easily mistake this palace for a museum; treasures are everywhere. Venetian chandeliers, stained glass windows, even a world class collection of crystal. Oh, and that's before you've even seen the Palace Library! Designed to replicate the one at Windsor Castle, it houses an impressive collection of rare manuscripts and one of the largest collections of the Koran in India. And, that's just inside the Palace... step outside to the Mughal, Rajasthani, and Japanese gardens that were the dreamworld of the Nizam.

While you no longer need a royal invitation to stay in one of the 45 rooms and 15 suites, you will certainly feel like a king or queen. The accommodations are inviting and charming with oak floors and colonial furnishings and luxurious modern amenities. The Historical Suites reflect a traditional style and are enhanced with delicate Edwardian artwork and fabrics hand selected by Her Highness Princess Ezra.

The Royal Jiva Spa uses traditional Indian practices for overall wellness, but it goes above and beyond body treatments...the spa even offers wellness cuisine designed with ayurvedic cooking principles. Don't worry... there's plenty of gourmet dining too!

At Taj Faluknuma Palace, you will truly trace the steps of Indian royalty. Whether you are playing snooker on the Nizam's custom-designed table or listening to the tales of the Palace Historian while enjoying the champagne sunset walk through the grounds, the experience is unparalleled.

TAJ FALAKNUMA PALACE
Engine Bowli, Falaknuma,
Hyderabad 500053, India
tajhotels.com

INDIA
JAIPUR

The Oberoi Rajvilās

Even in a country full of mysticism, romance, and cultural heritage, Jaipur stands out among India's treasured spots. Nicknamed the "pink city" because of its pink-hued buildings, Jaipur is a showpiece of Rajasthani architecture and a fascinating fusion of a legendary royal past merged with the frenetic pageantry of modern city streets.

On the outskirts of Jaipur is the exceptional Oberoi Rajvilās. This resort set on 32 acres of gardens, pools, and fountains is the perfect oasis. Rajvilās pays homage to the region's architecture and revives the majestic lifestyles of the Rajput princes with its recreated Rajasthani fort. Deluxe rooms are a blend of traditional flat-roofed houses and havelis (courtyard mansions) that are clustered in groups of four to six. The 54 deluxe rooms are richly furnished with colonial and traditional regional influences and have sunken marble baths that overlook private walled gardens. The 3 private villas feature individual swimming pools, and 14 private tents are set apart in two corners of the estate. These tents come with teak floors, embroidered interior canopies, furnishings covered in lavish fabrics, and sumptuous bathrooms.

"Take a break from sightseeing, relax in the peaceful surroundings at the swimming pool, or spend a few hours being pampered at the spa." Its wide range of holistic, ayurvedic, and western relaxation therapies will calm both body and mind.

Dine elegantly on Indian and Continental dishes at the resort's two restaurants or under the stars on the terrace

"Explore the countryside by elephant from Oberoi Rajvilās. As you sit atop a decorative wooden howda, you will wind along the riverbeds for an unforgettably memorable experience."

THE OBEROI RAJVILĀS
Goner Road
Jaipur, 302031, Rajasthan, India
oberoihotels.com

INDIA
JAIPUR

Rambagh Palace

Kings, princes, and their privileged guests once romped here but you too can enjoy the splendors of Rambagh Palace.

Built in 1835 for the queen's favorite handmaiden and later refurbished as a royal guesthouse and hunting lodge, it was christened Rambagh by the reigning Maharaja. His grandson loved it so much that he enlarged it and made it Rambagh Palace in 1925. It remained the permanent residence of the Maharaja of Jaipur until 1957, when the family converted part of it into a hotel.

"Rambagh Palace, a Taj Hotel, stirs the romantic in all of us with its remarkable history, elaborately detailed architecture, stately ornamental gardens, rich textures, art and antiques, and over-the-top grandeur."

The 46 rooms and 33 suites are traditional retreats with canopied beds and rich colors. Request the legendary Peacock suite, which overlooks the Mughal Terrace and the garden where the Maharaja used to celebrate "Holi," the festival of color and lights.

Play polo as the kings once played it or enjoy the game atop an elephant for a truly Indian experience. Succumb to a relaxing treatment inside the tented spa suites at the Jiva Grande Spa where the interiors are a love letter to India's magical past. From Mughal leitmotif and wooden floors to glittering chandeliers, royal pennants, and Indian love swings, this spa is truly one-of-a-kind

Not to be outdone, dining is an equally glamorous affair at Rambagh Palace. From royal feasts under starlit skies to evenings in private torchlit tents, romance is always part of the plan. Dine at Suvarna Mahal, the former palace ballroom, for a taste of the royal life.

RAMBAGH PALACE
Bhawani Singh Road
Jaipur 302 005 Rajasthan, India
tajhotels.com

INDIA
JODHPUR

Umaid Bhawan Palace

Towering over the desert capital of Jodhpur, Umaid Bhawan Palace is the last of the great palaces of India. One of the largest private residences in the world, it was built between 1928-1943 by the current Maharaja's grandfather. Designed as a symbol of a new Jodhpur and as a way to employ locals during the great famine of the time, this 347-room golden-yellow sandstone palace remains the principal residence of the Jodhpur royals.

Set within 26 acres of abundant gardens, Umaid Bhawan Palace is an Art Deco architectural masterpiece blending eastern and western influences – the soaring 105-foot cupola is inspired by the Renaissance, while the towers are purely Rajput. The 22 rooms and 42 suites are a testament to luxury.

"Umaid Bhawan Palace's public spaces are magnificently grand, unforgettable, and worthy of a stay just to be part of the elegance. While you are ensconced in these royal grounds, enjoy life as a Maharaja or Maharini would."

Visit the private museum, swim indoors at the Zodiac pool, wander the gardens, indulge at the spa where royal palace secrets are shared, or be driven in a vintage car.

Elegant dining completes the palatial experience. Whether indoors at Risala, in the colonnaded veranda at the Pillars, or in the Sunset Pavilion, (the highest elevation in all of Jodhpur), the experience is pure magic.

"I will always treasure the experience of sitting in the grand Rathore Durbar Hall for a Virtuoso lunch at the left hand of the Maharaja of Jodhpur. He and I reminisced about England and he shared family stories with me relating to his home, Umaid Bhawan Palace."

UMAID BHAWAN PALACE
Jodhpur 342006 Rajasthan, India
tajhotels.com

INDIA
MUMBAI

The Oberoi, Mumbai

Once known as Bombay, Mumbai is now known the world over as Bollywood. Call it what you will, but this city is India's most populated city with over 20 million people. Fast paced and Westernized, it is home to thriving businesses and is the world's largest producer of films. Grab a seat, since the world is coming to do business here, and when they do, they stay at The Oberoi, Mumbai.

"This modern tower in the city's business and shopping district of Nariman Point was designed with the contemporary traveler in mind; business and leisure guests feel right at home." It has sweeping views overlooking the Arabian Sea and Bay of Bombay from its prestigious Marine Drive location.

This hotel grabs you immediately with its 14-floor central atrium lobby and continues to impress with its dashing style. Fresh from a renovation, the 214 rooms and 73 suites are sleek and serene, but with high tech amenities and well-planned design elements, these accommodations function without a hitch. Got writer's block for tomorrow's presentation? Just gaze out your window at the bottomless views. Need to work off some steam? Hit the 24 hour fitness center, book a treatment at the spa, or head outdoors to the swimming pool.

Toast or take tea at The Champagne Lounge or enjoy the new Eau Bar for its lively nightlife. From international dining at Fenix, or Italian at Vetro and Enoteca, to the much talked-about Indian food at Michelin-starred Vineet Bhatia's Ziya, the only hard part about dining at The Oberoi is selecting your favorite spot.

"The Oberoi, Mumbai is a contemporary city hotel that lives up to all the outstanding Oberoi service standards."

THE OBEROI, MUMBAI
Nariman Point
Mumbai 400 021, India
oberoihotels.com

INDIA
MUMBAI

The Taj Mahal Palace

The Taj Mahal Palace has been a symbol of Bombay for over a century.

It is difficult to determine where the hotel's history ends and the city's begins, as the two have been inextricably linked since the grand hotel's opening. It served as the harbor's first landmark and it was also home to the city's first licensed bar. The Taj Mahal Palace has hosted everyone from Maharajas, dignitaries, and savvy travelers who have come to be a part of this legend since its opening in 1903.

at several spots. "From hot spots to time-honored favorites, dining at the Taj is as legendary as the hotel itself." In fact, the Sea Lounge, which has long been a part of the hotel's history, is a much-beloved Mumbai institution. It was once popular for matchmaking. Families would bring in prospective brides and grooms during cocktail hours at the Sea Lounge and everything from initial meetings to marriage proposals were conducted here!

Like the hotel itself, which effortlessly bridges past and present, the hotel's 516 rooms and 44 suites are at once historic and of-the-moment. Traditional furnishings and nods to India's history are at home with modern conveniences. Expansive views of the Arabian Sea are particularly pleasing from the modern tower accommodations, while those in the palace evoke the ambience of a bygone era. Even the palace hallways, lined with art and artifacts, celebrate the history.

THE TAJ MAHAL PALACE
Apollo Bunder
Mumbai 400 001, Maharashtra, India
tajhotels.com

"The Taj Mahal Palace has a mouthwatering array of restaurants. There are 10 different restaurants under one roof!" Choose from Sichuan cuisine at Golden Dragon, Middle Eastern delicacies at Souk, Japanese at Wasabi by Morimoto, and Indian specialties

INDIA
RANTHAMBHORE

The Oberoi Vanyavilās

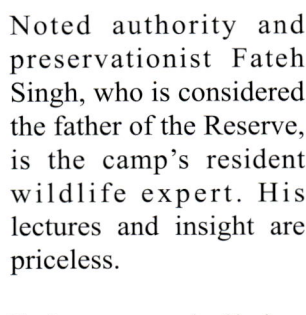

One of the world's most majestic creatures, the tiger is also one of the most elusive. Prized as trophies, tigers were aggressively hunted for decades and even neared extinction. Thanks to conservation efforts like the Ranthambhore Tiger Reserve, these animals are thriving once again.

The exotic Oberoi Vanyavilās, which translates to "jungle palace," is India's first luxury jungle camp. This one-of-a-kind retreat is adjacent to the Ranthambhore Tiger Reserve, where hopefully you will catch a glimpse. "Where else can you stay in a luxurious tent by night and spot the mysterious tiger by day?"

The 25 tents and public space comprise only a fraction of the 20 acres in an effort to preserve India's delicate environment. "These tents are nothing short of out of this world." Extremely spacious, they have an average of nearly 790 square feet. You may be in the Indian jungle, but inside you could be in any cosmopolitan resort with teak floors, embroidered canvas, chic campaign furnishings, tiger-patterned rugs, and luxurious bathrooms. Each tent is surrounded by a private walled garden with deck. Or, stretch out in the sun by the pool.

The Ranthambhore Reserve is home to a wide variety of wildlife, but you're here to earn your stripes as a tiger spotter.

Noted authority and preservationist Fateh Singh, who is considered the father of the Reserve, is the camp's resident wildlife expert. His lectures and insight are priceless.

Enjoy casual dining indoors or out, and in the evenings, listen to the local musicians play traditional Rajasthani music.

"Even if the tigers are elusive, it is only one of the reasons to enjoy the unforgettable Oberoi Vanyavilās!"

THE OBEROI VANYAVILĀS
Ranthambhore Road, Sawai Madhopur
Ranthambhore, 322001 Rajasthan, India
oberoihotels.com

INDIA
UDAIPUR

The Oberoi Udaivilās

Udaipur is a Rajashthan city of alluring palaces, havelis, and temples built around a shimmering, clear blue lake. Expertly blending Mughal design influences with Rajput intricate craftsmanship, Udaipur's architecture captivates and inspires.

Udaivilās opens your eyes to a magical world. Situated on Udaipur's famous Lake Pichola, it replicates a traditional Rajashthani palace and maintains a royal ambience. Its 30 acres of manicured grounds are filled with landscaped gardens, fountains, and pavilions, and its views toward the City Palace, one of Udaipur's major landmarks, are sensational. The resort adjoins a 20 acre wildlife conservatory where wild boar, peacocks, and Indian spotted deer roam freely.

The 82 rooms and 5 suites are elegantly appointed with a combination of traditional Indian and European furnishings and influences. The bathrooms, made entirely of marble, look out over private walled gardens. Most rooms have uninterrupted views of Lake Pichola and the City Palace, and all rooms have terraces. "My favorite accommodations are one of the 17 superior deluxe rooms with a semi-private pool, terrace, colorful umbrella, and all." Suites boast swimming pools and pavilions for relaxation or dining.

Take a break from sightseeing and dip in one of the outdoor pools. The striking spa brings an unprecedented level of relaxation to Udaipur. Savor fine Indian or Continental cuisine at Surya Mahal and Udai Mahal. While having a cocktail at the Bar, enjoy breathtaking views of Lake Pichola and the City Palace

Take a romantic sunset cruise on Lake Pichola while aboard a Gangore Nav, a traditional boat similar to those used during the famous Gangore festival 150 years ago.

"Oberoi Udaivilās is a favorite of mine. It is magic – pure and simple."

THE OBEROI UDAIVILĀS
Hardasji Ki Magri
Udaipur 313001, Rajasthan, India
oberoihotels.com

INDIA
UDAIPUR

Taj Lake Palace

Legend has it that young prince Maharana Jagat Singh II, who was barred by his father from enjoying the moonlight picnics with his bevy of courtesans, built his own lake island palace in the middle of Lake Pichola as an act of defiance. This palace, known as Jag Mandir, is today's Taj Lake Palace. What was once built as a rebellious act of passion by a young prince is now enjoyed by lucky travelers who make the trip to this romantic place on the waters of Lake Pichola.

The gleaming marble Taj Lake Palace is one of four lovely islands within Lake Pichola. Transformed into a romantic hotel by Maharana Bhagwat Singhji in 1963, the hotel became a part of Taj Hotels in 1971.

"Don't be surprised if the palace looks familiar…it was the secluded lair that lured Roger Moore in the James Bond film *Octopussy*."

Taj Lake Palace surrounds you with water views. Relive the history in the 66 rooms and 17 suites which have a rich, classical ambience. Live it up in the royal suites, where lavish appointments share the lifestyles of the House of Mewar. If only these walls could talk…imagine what the Chandra Prakash Suite would say. This impressive suite with decorative gilt moldings, sculpted marble columns, and fine fretwork screens, was the favorite of the Maharaja who held court here in the 1930s.

"Live the grand life here. Walk the grounds and hear the history while sampling caviar and Champagne, take an escorted shopping trip or a sunset sail on a 150-year-old ceremonial barge with resplendently dressed oarsmen. It is sure to satisfy your senses."

TAJ LAKE PALACE
Lake Pichola
Udaipur 313001, Rajasthan, India
tajhotels.com

INDIAN OCEAN
MALDIVES

Four Seasons Resort Maldives at Kuda Huraa
Four Seasons Resort Maldives at Landaa Giraavaru

Situated in the middle of the Indian Ocean, the Maldives are a collection of 1,200 tiny islands that dazzle your senses.

The Four Seasons Resort at Kuda Huraa indulges your fantasies with white sand beaches and perpetually warm turquoise waters from its garden village setting. A short speedboat ride from Malé, this secluded resort calls its own island all to itself. The resort's thatched-roof accommodations include 57 beach bungalows and 1 two-bedroom villa, plus 38 over-water bungalows perched on stilts above the blue lagoon. Six restaurants and bars are ready to satisfy, while the spa, reachable by traditional dhoni boat, completes the exceptional experience.

Enhance your stay with a cruise on the Four Seasons Explorer, a private 11 cabin catamaran. Cruise between the two resorts or take a several-day excursion.

When you really want to get away from civilization, hop aboard a seaplane for a scenic ride from Malé to the incomparable Four Seasons Resort Maldives at Landaa Giraavaru. Nestled on 44 acres of unspoiled wilderness in the heart of the Baa Atoll, the Maldives' only UNESCO World Biosphere Reserve, this hideaway is a true paradise. The 97 thatched-roof beach and water villas and 5 two-bedroom suites are privacy defined. Snorkel with turtles and manta rays in one of the country's largest natural lagoons and join pioneering conservation projects in the Marine Discovery Centre. There are seven restaurants and lounges with fine dining and fantastic settings. The Spa and Ayurvedic Retreat is a 2.5-acre retreat.

It just doesn't get much more exotic than this for a beach vacation where you can sail away to your own private island resort.

FOUR SEASONS RESORT MALDIVES AT KUDA HURAA
North Malé Atoll, Republic of Maldives

FOUR SEASONS RESORT MALDIVES AT LANDAA GIRAAVARU
Baa Atoll, Republic of Maldives
fourseasons.com

INDIAN OCEAN
MALDIVES

One&Only Reethi Rah

Go ahead and spread your wings. At this all-villa resort on one of the largest islands in North Male' Atoll, there's plenty of room.

One&Only Reethi Rah is exceedingly spacious. These luxurious villas, 37 with private pools, are among the largest resort villas in the world. Tucked within the lush tropical greenery, the 98 beach villas offer a secluded ambience, while the 32 over-water villas perched above the crystalline waters of the lagoon share a peaceful mood. Awaken to the sound of waves gently lapping at your waterfront verandah with steps leading directly into the ocean or sway in the soft Maldivian breezes in your hammock.

The good life is everywhere at One&Only Reethi Rah, especially at the sensational spa. There are eight thatched-roof treatment villas and two over-water couples' suites for an extra touch of romance. Blending Ayurvedic and Western therapies and traditions, all treatments are custom designed for your individual needs.

With 12 stunning beaches, adults only pool, infinity-edge freeform pool, and kids-only pool, you could spend your entire visit with your toes in sand, sea, and water, but should you choose to leave your chaise, there is plenty to occupy your time. From tennis to tubing, snorkeling to scuba diving, to dolphin expeditions, fill your days with fun and adventure.

Enjoy modern Japanese cuisine and Indian-Japanese tapas at Tapasake, lounge on an Arabian carpet on the beach and savor exotic Middle Eastern food at Fanditha, or watch the show unfold at the dramatic Reethi Restaurant's open kitchen.

Fringed by white sand coves and turquoise bays, One&Only Reethi Rah delivers contemporary beach elegance in the Maldives.

ONE&ONLY REETHI RAH
North Malé Atoll, Maldives
oneandonlyresorts.com

INDIAN OCEAN
MALDIVES

Soneva Fushi Resort & Spa

Sheltered from the rest of the world, Soneva Fushi is tucked away on one of the seventy inhabited private islands in the Maldives.

A blend of the owners' names, Sonu and Eva, Soneva Fushi is an unusual getaway and represents barefoot chic at its best. Incredibly romantic, it is a natural choice for honeymoons and special anniversaries.

Dine on fresh seafood and other culinary delights at the restaurant, but do not miss the lantern-lit dinner on a private beach or picnic on a deserted island.

Soneva Fushi was eco-friendly before it was chic; only two trees were removed to make way for this resort! Of course, it's easy to see why being green is so important when you're surrounded by all of this blue…the water here is pure magic.

If you have ever wanted to live out a Robinson Crusoe fantasy, this is definitely the place. In fact, the resort even named several suites and a villa after the legendary character! In total, 65 rooms, suites, and villas, most with private pools, are nestled within the lush, dense greenery of the island. Indigenous woods and subtle fabrics create havens of serenity while showcasing a relaxed, regional decorative style. Bathrooms seductively extend into private gardens. Each villa is further blessed by having its own stretch of pristine, powdery sand.

SONEVA FUSHI RESORT & SPA
Kunfunadhoo Island,
Baa Atoll, Maldives
sixsenses.com

Surrounded by a private shallow lagoon and enclosed by a coral reef, Soneva Fushi lures scuba divers and snorkelers. The Six Senses Spa is an integral part of the Soneva Fushi experience. Its jungle ambience isn't just a look – this spa takes many of its influences from nature.

INDIAN OCEAN
MALDIVES

Soneva Gili

Do you know that sensation you feel when floating on a raft in the water? It's a suspension of worry…in that time and place nothing can bother you. Want to sustain that feeling? Visit Soneva Gili, which has practically bottled that feeling. Leave your stilettos behind… Soneva Gili proudly touts a laid-back "no news no shoes" attitude.

Set on the crystal-clear turquoise waters of the largest lagoon in the Maldives, Soneva Gili will make you giddy with its accommodations. There are just 44 over-water villas and reachable only by boat, 7 Crusoe residences, plus the gigantic three-bedroom private reserve. The look? Remember the treehouse of your childhood? Well, jazz it up and set it on the water and you have Soneva Gili.

The thatched roofs, simple furnishings, and decks that stretch out over the water equal pure bliss and rustic chic. If you're really looking to run away from the world, stay in the Crusoe Residences, set out in the water away from the main island. They even come with their own row boats for accessing the main island, though you can always hop aboard the pontoon shuttle, too.

Six Senses Spa is a journey for the senses. Walk the plank, so to speak, since this spa is accessed by a wood planked walkway. Prepare yourself for an adventure in pampering with overwater yoga to Ayurvedic treatments in the thatched-roof champas.

Indulge in delicious food at two restaurants, but do opt for a romantic candlelit beach picnic or a sunset dinner cruise aboard a traditional dhoni.

Watch the sun rise or set from this exclusive hideaway…Soneva Gili is perfect for pure relaxation.

SONEVA GILI
Lankanfushi Island
North Malé Atoll, Maldives
sixsenses.com

INDIAN OCEAN
MAURITIUS

Four Seasons Resort Mauritius

Exotic? Yes, indeed. Welcome to the luscious Four Seasons Resort Mauritius at Anahita. Located east of Madagascar in the Indian Ocean, this island resort is a little slice of heaven with green Bambou Mountains in the distance and endless blue waters that put you in the lap of luxury.

Be tucked away inside one of the 91 spacious villas and 41 residence villas with two to six bedrooms, where the lines between indoors and out are gloriously blurred. Open-air bathrooms feature soaking tubs and outdoor showers. Natural woods and volcanic stone influence the interiors of these thatched-roof villas, where modern artwork adds a bold splash. Each villa has its own private terrace and plunge pool…make your own splash! Lagoon pool villas and the presidential suite are secluded on a private 11 acre island, Ile aux Chats.

The tranquil setting of this ancient volcanic island would be enough to satisfy most, but remember this is a Four Seasons, so expect world-class amenities. The oceanfront Ernie Els designed 18-hole golf course is the first of its kind in Mauritius and is certainly one of the most scenic spots for a round of golf.

Another highlight – the spa nestled within a vibrant mangrove. Treatments pull together Indian, African, Chinese, and European traditions while using indigenous ingredients.

The four restaurants and O Bar offer pleasurable dining in stunning settings. Bambou is poolside, with buffets and live entertainment in the evening, or have a bite with a view of the 18th hole at Le Club. Dine at the open-air Acquapazza set on the private island, Ile aux Chats, or tuck into a steak at Beau Champ, overlooking the lagoon.

FOUR SEASONS RESORT MAURITIUS
Beau Champ
Mauritius
fourseasons.com

INDIAN OCEAN
MAURITIUS

The Oberoi, Mauritius

Surrounded by the turquoise waters of the Indian Ocean, Mauritius is a divine destination blessed with sandy beaches and blanketed in golden sunshine. Dreaming of a tropical idyll where you can truly get away from it all? Mauritius is your salvation.

Located on the northwest coast of Mauritius in the stunning Baie Aux Tortues, The Oberoi is exceptionally private and exclusive. Marvel at the glittering blue lagoon or look out over the majestic range of green mountains on the horizon from this 20 acre property. The Oberoi perfectly blends Mauritian culture and heritage while incorporating Chinese, French, Indian, and African cultures for a modern melting pot of design.

The 48 pavilions and 23 villas are luxurious and most have private swimming pools set within sub-tropical gardens. Natural fabrics in subtle colors are used in the interiors, and original Mauritian artwork abounds. Elevated dining pavilions, featured at all villas, have fantastic views of the Indian Ocean and lagoon and make private dining even more enchanting.

Water sports are abundant and two swimming pools delight swimmers and sunbathers alike. The Spa echoes the resort's tranquil, serene ambience with treatment rooms overlooking private gardens. A strong commitment to holistic therapy is evident at the spa, and many Mauritian fruits and vegetables are used in the treatments performed by Indonesian-trained therapists.

The kitchen expertly blends Creole, Asian, and European flavors at the thatched-roof restaurant. With a cool drink in hand, the bar, with a beachfront setting that includes an 18th century ruin, is an exotic place to unwind!

THE OBEROI, MAURITIUS
Turtle Bay
Pointe aux Piments, Mauritius
oberoihotels.com

INDIAN OCEAN
MAURITIUS

One&Only Le Saint Géran

Tucked away in the Indian Ocean island nation of Mauritius, One&Only Le Saint Géran is a peaceful hideaway set on the shimmering white sands of a private peninsula. It is a place where thousands of coconut palm trees sway in the gentle breezes and sunshine warms your body and soul. Stress has met its match…let your worries disappear at the quietly luxurious One&Only Le Saint Géran.

Cosmopolitan dining is one of the highlights of a visit to One&Only Le Saint Géran. Prime is a chic and sophisticated steakhouse with a modern look and flavor, while Rasoi by celebrated chef Vineet Bhatia ups the luxe factor. Bhatia's London restaurant was called the best Indian restaurant in the world, but you can taste his award-winning cuisine while sitting along the water's edge with views of the green sugarcane-clad mountains and the private lagoon.

The 162 suites and the gigantic two bedroom villa share a breezy and beachy British Colonial décor. Beds done up with Egyptian cotton sheets and piled high with pillows, rattan furnishings, and spice-colored accents create a soothing and sophisticated retreat. All accommodations have private terraces or balconies facing the ocean and cove with bountiful tropical gardens.

Build sand castles with the kids or just bliss out at the beach at this laid-back resort. The sheltered lagoon with its calm waters is ideal for water sports, or play a round of golf on the Gary Player 9-hole course with its own clubhouse and golf academy. Steal away to the spa, where a world of serenity set within the lush gardens awaits your arrival.

ONE&ONLY LE SAINT GÉRAN
Mauritius
oneandonlyresorts.com

INDIAN OCEAN
SEYCHELLES

Four Seasons Resort Seychelles

You daydream at your desk gazing at that screen saver with its perfect tropical island. You wonder…is it real? Yes, it's definitely real and if you put down that mouse and pack your bags, that exotic paradise is waiting for you in the Seychelles. This archipelago in the Indian Ocean sits off the East African coast just north of Madagascar. In total, there are 115 islands, but only about 20 are inhabited, making it the ultimate spot for chic castaways.

Leave the world behind when you stay at the Four Seasons Resort Seychelles. This resort snuggles into a hillside overlooking a splendid stretch of beach. The accommodations are a luxurious take on the Robinson Crusoe fantasy. The 62 treehouse-style villas and 5 suites are perched on stilts overlooking the sea and are the last word in sophisticated solace. Tucked into the jungle-covered hillside, these expansive accommodations afford spectacular views and boast great creature comforts like sleek design and infinity-edge plunge pools.

From the beach and water sports to the oceanfront pool, it's all about together time at the Four Seasons Resort Seychelles. Spend quality time with loved ones or celebrate a honeymoon or special anniversary in this incomparably romantic setting. Learn about ancient rituals and traditional therapies at the locally-influenced spa, where treatments awaken your senses.

Certainly your taste buds will be stimulated at the Four Seasons, where four restaurants and lounges tempt you with an array of flavors. From Creole specialties to dishes hailing from the Mediterranean and Southeast Asia, the restaurants present a taste of the world.

FOUR SEASONS RESORT SEYCHELLES
Petite Anse, Baie Lazare
Mahé, Seychelles
fourseasons.com

LEBANON
BEIRUT

Four Seasons Hotel Beirut

Where can you find ancient treasures and pulsating nightlife all rolled into one? Beirut! This capital city of Lebanon is often referred to as the "Paris of the Middle East." It brims with history and culture, but this city really comes alive at night, when a dizzying array of beautiful people hit the streets to dance in the hot nightclubs until dawn.

Whether you are traveling to Beirut on business or simply want to take in the intoxicating pleasures of this Middle Eastern city, the Four Seasons Hotel is the city's best. Set on the edge of the Mediterranean, it is cutting-edge contemporary and embodies the new Beirut. Soaring skywards, the sail-topped hotel is a landmark in the waterfront Corniche. While staying here, you are only a stone's throw from the Marina. Downtown businesses are within easy reach, as are the dynamic historic sites of Martyrs' Square and the Roman Baths. Do a little shopping in Al-Hamra, but stay up late and hit the cafés and nightlife of Gemmayzé with the locals.

The city's French link is celebrated in the 170 rooms and 60 suites where leading French designer Pierre-Yves Rochon has imparted his signature sense of style. Suede-upholstered headboards and contemporary furnishings are at home with classic elements. Naturally, the waterfront setting makes for great views; floor-to-ceiling windows and private terraces definitely take advantage of those vistas!

From elegant settings to relaxed venues, the five restaurants, lounges, and bars live up to Beirut's reputation for fine entertaining. The Roof is not just one of the city's hippest spots – it's the highest!

FOUR SEASONS HOTEL BEIRUT
1418 Professor Wafic Sinno Avenue
Minet El Hosn, Beirut, Lebanon 2020 4107
fourseasons.com

OMAN
ZIGHY BAY, DIBBA

Six Senses Zighy Bay

This is the place for those who have seen it all and done it all. It just doesn't get much more exotic than Oman. If you want a getaway where running into your country club pals is next to impossible, head for Six Senses Zighy Bay.

It may be only a 90-minute drive from Dubai, but Six Senses Zighy Bay is worlds away. It is best described in one word; striking. Designed to mimic Omani villages, the resort has a dramatic setting flanked by mountains on one side and the glorious beach at Zighy Bay on the other. The rugged mountains which rise above the coast along the northern Musandam Peninsula have a fjord-like look.

All 79 pool villas, the private reserve, and 2 retreats ooze simple sophistication with dark woods, crisp white linens, and exotic accents. Exceedingly private, the villas all have their own infinity pools shaded by palms.

To do or not to do is the question at Zighy Bay. Veg out on the beach, be luxuriously lazy, picnic in the mountains, or spring into action with an exciting adventure like paragliding. Retreat to the Six Senses Spa for a little R&R.

Feast on international and regional specialties in a romantic candlelit setting with views over the Gulf of Oman.

The resort's off the beaten path locale makes for unusual arrivals. Come by speedboat or take the winding drive in a 4 x 4 vehicle. First impressions are truly lasting at Six Senses Zighy Bay.

SIX SENSES ZIGHY BAY
Zighy Bay, Musandam Peninsula
Dibba, Sultanate of Oman
sixsenses.com

SYRIA
DAMASCUS

Four Seasons Hotel Damascus

Syria is a mystifying place. It is the crossroads of Asia, Africa, and Europe and was a leading stop on the Silk Road. Its religious history is powerful, with roots in Islam and Christianity running deep. Its abundance of ancient mosques, churches, souks, and ruins brings out the history buff in all of us. Syria is home to both Castle des Chevaliers, considered by many to be the greatest fortress in the world, and Palmyra, one of the best-preserved ruins of a Roman city.

If the mesmerizing history has you feeling weary, visit the Balloran Spa for a rejuvenating and relaxing treatment.

Six restaurants make Four Seasons Hotel Damascus a dining destination. Il Circo specializes in Italian dining, while the Pool Bar and Kithara delight with their laid-back ambience. From its detailed yellow interior to its traditional Aleppo cuisine of northern Syria, Al Halabi is Damascus dressed up at its best.

Did you know that Damascus is the oldest continuously inhabited city in the world and dates back to 9000 BC? Depart for Damascus and you will. When visiting, make the lovely Four Seasons Hotel your home. Towering over an ancient garden and with ruins in sight, the city center location makes it an easy walk to the many businesses and shops that have sprouted up amidst the ancient treasures.

The 231 rooms and 66 suites are styled with a fashionable and contemporary European elegance. Soft pastel walls, celadon bedspreads, walnut furnishings… the soft tones create a soothing haven in this vibrant city. Take in the views, which look out over the city and Mount Kassion in the distance.

FOUR SEASONS HOTEL DAMASCUS
Shukri Al Quatli Street, P.O. Box 6311
Damascus, Syria
fourseasons.com

UNITED ARAB EMIRATES
DUBAI

Al Maha Desert Resort & Spa

Just 45 minutes outside the glittering lights of Dubai, Al Maha Desert Resort & Spa promises a singular experience. This unique Luxury Collection property is set in almost 60,000 acres of pristine desert sands in a conservation reserve. Al Maha is the embodiment of a Bedouin's fantasy in a natural desert oasis.

The 35 Bedouin tented suites, 2 Royal tented suites, and 2 Emirates tented suites all share an incredibly enchanting ambience. Strikingly simple, the exteriors are dramatic and eye-catching, while inside, the accommodations sport a well-collected safari look with handcrafted furnishings and artifacts. Tented canopy ceilings and indoor plumbing complete the utterly one-of-a-kind atmosphere. The wooden deck with private swimming pool of each tented suite creates your own private oasis.

As if the shifting sands of the desert weren't enough to capture your heart, Al Maha offers plenty of distractions. From falconry, archery, and horseback riding to wildlife desert drives and camel trekking, there are a multitude of ways to explore this desert wonderland.

The Spa is a center of well-being and offers a local take on relaxation. Enjoy panoramic views of the desert and distant Hajar Mountains from the traditional gathering place in the library or while cooling off in the main swimming pool.

With a variety of options from the Middle East and Mediterranean, and with special theme menus featuring Indian, Sri Lankan, and Japanese dishes, Al Maha's cuisine allows you to dine like an Arabian prince or princess at Al Diwaan. For an out-of-this-world experience, dine on the dunes. Lit by torches, this dining experience is something you won't easily forget.

AL MAHA DESERT RESORT & SPA
A LUXURY COLLECTION RESORT & SPA
Dubai Desert Conservation Reserve
Dubai, Al Ain Road
Dubai, United Arab Emirates
luxurycollection.com/almaha

UNITED ARAB EMIRATES
DUBAI

Armani Hotel Dubai

Dubai is to the Middle East what Las Vegas is to the United States. Big, brash, greedily over-the-top. Gilding the lily? Dubai does that and so much more.

Take a break from the glitz and glitter and stay at the Armani Hotel Dubai. This minimalist masterpiece is exclusively located in Burj Khalifa, the world's tallest building. Legendary Italian fashion designer Giorgio Armani is well known for his impossibly chic, red carpet-ready couture, but the Dubai property marked the designer's first foray into hotels.

Armani Hotel Dubai is nothing short of the antithesis of typical Dubai.

Soft color tones in creams, mochas, and grays…clean-lined furnishings with hints of shiny chrome…it's so much more Milan than Middle East.

Step into a world of sophisticated serenity at the Armani Hotel Dubai. Armani oversaw every design detail and his streamlined sensibility is everywhere, starting with the hallways where low lighting, rich dark colors, and a lack of doorknobs keeps everything seductively sleek. With details like Italian handcrafted leather walls, Japanese tatami floors, and Brazilian green marble, the 160 rooms usher in a sense of calm.

From luxurious treatments to bespoke Armani scented oils, the experience at the spa is über-Zen.

Dining selections are marvelous. Each venue echoes the hotel's contemporary cosmopolitan flavor…choose from Tuscan country fare, gourmet Indian, modern Japanese and more at seven other spots in the Armani Hotel Dubai. The two hipper-than-thou nightclubs are the preferred spots of international jet setters.

ARMANI HOTEL DUBAI
Burj Khalifa
1 Emaar Boulevard
Dubai, Dubayy, UAE
armanihotels.com

UNITED ARAB EMIRATES
DUBAI

Burj al Arab

Despite its young age, this hotel is a Dubai landmark. Soaring more than 1,000 feet above the Arabian Gulf on Jumeirah Beach, the sail-shaped building is known the world over for its distinctive and dramatic architecture. It dominates the Dubai skyline and is one of the most photographed structures in the world. At night, Burj al Arab is illuminated by choreographed lighting representing water and fire. And that's just the outside.

Inside, Burj al Arab spares no expense in creating a dazzling first and lasting impression, starting with one of the world's tallest atriums, extending to the helipad on the 28th floor, and continuing to a restaurant which seems to be suspended in the air. All this, and a fleet of Rolls Royces to ferry you about town, plus helicopters to spirit you away in style.

Burj al Arab's accommodations will certainly catch your eye. Done up with vibrant colors and attention-grabbing and glittering accents, the 202 suites are incredibly spacious and showcase lovely views of the Gulf.

Spoil yourself at the gigantic Assawan Spa with over-the-top princely pampering. Two indoor pools…two solariums…squash court…this place has it all.

The array of restaurants will floor you…feast on Arabic cuisine in the Royal Dining Hall or dine Jules Verne style at Al Mahara, to sample succulent seafood as you watch tropical fish swim by your table. Al Muntaha, which translates to "the top," certainly lives up to its name…this restaurant seemingly flies over the water with its floor-to-ceiling windows. In total, six restaurants are on hand to keep you sampling.

BURJ AL ARAB
Jumeirah Beach Road
Dubai, UAE
jumeirah.com

UNITED ARAB EMIRATES
DUBAI

Raffles Dubai

Only in Dubai would you have a hotel that resembles a sailing ship and another that looks straight out of Giza. Raffles Dubai, inspired by the great pyramids of Egypt, is an architectural sensation.

Raffles puts you in the center of Dubai. Just around the corner, indulge in some serious retail therapy. The hotel adjoins Wafi, one of the city's most exclusive shopping and leisure destinations, with hundreds of boutiques selling international haute couture, jewelry, and gifts. Nearby souks, including the impressive Khan Murjan, offer authentic crafts by artisans from the region.

The hotel has some of the most spacious rooms in the city, and each has a generously-sized private balcony. The contemporary 192 rooms and 56 suites feature welcoming woods and bold tones, while handcrafted accents and elegant fabrics elevate the level of luxury. The sophisticated design offers a sensual blend of Middle Eastern and Asian ambience.

Raffles Dubai is home to an eclectic selection of restaurants, suitable for all moods and preferences. There is something for everyone from foodies to fashionistas, including a lovely afternoon tea. Chinese… Continental… it's all here, but the shining star is certainly Red Lounge Terrace. From its hip small bites menu to its breathtaking views to its beautiful people crowd, it is not to be missed.

The full service Spa is an oasis of relaxation, but the jewel-in-the-crown is definitely the private garden sanctuary in the Raffles Botanical Garden. Enjoy a treatment or just take a stroll through this lush 10,000-square-foot tropical garden, inspired by ancient Egyptian gods and the life elements of earth, air, fire, and water at Raffles Dubai.

RAFFLES DUBAI
Sheikh Rashid Road, Wafi
Dubai, UAE
raffles.com

UNITED ARAB EMIRATES
DUBAI

The Ritz-Carlton Dubai, International Financial Centre

The city of Dubai is waiting for you at The Ritz-Carlton, Dubai International Financial Centre.

This elegant retreat stands 14 stories high in the heart of the business district. It has a direct walkway to The Gate, making it a perfect base for those conducting business in this dynamic city. The hotel is situated just five minutes from the Dubai Convention Centre, Dubai Mall, and Burj Khalifa, the world's tallest building. The Ritz-Carlton is also adjacent to the Dubai International Financial Centre's main building and offers easy access to and from Sheikh Zayed Road. Of course, with plenty of Ritz-Carlton niceties, you don't need to be here on business to take pleasure in the luxurious amenities.

The 261 rooms and 80 suites effortlessly bridge contemporary European élan with Asian panache. Silk bed coverings, accent pieces, and artwork hint of Asia, while elegant furnishings are rooted in Europe. It is soothing and sophisticated in a city known for its often wild style.

Meet for afternoon tea or drinks at the Lobby Lounge & Terrace, with its dramatic views of the courtyard waterfall or indulge in caviar or bites at No. 5 Lounge & Bar. Whether you are doing deals or simply want to dine, the restaurants present a number of choices. From the French brasserie-style Can Can to the traditional steakhouse ambience at Center Cut to the gourmet Thai food at Blue Rain, dining is delightful at The Ritz-Carlton, Dubai.

THE RITZ-CARLTON DUBAI INTERNATIONAL FINANCIAL CENTRE
Gate Village, DIFC
Dubai, UAE
ritzcarlton.com

The Spa is a hedonist's heaven with a calming indoor pool and an extensive holistic treatment menu. Choose your background music from a music menu, or bring your own tunes to listen while you luxuriate.

AUSTRALIA

BHUTAN

BORA BORA

CAMBODIA

CHINA

FIJI

INDONESIA

JAPAN

Asia & Pacific

LAOS

MALAYSIA

MYANMAR (BURMA)

NEW ZEALAND

SINGAPORE

THAILAND

VIETNAM

AUSTRALIA
GREAT BARRIER REEF

Qualia

You don't need to be an underwater enthusiast to appreciate the incredible beauty of the Great Barrier Reef. With its sparkling turquoise waters home to thriving coral and a mesmerizing array of marine life, the Great Barrier Reef is one of the world's most fascinating and beautiful destinations. You've come all this way to see it…so why stay anywhere but right in the middle? At Qualia, the Great Barrier Reef envelops you in all of its mighty glory.

Qualia is situated on the secluded northernmost tip of Hamilton Island, one of the 74 islands that comprise the Whitsunday Islands. This luxury resort is tucked away from it all and is a privileged place where 60 private pavilions look out over the Coral Sea and the Whitsundays.

Absolute relaxation is the mantra at this luxuriously understated showpiece. The light-filled pavilions face the water and are surrounded by lush, tropical jungle. Natural materials like timber, stone, and glass create a soothing sophistication, but wherever you are, it's always about the view. My, what a view it is! Endless blue horizon edged with islands…it is the embodiment of a daydream.

Qualia's guest-only facilities include two private swimming pools and a spa that takes relaxation to the top. Have you ever enjoyed a hot stone massage with 300 million-year-old stones before? You will here!

Dine on modern Australian cuisine for lunch at Pebble Beach or for dinner in the romantic setting of Long Pavilion. The chef behind Qualia's two restaurants personally visited every top resort in the South Pacific before settling on the menus… his competitive edge results in a pleasure for your palate.

QUALIA
Great Barrier Reef
Australia
qualia.com.au

AUSTRALIA
SYDNEY

Park Hyatt Sydney

Itching for something new in Sydney? It's all yours at the "new" Park Hyatt, which just opened after total renovations.

The iconic Park Hyatt Sydney has been a waterfront fixture in the Rocks district for 21 years. It has always been synonymous with contemporary styling, but after its multi-million dollar total redesign, it is the pinnacle of modern sophistication. Rich chocolate, cream, and beige hues set a soothing tone in the public and private spaces.

The harbor view 152 rooms and 3 spectacular rooftop suites really shine with custom-designed furnishings and lighting, and with artwork by renowned Australian artists commissioned specifically for the new design. These accommodations really bring the outdoors in with floor-to-ceiling glass doors that open onto spacious private balconies with unparalleled harbor views.

Work out in the state-of-the-art fitness center or swim laps in the pool but be sure to save time for several treatments at the beautifully modern Spa.

Enjoy the casually elegant ambience of the Park Hyatt in The Living Room, where all day long you can refresh and refuel in a stylish setting. You may initially come for the views, but stay for the food at the sensational restaurant. Designed with floor-to-ceiling windows to capture postcard-perfect views of Sydney Harbour, the restaurant impresses diners with more than just a pretty scene. The modern Australian cuisine is a revelation!

"The Park Hyatt Sydney sitting on the water's edge is a relatively low contemporary building surrounded by all the skyscrapers, but there is no question that this luxury hotel has the best view of the spectacular Sydney Opera House and the harbor. It is my personal favorite."

PARK HYATT SYDNEY
7 Hickson Road, The Rocks
Sydney 2000, Australia
parkhyatt.com

BHUTAN

Amankora

Bhutan has a stunning landscape of soaring peaks and low-lying plains. This remote country tucked between Tibet and India is the sole surviving Himalayan Buddhist kingdom.

Amankora promises an unforgettable journey through the mystical valleys of Bhutan. Historically isolated, the valleys offer a bit of a "country within a country" experience, and Amankora celebrates these differences in a series of five lodges complete with spas and fine dining.

Most journeys start at Paro. The 24 suite Paro is set within a pine forest and on clear days offers uninterrupted views onto Mount Jumolhari, the home of the Gods of the Kingdom in the clouds. Visit the nearby 17th century ruins of Drukyel Dzong.

You can also choose to begin at the 16 suite Thimpu lodge in a blue-pine forest of the Motithang area, close to the capital's sightseeing and shopping.

Next up, visit Punakha in the lush green of the Dochu La Pass and near the impressive monastery fortress of Punakha Dzong. There are 8 suites at this unique lodge, which is accessed by crossing a suspension bridge over the Mo Chhu, and is centered by a traditional Bhutanese farmhouse.

Discover the remote wilderness of the Phobjikha Valley with stunning views across a gorge to the 16th century monastery of Gangtey Goemba at the 8 suite Gangtey lodge. There are few visitors in this secluded valley, making it all the more remarkable.

In sharp contrast, the 16 suite Bumthang is located directly in the centre of Bumthang Valley. The courtyard rests adjacent to the Wandichholing Palace and 29 temples and monasteries are nearby.

Take five at Amankora… to meditate or sightsee…it's spiritual.

AMANKORA
Bhutan
amanresorts.com

BORA BORA

Four Seasons Resort Bora Bora

Nothing says romance quite like Bora Bora. The most famous of French Polynesia's Leeward Islands, this tropical paradise is impossibly beautiful. Gaze out at its turquoise waters and white sand beaches and you'll soon see why author James Michener declared it the most beautiful island in the world.

"Escape to your own Utopia at the Four Seasons Resort Bora Bora." Set on its own private motu (small islet), the resort is nestled around the outer beaches of Bora Bora lagoon. The 100 overwater bungalows are perched on stilts above the turquoise lagoon. While 7 beachfront villas nestled along a stretch of semi-private beach offer private plunge pools. From the roofs thatched with pandanus leaves to teak wood furnishings and bold works of art, The Four Seasons celebrates the traditions of Polynesia inside and out.

You have come for the beach and that glorious turquoise water, so dig your toes in the sand or sun by the shimmering pool. Sail away on the catamaran, hunt for black pearls nearby, or spend some downtime in the architecturally stunning spa where overwater yoga is a highlight.

Bora Bora's beauty isn't just for couples – the Four Seasons invites families to play together in paradise. Little ones have their own club and young adults even have their own island - Chill Island.

Four restaurants and bars showcase the fresh and delicious cuisine of the South Pacific. Snack in the sun or sup under the stars at this magical getaway.

"Surrounded by the breathtakingly beautiful turquoise waters, you will immediately unwind. So much so that you will never want to leave the Four Seasons!"

FOUR SEASONS RESORT BORA BORA
Motu Tehotu, BP 547
98730 Bora Bora, French Polynesia
fourseasons.com

BORA BORA

The St. Regis Bora Bora Resort

Fall in love with The St. Regis Bora Bora Resort. This luxurious hideaway delivers signature St. Regis service. With several private swimming pools suspended over the lagoon and a private helicopter pad, The St. Regis Bora Bora promises an exceptional holiday.

This exotic getaway feels intimate, with just 90 bungalows and one royal residence, but it is the incredible amount of space that makes it really stand out. The overwater villas are some of the largest in the region with over 1,550 square feet. The interiors set a joyful, tropical tone. Daydream in your own private garden or stretch out on the pontoon decks of the overwater villas.

Bring the little ones along. The Kids Creativity Club isn't just babysitting – this program keeps them engaged with nature activities, Polynesian crafts, and an array of indoor and outdoor adventures. Kids even have their own secluded beach!

While the kids are building castles, go straight to the spa situated on its own private island, where a world of pampering and well-being is pure magic. Enjoy a massage in an open-air cabana or nod off during a blissful Tahitian influenced treatment. From pure mother of pearl to monoi oils, the bounty of nature is shared at the spa.

With all-day Mediterranean dishes at Te Pahu, sushi at Sushi Take, a swim-up bar at Aparima, and Lagoon by Jean-Georges Vongerichten, expect nothing but superior dining.

"The St. Regis Bora Bora Resort brings exotic beach and French Polynesian sophistication together. I am particularly fond of this property, as the owner invited me along on an extensive hard hat tour and incorporated so many of my suggestions."

THE ST. REGIS BORA BORA RESORT
Motu Ome'e BP 506
98730 Bora Bora, French Polynesia
stegis.com/borabora

CAMBODIA
PHNOM PENH

Raffles Hotel Le Royal

Phnom Penh is Cambodia's capital and this lovely city on the banks of the Mekong River is filled with historical and cultural treasures. The Royal Palace is a must see attraction. Inside the yellow walls of the palace compound are several structures, including the impressive Silver Pagoda. For an in-depth look at the ancient Khmer civilization, visit the fascinating National Museum with its 5,000 artifacts, but make sure to take a scenic cruise on the Mekong River.

Raffles Hotel Le Royal is the perfect choice in Phnom Penh. This classic hotel in the center of the city is the number one hotel and represents the best of the past and present. The grand Hotel Le Royal still reflects the European colonial era in Asia.

First opened in 1929, it has played host to writers, artists, and international travelers for decades. The rich past is felt everywhere, including in the traditionally decorated 170 rooms and 37 suites. Each, of course, is fully updated with modern amenities, and the rooms feature Cambodian style.

The Raffles Amrita Spa is a lovely retreat for a rejuvenating massage or beauty treatment, while the outdoor pool is a particularly refreshing spot during the warm Cambodian days.

Everyone comes to dine and drink at Raffles Hotel Le Royal. This hotel has been a meeting place ever since its opening. From afternoon tea and sumptuous buffets to elegant Khmer and Continental cuisine, the five restaurants and bars present tantalizing array of choices. Don't miss the famous Elephant Bar, where you can enjoy the Airavata, a cocktail of secret ingredients, or indulge in their special Million Dollar Cocktail.

RAFFLES HOTEL LE ROYAL
92 Rukhak Vithei Daun Penh
Sangkat Wat Phnom
Phnom Penh, Cambodia
raffles.com

CAMBODIA
SIEM REAP

Raffles Grand Hotel d'Angkor

You visit Athens for the Acropolis and similarly, you travel to Cambodia to see Angkor Wat. This temple complex, built for King Suryavarman II in the early 12th century, is the world's largest religious building. More than just a landmark or monument, Angkor Wat will captivate you with its mystique.

Raffles Grand Hotel d'Angkor is just five miles from Angkor Wat. This hotel in the center of Siem Reap has been a favorite choice of savvy travelers since the early 1930s. Set within 15 acres of beautifully landscaped French gardens, Raffles Grand Hotel d'Angkor shares the spirit of old-world Cambodia with the modern elegance of European sophistication. Share in the storied history by staying at this renowned hotel, where the original elevator now serves as a focal point in the lobby.

Raffles Grand Hotel d'Angkor is comprised of the historic Main Building as well as new wings designed to replicate the same architectural style. Inside, the 119 rooms and 20 suites are decorated with traditional and informal furnishings with French-Indochina accents. " I personally recommend splurging on one of the six cabana suites situated off the enormous swimming pool… with private terraces, they feel like mini villas."

Swim in the pool, which mimics the reflecting pools at Angkor Wat, or wander through the bountiful gardens. Take time to indulge at the Raffles Amrita Spa where East meets West.

Dining at Raffles Grand Hotel d'Angkor includes a variety of culinary delights. From casual and poolside to traditional and elegant, the six restaurants and bars present an enticing array.

"After busy days of visiting temples, returning home to Raffles Grand Hotel d'Angkor is bliss."

RAFFLES GRAND HOTEL D'ANGKOR
1 Vithei Charles de Gaulle, Khum
Svay Dang Kum
Siem Reap, Kingdom of Cambodia
raffles.com

CAMBODIA
SIEM REAP

La Résidence d'Angkor

Walk the paths of the ancient temple of Angkor Wat and wonder at the history of this man made Wonder of the World and UNESCO Heritage Site. Angkor Wat and the extensive complex of temples in the Siem Reap area are the remains of an ancient 8th to 12th century Khmer civilization.

"Learn about the culture and religion of this foreign land. Sightseeing isn't just about seeing…it's about experiencing something new, even if exhausting! So, when the wondrous Angkor Wat has sapped your energy, revive at the intimate La Résidence d'Angkor."

This Orient-Express hotel enjoys a lovely and secluded setting on the banks of the tree-lined river. Revel in the quiet beauty of this Khmer-style hotel. Its peaceful ambience is best experienced at the delightful pool, where 45,000 hand glazed tiles, each reflecting a different shade of green, create a stunning effect.

The 62 spacious accommodations celebrate the traditional Khmer style with bamboo, hardwoods, and jewel toned cottons and silks. Floor-to-ceiling windows add to the airy ambience.

Kong Kea Spa is an award-winning facility that pampers guests with ancient Roman therapies. Enjoy a treatment while gazing out over your own private bamboo garden. It is tranquility defined.

If you simply can't tear yourself away from that gorgeous pool, the Pool Bar is your salvation with snacks and beverages to keep hunger at bay. The BBQ Restaurant is a nice casual outdoor spot for freshly grilled meats, while the Martini Lounge heats things up with its swanky style. "Watch traditional Khmer dancers as you feast on classic Cambodian cuisine at The Dining Room. It goes beyond dinner theater."

LA RÉSIDENCE D'ANGKOR
River Road
Siem Reap, Kingdom of Cambodia
residencedangkor.com or
orient-express.com

CHINA
BEIJING

The Peninsula Beijing

Beijing is an enthralling city with a fascinating mix of old and new.

"The streets were crowded with bicycles and people wearing dull official jackets on my first visit in the summer of 1983. While cars and color are everywhere today, you still feel the traditions of this Chinese capital city."

The Peninsula Beijing is known worldwide for its standards of excellence. From state-of-the-art electronics that allow guests to control room temperature, lighting, and entertainment with literally a touch of a finger to sophisticated, contemporary furnishings, the 468 rooms and 57 suites are sure to please.

The amenities are first class… even Rolls Royce Phantoms are available. The Peninsula Spa by ESPA is a fitness and wellness enthusiast's dream come true with a fully equipped workout facility, indoor pool, and comprehensive treatment menu.

The Peninsula's central location means Beijing's major sightseeing and shopping is right around the corner, but you don't even need to leave the hotel to find something to take home. The Peninsula Arcade has over 50 tantalizing boutiques.

The Peninsula's dining is truly transporting. Open the heavy wooden doors of Huang Ting to experience the atmosphere of a traditional nobleman's home. Aged pine flooring and carved timber screens set the mood for the Cantonese cooking spotlighted here. Watch the buzz of Beijing all around you in the Lobby Lounge, which is perfect any time of the day, but Jing is the don't miss spot with award-winning fusion dining and a glamorously modern ambience.

"The colorful Chinese dragon gate marks the entrance to this iconic hotel that like the city, retains its heritage while marching forward to the future."

THE PENINSULA BEIJING
8 Goldfish Lane, Wangfujing
Beijing 100006, China
peninsula.com

CHINA
BEIJING

Raffles Beijing

Be a part of Beijing's history at Raffles Beijing, formerly known as Grand Hotel de Pékin.

Raffles Hotel has gracefully reinvigorated this landmark, which has been a part of Beijing since the early 1900s. Situated a few blocks from Tiananmen Square and overlooking the Forbidden City, this property has hosted countless political and cultural events.

Comfortably sophisticated, the 147 rooms and 24 suites define tradition and offer an artful blend of Asian accents and European style, plus modern conveniences and technological advances.

The hotel's ideal location places it right in the middle of everything. You can enjoy a leisurely breakfast and still make your business meeting, or if you're on vacation, the hotel is just steps from the famous sights.

Take a dip in the indoor pool, then ring the valet for a basket filled with reading materials and music delivered to you poolside. Work out, then fit in a treatment at the spa.

East 33, which takes its name from the hotel's address, showcases Eastern and Western cuisines, but you can revisit the grandeur of the 1920s at the Writers Bar and Jaan Restaurant, which retains its original dance floor and sparkling crystal chandeliers.

"It was still the Grand, filled with American ex-pats running overseas operations from the hotel, on my 1983 visit. The kiosk was the only place to legally purchase English-speaking publications. Gratuities were banned, so at our guide's request, we provided an armful of publications that he wanted to share with his young Chinese friends. On a recent visit, I was greatly impressed by the many beautiful changes at the "new" Raffles Beijing."

RAFFLES BEIJING
33 East Chang An Avenue
Dongcheng District
Beijing 100004, China
raffles.com

CHINA
BEIJING

The Ritz-Carlton Beijing, Financial Street

Business taking you to Beijing? Stay in the center of the buzzing Financial District at The Ritz-Carlton Beijing, Financial Street. Its address is smack in the middle of China's new Wall Street. Located at the intersection of Taipingqiao and Jinchengfangdong and connected to the Second Ring Road, this hotel offers unrivaled access to everything within Beijing.

This ultra-modern tower crafted of chrome and glass fits perfectly at home in this dynamic and thriving business center. "Outside, the city's businesses are steps away, but inside, this hotel is a warm and inviting home." The 203 guest rooms and 50 suites are well-appointed and utterly luxurious. Soft color tones punched up with bold accents and elegant, contemporary Chinese furnishings ensure a soothing ambience.

If you need to exercise pre-meeting or unwind post-meeting, The Ritz-Carlton Spa, Fitness & Salon is on hand for your needs.

Dining is a true delight. Enlightened vegetarian dishes and seafood are the focus at Greenfish, where brilliant colored glass and mosaic tiles set an upbeat mood. Take tea or enjoy a cocktail at the Tea Apothecary. "Embark on a culinary journey featuring seven regional Chinese cuisines, including modern interpretations of Sichuan, Cantonese, and Beijing dishes at Qi. The color red, viewed by the Chinese as good luck, sets the stage for this stunning space." Pasta was supposedly brought to Italy from China by Marco Polo, so it's no surprise that the hotel includes a trend-setting and delicious Italian restaurant, Cépe, in its fantastic repertoire.

"Stay at the thoroughly modern and welcoming Ritz-Carlton Beijing, Financial Street and make your trip a pleasure."

THE RITZ-CARLTON BEIJING, FINANCIAL STREET
1 Jin Cheng Fang Street East, Financial Street
Beijing 100140, China
ritzcarlton.com

CHINA
BEIJING

The St. Regis Beijing

The St. Regis is in the exclusive embassy district. It neighbors the historic Beijing International Club, the famed meeting place of dignitaries, foreign correspondents, and government officials.

The first hotel to be branded as a St. Regis in the Asia Pacific region, The St. Regis Beijing brings unparalleled luxury to this city. The 156 rooms and 102 suites feature rich polished woods, dramatic artwork, glorious views, and all the contemporary comforts, including St. Regis signature 24 hour butler service. "With many suite categories available, among them the Diplomat, Statesman, and Ambassador, my tried-and-true favorite is the Statesman."

The St. Regis offers a host of amenities. The fitness center has it all – Pilates, yoga, even ballet classes are among the offerings. Jump feet first into the glass-enclosed Roman-style swimming pool, then warm up in the two natural hot spring water Jacuzzis. There is even a children's pool. Challenge friends or family to a game in the 8-lane bowling alley or spend downtime together at the spa, where natural hot springs are the basis for many of the therapeutic treatments.

East meets West in the restaurants. The Garden Court is a lovely brasserie for all day dining and a delicious buffet, while Danieli shines with Italian food and is considered Beijing's best Italian restaurant. Astor Grill is popular for steaks, the Wine and Garden Lounges are comfortably chic, but Celestial Lounge is the spot for Chinese cuisine in a traditional setting.

"This less congested area of Beijing creates a calming atmosphere. Only minutes from everything, I love the location, the spacious accommodations, and the tranquil, contemporary feeling of The St. Regis Beijing."

THE ST. REGIS BEIJING
21 Jianguomenwai Dajie
Beijing 100020, China
stregis.com/beijing

CHINA
BEIJING · GUILIN · XIAN

Shangri-La Hotel, China World Summit Wing, Beijing
Shangri-La Hotel, Guilin • Shangri-La Hotel, Xian

Shangri-La brings together the many faces of China in its luxury hotels.

"Climb new heights at the Shangri-La Hotel, China World Summit Wing." This luxurious hotel occupies the top floors of the city's newest landmark, the China World Tower, which soars 81 floors above the China World Trade Center complex. "All 249 guest rooms and 29 suites are the ultimate in modern design and boast floor to ceiling windows for soaring views. Add four restaurants, two bars, CHI, The Spa, a stunning indoor pool, and you have Beijing's sleekest most phenomenal new hotel."

All visitors to China should visit Guilin. The well-recognized sky-reaching mountains and crystal-clear rivers

have been captured by Chinese artists for centuries. Shangri-La, Guilin is number one in the city. Overlooking the picturesque Li River, the 432 rooms and 17 suites feature luxuriously tailored interiors with beautiful views of the lush landscaped gardens or the river. Relax at the pool and spa or delight while dining in one of the many delicious restaurants and bars.

The Shangri-La, Xian is a history buff's haven. Xian, an ancient capital of China and one-time stop on the legendary Silk Road, is most notable for the Terracotta Army. Like the pyramids are to Egypt, the 3rd century BC Terracotta Warriors are to China. Only discovered in 1974, you come to see this important archeological site and it is only a short distance from the hotel. After a busy day, return to this hospitable hotel's 382 rooms and 8 suites with views of the landscaped gardens and the city, a luxurious spa, and four trendsetting restaurants.

CHINA WORLD SUMMIT WING, BEIJING
No 1 Jianguomenwai Avenue
Beijing 100004, China

SHANGRI-LA, GUILIN
111 Huan Cheng Bei Er Lu
Guilin 541004, China

SHANGRI-LA, XIAN
38B Keji Road
Xian 710075, China
shangri-la.com

CHINA
HONG KONG

Four Seasons Hotel Hong Kong

Surrounded by the South China Sea, Hong Kong is the gateway to China and the Far East. First settled by the Chinese in the 7th century, Hong Kong was under British rule from 1842 to 1997. Hong Kong is a thriving center for international business.

Set in Hong Kong's Central on the waterfront overlooking Victoria Harbour, the 55-story Four Seasons Hotel Hong Kong is exceptional. In the shadow of the prestigious 88-story International Finance Centre, it offers unrivaled access to Hong Kong businesses in the financial district.

"I love the chic, contemporary décor of the 345 rooms and 54 suites, all with alluring views of the city. The silk-covered walls in soothing neutral shades, detailed wood trimmings, and Chinese influenced touches like authentic ink paintings are so perfect. I often say this dash of modern flair represents the 'new' Four Seasons room style."

The enormous Spa with 17 treatment rooms is a masterpiece of wellness. These superior facilities are unmatched, while the treatments are a delightful mix of relaxing and rejuvenating therapies. "Then add the outside swimming pool and you are all set!"

The Four Seasons draws diners from all over. Meet for drinks at The Lounge or the chic lobby level Blue Bar. Traditional Japanese can be sampled at Inagiku at ifc, an outpost of the renowned Tokyo restaurant. Independently operated, it is as much entertainment as it is sustenance. The clear winners are Caprice and Lung King Heen, both having been awarded three Michelin stars each. Enjoy authentic French cuisine in an open-kitchen setting at Caprice, while the stylish Lung King Heen highlights contemporary Cantonese.

FOUR SEASONS HOTEL HONG KONG
8 Finance Street, Central
Hong Kong, China
fourseasons.com

CHINA
HONG KONG

Mandarin Oriental, Hong Kong

Deeply rooted in Asian culture, the Mandarin Oriental, Hong Kong is one of the world's finest hotels.

The Mandarin Oriental is situated in the heart of Hong Kong's financial district and overlooks Victoria Harbour. All of Hong Kong is easily explored from here.

Mandarin Oriental preserves its Chinese heritage. It has an impressive collection of Chinese art with many rare and unique pieces gracing the public and private rooms. "The Mandarin Oriental, Hong Kong is gearing up to celebrate 50 years of luxury hospitality in 2013." Dramatically and completely redesigned, the Mandarin Oriental's 430 rooms and 71 suites are a celebration

of China, where light woods, lustrous silks, and Chinese art are sophisticated and serene.

Reminiscent of 1930s Shanghai, the spa adds an element of mystery to your journey where traditional Chinese and Ayurvedic principles are taken to heart. Get some exercise at the fitness center or swim laps in the elegant indoor pool.

The Mandarin Oriental's ten restaurants and bars cross all cultures for inspiration and are as populated by locals as they are by guests. The Clipper Lounge has even been called "Hong Kong's living room." Mandarin Oriental has you covered with Michelin starred cuisine running the gamut from Chinese and French cuisine to British classics.

"I personally think the stunning Man Wah restaurant overlooking the Harbour is the finest Chinese restaurant in the world. For me, no trip to Hong Kong is complete without dining on their succulent Peking duck. I have been known to take a later flight just to have it again! I have been returning to the Mandarin Oriental, Hong Kong since my first trip in 1983."

MANDARIN ORIENTAL, HONG KONG
5 Connaught Road, Central
Hong Kong, China
mandarinoriental.com

CHINA
HONG KONG

The Peninsula Hong Kong

Not just a hotel, The Peninsula is a Hong Kong landmark. Opened in 1928, The Peninsula is genteel and its superb service is world-renowned.

The Peninsula shares a privileged lifestyle with its lucky guests. Be whisked away by a chauffeured Rolls Royce, or arrive by helicopter if you are in a hurry.

The hotel is located in the heart of Kowloon and overlooking the Harbour to Hong Kong Central. The 346 rooms and 54 suites sparkle. Floor-to-ceiling glass walls in the tower allow for uninterrupted views of the harbour…enjoy the views through the specially commissioned telescopes

"The Peninsula Spa is the best city retreat anywhere. From the moment you enter, all of your senses are immediately awakened and relaxation begins. From the trickling water features, to the aromatic fragrance, to the stunning Asian décor, to the soothing lighting, to the stupendous views, you shouldn't miss this treat."

The Peninsula's delights extend to dining. Gaddi's is a Hong Kong institution, notable for its elegant setting and gourmet French cuisine. Specializing in Pacific Rim cuisine, Felix occupies the top two floors of the tower and has a trendy décor styled by international tastemaker Philippe Starck. Perhaps one of the most unique features of this hotel is The Peninsula Academy. Immerse yourself in the local culture and learn about its many fascinating traditions. From tai chi and feng shi to Cantonese cooking and medicine, there's nothing like it.

"The Peninsula is the grand dame of this vibrant city, but she does not rest on her laurels. The hotel has always been setting luxury standards that welcome guests back home."

THE PENINSULA HONG KONG
Salisbury Road, Kowloon
Hong Kong, China
peninsula.com

CHINA
HONG KONG

The Ritz-Carlton, Hong Kong

Soar to new heights to experience The Ritz-Carlton, Hong Kong.

Not many hotels can say they have changed the landscape, but the Ritz-Carlton has literally redrawn the Hong Kong skyline. It is the world's tallest hotel! Dramatically towering and dominating the cityscape, The Ritz-Carlton goes beyond spectacular views to offer unrivaled sights.

While the bird's eye view from 102 to 118 floors of Victoria Harbour and the New Territories is simply marvelous, The Ritz-Carlton's modern panache is eye-catching enough to draw your attention away from the views – at least for a little while! The 232 rooms and 80 suites are luxurious aeries in the sky.

Sleek and contemporary styling defines the look, while Asian silks and accents add a sense of place. And the service? It's far reaching.

Leave your stress behind at the ESPA Spa, located on the 116th floor. Unwind in a sophisticated setting where you can contemplate the world through floor to ceiling windows.

The Ritz-Carlton has a soft spot for guests with a sweet tooth. The Chocolate Library is no mystery – enjoy everything from chocolate-based savory dishes to chocolate afternoon tea. Pastry Gems looks like haute couture, but they are edible confectionaries. "From the Italian dishes at Tosca to the all-day dining at The Lounge to the Chinese cooking at Tin Lung Heen (Dragon in the Sky), The Ritz-Carlton's restaurants are bold, artistically designed settings." Of course, there is nothing better than toasting with champagne and dining at Ozone, the world's highest bar on the 118th floor.

"Wow! The new Ritz-Carlton, Hong Kong is extraordinary. Be impressed by it all… precious woods, metals, stones, crystals…even alabaster-topped bathroom sinks…stupendous views…sterling service… dynamite dining…it is a modern marvel."

THE RITZ-CARLTON, HONG KONG
International Commerce Centre,
1 Austin Road West
Kowloon, Hong Kong, China
ritzcarlton.com

CHINA
SHANGHAI

Four Seasons Hotel Shanghai

The port has played a major role in Shanghai's history. Opened to foreign trade in 1842, British, French, and Japanese have all left their mark on Shanghai, resulting in an unusual fusion of international cultures.

"Having not been in Shanghai for 28 years, this futuristic 21st century city was not recognizable to me. The modernization and huge international development makes it a modern boomtown."

In the heart of this dynamic city, a short distance from prestigious shopping, entertainment and business in the Nanjing and Huaihai road areas, the Four Seasons Hotel Shanghai was the first Four Seasons in mainland China and set new standards of luxury in China.

The 37-story Four Seasons Hotel Shanghai invites you to take your place in one of the elegantly designed 342 rooms and 78 suites that includes 51 Executive Suites. Traditional Chinese colors and printed silks rest comfortably alongside classic-style furnishings.

The hotel's spa Qin, which is pronounced "chin" and means to "affect deeply," is a stylish urban oasis specializing in relaxation and beauty with roots in Chinese medicine. There are over 37 different therapies which include everything from acupuncture and foot reflexology to manicures and massages.

Whether you are entertaining business associates or just enjoying a quiet dinner for two, the Four Seasons delivers with a wonderful array of choices. Fill your plate with international delicacies at Café Studio or enjoy dim sum and gourmet Chinese at Si Ji Xuan. If Japanese food and teriyaki call your name, visit Shintaro, while Steak House appeals to the carnivore in all of us.

"Let the Four Seasons Hotel Shanghai welcome you in contemporary comfort and luxury."

FOUR SEASONS HOTEL SHANGHAI
500 Weihai Road
Shanghai 200041, China
fourseasons.com

CHINA
SHANGHAI

Grand Hyatt Shanghai

Shanghai has roots extending back more than 5,000 years as a simple fishing village, but that is hard to believe when you visit today. It has grown to become China's largest city with nearly 19 million residents.

Located in the center of Pudong and Lujiazui business district, the Grand Hyatt Shanghai occupies the 53rd to 87th floors of the Jin Mao Tower building, one of the world's tallest buildings. This Tower is a Shanghai landmark and its easy access to Shanghai's Stock Exchange, World Financial Center, and International Convention Center makes it a natural choice for business travelers.

"The building is a masterpiece of contemporary design highlighting the new face of Shanghai, so it is appropriate that the Grand Hyatt shows off a sleek style." Naturally, the views of the Bund and Huang Pu River are astounding. Did you know that number 88 is considered an auspicious number in China and is said to represent great wealth and prosperity? It is the hotel's street address.

"It takes a mere 47 seconds to reach the lobby and your room." Inside the 510 rooms and 45 suites, the look is chic with floor to ceiling windows. Chinese elements like Tang Dynasty poems in gold calligraphy effortlessly blend with contemporary furnishings.

Visit the Club Oasis Spa for a rejuvenating treatment. Bring new meaning to the phrase "runner's high" at the fitness center and indoor swimming pool, one of the highest in the world.

You can sample sushi, go for Italian, sup on Shanghai regional cooking, or delight in Cantonese all without leaving the hotel at the six restaurants. Cloud 9 is a hot spot with dancing to the DJ.

GRAND HYATT SHANGHAI
Jin Mao Tower
88 Century Boulevard
Pudong, Shanghai 200121, China
grandhyatt.com

CHINA
SHANGHAI

Park Hyatt Shanghai

Great location, design reminiscent of Milan, and top-notch amenities. You're at the Park Hyatt Shanghai, a sophisticated and modern Chinese residence-style hotel located in the heart of the Lujiazui business district in Pudong.

Like its cousin the Grand Hyatt, the Park Hyatt reaches for the sky – literally! It occupies floors 79 to 93 of the Shanghai World Financial Center, otherwise known as "The Vertical Complex City."

Park Hyatt, soaring above Shanghai, delivers an exemplary experience. Take in the sweeping views of the city skyline and Huangpu River from the 160 rooms and 14 suites. Rooms are crisp and contemporary with white-on-white bedding and rich chocolate brown hues. Intriguing artwork and objects create a modern museum-like feel, while rain showers and state-of-the-art technology up the comfort factor.

You might be in the middle of the hustle and bustle, but you'd never know it, especially at the serene Water's Edge Spa. Fit in a workout, swim a few laps, try tai chi with a master, or book a massage to work out the kinks.

Enjoy casual bites and a buffet at Pantry or dress it up a bit at The Dining Room, where fine European food is the focus. The formal setting is perfect for an important meeting or occasion, and the views are mesmerizing.

"100 Century Avenue Restaurant is the feather in the Park Hyatt's cap. It overlooks the city from the 91st floor but keep your attention focused inside, since the multiple open kitchens really put on a show. From the 500-label wine list to steak, sushi, and seemingly endless selections, this restaurant truly is the Park Hyatt Shanghai."

PARK HYATT SHANGHAI
100 Century Avenue
Pudong, Shanghai 200120, China
parkhyatt.com

CHINA
SHANGHAI

The Peninsula Shanghai

Is Shanghai truly the "Paris of the East?" It certainly has a glamour and style all of its own, plus The Peninsula Shanghai!

"A wonderful hotel that bridges the past and the present with panache." The Peninsula sits in good company. In fact, it is difficult to find a better location than here, where the hotel fronts the world-famous Bund and has spectacular views of the Huangpu River, Pudong, and the gardens of the former British Consulate.

The 191 rooms and 44 suites delightfully blend old and new with handsome Art Deco design in noble blue or celadon green. Large marble bathrooms, walk-in closets, the newest Peninsula room technology, and state-of-the-art amenities make life so comfortable.

The Peninsula Spa by ESPA has a stunning design complete with neo-classical decor in French navy and ivory tones and rich dark wood floors. Pop in for a manicure or spend an afternoon at the spa and indulge in signature treatments like the Oriental Thermal Infusion or Bamboo Harmonizer. Don't miss a dip in the pool…it's probably the world's only indoor pool with a fireplace.

The Peninsula Shanghai's restaurants and bars are as striking as they are delicious. Take tea in the grand Lobby, enjoy cocktails and dancing at Salon de Ning, or people watch at The Compass Bar. Sir Elly's Restaurant, Bar and Terrace is "the" place for drinks and modern European cuisine and has glorious views across the Bund skyline, while YI Long Court dishes up fabulous Cantonese cuisine.

"This classically elegant hotel pulls out all the stops with its quiet luxury, so stay at The Peninsula Shanghai and revel in this new level of excellence."

THE PENINSULA SHANGHAI
No. 32 The Bund
32 Zhongshan Dong Yi Road
Shanghai 200002, China
peninsula.com

CHINA
SHANGHAI

The Ritz-Carlton Shanghai, Pudong

The Ritz-Carlton Shanghai, Pudong occupies the upper floors of a modern 58-story tower situated on Century Boulevard in the financial center of Shanghai.

The 226 rooms and 59 suites are located on floors 39-51 with terrific views of the city, Bund or river, but the interiors are as dazzling as the city's skyline. Infused with a seductive sophistication, the rooms blend rich woods and bolder colors with magnificent artwork, creating a residential ambience – perfect for business or vacation. Ritz-Carlton service will exceed your expectations.

"Shanghai was old world China when I first visited in 1983… everything was tired, but you could visualize Shanghai's heyday and even find some reasonable antique Chinese porcelains. I treasure the ones I found there. Today, little of that remains in this modern city of architectural wonders. On a recent visit to The Ritz-Carlton Shanghai, Pudong I admired its museum quality contemporary Asian artifacts, but I saved time to view some of the ancient Chinese art at the Shanghai Museum."

A contemporary showpiece, The Ritz-Carlton Spa by ESPA, indoor pool, and 24-hour fitness center await your pleasure. No matter which of the five restaurants you choose, The Ritz-Carlton goes above and beyond. Take in the scene at Scena, where Italian fine dining whets your appetite. The rich reds and purples of Jin Xuan create a moody setting for fine Cantonese cooking. Afternoon tea and cocktails with live jazz are the beat at Aura, while the light and airy Aroma entices all day long. Go up to the 58th floor to Flair, enjoy Asian tapas, a raw bar, light meals and cocktails, but savor the ever-changing Shanghai views.

THE RITZ-CARLTON SHANGHAI, PUDONG
Shanghai IFC, 8 Century Avenue
Shanghai, Lujiazui, Pudong 200120, China
ritzcarlton.com

CHINA
LHASA, TIBET

The St. Regis Lhasa Resort

You don't need to be the Dalai Lama to find inner peace…at least not if you're staying at The St. Regis Lhasa Resort. Situated on the Tibetan Plateau 12,000 feet above sea level, this resort is the closest thing to heaven as the highest region in the world.

This sensational new resort is the hottest thing to hit Tibet. It offers unprecedented levels of luxury in this "rooftop of the world."

Its impressive architecture will grab you immediately. Styled with a mesmerizingly modern interpretation of typical Tibetan structures, The St. Regis left no stone unturned in its pursuit of excellence. Walk into the lobby…it's perfectly fine to blame your lack of air on the elevation since it really is breathtaking.

The 122 rooms, 28 villas, and 12 suites are a revelation. Lit with a soft golden glow, they have a classic take on Tibet while incorporating sensual and sleek modern styling. The 24-hour butler service elevates the luxurious experience.

The over-the-top Iridium Spa will have you thanking the Gods for their generosity. After all, it is the first luxury spa in all of Tibet. Glorious interiors are just part of the picture, though the gold-tiled pool will linger in your memory for quite some time. Yoga, Pilates, and a whole host of exotic treatments are on hand to have you surrendering any stress at the giant wood doors.

The five fine dining options bring new meaning to the words "rooftop dining," since you are feasting on Tibetan, Chinese, and Continental cuisine on the world's rooftop.

Are you truly blessed or are you just at the sublime St. Regis Lhasa Resort?

THE ST. REGIS LHASA RESORT
No.22, Jiangsu Road
Lhasa, Tibet (Xizang) 850000, China
stregis.com/lhasa

FIJI

InterContinental Fiji Golf Resort & Spa

Few things communicate "vacation" quite like Fiji. It really isn't possible to worry about anything when you are on this unspoiled island in the South Pacific.

For a family friendly playground in this blissful part of the world, select the InterContinental Fiji Golf Resort & Spa. There truly is something for everyone of every age. Located on the beautiful, picturesque Natadola Beach on Fiji's main island of Viti Levu, the InterContinental is a beach lover's paradise. Swim or snorkel in the surf, horseback ride, do nothing by the adults-only infinity pool, or play in the activity pool with the kids. Its shallow areas and water fountain zones practically beg for little feet to jump and splash around. Kids can also play at the resort's kids club, appropriately named Planet Trekkers.

Don't worry – there's plenty of fun for adults, too! Grab your clubs and play a round on the scenic 18-hole championship golf course. The spa shares the native Fijian warmth and generosity of spirit so feel the worry melt away.

The 180 rooms and 91 suites are artistically designed with local woods and accents to set a sense of place. In the Lagoon, Beachfront and 55 Hilltop Suites, relax on the terrace, soak in a Cleopatra bath, or snooze on the daybed.

The five restaurants and bars offer a variety of stunning locales. From poolside at Toba Bar & Grill to the sleek styling and stunning views overlooking the lagoon and the island of Navo at Navo to Sanasana's spot alongside the sugar cane train track looking out over Meke Lawn, each spot is more inspiring than the next.

THE INTERCONTINENTAL FIJI GOLF RESORT & SPA
Natadola, Fiji
ichotelsgroup.com

FIJI

Laucala Island

If you have ever wanted to just pack up and run away from it all, you should head straight to Laucala Island. An exclusive private island, this is the paradise of your dreams. Thatched-roofed villas sprinkled on the sides of a cliff…sugar-soft white sand beaches…dazzling turquoise waters…swaying palm trees…Laucala Island brings your dreams to life.

This stunning resort is the ultimate exotic hideaway in the Fijian Pacific archipelago. You will feel away from the everyday at this gorgeous retreat that is perfect for honeymoons and romantic getaways. Just 25 private villas maximize privacy, peace and quiet. Each villa has been built in the Fijian residential tradition…all spaces effortlessly flow to the next, from the interior areas, to your private outside terraces, to your tropical garden, to your infinity pool, to your indoor - outdoor bathrooms. The contemporary design reflects the resort's deep commitment to nature with furnishings of native woods.

The best thing to do at Laucala Island is nothing at all, so bask in the warmth of the sun, cool off in the tranquil, crystal clear lagoon or relax with a spa treatment. Whether you want to explore the area's rain forests, enjoy horseback riding, go yachting, play golf or go fishing, it is all here.

Feast on fine dining at the elegant Plantation House Restaurant. For a taste of Asia, visit the lovely Seagrass Restaurant. Snack on finger food by the Pool or tuck into the barbeque at the Beach Bar. Sundowners at Rock Lounge are a perfect way to end a special day, but nothing matches the romance and magic of a candlelight dinner on the private beach.

LAUCALA ISLAND
Fiji
laucala.com

FIJI

The Wakaya Club & Spa

Imagine a spot untouched by civilization - a place so pristine, it was undeveloped for centuries. It's not a fantasy…it's The Wakaya Club & Spa. This spectacular island in the Fiji archipelago was first spotted in 1789 by Captain William Nigh, who sailed right past on his famous ship The Bounty. Uninhabited for 140 years, David and Jill Gilmour purchased the island in 1973 and in 1990 opened their dream of an eco-minded luxury resort.

From Nadi, board the resort's Grand Cessna Caravan aircraft for arrival at this secluded 2,200 acre getaway where warm and friendly islanders will totally pamper only 32 guests.

There are 10 freestanding waterfront Fijian suites (bures) or large private cottages; each with living room, bedroom, bathroom, secluded garden and two covered outdoor decks. The Governor's is a larger one bedroom and Ambassador's has two bedrooms. But the last word in South Pacific luxury is Vale O (House in the Clouds), a 12,000 square foot villa on a 16 acre hilltop estate with stunning panoramic ocean views. Be secreted away to this storybook setting with top five-star comforts.

The Wakaya Club & Spa will enchant you at every turn. Choose to be as active or as pleasurably lazy as you'd like…offering a variety of land and water activities from nature hikes, golf, tennis, and croquet, to a spa with organic ingredients and holistic treatments. The coral reefs make for excellent scuba diving and snorkeling, or go sea kayaking.

You'll be living off the land at Wakaya; organic is a given. The exceptional gourmet dining is Pacific Rim-style cuisine and sources its ingredients either on island or locally.

THE WAKAYA CLUB & SPA
Fiji
wakaya.com

INDONESIA
BALI

Amandari

It's not just about beaches and postcard-worthy sunsets in Bali. This culturally rich country has a whole other side. Ubud is the center of Bali's artistic soul. Located in the mountainous region of the north, it is a verdant land of pure magic. See the other side of Bali at the exceptional Amandari.

Amandari, which means "peaceful spirits," is located in the village of Kedewatan in Ubud. Set high above the winding Ayung River gorge, the resort's design is based on a traditional Balinese village. Walk the path of enlightenment literally at Amandari. The pathway that runs through the resort and down the valley to the river below is considered sacred land. Every six months for hundreds of years, local villagers have taken the path through the resort grounds down to a pool of holy water. Just above this spring-fed pool sit three modest shrines and a 7th-century tiger statue carved in stone.

Even if you're not on the path to inner peace, Amandari will delight you. The 30 thatched-roof suites, set within walled gardens, are linked by pebbled walkways. The simple and soothing design makes use of local materials – both coconut wood and teak dominate the interiors. Pool suites have private pools, while all have enchanting views of the Ayung River Gorge or surrounding rice paddy fields.

Imagine experiencing a treatment at the spa, where two open-air bales surrounded by a lotus pond seemingly float above the water.

"Whether you want to seek out the artists in Ubud, visit nearby temples and monuments, hunt for jewelry in Celuk, or wander along a rice paddy, Amandari awaits your return."

AMANDARI
Kedewatan, Ubud
Bali, Indonesia
amanresorts.com

INDONESIA
BALI

Bulgari Resort, Bali

This Balinese luxury resort really shines…maybe not surprising since it was the creation of the renowned Italian jewelry company.

The Bulgari Resort, Bali is located near Uluwatu on the southern tip of the Jimbaran Peninsula. Perched on a cliff 450 feet above the water, this stylish resort has glorious views of the Indian Ocean. The Bulgari Resort marries the natural beauty of Bali and its time-honored traditions with the slick lines and high style of Italian design principles.

In a place where each rock was hand cut and chiseled onsite, expect to be wowed by the interior design. The 59 villas are truly a vision of beauty. From the walls made of volcanic stone and palimanan to the handwoven Balinese fabrics to richness of bangkiray, a Javanese mahogany used in the windows and door frames, the details are enchanting. Add unobstructed views, a plunge pool and patio, and lush tropical foliage and you have a definition of paradise.

Set in a Balinese temple, the Spa is a haven of tranquility at the water's edge. Focusing on Ayurvedic principles, the spa uses ESPA and Bulgari products.

Serenity will be found on the perfect white sand beach, reachable by an inclined elevator, or at the seductive infinity pool. The private beach is protected…you may spot dolphins frolicking as you stretch out in the sun. Feeling a bit hungry while your toes are in the sand? Pop over to La Spiaggia for succulent seafood and cocktails. Nothing beats the strikingly sophisticated settings of Il Ristorante, set next to an ornamental lake, and the cliff edge Sangkar Restaurant, with its delicious Indonesian culinary creations.

BULGARI RESORT, BALI
Jalan Goa Lempeh, Banjar Dinas Kangin
Uluwatu, Bali 80364, Indonesia
bulgarihotels.com

INDONESIA
BALI

Four Seasons Resort Bali at Jimbaran Bay
Four Seasons Resort Bali at Sayan

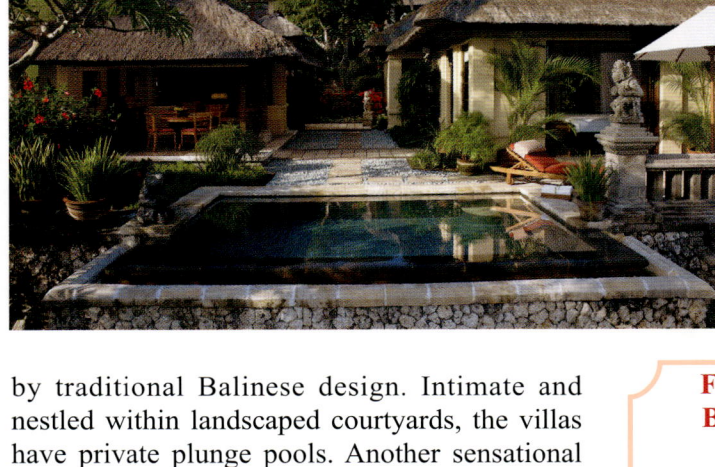

Exotic, mystical, and stunningly beautiful, Bali is truly an "island of the gods." Stay at both the beachfront Four Seasons Resort at Jimbaran Bay and at the stunning jungle setting Four Seasons Resort Bali at Sayan.

The Four Seasons Resort at Jimbaran Bay is an ideal Balinese beach resort. Situated on the southern tip of the island, this superb location affords views of Jimbaran Bay and across to Mount Agung, the physical and spiritual center of Bali.

Taking Balinese tradition, the Four Seasons Resort is built as a series of villages. The 147 villas show off Indonesian furnishings and are influenced by traditional Balinese design. Intimate and nestled within landscaped courtyards, the villas have private plunge pools. Another sensational feature? The outdoor showers – bathing is just magical! Taste everything from Indonesian to Italian at the four open-air restaurants and lounges. Soak up Balinese rituals with native herbs, flowers, and spices at the Spa.

Be ensconced in the verdant beauty of terraced rice fields of Ubud at Four Seasons Resort Bali at Sayan. The riverside resort rests on 17 acres of terraced rice slopes and has stunning architecture that blends perfectly with the natural setting. Suspended teak walkways lead you to the resort's 18 suites and 42 private villas, complete with lily ponds and plunge pools. Indigenous artwork and locally woven textiles add to the regional flavor of the resort. Three restaurants take full advantage of the wondrous setting, while the stand-out spa is a temple of serenity.

"Bali is a magical place and the genuinely caring spirit of the people makes your stay at both Four Seasons Resorts in Bali a very memorable occasion."

FOUR SEASONS RESORT BALI AT JIMBARAN BAY
Jimbaran, Denpasar
80361 Bali, Indonesia
fourseasons.com

FOUR SEASONS RESORT BALI AT SAYAN
Sayan, Ubud, Guanyar
80571 Bali, Indonesia
fourseasons.com

INDONESIA
BALI

The Oberoi, Bali

The Oberoi, Bali was the world's first villa resort concept. Built in 1978, this cutting-edge property continues to impress and has been an award winner since its opening.

Nestled on 15 acres of tropical gardens on Bali's beautiful Seminyak Beach, The Oberoi resembles a traditional Balinese-style village with secluded villas and luxurious cottages tucked amid the fragrant frangipani and colorful flowers.

The spacious 14 villas and 60 lanais are nestled behind coral stone walls and have courtyard gardens with rock ponds. Handcarved wooden beds and furnishings, local artwork, and the indoor - outdoor ambience give these accommodations an authentic look and feel. Secluded and romantic, The Oberoi is a favorite of honeymooners.

The Spa is simply sensational. Book an open air massage pavilion for a truly memorable experience. Overlooking a pond filled with carp, water lilies, and tropical plants, it is difficult to find a place better suited to relaxation. From Balinese deep-pressure massage to Javanese mandi lulur treatments, the spa takes its inspiration from traditional culture.

"The Oberoi, Bali sits on Bali's best powder sand beach, and sunsets are stunning."

Breakfast by the beach at Frangipani or cool off with a cocktail at the colorful Kayu Bar. Sit under the thatched roof at Kura Kura, where Indonesian, Asian, and Continental cuisine are on the menu. Be transfixed by the traditional Balinese performances which blend dance, music, and song with brilliant costumes, masks, and headdresses at the Amphitheater. It is all part of the exceptional Oberoi, Bali experience.

"Mr. M.S. Oberoi was a visionary in luxury resort design. Today, as Chairman, his son P.R.S. Oberoi with his son Vikram Oberoi continue the tradition of excellence in hotel design and hospitality."

THE OBEROI, BALI
Seminyak Beach
Jalan Kayu Aya, Denpasar
80361, Bali, Indonesia
oberoihotels.com

INDONESIA
BALI

The St. Regis Bali Resort

Be mystified by the stunning beauty of Bali at The St. Regis Bali Resort. This exclusive all suite and villa resort is perfectly positioned on the beachfront in Nusa Dua, considered one of Bali's top spots.

Take in the views of the Indian Ocean and prestigious Bali Golf & Country Club while enjoying the creature comforts of this calm and serene setting.

This stylish resort features 80 suites, 42 villas, and 2 residences with panoramic ocean and lush garden views. The interiors reflect the vibrancy and artistry with beautiful woods, brilliantly colored art, and unusual objets d'art. St. Regis prides itself on superior levels of service… so much so that each villa features a Butler Quarter with a separate entrance for 24 hour personalized butler service.

With its beachfront location, swimmable lagoon, and inviting pools, The St. Regis Bali Resort is heaven for sun seekers and water lovers, but there are plenty of other ways to fill your days during a stay. Play golf at the adjacent Bali Golf & Country Club or be taken away from it all at the Remède Spa, where you can practice yoga or meditation or be pampered totally.

Revel in the casual elegance of Kayuputi with its relaxing indoor and outdoor dining, or sample Asian and Western fare at Boneka. Have a hankering for a ham sandwich? Visit the Gourmand Deli. Nothing says Bali quite like a cocktail at sunset…order one at the Vista Bar or the King Cole Bar.

THE ST. REGIS BALI RESORT
Kawasan Pariwisata, Nusa Dua
Bali 80363, Indonesia
stregis.com/bali

INDONESIA
LOMBOK

The Oberoi, Lombok

Lombok, a neighboring island of Bali, is one of Indonesia's exotic gems.

Be transported to paradise while staying at the romantic and alluring Oberoi, Lombok, where 24 acres of lush grounds right on the beach will be your heavenly home.

"The Oberoi, Lombok will capture you immediately. As you enter the temple-inspired reception area, you will be mesmerized by its tranquil beauty with terraced reflecting infinity pools, dotted with palms and secluded bale bengongs stretching out to the sea."

This picturesque and peaceful haven has 30 terrace pavilion rooms and 20 luxurious villas. The terrace pavilion rooms offer a beautiful setting, while the thatched roof villas are set within stone walls and are exceptionally spacious with beamed, vaulted ceilings, fabulous bathrooms inside and out, and rock pond gardens. Indonesian furnishings and decorative objects show off a pride of place.

Naturally, the beach and shimmering pools are the major draw, but the Spa runs a close second. Explore the local culture by indulging in traditional beauty treatments...the Mandi Lulur treatment is a favorite of Indonesian brides who pamper themselves prior to a wedding with this massage and tropical flower bath.

Toast day's end at Tokek Bar, with views across to Mt. Rinjani, and feast on Asian cuisine at The Lumbung Restaurant, an open-sided thatched pavilion set in a landscaped coconut grove with dreamy ocean views. Nothing quite captures the magic of Lombok like the candlelit path to the Ampitheater, where you will be entertained by Sasak dancers.

"When I think of tranquil, exotic luxury, The Oberoi, Lombok always comes to mind. It is one of those rare places where time seems to stand still."

THE OBEROI, LOMBOK
Medana Beach, Tanjung
83352, Lombok, Indonesia
oberoihotels.com

JAPAN TOKYO

Mandarin Oriental, Tokyo

Tokyo is a fast-paced, electrifying city with so much to offer eager travelers. It is a place where old and new collide on a daily basis. Innovative, yet traditional, Tokyo promises a unique experience.

Perhaps nothing best demonstrates this quirky blend of past and present quite like the 400-year-old Nihonbashi neighborhood. Known as the center of Japan, it is indeed centrally located within Tokyo. Home to thriving modern businesses, it also retains its old world ambience. Where else can you conduct business with a world recognized company and walk just steps away to browse in centuries old shops?

This heart of Tokyo is also home to Mandarin Oriental, Tokyo. Like its locale, the hotel blends history with high-tech. Take the high-speed elevator up 38 floors and open your eyes to all of Tokyo before you. The hotel's lobby showcases stunning panoramic views, as do the 157 rooms and 21 suites. The boundaries of the spacious accommodations seem to have an endless sense of space with mellow colors, sleek furnishings, and glass walls. Mandarin Oriental, Tokyo sets a serene overtone.

It's perfectly fine to have your head in the clouds at the Spa, where vertiginous views are the backdrop for a wellness journey.

Mandarin Oriental, Tokyo delivers a prize-winning showcase of ten restaurants and bars. Gorgeous settings with modern flair are in keeping with the hotel's of the moment attitude. Italian, sushi, and fine cakes prepared by a pastry chef who won first place at the World Pastry Championship are just some of the choices. And then there are the three showstoppers; the Chinese, French, and Tapas spots that have all earned Michelin stars.

MANDARIN ORIENTAL, TOKYO
2-1-1 Nihonbashi Muromachi
Chuo-ku, Tokyo 103-8328, Japan
mandarinoriental.com

JAPAN
TOKYO

Park Hyatt Tokyo

Park Hyatt Tokyo calls the business and entertainment Shinjuku district home. This contemporary hotel occupies the top 14 floors of 52-story Shinjuku Park Tower. Great views? Of course! The Park Hyatt frames sweeping views of the city and Mt. Fuji from its dramatic perch.

Step off the busy street into the chic atmosphere of the Park Hyatt. This Tokyo outpost of the top-tiered Hyatt hotels echoes the modern sensibility and comfortable vibe of its sister properties all over the world. Designed with the contemporary business traveler's needs in mind, the 154 rooms and 23 suites have a residential ambience. When you retreat to your room after a busy day, you'll feel like you're coming home to a Tokyo apartment, rather than a hotel room. Why? The modern Japanese interior design, extensive private art collection, and plentiful creature comforts create a welcoming look and feel.

The Park Hyatt offers all of the first-rate amenities of a luxury hotel. Whether you want to work up a sweat, swim laps in the indoor pool, or succumb to the gentle relaxation of a spa treatment, Club on the Park Spa is one of the best.

Enjoy the laid-back luxury at Park Hyatt Tokyo, especially in its four restaurants. Have a business dinner or meet up with friends. Sample regional specialties at the Japanese Kozue Restaurant or take a virtual trip to Paris at the French brasserie-style Girandole. "Of course, the crowning achievement at the Park Hyatt Tokyo is its New York Grill, located on the top floor. International cuisine with a hip and energetic vibe...sounds like another New York I know and love."

PARK HYATT TOKYO
3-7-1-2 Nishi Shinjuku, Shinjuku-Ku, Tokyo, 163-1055, Japan
parkhyatt.com

JAPAN
TOKYO

The Peninsula Tokyo

Perfect for business or pleasure, The Peninsula Tokyo has a prestigious location opposite the impressive Imperial Palace.

This contemporary, yet regal, hotel is ideally located in the heart of the financial district of Marunouchi and the world famous neon lights of the Ginza. The convenient address definitely makes getting to your morning meeting on time a cinch, or on time for a day of sightseeing, especially after a luxurious night's sleep in one of the 267 rooms and 47 suites. The accommodations' style is inspired by Japanese heritage with simple, straight lines in the furnishings, sumptuous materials, and uncluttered space. State of the art technology (don't worry; it just requires one touch) makes everything run like clockwork.

Squeeze in a little looking or shopping time as you are just minutes by foot from some of the finest shops in the world in the Ginza. But even if your visit is confined to the hotel, you'll still be in seventh heaven. There is so much to love at this hotel, where the Peninsula Spa by ESPA totally relaxes you. You can swim laps in the indoor pool with a view of the Imperial Gardens or slow down with a soothing massage. Just in case you are feeling the love, there is even a wedding chapel, so expect to see Japanese brides in formal kimono traditional.

Sip tea in the lofty Lobby for the famous Afternoon Tea or dig in to delicious Cantonese at Hei Fung Terrace. With Japanese Kaiseki at Kyoto Tsuruya, international cuisine at chic Peter, and light dishes and nibbles at The Peninsula Boutique & Cafe, The Peninsula Tokyo anticipates your every mood.

THE PENINSULA TOKYO
1-8-1 Yurakucho, Chiyoda-ku
Tokyo, 100-0006 Japan
peninsula.com

JAPAN
TOKYO

The Ritz-Carlton, Tokyo

Be entranced by the sheer drama of it all at The Ritz-Carlton, Tokyo. You will quite literally have the city spread out before you while staying at this hotel located on the top nine floors of Tokyo's tallest skyscraper. From the panoramic views to the first-class service to the elegant atmosphere, The Ritz-Carlton does Tokyo in style.

The Ritz-Carlton is situated within Tokyo Midtown Tower in Roppongi, Tokyo's business, entertainment, and diplomatic hub. Outside it may be glittering lights and the frenetic pace of one of the world's busiest cities, but inside, it is sophistication – pure and simple. The 212 rooms and 36 suites echo the hotel's contemporary elegance with fine woodwork, hand-tufted carpets, alluring Japanese patterned wall coverings, and modern art.

Take in the city vistas, Tokyo Tower, and Mt. Fuji from the comfort of your private room or while enjoying the hotel's wide variety of amenities, including the outstanding Spa and Fitness by ESPA. This facility has it all - indoor pool, dry sauna, steam sauna, nine spa treatment rooms, one spa suite, fitness studio and more.

The hotel outdoes itself when it comes to fine dining with eight options. Feast on French seafood at Azure 45 or visit the Lobby Lounge for tea and cocktails. There are places, like the Cafe & Deli, to pick up a tasty snack on the go, but be sure to set aside time to visit Hinokizaka. It is out of this world and delivers the true essence of traditional, yet contemporary Japanese cuisine. There are traditional counters for sushi, teppanyaki, and tempura, plus a 200-year-old Japanese teahouse for private dining – all with breathtaking cityscapes.

THE RITZ-CARLTON, TOKYO
Tokyo Midtown, 9-7-1,
Akasaka, Minato-ku
Tokyo, 107-6245 Japan
ritzcarlton.com

LAOS
LUANG PRABANG

La Résidence Phou Vao

Laos is a mystical, unspoiled land of forested hills and roaring waterfalls. The Mekong River slices through the entire length of this beautiful country, where Buddhist culture runs deep. From its modern towns and rural villages to tribal settlements, this former French Indochinese state is a fascinating place untouched by mass tourism.

One such place is Luang Prabang, the ancient capital of the Kingdom of a Million Elephants. This World Heritage town is a stunning sight with mountainous land and a treasure trove of temples and sights, including the impressive Royal Palace Museum, home to a massive golden Buddha.

While making Luang Prabang a stop on your journey, make the unforgettable La Résidence Phou Vao your home. This Orient-Express hotel, perched on the small hill of Phou Vao (the Hill of Kites), has an unparalleled setting with inspiring views overlooking Mount Phousi, Luang Prabang's sacred mountain, and the golden dome of the Wat Chomsi.

The 32 rooms and 2 suites feature simple furnishings and Laotian tiles to showcase a strong local pride. Whether you are facing the lush tropical gardens, the cliff edge infinity edge pool, or gazing out at the old city of Luang Prabang and its Phousy Temple, the views are magical.

The Mekong Spa, set next to a water lily pool, is the embodiment of tranquility. Relax at this refined facility and step back in time to a more gracious era.

Phou Savanh Restaurant is the finest restaurant in Luang Prabang. Inside, it is an elegant affair, while outdoors is romantic with lanterns and candles hung in the shrubs and trees of the hotel's abundant gardens.

LA RÉSIDENCE PHOU VAO
La Résidence Phou Vao
Luang Prabang, Laos
residencephouvao.com or
orient-express.com

MALAYSIA
LANGKAWI

Four Seasons Resort Langkawi

One of just four inhabited islands in an archipelago of 99 islands in the Andaman Sea, Langkawi is unbelievably intimate and astonishingly beautiful. Tropical flora and fauna, crystal-clear emerald green hued waters, lush mountainous rainforests…it is an Eden. Its seclusion once made it a haven for pirates, but today's visitors will find treasures at the Four Seasons Resort Langkawi.

Get a new lease on life at the Four Seasons Resort Langkawi. It is a place where to do lists are banished. "From bird watching and kayaking to snorkeling and biking, you can do it all, but do not miss a mangrove safari, led by a naturalist, to explore this marine ecosystem forest.

Of course, you might be convinced to stay put…this resort will certainly have a hold on you. Malaysia is a bit of a melting pot, and you'll see the confluence of Asian, Arabic, and Indian cultures all over the resort, but especially within the striking 68 pavilions and 23 villas, set within the lush gardens or dotted along the beach.

From Malay and Mediterranean to seafood and steaks, the four restaurants and bars present an enticing array of selections, but it is the dramatic open air settings with romantic views of the Andaman Sea that will have you wanting to return

The Spa looks a bit like Morocco meets Malaysia with its Moorish architecture. Retreat to a place where worries dissipate immediately upon entrance. Six spa pavilions seemingly float amongst reflecting ponds; it is tranquility defined.

"For me, the exotic spa at the Four Seasons Resort Langkawi is the most stunningly beautiful and relaxing experience I have encountered in my worldwide travels."

FOUR SEASONS RESORT LANGKAWI
Jalan Tanjung Rhu, Kedah Darul Aman
Langkawi 07000, Malaysia
fourseasons.com

MYANMAR
YANGON

The Governor's Residence

Step back in time to the glamour of the 1920s in Burma. The Governor's Residence, an Orient-Express hotel, is the former mansion of the governor of the southern states of Burma.

Set within Yangon's embassy district, this hotel is surrounded by blooming gardens dotted with lotus pools. Here, the traditions of a bygone era seem alive. Take a seat in a teak armchair on the fan-cooled veranda or dine by lantern light as the balmy breezes carry the scent of tropical flowers. You will have no trouble connecting with the past.

While the hotel retains its colonial-era ambience, the guest accommodations have an informal Burmese flair.

The 45 deluxe rooms and 2 junior suites are decorated with teak furniture and Oriental cottons, with lovely views over the gardens or free-form fan-shaped swimming pool.

"Drink in the history of Burma, now known as Myanmar, at The Governor's Residence." The Mandalay Restaurant, in the original former residence of the Kaya Governor, overlooks the private garden and serves delicious Asian and European cuisine. In the evenings, spend time at the open air colonial style Mindon Lounge, which overlooks the beautiful green ceramic pool and gardens, and hosts traditional Myanmar dance and music.

Rudyard Kipling once referred to this country as "quite unlike any land you know."

"A few years ago, I visited this mystical land and felt like I was in a time warp. You will journey back hundreds of years to unspoiled simplicity while sailing up the Ayeyarwady River on the Road to Mandalay, a luxury Orient-Express riverboat, and then stay at the atmospheric Governor's Residence. It was a remarkable and memorable trip."

THE GOVERNOR'S RESIDENCE
35 Taw Win Road, Dagon Township
Yangon, Myanmar
governorsresidence.com or
orient-express.com

NEW ZEALAND
FEATHERSTON

Wharekauhau Country Estate

The name is a tongue twister, but after you have been here you'll never forget it.

Wharekauhau (ferry-ko-ho) is unbelievably gorgeous. Rising above Palliser Bay and looking to the rugged coastline of the sea, this 5,500 acre working farm which began life as a sheep station in 1840 promises something different. How many resorts have you visited where 16,000 to 20,000 lambs are born each spring? Just as each season brings its changes, something different happens each week at Wharekauhau.

Of course, Wharekauhau isn't just a typical farm; it is a luxurious and unique retreat. You won't be forsaking any creature comforts either. Comprised of the Edwardian-style manor house, 15 exquisite guest cottages sprinkled throughout the estate, and the grand three bedroom Château Wellington, Wharekauhau delivers an exceptional and intimate guest experience.

At Wharekauhau, you can wind down with a glass of New Zealand wine and wander the gardens or you can wind up and participate in a number of activities. Hike, horseback ride, helicopter tours, and four wheel drive safaris are just some of the thrilling adventures. Prefer something less exhilarating? Take a tour of the farm, sheep shearing in season, explore the coastline, or visit nearby vineyards.

Mingle with other guests during dinner, where you will feel that you've been invited to a private dinner party. Should you prefer more privacy, private dining rooms are available. The menu always adapts to the seasons, but you can expect delicious dining on classics like rack of lamb, beef, venison, fish, and other New Zealand specialties. Local produce and award-winning wines are a highlight of the gourmet dining at Wharekauhau.

WHAREKAUHAU COUNTRY ESTATE
Western Lake Road, Palliser Bay
RD3 Featherston, Wairarapa, New Zealand
wharekauhau.co.nz

NEW ZEALAND
GLENORCHY

Blanket Bay

Blanket yourself in utter beauty at Blanket Bay.

Nestled amidst the snow-capped peaks of the Southern Alps on the shores of Lake Wakatipu, Blanket Bay encourages you to leave your cares behind.

This resort is just 45 minutes from Queenstown in the countryside that lured miners during the 1860s gold rush. Today, you will discover a place of quiet serenity, and the treasure? Cherished memories at Blanket Bay.

Unwind in 5 intimate lodge rooms, 3 generous lodge suites in the Main Lodge, and 4 superb chalet suites that all provide the ultimate in rustic refinement. From the abundant use of natural materials to the magnificent lake and mountain vistas, Blanket Bay displays its setting everywhere.

New Zealand is widely known as an adventurer's Eden and Blanket Bay responds with a heart-racing array of activities. Fill your days with everything from fly-fishing and heli-skiing, hiking and kayaking, skydiving and 4WD tours, horseback riding, and vineyard tours, and even flight-seeing over the World Heritage Fjordland National Park and Milford Sound. "I loved jetboating on the Dart River and the helicopter tour over high peaks, but only watched the adrenaline high bungee jumpers."

Return home to Blanket Bay for an adventure in the culinary arts. The Lake View Dining Room, with beamed ceiling and stone fireplace, is just perfect for elegant dining, but if the weather permits, take a seat on The Terrace for an unforgettable setting under the stars. "The dining here is a revelation. Artfully prepared and plated, the dishes are a feast for the eyes and palate and served with fine New Zealand wines. Yes, Blanket Bay is one of my favorite places!"

BLANKET BAY
Rapid 4191
Glenorchy, New Zealand
blanketbay.com

NEW ZEALAND
HAWKE'S BAY & MATAURI BAY

The Farm at Cape Kidnappers & Kauri Cliffs

With emerald green pastures and jagged cliffs jutting into the sea, New Zealand is a country blessed with stunning beauty. Take in this majesty at these Relais & Chateaux exceptional sister properties.

The Farm at Cape Kidnappers is nestled on 6,000 acres of rolling pastures in Hawke's Bay. This working sheep and cattle farm promises a scenic country getaway with panoramic Pacific Ocean views. It's pure cosmopolitan country…buildings blend river stone and weathered wood… inside, 24 suites share a fresh and light interior design with country casual furnishings. The four bedroom owner's cottage is ideal for families. Play a round of golf on the Cape Kidnappers course, ranked the 41st best golf course in the world by *Golf Magazine*. "Take time to visit some of New Zealand's finest local wineries with delicious dining and wine tastings. I sure did. But I loved everything about The Farm at Cape Kidnappers, including its superb cuisine and own wine."

See another side of New Zealand at Kauri Cliffs. This award-winning lodge is located on the Bay of Islands in the North Island. Spectacular ocean views are just part of this 6,000 acre property near Matauri Bay where the 22 suites and two bedroom owner's cottage offer a world of sophisticated serenity. "Relax at the spa, nestled at the edge of a Totara forest or go to the farm and watch a sheep dog move hundreds of sheep from one pasture to another." Play challenging golf (6 holes played alongside the cliffs and 15 holes have Pacific Ocean views) on one of the 100 greatest golf courses in the world, according to *Golf Magazine*.

THE FARM AT CAPE KIDNAPPERS
446 Clifton Road
Te Awanga, Hawke's Bay, New Zealand
capekidnappers.com

KAURI CLIFFS
Matauri Bay Road
Matauri Bay, Northland, New Zealand
kauricliffs.com

NEW ZEALAND
TAUPO

Huka Lodge

On the banks of the Waikato River with the mighty cascades of Huka Falls just below, Huka Lodge shares New Zealand's pristine landscape of verdant fields and crystal clear water.

It was those waters that first drew Irish fisherman Alan Pye, who came to Taupo after hearing it was an angler's dream. He established Huka Lodge more than half a century ago. Its early roots were simple with a basic lodge and canvas tents, but Huka Lodge's reputation as an idyllic retreat grew. Its original rustic spirit remains, but today's guests are treated to luxurious accommodations and fine cuisine.

Be one with nature without forsaking any of life's comforts at Huka Lodge, where 17 acres of park like grounds live up to the name of the "great" outdoors. Come inside to the Main Lodge, where a roaring log fire takes the chill out of the air and you will instantly feel at home. With just 18 junior lodge suites, one lodge suite, the two bedroom Alan Pye Cottage and the four bedroom Owner's Cottage, Huka Lodge maintains an intimate atmosphere. Tucked along the riverbank with rich wood floors and a cheery country vibe, they create an understated elegance.

Of course, no time at Huka Lodge would be complete without trying your hand at fishing, but with everything from hunting and hiking to horseback riding, there are a plethora of recreational pursuits.

Dining at Huka Lodge is like being in a chef's private home; expect nothing less than the best when it comes to fine food and wine.

"The idyllic setting, welcoming atmosphere, and delicious food make Huka Lodge a top choice of mine."

HUKA LODGE
271 Huka Falls Road
Taupo 3377, New Zealand
hukalodge.co.nz

SINGAPORE

The Fullerton Hotel & The Fullerton Bay Hotel

See the different sides of Singapore at The Fullerton Hotel and The Fullerton Bay Hotel.

The Fullerton Hotel opened in 2001, but the historic building was built in 1928 and was the one-time home of the General Post Office, The Exchange, Chamber of Commerce, and The Singapore Club. "After a $400 million renovation, this hotel with 400 rooms and suites has breathed new life into this landmark building." Doric columns and porte cocheres are the distinguished features of the Palladian-style exterior, while inside, the accommodations are modern and serene.

Rest by the infinity pool along the Singapore River or visit the sleek Asian spa for a soothing treatment. Stay on track with your fitness regimen at the fully equipped fitness center. Fine dining is a hallmark at Town Restaurant, Jade, and The Courtyard, but don't miss the great views along the river at The Lighthouse or the charming confines of the Post Bar, with its original ceiling and pillars of the Post Office.

For a thoroughly modern look of Singapore, stay at The Fullerton Bay Hotel. This latest addition to the sparkling Marina Bay waterfront boasts spectacular views of the bay and Singapore skyline.

The 100 accommodations are completely of the moment with polished rosewood and latticed screens, as well as leather and chrome. Modern and sleek, the rooms and suites are chic havens and many have balconies. The crowning glory is certainly the rooftop pool, an oasis in the heart of the city center. At night, it transforms into a dynamic rooftop bar. Clifford, The Landing Point, and Lantern all showcase sparkling settings with trend-setting food and stylish crowds.

THE FULLERTON HOTEL
1 Fullerton Square
Singapore 049178
fullertonhotel.com

THE FULLERTON BAY HOTEL
80 Collyer Quay
Singapore 049326
fullertonbayhotel.com

SINGAPORE

Mandarin Oriental, Singapore

Singapore, known as the Lion City, has one of the world's busiest seaports, a thriving financial district, world-class shopping, and some of the best cuisine in the world. When visiting, why stay anywhere but right in the middle of it all?

"Mandarin Oriental, Singapore puts you in the heart of the best dining and entertainment with its prestigious Marina Bay location, yet it is only a short distance away from the financial area and the city's attractions."

The recent refurbishment of the Mandarin Oriental, Singapore echoes the brand's signature blend of Asian style with marvelously modern features. Featuring floor to ceiling windows with views stretching over the city skyline, ocean, or harbor, the 468 rooms and 59 suites have stylishly designed interiors with a contemporary flair and subtle Oriental touches.

Retreat to an urban sanctuary at the Mandarin Oriental, Spa. This luxurious spa melts away the stresses inflicted by the hectic pace of the city… you won't find yourself worrying about a thing after a rejuvenating massage or therapeutic body treatment.

Speaking of tranquil spots, snag a chaise by the shimmering pool, set within lush gardens. You can swim laps or just lounge…there is even a separate children's pool for little splashers.

Celebrate a deal over drinks at Axis Bar, where harbor views and dramatic design put everyone in a happy mood. Six restaurants and bars take advantage of sparkling harbor views and present a veritable worldwide journey. Choose from Italian at Dolce Vita, where the living and dining really is good. Enjoy Cantonese at Cherry Garden, fusion at Melt, and Japanese at Wasabi Bistro, or sink your teeth into a juicy steak at Morton's.

MANDARIN ORIENTAL, SINGAPORE
5 Raffles Avenue, Marina Square
Singapore 039797
mandarinoriental.com

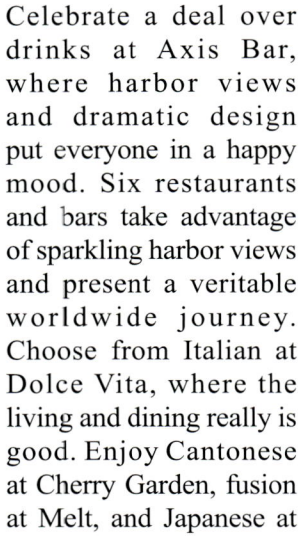

SINGAPORE

Raffles Hotel Singapore

Raffles Hotel Singapore is a legend. For more than 120 years, this graceful landmark has been a Singapore icon. Its British colonial architecture set within tropical gardens seems straight out of a novel – but wait, it is! Both Rudyard Kipling and Somerset Maugham immortalized Raffles in their classic novels. The hotel was declared a national monument in 1987.

Travel back in time without feeling like you've left modern day comforts behind at Raffles Singapore. The 105 suites share an elegant ambience with teakwood floors, Oriental carpets, and period furnishings.

Take a tour of the historic gardens or visit the Raffles Museum, which spotlights the golden age of travel. You can also stretch out in the sun by the pool or spend some down time at the Spa.

Raffles Singapore has always taken pride in its fine dining and entertainment. It was the place to be in 1887 and continues to lure those in the know today with 15 distinctive restaurants and bars. Some still offer time-honored traditions, while others are embarking on new traditions. The Tiffin Room specializes in curry as it did over a century ago. From billiards rooms that once held a tiger to a bar that created the renowned Singapore Sling cocktail, history was, and continues to be made, at Raffles Singapore.

"On St. Patrick's Day 2006, the Indian garbed doormen suggested I go inside to await the imminent appearance of HRH Queen Elizabeth. What a memory to be so close as she gracefully descended the lobby's grand staircase in her green silk ensemble with a marvelous, whimsical hat."

RAFFLES HOTEL SINGAPORE
1 Beach Road
Singapore 189673
raffles.com

SINGAPORE

The Ritz-Carlton Millenia, Singapore

The Ritz-Carlton Millenia is a modern architectural marvel on the Singapore skyline. This contemporary hotel dominates more than seven acres in the heart of Marina Centre.

It's not just the architecture that is a work of art…the extensive 4,200 piece contemporary art collection is one of Southeast Asia's finest. From Dale Chihuly's magnificent glass sculpture titled 'Sunrise' to Frank Stella's striking three-ton roof sculpture suspended from the ceiling, art is everywhere. Another artful spot is the award-winning seven acres of landscaped gardens that are a true oasis in this bustling city. Lounge on a chaise by the pool set within this colorful and fragrant setting.

This distinctive hotel is the ideal place from which to marvel at the city's skyline or explore the wonders of Marina Centre. You won't find a more interesting mix of dining and entertainment options, yet still close to shopping and business areas.

The 528 rooms and 80 suites feature unobstructed views of the Singapore skyline or Marina Bay. The décor is classic contemporary, but this hotel really sparkles when it comes to service. From cutting-edge amenities to white glove treatment, The Ritz-Carlton is first in class.

Singapore's melting pot culture is best seen at the hotel's restaurants. From traditional afternoon tea and classic Cantonese cuisine to Japanese and sushi, seafood buffets, and Sunday champagne brunch, there is a little bit of something from everywhere here.

"It is hard to beat sitting on the edge, in a bath brimming with bubbles, sipping a glass of Champagne, and watching the sun set over the spectacular skyline of Singapore. That is just one of the wonderful memories I have of The Ritz-Carlton Millenia."

THE RITZ-CARLTON MILLENIA, SINGAPORE
7 Raffles Avenue
Singapore 039799
ritzcarlton.com

THAILAND
BANGKOK

Four Seasons Hotel Bangkok

Start your trip to Thailand off with a bang in the incomparable city of Bangkok. This place is exhilarating, if slightly exhausting. It is a riot of colors, sounds, smells…a true feast for the senses. "There are lots of temples to explore, busy markets to wander, fittings for custom made clothes…the list is endless."

Make your home at the Four Seasons Hotel Bangkok, located within the bustling business and shopping district, and celebrate the heritage of Thailand with a fresh and modern approach. The 312 rooms, 35 suites, and 7 garden cabanas showcase a glorious harmony of past and present. Shimmering silks, traditional Thai design, and artwork show off a tremendous attention to detail. "Spacious and sophisticated with rich colors, the accommodations offer a refined respite from the hectic world just outside the door."

Surrounded by lush tropical gardens with a waterfall and lotus ponds, the outdoor pool is a showpiece at the Four Seasons. Snooze in the sun as the warm breezes carry the tropical scents. It will be hard to believe you are in busy Bangkok while resting in this sanctuary. "Take time away from the hustle and bustle for a rejuvenating treatment at the sexy and sleek spa."

The Four Seasons' location makes it easy to get anywhere, but you won't need to travel far for fine dining. Enjoy Madison's Manhattan-style steaks, sample Japanese at Shintaro, or tickle your taste buds at Spice Market. Both The Lounge and The Terrace invite you to unwind with a cocktail, but nothing matches Biscotti, named by *Condé Nast Traveler* as one of the tastiest restaurants in the world.

FOUR SEASONS HOTEL BANGKOK
155 Rajadamri Road
Bangkok 10330, Thailand
fourseasons.com

THAILAND
BANGKOK

Mandarin Oriental, Bangkok

Nothing in Bangkok is quite like the Mandarin Oriental. This hotel, known as The Oriental for generations, first opened its doors over 135 years ago. Set right on the Chao Phraya River, the ancient River of the Kings, this hotel is truly legendary. From Noel Coward to James Michener, this historic hotel has inspired legions of writers.

The hotel's character really comes alive in the 358 rooms and 35 suites. The literary connection is also palpable… enjoy quotes from famous authors placed on your pillow at turn down or get bookish in one of the themed Authors' Suites. "The interiors are polished and exquisite, enhanced with the shimmer of Thai silk and furnishings from the Orient."

From Thai cooking classes and cultural programs to three pools and a spa considered one of the best in Asia, Mandarin Oriental certainly does not disappoint when it comes to fantastic features.

Indulge at Mandarin Oriental's nine distinctive dining venues…China House dishes out contemporary Chinese cooking in an art deco setting reminiscent of 1930s Shanghai. French, Italian, International… it's all here. Of course, Sala Rim Naam stands out in the crowd for its unique setting across the river from the hotel in a pavilion crafted of teak and bronze. It is a true celebration of ancient Siam with traditional dishes and classic Thai dance and music.

"Ever since my first visit in 1983 to the Mandarin Oriental, I continue to treasure the river view from my beautiful room, the savory breakfast on the Riverside Terrace, and my table at Lord Jim's for the best seafood in town. The Mandarin Oriental is Bangkok at its best."

MANDARIN ORIENTAL, BANGKOK
48 Oriental Avenue
Bangkok 10500, Thailand
mandarinoriental.com

THAILAND
BANGKOK

The Peninsula Bangkok

The Peninsula effortlessly blends European elegance and Thai style on the west bank of the Chao Phraya River. "All of Bangkok's major sights… from the royal residence of the Grand Palace, to the Reclining Buddha Temple, to a klong boat excursion to see the life of the river…all are nearby. A little inside tip – never, man or woman, wear shorts or a sleeveless top, as you won't be allowed inside the Grand Palace." Hop aboard the hotel's unique green-roofed boat for easy transport across the busy river.

Thanks to The Peninsula's w-shaped architecture, all of the gracious 305 rooms and 65 suites face the river. The interiors are a delightful mixture of European and Asian design. There are just 10 rooms and 2 suites per floor at this hotel, which is renowned for its exceedingly spacious accommodations. Trust me, after spending a day out on Bangkok's busy streets, you will be delighted with the extra elbow room!

The ESPA Spa is incredibly beautiful with traditional Thai design elements and accents. Set within a tranquil riverside garden, the Thai Colonial-style structure houses a wealth of opportunities for rejuvenation. If working up a sweat is more your style, the hotel's comprehensive fitness center with tennis courts is on hand.

"For me, the three-tiered outdoor swimming pool is definitely the hotel's clear winner. Stretching toward the river, the pool's terraces have waterfalls, bridges, and abundant tropical flowers. Even salas, intricately carved wooden pavilions, are located poolside."

Taste delicious Thai and Chinese cooking at The Peninsula's four restaurants which run the gamut from elegant indoor affairs to casual riverside terraces.

THE PENINSULA BANGKOK
333 Charoennakorn Road, Klongsan
Bangkok 10600, Thailand
peninsula.com

THAILAND
BANGKOK

The St. Regis Bangkok

Come see the sleek and chic side of Bangkok at The St. Regis. This sexy hotel is a new address on Rajadamri Road with proximity to major businesses and superb restaurants.

It all begins with a first impression and The St. Regis wows immediately at reception. The look is dramatic and modern, cream-colored chairs sidle up to gleaming dark wood desks, while zebra-patterned rugs and unusual objects set a splashy tone. The rich chocolate browns and cappuccino tones create a warm and inviting ambience.

In stark contrast, the 176 rooms and 51 suites are done in a soft palette of grays and blues. Light and airy yet infused with a chic impression, the accommodations bear the inimitable St. Regis sophistication. Elegant silks and contemporary local artwork are among the details that make these rooms and suites stand out.

From poolside drinks and snacks to regal afternoon tea to classic cocktails and live music at the New York-style St. Regis Bar and wine at Decanter, The St. Regis Bangkok knows how to entertain. Enjoy delicious Italian cuisine in the striking and trend setting restuarant JoJo or go all out at Viu, where you can traipse across the globe in this three-room restaurant with international leanings.

Surrounded by lush tropical plants, the pool terrace overlooks the cityscape and the Royal Bangkok Sports Club's golf course. Open to guests only, the pool feels private and exclusive. Spend time at the Elemis Spa for a reinvigorating treatment.

THE ST. REGIS BANGKOK
159 Rajadamri Road
Bangkok, 10330 Thailand
stregis.com/bangkok

THAILAND
CHIANG MAI

Four Seasons Resort Chiang Mai

What a difference an hour makes! It may be just a one-hour flight from Bangkok, but Chiang Mai is a far cry from the hectic city. Instead, this inspirational place is defined by a mountainous landscape dotted with terraced rice paddies and lush vegetation. Its beauty and spirit is infectious and has even earned it the nickname "the rose of the north." From centuries-old temples to handicrafts, the area is brimming with artistry and the best place to experience this uniquely beautiful setting is the Four Seasons Resort Chiang Mai.

This resort is truly a world unto itself with 64 pavilions, 12 pool villas, 17 residences, and 5 residence villas.

The interiors reflect their locale with polished teak wood floors, rich Thai cottons, and striking Siamese art. "Covered outdoor verandas, known as salas, are a special feature of each accommodation. Whether you stretch out on the daybed or dine under the stars, the salas are perfect for reading, meditation, and daydreaming."

Set within gardens, the stunning spa sources Thai herbs and aromatic oils from traditional rural origins. The swimming pool, amidst the terraced rice paddies, feels almost surreal.

Another integral part of the Four Seasons Resort is its cooking school, where you will take home a treasured memory and master several Thai favorites. Six restaurants and bars are available should you decide to leave the cooking to the professionals.

"One morning before sunrise, pay tribute to the monks as you provide their alms for the day before visiting a Hmong or Akha hilltribe settlement…then return for a hearty breakfast…do take advantage of the pleasures of the Four Seasons Resort Chiang Mai."

FOUR SEASONS RESORT CHIANG MAI
Mae Rim-Samoeng Old Road
Mae Rim, Chiang Mai 50180, Thailand
fourseasons.com

THAILAND
CHIANG MAI

Mandarin Oriental Dhara Dhevi, Chiang Mai

Inspired by traditional Lanna culture, Mandarin Oriental Dhara Dhevi is divine. Set near the major attractions of Chiang Mai, this resort rests on 60 acres of stunning grounds and is a glorious world unto itself.

"Dramatic and dazzling." These two words best describe the sensational architecture of this showstopper. The Mandarin Oriental envelops you in its majestic beauty. The 54 colonial-style suites and 64 private teakwood villas are luscious. The attention to detail is marvelous, the look is at once soothing with traditional, elegant Thai furnishings. Nestled within the lush greenery, the accommodations are intimate and exclusive. Many villas boast private plunge pools.

"Mandarin Oriental Dhara Devi is home to a world-class destination spa. Inspired by an ancient Mandalay palace, the design is truly breathtaking. It is an inspiration and even incorporates the spa's principles in its design – the seven-tiered roof is symbolic of the seven steps to nirvana." Spiritual, physical, and emotional well-being is the guiding force behind this spa with a world renowned Ayurvedic center. Put yourself on the path to enlightenment, even if just for a day or two.

Soak up the sun by two swimming pools or duck indoors to learn the secrets of Thai cooking at the culinary academy. Unique to the Mandarin Oriental Dhara Devi resort is the Ban Sam Lang, the arts and crafts village, comprised of three northern Thai houses brought here from surrounding villages. Immerse yourself in ancient Lanna culture and learn about everything from traditional crafts to celebrations and rice cycles.

"Dine around the world at the Mandarin Oriental Dhara Devi, offering elegant French at Farang Ses, regional Chinese at the opulent Fujian, reminiscent of a 1930s Shanghai mansion, and even a traditional tea shop, but do not miss Le Grand Lanna, which I think is one of the best Thai restaurants in the country."

MANDARIN ORIENTAL DHARA DHEVI, CHIANG MAI
51/4 Sankampaeng Road Moo 1 T. Tasala A. Muang
Chiang Mai 50000, Thailand
mandarinoriental.com

THAILAND
CHIANG RAI

Four Seasons Tented Camp Golden Triangle

The Golden Triangle is a mystical place. Bordered by Burma (Myanmar) to the north and Laos to the east, this mountainous region of northern Thailand is home to some of Thailand's oldest civilizations. Shrouded by clouds and mist, it is brimming with mystery on the Mekong Delta.

The Golden Triangle is a 75,300 square mile area where the borders of Thailand, Laos, and Burma converge. This crossroads presents a collision of cultures along with captivating scenery. To truly experience this unique destination, stay at the Four Seasons Tented Camp Golden Triangle.

This retreat is set amid exotic bamboo jungles with just 15 freestanding tented accommodations. While many hotels boast lovely views of scenic countryside, not many can claim to have views of three different countries! Handcrafted furnishings, hand-hammered copper bathtubs; it's straight out of the 19th century adventurer's handbook.

Of course, you're not here just to stay snuggled inside your tent; you're here to commune with one of nature's most fascinating animals... the elephant. Become acquainted by bathing these gentle giants. Soon, you'll be meandering the jungles and mountain trails together. Touring will include visiting hilltribe settlements, particularly the Karen Hill group, recognized for their "longneck" women. Board a traditional long tail boat for an excursion along the mighty Mekong River. Back at the resort, more traditional ways of relaxation include the free form pool and the indoor-outdoor spa.

The readers of *Condé Nast Traveler* voted Four Seasons Tented Camp Golden Triangle the number one resort in 2010 on their "Best in the World" Top 100 list. Within hours of arrival, you will be trumpeting its praises too.

**FOUR SEASONS
TENTED CAMP
GOLDEN TRIANGLE**
Chiang Rai 57150, Thailand
fourseasons.com

THAILAND
KOH KOOD

Soneva Kiri

If you have ever wanted to flee civilization and escape to a total paradise, you may have just found your Eden at Soneva Kiri. This exceptional hideaway calls the Thai island of Koh Kood its home. The island's lush rainforest and white sand beaches will call to you.

Koh Kood is tucked away in the Gulf of Siam, but all you need to do to arrive here is hop aboard the resort's private plane for a one-hour flight from Bangkok. As you careen across the sea, marvel at the beauty of this unspoiled stretch of Thailand. Soon enough, you'll be digging your toes in that sugar soft sand.

Arrive at Soneva Kiri and you will soon discover a new approach to vacationing. You won't be checking in with the office or texting your friends back home. Instead, put yourself on island time Six Senses style, with its "no news, no shoes" laid-back vibe.

The 28 pool villas and 8 private residences are the embodiment of Six Senses' signature beachy, breezy, boho chic style. Crisp white linens and simple wood furnishings feel local and luxurious at the same time. Green living is golden at this resort, which prides itself on cutting-edge eco sensitivity.

There is so much to do at Soneva Kiri, with plentiful water sports, jungle treks, fishing tours, boating excursions, and more, but what may be most memorable is what you don't do. Spend time doing nothing on the private beach or meditate with a heavenly treatment at the Six Senses Spa.

From it sheer diversity of selections to its stunning settings, dining at Soneva Kiri is always a delightful event.

SONEVA KIRI
110 Moo 4, Koh Kood Sub-District
Koh Kood, Trat 23000, Thailand
sixsenses.com

THAILAND
KOH SAMUI

Four Seasons Resort Koh Samui

Koh Samui is just one of the 60 islands that make up an archipelago off Thailand's east coast. Set in the crystal clear blue-green waters of the Gulf of Siam, Koh Samui is a place where coconut palm trees sway in gentle breezes and white sand beaches await your arrival.

Experience the best of this secluded and peaceful refuge at the Four Seasons Resort Koh Samui. This exclusive resort is nestled on the northwestern tip on peaceful Laem Yai Bay. Just minutes from town but offering a tucked-away ambience, the Four Seasons Resort delivers an exceptional experience. Explore the historic temples, waterfalls, and striking limestone rock formations nearby, or simply unwind in the tranquil setting of this coastal resort.

The 60 one bedroom villas, nestled on the hillside or just steps from the beach, are perfect for romantic getaways, while the 14 one to five bedroom residence villas are ideal for those seeking more space with families. Enjoy the beautiful setting and astonishing panoramas of Laem Yai Bay, the island of Pha Ngan, or the Gulf of Siam from your outdoor deck with private infinity pool.

Delve into Thailand's rich heritage and culture at the spa, where ancient healing techniques will wipe away any tension. Treatment rooms are housed in individual salas or Thai-style covered verandas. Should you choose to keep your toes firmly planted in the sand, the spa offers beachfront treatments as well. The resort's two pleasure boats are on hand to ferry you to exotic islands and private beaches.

Three restaurants and bars spotlight succulent seafood with a classic Thai zing at Four Seasons Resort Koh Samui.

FOUR SEASONS RESORT KOH SAMUI
219 Moo 5, Angthong
Koh Samui, Surat Thani 84140, Thailand
fourseasons.com

THAILAND
KRABI

Phulay Bay, A Ritz-Carlton Reserve

There is a saying that the best never rest…it's certainly true of Ritz-Carlton. While this exceptional brand of luxury hotels may be best known for its elegant hotels in international cities, it will soon be synonymous with exceptionally private and unique boutique resorts – at least if this first star is any sign.

Phulay Bay, A Ritz-Carlton Reserve, is unbelievably exclusive. This luxurious resort on the Andaman Sea is stunning and captivating. Beautiful beaches, clear waters, sunny skies…it's better than any picture. Phulay Bay is in Krabi, not far from Phuket, but far less developed. From here, you can explore temples and monasteries or ply the waters on traditional decorated Thai boats. Definitely do not miss a visit to Phang Nga Bay, a particularly scenic place where soaring peaks rise out of calm waters.

All 54 exceedingly spacious pavilions and villas are romantic sanctuaries accented with an Art Deco feel and contemporary Thai design. Views of private tropical gardens or the glistening ocean are mesmerizing…relish them from the privacy of your own veranda with lounge bed. From rainforest showers outdoors, to gigantic indoor bathrooms, to dedicated 24-hour butler service, no luxurious touch is forgotten.

ESPA at Phulay Bay is a gorgeous spa that is a destination unto itself with a spa vitality pool and wellness studio.

Phulay Bay isn't restricted just to adults. Bring the whole family along and let the kids learn traditional Thai crafts, baking, and even kids yoga. Adults will want to take a cooking class to impress friends at their next dinner party, but first sample the many delicacies served at Phulay Bay.

**PHULAY BAY,
A RITZ-CARLTON RESERVE**
111 Moo 3 Nongthalay, Muang
Krabi 81000, Thailand
ritzcarlton.com

THAILAND
PHUKET

Amanpuri

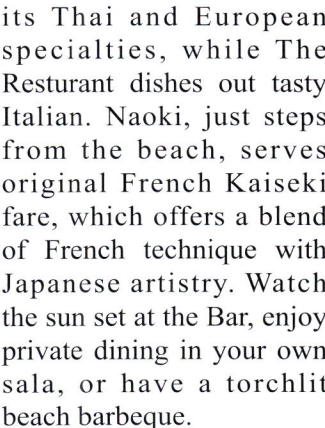

Sometimes you just can't improve on perfection. It's definitely true when considering Amanpuri. Built in 1987, Amanpuri, which means "place of peace," was the flagship property for Amanresorts. Some things never change, and this resort continues to improve and impress adult guests with its graceful Thai style and seamless service.

Amanpuri is nestled on a coconut palm plantation overlooking the Andaman Sea on the west coast of Phuket, one of Thailand's most world-famous resort destinations. The 40 Thai styled pavilions welcome you to a world of simple pleasures with exquisite, classic Thai décor. Outdoor salas with sun decks and dining terraces allow you to relax in this beautiful setting, while those who are staying in pool pavilions will enjoy the luxury of a private pool.

Amanpuri overlooks a perfect swimming beach, but equally tempting are the two stunning swimming pools. Another fantastic component of Amanpuri is its sensational spa. Thai-style pavilions, light filled with abundant use of glass, invite you to unwind in the lap of luxury. Participate in a guided yoga or meditation session held at daybreak (and other times, of course!) in the open-sided teakwood salas set high on the hillside.

Enjoy poolside dining at the Terrace, with its Thai and European specialties, while The Resturant dishes out tasty Italian. Naoki, just steps from the beach, serves original French Kaiseki fare, which offers a blend of French technique with Japanese artistry. Watch the sun set at the Bar, enjoy private dining in your own sala, or have a torchlit beach barbeque.

Amanpuri epitomizes a sophisticated, luxury retreat in Southeast Asia, so put it on your wish list.

AMANPURI
Pansea Beach
Phuket 83000, Thailand
amanresorts.com

VIETNAM
CON DAO & NINH VAN BAY

Six Senses Con Dao & Six Senses Ninh Van Bay

There really is only one word to describe Six Senses Con Dao... wow! From the natural beauty of this national and marine park setting to the stunning architecture and design that makes cutting edge look old fashioned, Six Senses has cornered the market on style. Snuggled along a mile of pristine beach, Six Senses Con Dao is magically remote, yet reachable by a 45-minute flight from Ho Chi Minh City. This is Vietnam like you have never seen it before.

The 50 villas are sensational spaces with private infinity pools and unobstructed views of the East Vietnam Sea. Beds are romantically draped with gauzy netting in these light-filled spaces. All building materials are natural, sustainable, and reclaimed – there are more than a thousand beautifully carved antique panels. Unwind on the beach, step aboard a boat, or visit the Six Senses Spa. Time stands still in this serene spot.

Sail away to Six Senses Ninh Van Bay for another view of Vietnam. This resort is accessible only by boat and offers a world of sophisticated seclusion. The 58 pool villas are located on the beach, sprinkled along the hillside, and over natural rock formations...creating an out of another world experience... even with private swimming pools. The calm waters of the bay are perfect for water sports. After you've exhausted your muscles from all those aquatic adventures, visit the Six Senses Spa for a reinvigorating treatment. In this paradise, you will want for nothing. Dine by the bay, the pool, or the rocks for a breathtaking setting that complements the fresh seafood and produce prepared with international influences or celebrate in the wine cellar.

SIX SENSES CON DAO
Dat Doc Beach, Con Dao District
Ba Ria, Vung Tau Province, Vietnam
sixsenses.com

SIX SENSES NINH VAN BAY
Ninh Van Bay, Ninh Hoa
Khanh Hoa, Vietnam
sixsenses.com

VIETNAM
HANOI

Sofitel Legend Metropole Hanoi

What's in a name? If it's the Sofitel Legend Metropole Hanoi, it's a hint of its past. This hotel truly is a legend and number one in Hanoi. World travelers have been coming to this hotel since 1901. Nothing captures the elegance and grandeur of the French Colonial era like the Sofitel Legend Metropole Hanoi.

Perfectly positioned in the heart of Hanoi, The Metropole was the first Sofitel Legend property in the world. It's easy to see why this hotel company chose this property as its standard setter. Its grand and graceful building with a significant history is an unbeatable combination that classifies it as a Legend, the newest Sofitel luxury brand.

The 342 rooms and 22 suites are divided between the historic Metropole wing and the neo-classical Opera Wing. Step inside your door to a private world of luxurious details with traditional decor… rich dark woods, crown molding, elegant bathrooms. From the artwork to the objets d'art, traces of Vietnam and its French Colonial past are displayed throughout these sumptuous rooms and suites.

Take a break from sightseeing to spend time at the lovely outdoor swimming pool and certainly make time for a treatment at the spa. The newly established Le Spa du Metropole is a sensual retreat blending French and Asian touches. Rituals, therapies, and traditions marry East and West for a comprehensive treatment menu.

Whether enjoying traditional French bistro cuisine at Le Beaulieu, Vietnamese specialties at Spices Garden, or modern interpretations of Italian at Angelina, or the not to be missed Sunday Brunch, the three restaurants at Sofitel Legend Metropole are the places to be and be seen in Hanoi.

SOFITEL LEGEND METROPOLE HANOI
15 Ngo Quyen Street, Hoan Kiem
Hanoi 10000, Vietnam
sofitel.com

VIETNAM
HOI AN

The Nam Hai

Serenity now. This catchphrase is most often used during times of tension, but it might as well be the mantra at the luscious Nam Hai. This strikingly modern resort in central Vietnam's Hoi An is unbelievably gorgeous. Set amidst lush landscaping with unobstructed views of the sea, the setting alone packs a powerful punch, then blend it with chic, contemporary design, gracious and exceptional service, and plentiful amenities… and you have one of Asia's finest resorts.

All villas face the beach, so you will fall asleep to the sound of the gentle lapping of waves. The 60 hotel villas are designed with a seductive and cosmopolitan look, where unique artwork and objects set a soothing tone. Outdoor showers set within private gardens, intuitive butler service…it's all here. The 40 pool villa residences are the height of luxury and have one to five bedrooms…the best choice if traveling with the family, plus stunning private infinity pools.

The facilities exceed expectations. A pristine white sand beach and three swimming pools sparkle and shimmer in the sunlight. Play tennis, visit the fitness center, let the kids play at their own club, or play golf on the 18-hole Colin Montgomerie-designed course nearby. The spa, surrounded by pools filled with lily pads, is an ultra-sophisticated retreat where you will surrender your stress at the door.

The Dining Room, The Beach Restaurant, and The Bar all show off a sassy style with sharp designs. Close your eyes and taste the tantalizing cuisine as you watch the sun set over "China Beach," there's no mistaking The Nam Hai's location for anything but a tranquil paradise in Vietnam.

THE NAM HAI
Hamlet 1, Dien Duong Village,
Dien Ban District
Hoi An, Quang Nam-Da Nang, Vietnam
thenamhai.com

VIETNAM
SAIGON

Park Hyatt Saigon

Tomato, tom-ah-to. Saigon, Ho Chi Minh City. Call it what you will, but this Vietnam capital is one of the most exciting places to visit in Southeast Asia and there's just one place in the city that delivers it all – the Park Hyatt Saigon.

This colonial-style hotel is located at Lam Son Square in the heart of Saigon. You'll be only minutes from all the major attractions, exciting restaurants, and parks. If you happen to be there on business, the Park Hyatt is a perfect base, as it is in the central business district.

The Park Hyatt Saigon strays from the brand's typical modern Milanese design. Instead, the 223 rooms and 21 suites are designed with a definitive colonial style in honor of the city's European heritage. You'll find wooden shutters framing the windows, two poster beds, and other charming traditional touches in these very comfortable accommodations.

Park Hyatt Saigon delivers a delightful guest experience. Unwind by the stunning outdoor swimming pool, set within lovely landscaped gardens, but save time for touring historical and cultural sights…don't miss the local markets, from flowers to silks to fish. Cooking classes immerse you in the local culture…first visit the market with a chef and then learn the tricks of the trade.

Visit Saigon's best urban sanctuary at Xuan Spa. Xuan, which means "spring," is an oasis from the busy city with soothing spa treatments.

The Park Hyatt's two restaurants and two bars are the center of the city's social life. Visit Square One for delicious regional cuisine, while Opera delivers a powerful performance with its elegant Italian dining.

PARK HYATT SAIGON
2 Lam Son Square, District 1
Ho Chi Minh City, Vietnam
parkhyatt.com

CANADA

UNITED STATES

MEXICO

COSTA RICA

North America • Central America • South America

ARGENTINA

BRAZIL

COLOMBIA

PERU

CANADA
BANFF

The Fairmont Banff Springs

You don't get much more legendary in Canada than at The Fairmont Banff Springs. Constructed in 1888, this grand resort sparked tourism to the Canadian Rockies. As if its superior location - in the heart of Banff National Park, a UNESCO World Heritage Site – wasn't enough, the hotel is itself a National Historic Site.

It may have a serious history behind it, but this grand resort, modeled after a Scottish baronial castle, is as modern today as it was in 1888. Though the resort has a considerable size with 689 rooms and 79 suites, the rooms maintain an unparalleled intimacy. Superbly inviting, they are cozy with sweeping Alberta mountain views. For an added level of comfort, you can bring Fido along with your family.

Winter, spring, summer, and fall, Banff offers something for all. Skiing is a natural draw, with three area mountains. The resort's spectacular 18-hole Stanley Thompson-designed golf course and the 9-hole Tunnel Golf Course are perfect for enjoying clear Canadian days. If you're more sybaritic, Willow Stream delights the senses with soothing waterfalls and mineral pools, terraces with views of the Bow Valley, and wonderful treatments. From swimming pools to a bowling alley, there are plenty of ways for parents and children to enjoy family time together in the Canadian Rockies.

With a dozen restaurants and lounges, The Fairmont Banff Springs really does have food for every mood. The selections run the gamut from elegant to relaxed, but you can expect the same dedication to service throughout this entire resort.

Come be a part of the legend at the beautiful Fairmont Banff Springs.

THE FAIRMONT BANFF SPRINGS
405 Spray Avenue
Banff, Alberta, Canada T1L1J4
fairmont.com

CANADA
JASPER

The Fairmont Jasper Park Lodge

Majestic peaks reaching to the heavens… mountains have a spiritual pull. They take us away from the everyday and remind us that nature is mighty and majestic. One of the best places to reconnect with the great outdoors is Canada's Jasper National Park. This mosaic of mountain peaks is Canada's largest park and a UNESCO World Heritage Site.

Nestled on 1,000 pristine acres within the park, The Fairmont Jasper Park Lodge brings you unprecedented access to this mountain setting. The historic resort is comprised of a village of heritage log cabins connected by picturesque paths. It puts luxury into the log cabin. It looks every bit the mountain lodge it claims to be - only better! Massive stone fireplaces with crackling fires…hunting trophies hung on the walls…even paneled wood interiors that remind of simple log cabins, The Fairmont Jasper Park Lodge brings you rustic interiors with a sophisticated edge.

Alpine-themed patterns and artwork along with warm wood furnishings create a country charm in the 336 rooms and 110 suites. Surrounded by incredible views of majestic mountains and the blue-green Lac Beauvert, the accommodations are inviting and relaxing. Traveling with family? Stay in one of the ten signature cabins, offering plenty of space for the kids.

There is so much to do in this veritable playground. Hiking, biking, rafting, golf, dog-sledding…you name it and The Fairmont delivers. After a busy day, slow down and enjoy a fir-infused stone massage, mountain mineral ritual, or a maple-butter body wrap. For a local taste, visit one of eight restaurants.

The Fairmont Jasper Park Lodge is a perfect country retreat in the glorious Canadian Rockies.

**THE FAIRMONT
JASPER PARK LODGE**
Old Lodge Road
Jasper, Alberta, Canada, T0E1E0
fairmont.com

CANADA
LAKE LOUISE

The Fairmont Chateau Lake Louise

Go ahead and rub your eyes. Wipe your glasses. It's understandable. You have just taken your first glance at Lake Louise and you're making a call to your optometrist. That color can't possibly be real, right? Contrary to your first impression, Mother Nature doesn't have Photoshop. That surreal blue-green color… it's natural. Originally named Emerald Lake, it was renamed Lake Louise after Queen Victoria's fourth daughter, but you can call it yours while staying at The Fairmont Chateau Lake Louise.

The mountains have long been the draw, first luring climbers and now skiers, who carve fresh tracks on powdery slopes, even heli-skiing. Lake Louise hosts World Cup skiers annually. The Spa is a pleasant diversion from heart-pumping activities. Wind down with a hot stone massage in the tranquil space.

The wide range of restaurants includes everything from a deli to a formal dining room.

Make others green with envy when you stay at The Fairmont Chateau Lake Louise.

This hotel set on the edge of the rapturous lake rests in the heart of Banff National Park. Open since 1890, it began as a simple one-story log cabin and grew to become the impressive Chateau, luring Hollywood. It has even been known as "Hollywood North," both for the amount of movies shot here and for the film stars who have vacationed here.

It is easy to see what brought them…the elegant and polished 458 rooms and 96 suites are a delight. Sharing an updated country appeal, the accommodations are relaxing and welcoming, especially after a long day of hitting the slopes, fishing, boating, hiking, or other outdoor pursuits.

THE FAIRMONT CHATEAU LAKE LOUISE
111 Lake Louise Drive
Lake Louise, Alberta, Canada, T0L1E0
fairmont.com

CANADA
TORONTO

Four Seasons Hotel Toronto

It was 1961 and Isadore Sharp built his first hotel on Jarvis Street in Toronto. He had no experience in the hotel business, as a former architect and builder of apartments and houses (that's him on the ladder). Without a vision or grand scheme, Sharp started Four Seasons Hotels and Resorts with only one hotel. Little did he know that his philosophy of featuring superior design, top quality amenities…like a good bed…and a deep commitment to service, would revolutionize the hotel industry. It would later become a world-renowned brand and synonym for luxury.

Bid goodbye to the existing Four Seasons building. Just 400 yards east on Yorkville Avenue, the Four Seasons brings you the best of the best in a brand new bright and shiny package. This skyscraper, set in the heart of Toronto's Yorkville Village, is still steps from Bloor Street boutiques and minutes from Bay Street business.

"We all wait with baited breath to see the newest vision to be inaugurated in mid-2012." Of course, the 217 rooms and 42 suites will have a sleek, contemporary atmosphere filled with natural light and abundant creature comforts.

It will feature the largest luxury hotel spa in Toronto, complete with 16 treatment rooms, including a couples spa suite, and access to an indoor pool. The new bar and restaurant will be a focal point in the city to mix with taste makers for drinks or cool cuisine.

"What began with one hotel has grown to become a world-recognized legend with 85 luxury hotels in 35 countries. Fifty years later, Four Seasons continues to shape the way we experience the world."

FOUR SEASONS HOTEL TORONTO
60 Yorkville Avenue
Toronto, Ontario, Canada M5R 2B1
fourseasons.com

CANADA
TORONTO

The Ritz-Carlton, Toronto

Whether you are left or right brained, you'll love the exciting Ritz-Carlton, Toronto. This luxury hotel is the newest thing to hit the city and welcomes guests to an inviting home. Its location in the heart of the busy financial and theater districts makes it ideal for all travelers. Across from Roy Thomson Hall and steps from the Toronto International Film Festival Bell Lightbox, The Ritz-Carlton shares an artistic flair with its privileged guests.

Surround yourself in classic elegance in the 211 fashionably appointed guest rooms and 56 dramatic corner suites. Floor to ceiling windows frame magnificent city or lake views. Ritz-Carlton thinks of everything…they even offer heated perimeter flooring to chase away the Canadian chill! Contemporary furnishings are as stylish as they are comfortable, and the amenities are first-rate.

The large Urban Sanctuary and Spa is absolutely marvelous. It may be in the heart of downtown Toronto, but this spacious and serene facility gets its inspiration from Canada's great outdoors. Bathed in light and sharing a tranquil spirit, the Spa encourages you to practice yoga, work up a sweat, swim laps in the pool, or simply relax with a nature-based treatment.

The Ritz-Carlton, Toronto puts on quite a show with two bars and a restaurant. Hip and happening, choose DEQ for breathtaking views of Simcoe Park and the CN Tower. With comfortable furnishings, an expansive outdoor patio and open-air firepit, DEQ features all-day dining. Before or after a performance at Thomson Hall, hit up the trendy TOCA Bar. Of course, the star is Tom Brodi and his TOCA restaurant. His creative menu is peerless.

THE RITZ-CARLTON, TORONTO
181 Wellington Street West
Toronto, Ontario M5V 3G7 Canada
ritzcarlton.com

CANADA
VANCOUVER

Shangri-La Hotel, Vancouver

Few cities can offer a true blend of urban delights and rugged nature, but Vancouver does it with aplomb. This vibrant Canadian city is nestled between the Coast Mountain Range and the Pacific Ocean. It is the gateway to world-renowned Whistler and is the home port for many Alaskan cruises, but this city isn't just a pass-through. Save a day or two to explore the region. "I highly recommend an excursion to the San Juan Islands to spot the resident pods of orca whales."

There is no better place to experience the vivacity of Vancouver than at the Shangri-La Hotel. This property marks the hotel company's expansion into Canada and what an impression it has made! Located in the heart of downtown, the hotel occupies the first 15 floors of a 61-story landmark building; the tallest n the city. It's not just stature; this hotel has serious style.

The luxurious 80 guest rooms and 39 suites are gorgeously decorated in a contemporary Asian style. Warm latte tones and golden hues create a palpable richness in the accommodations, many of which feature private balconies and stunning views of the city.

Visitors can enjoy personalized spa treatments at CHI, The Spa or even sip a natural juice or healthy light meal served bento box-style at Ginger.

Xi Shi lounge is stunning and celebrates Shangri-La's Asian heritage. Xi Shi is the ancient Chinese goddess of the lotus blossom…if you think you've spotted her it's just the waitresses sporting traditional Shanghai cheongsams. Vancouver's coastal setting inspires the seafood focused menu at MARKET by Jean-Georges, the hottest restaurant in town.

SHANGRI-LA HOTEL, VANCOUVER
1128 West Georgia Street
Vancouver, B.C. V6E 0A8 Canada
shangri-la.com

CANADA
WHISTLER

Four Seasons Resort Whistler

What Pebble Beach is to golf, Whistler is to skiing. Home to both Whistler and Blackcomb Mountains, this British Columbia town is consistently regarded as North America's best ski destination. The world watched as the Olympic Games were held here in the Winter of 2010, but you don't need to be a gold medal athlete to appreciate the many charms of this alpine village.

Four Seasons Resort Whistler is without a doubt the number one resort in Whistler. Stay at this incomparable resort for five-star comfort. The 178 rooms and 95 suites are a lesson in casual sophistication. These spacious accommodations perfectly capture the spirit of a luxurious mountain residence with cozy gas-burning fireplaces and warm, elegant surroundings. Enjoy superb views from your private balcony.

Whether you strap on skis or a snowboard, lace up your sneakers for a thrilling bike ride, or clip into a lifejacket for a river rafting excursion, the hotel guides you every step of the way.

Surrounded by the stunning snow-capped peaks, glistening glaciers and alpine meadows, the Spa is the ultimate retreat. The views aren't the only stunner…enjoy luxurious spa treatments using seaweed, fresh fruits, wild flowers, pure essential oils, and clay harvested from British Columbia's glacial lakes.

Fifty Two 80 Bistro and Bar is the perfect après ski locale. Sip a mountain mojito or wine indoors, on the inviting heated terrace, or by the wood-burning fire pit. Named for the curvature on the side of a ski or snowboard, Sidecut shares glorious views of Whistler and Blackcomb mountains with wholesome food.

Whistle a happy tune at the Four Seasons Resort Whistler.

FOUR SEASONS RESORT WHISTLER
4591 Blackcomb Way
Whistler, British Columbia, Canada V0N 1B4
fourseasons.com

ARIZONA
SCOTTSDALE

The Phoenician

From sunshine and spas to emerald green golf courses and alluring art galleries, Scottsdale has something for everyone. "There are numerous resorts in this ultimate desert vacation destination, but if you want award-winning golf, a first-rate spa, fine dining, and more pools than you can count, make a beeline for The Phoenician."

Nestled at the base of Camelback Mountain on a 450 acre property, The Phoenician is the epitome of a luxury resort. "The professional staff makes you feel so special, but take a look at the mind-boggling array of activities and you might just need to extend your vacation!"

Play a round of golf or meet your match on the championship tennis courts. Wander through the striking Cactus Garden, where you might run into a roadrunner. Nine pools and a waterslide will cool you down after a hard day's play. The Centre for Well-Being is one of the leading spas on the west coast.

"This large resort has 392 spacious guest rooms, but I would suggest staying in one of the 119 casita rooms or 72 luxurious canyon suites." They share a desert-influenced décor with serene earth tones and local artwork. The hotel's $25 million art collection is enjoyed throughout the public and private spaces. For even more seclusion, opt for a casita or villa, tucked away from the heart of the resort.

If you can't find something sweet or savory to tempt you at The Phoenician's ten restaurants and lounges, then you certainly are out of luck, because this resort really does cover all the bases. From casual coffee spots to gourmet restaurants and everything in between, it's all here.

**THE PHOENICIAN,
A LUXURY COLLECTION
RESORT**
6000 East Camelback Road
Scottsdale, AZ 85251
luxurycollection.com/phoenician

ARIZONA
TUCSON

Canyon Ranch

Canyon Ranch needs no introduction. This destination spa was a game changer and pioneered the idea of a spa vacation.

"Whether you are looking to jumpstart a new exercise regimen, want to start eating better, or simply want to get away from it all and unwind in a beautiful natural setting with plenty of spa treatments, Canyon Ranch is at your service with 4, 7, and 10 day programs."

Set on the edge of Tucson on 150 acres in Arizona's Sonoran Desert, Canyon Ranch enjoys year-round sunny weather and clear desert air. This is a stress-free zone; a place where you can reconnect and take control of your body, spirit, and mind.

The one-story Southwestern-style 124 rooms and 43 suites are clustered throughout the grounds. The interiors are designed to match the spirit of the American Southwest…spend time on your private porch as you gaze out at the stark beauty of the desert or simply meditate.

Whether you are a fitness fanatic or a complete newbie, Canyon Ranch offers something to fit your level and interests. Participate in something new with 40 different indoor and outdoor activities regularly scheduled. Work on your nutrition know-how with food and nutrition programs or learn to battle stress with meditation and behavioral changes.

Maybe you'd prefer to work out your issues at the Spa? That's perfectly fine, since this marvelous spa encourages you to take advantage of its sensational treatments.

"Banish any thoughts you may have about spa cuisine… Canyon Ranch bucks the tasteless trend and delivers exemplary food. You'll even dine on delicious items like lobster, lamb chops, even hot fudge sundaes!"

CANYON RANCH
8600 E. Rockcliff Road
Tucson, AZ 85750
canyonranch.com

ARIZONA
TUCSON

The Ritz-Carlton, Dove Mountain

Steal away to the Sonoran Desert.

"The Ritz-Carlton, Dove Mountain, opened in 2009, is a luxury resort in an undeveloped and natural setting that has it all – and it's tied up with a Ritz-Carlton blue ribbon. Jack Nicklaus golf, a glorious spa, fine dining, elegant accommodations…what else could you possibly need?"

This resort takes the spirit of the Southwest and glams it up in its 165 rooms and 44 suites. These casual and comfortable accommodations feature mesquite woods, rich colors and unique patterns associated with the American desert, yet Ritz-Carlton manages to modernize the look and feel with a chic and contemporary edge.

There is fun for the whole family at The Ritz-Carlton, Dove Mountain. Enjoy world class hiking on 20 miles of trails, challenge yourself with rugged mountain biking, or take a guided desert jeep tour through the majestic Saguaro forest. Southern Arizona is the Astronomy Capital of the World with over 350 nights of stargazing each year…look through the hotel's professional telescope to see if you can spot Orion.

Of course, Arizona is a world-class golf destination, so it should come as no surprise that the Jack Nicklaus designed course is a true winner. Challenging, scenic…it is a golfer's dream.

If your tastes lean more toward practicing downward dog than putting, you'll be thrilled with the offerings at this Southwestern spa.

After you've played golf, hiked the trails, splashed with the kids in the pools and careened down the slide, or chilled out in the sun, it's time to enjoy five restaurants with delicious American food with a Southwest focus in casually sophisticated settings at The Ritz-Carlton, Dove Mountain.

THE RITZ-CARLTON, DOVE MOUNTAIN
15000 North Secret Springs Drive
Marana, AZ 85658
ritzcarlton.com

CALIFORNIA
LAGUNA BEACH

Montage Laguna Beach

Laguna Beach is that perfect Southern California town, where the crash of the surf is a soundtrack for a luxuriously laid-back lifestyle. It is a place where sun-bleached surfers, A-listers, and artists all converge to soak up the rugged natural beauty and catch some of that contagious spirit.

Join the crowd at Montage Laguna Beach. Perched on a bluff overlooking the Pacific Ocean and the sunny beaches of the golden state, it doesn't get much better than this scenic spot. Montage's Craftsman style architecture sets a relaxed tone on 30 lushly landscaped acres. The boutiques and galleries of Laguna Beach are nearby, but celebrate California's coast at Montage.

The 190 rooms and 60 suites share the intimate ambience of an upscale beach house with country-style furnishings and artwork by noted California artists. Enjoy the spectacular coastline views from your private balcony.

The shimmering oceanfront mosaic pool is Montage's centerpiece. For added privacy and exclusivity, take a private poolside cabana, while the adjacent bar and grill caters to your needs throughout the day. Children's programs are plentiful, whether Paintbox Petite for little ones, Paintbox for 5 to 12 year olds, or M-Teens.

Spa Montage is a delight and makes living better an art form. Sunset yoga, decadent therapies, and beauty treatments are all part of the perfect package here.

"From the lobby to the bar to the four restaurants, casual sophistication permeates the entire resort. Far from fussy, the atmosphere is as breezy as the soft ocean winds. Add panoramic views of the Pacific Ocean and you have the wonderful and memorable Montage Laguna Beach."

MONTAGE LAGUNA BEACH
30801 South Coast Highway
Laguna Beach, CA 92651
montagelagunabeach.com

CALIFORNIA
LAGUNA NIGUEL - DANA POINT

The Ritz-Carlton, Laguna Niguel

Bathed in sunshine and cosseted by ocean breezes, The Ritz-Carlton, Laguna Niguel is an idyllic resort. This resort offers the perfect blend of luxury and natural beauty from its dramatic setting perched atop a 150 foot bluff overlooking the Pacific Ocean.

Halfway between Los Angeles and San Diego, Laguna Niguel is a delightful destination. Southern California's laid-back lifestyle is on display in this spot near the charming artists' colony of Laguna Beach.

The Ritz-Carlton is the picture of seaside elegance. "All 366 guest rooms and 30 suites have a contemporary décor and balconies that bring the outside in. Rooms show off beautiful views of the pool, garden, and coastline…naturally my favorites have sweeping views of the Pacific!"

From your toddlers and teens to furry four-legged pets, this resort spoils them all Ritz-Carlton rotten. Entertain and educate (shh—don't tell them!) with one of the fascinating adventures featured at The Ambassadors of the Environment program, run by noted conservationist Jean-Michel Cousteau.

Of course, the best way to take advantage of the radical coastal setting is by hanging ten – this SoCal spot is a surfing haven and was even memorialized in the iconic film *The Endless Summer*. Learn the basics or sharpen your skills with top-notch instructors.

Aquatic adventures aside, there's world-class golf at half a dozen area courses.

Visit the spa or soak up the rays poolside at one of two pools. Those lazy days of summer surely never end at The Ritz-Carlton.

"From your ocean facing balcony to the blufftop lounge to Raya restuarant at The Ritz-Carlton, Laguna Niguel, the sun setting over the Pacific Ocean is a lasting memory."

THE RITZ-CARLTON, LAGUNA NIGUEL
One Ritz-Carlton Drive
Dana Point, CA 92629
ritzcarlton.com

CALIFORNIA
LAKE TAHOE

The Ritz-Carlton, Lake Tahoe

World-class skiing, thrilling water sports, and exciting nightlife are just some of the reasons travelers love Lake Tahoe, but there is just one luxury resort that brings it all together in one spectacular mountain setting - The Ritz-Carlton, Lake Tahoe.

Perched mid-mountain in the Highlands Village at Northstar, The Ritz-Carlton offers ski-in, ski-out access to the legendary trails of this leading ski destination. Grab a seat on the high-speed gondola, which ferries guests across to the Village at Northstar for skiing, ice skating, shopping, dining, and bars. The ski valet ensures that schlepping those skis is not part of your stay. During the summer, the mountain concierge will direct you to the most scenic mountain biking trails, arrange boat trips on nearby Lake Tahoe, or book tee times at local golf courses.

The 153 rooms and 17 suites are the embodiment of modern mountain décor with autumnal color tones, updated plaid patterns, and stone fireplaces. Sink into one of the rich leather club chairs and gaze out at the magical mountains and Martis Valley views or enjoy the view from your balcony.

Enjoy après-ski in the heated pool overlooking the slopes, but no visit is complete without a stop at the outstanding spa. You can soothe tired muscles with a massage, detoxify in the dry-heat lodge, or invigorate in the pinyon pine steam room.

The fresh air and plentiful alpine adventures are sure to work up an appetite. Good thing that The Ritz-Carlton has some of the best dining around, especially at Manzanita. Acclaimed chef Traci Des Jardins struts her stuff with her signature French-inspired California cuisine.

THE RITZ-CARLTON, LAKE TAHOE
13031 Ritz-Carlton Highlands Court
Truckee, CA 96161
ritzcarlton.com

CALIFORNIA
LOS ANGELES - BEVERLY HILLS

The Beverly Hills Hotel

The Beverly Hills Hotel is a classic. "It just doesn't get more Hollywood than this hotel, as it prepares to celebrate its 100th anniversary in 2012." This legendary Dorchester Collection hotel, affectionately known as "the pink palace," is a landmark in the true sense of the word. Look at old pictures of Beverly Hills and all you will see is this icon hovering above Sunset Boulevard.

The Beverly Hills Hotel has long been a playground and meeting place of the silver screen's most famous stars. The stories are endless… Katharine Hepburn dove fully clothed into the pool and Marilyn Monroe took up residence while filming *Let's Make Love*. "Today, you'll likely find movie producers brokering deals over meals and gorgeous guys and dolls hoping for stardom…maybe you will be discovered here."

Surrounded by 12 acres of lush gardens and exotic flowers, The Beverly Hills Hotel has 187 rooms and 23 unique bungalows. These bungalows are almost as legendary as the hotel itself. Elizabeth Taylor even honeymooned with six of her eight husbands in the bungalows here. Three new Presidential bungalows are the hottest thing in town.

La Prairie Spa and a fitness center keep you bikini ready…good thing, since that famous pool is waiting.

The hotel's retro glamour extends to the restaurants, especially at The Fountain Coffee Room, where a traditional soda fountain counter lined with green stools looks straight off a movie set. Other spots include the poolside Cabana Café and a bar, but it is the Polo Lounge that functions as a private club for Hollywood.

"You have to hand it to this old gal…she's still got it!"

THE BEVERLY HILLS HOTEL
9641 Sunset Boulevard
Beverly Hills, CA 90210
dorchestercollection.com

CALIFORNIA
LOS ANGELES - BEVERLY HILLS

Beverly Wilshire, A Four Seasons Hotel

Catch a glimpse of glamour at The Beverly Wilshire, A Four Seasons Hotel.

Located at the intersection of Rodeo Drive and Wilshire Boulevard, you can't get any closer to the gilded life of Beverly Hills than at this prestigious hotel where legendary shopping is quite literally steps away. "Feeling like you've been here before? You're not suffering from déjà vu – this hotel was itself a leading lady in the film *Pretty Woman*."

The Italian Renaissance landmark hotel is comprised of two wings with two very different personalities. Bridging old and new, the hotel's historic Wilshire Wing in the original building dates to 1928 and sits at the corner of Wilshire and Rodeo, while the Beverly Wing is more contemporary and looks across Beverly Hills and Los Angeles. The side-by-side buildings are connected by a beautifully designed central porte cochère. The interior design of the 258 rooms and 137 suites is similar, offering both traditional and contemporary décor in gentle shades for a light, airy appeal.

Living the luxe life is just so easy at The Beverly Wilshire, especially at the Mediterranean-style pool, where you can lounge on a day bed in the sun or shade. The Spa at Beverly Wilshire is a modern wonder for taking a break.

Tuck into a perfect steak at CUT by Wolfgang Puck, where cutting-edge also describes the white-on-white design created by Richard Meier, the acclaimed architect of L.A.'s Getty Center, among other things. If people watching is on your radar screen, stop by The Blvd for a great scene.

"The Beverly Wilshire, and its restaurants, remains one of the best places to see and be seen."

BEVERLY WILSHIRE, A FOUR SEASONS HOTEL
9500 Wilshire Boulevard
Beverly Hills, CA 90212
fourseasons.com

CALIFORNIA
LOS ANGELES - BEVERLY HILLS

Montage Beverly Hills

Montage Beverly Hills may have only opened in 2008, but this stately hotel has heart and soul. "It's as if the Montage took the best of Beverly Hills, sprinkled in Spanish, Italian, and Moroccan influences, and blended it together. The result is a sophisticated hotel with a sumptuous vibe…it's in perfect keeping with its Beverly Hills neighbors."

The 146 rooms and 55 suites are a testament to Montage's dedication to the finest things in life. The accommodations have traditional and classic roots with an extra oomph for added luxury. Enjoy panoramic views of Beverly or Canon Drives…if you're really lucky, you'll have a room with a balcony overlooking the adjacent Beverly Canon Gardens. This is Beverly Hills, baby.

On the roof, a stylish oasis awaits. The mosaic-tiled swimming pool is one of Montage's highlights. Private poolside cabanas, a rooftop bar, lush landscaping, even panoramic views of the Hollywood Hills are all part of the sensational experience.

"Once the shops of nearby Rodeo Drive have worn you out, slip off those stilettos and step into a world of ultimate luxury at the lavish two story 20,000 square foot Spa Montage, where comprehensive doesn't even begin to describe this Mediterranean-style temple of luxurious serenity."

Enjoy the elegant surroundings of the Lobby Lounge, where you can take afternoon tea or cocktails. The sunny, poolside setting of the Conservatory Grill is a perfect match for its healthy California cuisine, sourced from the local farmers market, but for a dramatic and romantic setting, choose Scarpetta. This seductive spot may seem straight out of the Mediterranean, but it's all mmm… Montage Beverly Hills.

MONTAGE BEVERLY HILLS
225 North Canon Drive
Beverly Hills, CA 90210
montagebeverlyhills.com

CALIFORNIA
LOS ANGELES - BEVERLY HILLS

The Peninsula Beverly Hills

You can hide from the flashing bulbs of the paparazzi while staying at The Peninsula Beverly Hills. "Even if your last name isn't in lights, this oasis of elegance in the heart of Beverly Hills has been treating guests like A-listers for 20 years."

The refined French Renaissance-style Peninsula is enhanced by glorious gardens filled with an extraordinary selection of flowers, trees, and shrubs. As you listen to the birdsong in this delightful setting, complete with trellises and trickling fountains, it may be hard to believe that you're in the middle of the busy city. Oh, but you are in Beverly Hills, so if you have an inkling for a little Rodeo Drive shopping, simply ring the front desk and ask to be chauffeured over – in one of the hotel's Rolls Royces, of course!

The 193 rooms, 36 suites, and 16 villas are elegantly appointed with fine furnishings, fabrics, marble floors, and fine artwork. The luxurious villas are tucked away within the gardens and filled with handwoven carpets, imported raw silks, and custom furnishings.

The rooftop garden pool and terrace feature private cabanas for ultimate relaxation. Retreat to the classical Peninsula Spa for seriously sophisticated soothing and pampering.

Fine dining is part of the first class experience. Whether you dine in the airy salon-style setting of the Living Room, snack poolside, or have drinks at the bar, it is superb, but the hotel's golden child is The Belvedere Restaurant. Revered for its power breakfast, this establishment has garnered top awards for 16 consecutive years.

"Celebrities will come and go in this town, but The Peninsula always is a star."

THE PENINSULA BEVERLY HILLS
9882 South Santa Monica Boulevard
Beverly Hills, CA 90212
peninsulahotels.com

CALIFORNIA
LOS ANGELES

Hotel Bel-Air

Cross the arched bridge and enter the unhurried, romantic world of Hotel Bel-Air. Its 12 acres of lush grounds, intimate courtyards, trickling fountains, and wrought-iron balconies have been cossetting guests for 65 years.

"Like many aging beauties, the Bel-Air was closed for 2 years for a big nip and tuck. This legendary Dorchester Collection hotel reopened to rave reviews in late 2011. Hotel Bel-Air has reclaimed its role as the ultimate hideaway."

Famed interior designer Alexandra Champalimaud has infused the 58 guestrooms and 45 suites with a stylish retro Hollywood glamour. The design schemes harken back to the 30s, 40s, and 50s and blend American and international influences. "Natural wood ceilings, bold furnishings, and glorious garden views…good things do come to those who wait!"

The hotel's total revamp includes the addition of a well-equipped fitness center and a fantastic La Prairie Spa. The signature oval-shaped pool set among hanging palms is one of the best spots, but nothing matches the hotel's Swan Lake. Whether you are popping the question, celebrating a birthday or anniversary, or simply enjoying a beautiful sunny southern California afternoon with a friend, it is priceless.

Echoing the old Hollywood glamour seen throughout the hotel, the signature restaurant and bar are headed up by none other than renowned celebrity chef Wolfgang Puck. His history with the hotel dates back to the early 1980s… he even created the Bel-Air's famous tortilla soup.

"A beautiful white evening gown photographed during a photo shoot in front of the Swan Lake so captivated me that I had the gown copied for my daughter Jennifer's cotillion."

HOTEL BEL-AIR
70 Stone Canyon Road
Los Angeles, CA 90077
dorchestercollection.com

CALIFORNIA
LOS ANGELES

Four Seasons Hotel Los Angeles at Beverly Hills

The sixteen-story Four Seasons Hotel Los Angeles at Beverly Hills affords panoramic views of Beverly Hills and the Hollywood Hills. Located on a quiet residential street, the hotel exudes a sense of calm, while its central location makes it an ideal base for business and leisure travelers.

"The recent renovations from top to bottom at the Four Seasons LA are simply fabulous." The hotel's 188 rooms and 97 suites are the picture of contemporary elegance with chic furnishings and soft colors. You will want for nothing.

Whether you need primping or pampering, the Four Seasons is on hand to cater to your needs. A variety of services are available in the privacy of your room, but for a truly relaxing getaway, steal away to the Spa for a whole host of enticing selections. In addition to regular treatment rooms, the spa boasts a private poolside cabana. From reflexology and massage to a manicure and pedicure, you can take the spa outside. "The terrific rooftop pool is a very 'in' place for sunning and socializing."

Four Seasons gives you the best of both worlds when it comes to dining. Windows Lounge is a relaxing spot for appetizers and drinks, but come Fridays and Saturdays, this place revs up the volume with its DJ dance party. Grab a casual bite at the poolside Cabana or throw on heels and a dress to dine in the sultry setting of Culina, Modern Italian. Named by *Esquire* as one of the nation's best new restaurants, it also features LA's only crudo bar.

"The Four Seasons Hotel Los Angeles at Beverly Hills is a winner."

**FOUR SEASONS HOTEL
LOS ANGELES AT BEVERLY HILLS**
300 South Doheny Drive
Los Angeles, CA 90048
fourseasons.com

CALIFORNIA
LOS ANGELES

The Ritz-Carlton, Los Angeles

Downtown Los Angeles is new and different with the addition of The Ritz-Carlton, Los Angeles.

This hotel is still a baby having opened in 2010, but it can party like a rock star. Part of the soaring 54-story luxury tower at LA Live, the hotel is steps away from the entertainment of the Staples Center, the Nokia Theatre, and The GRAMMY® Museum. Hence that vibrant rock star personality!

The 109 rooms and 14 suites are dressed to impress with a cool, clean, totally Californian sophistication. Contemporary furnishings and largely white palettes keep these rooms looking fresh and hip. Of course, panoramic views don't hurt either, and it's safe to say that you will enjoy the best views of Los Angeles from this stunning downtown tower.

The Spa is sleek and sophisticated and will treat you like an Oscar winner, even if your last time on the stage was your 8th grade play. Enjoy the signature Champagne welcome, then indulge in decadent treatments with names like Cashmere and Truffle or the Fountain of Youth facial.

Whether you are working out in the fitness center, chilling out by the 26th floor private rooftop pool, or toasting with pals at Ion, the rooftop pool bar, the views are simply incomparable.

Snack on light bites and wine at Glance Wine Bar or sip cool cocktails at The Mixing Room. The über-hip LA Market by Kerry Simon offers modern American cooking with a taste for nostalgia. WP24 by Wolfgang Puck is super-sleek and features his take on modern Chinese cuisine.

The Ritz-Carlton, Los Angeles is the nerve center of it all in thriving downtown.

THE RITZ-CARLTON, LOS ANGELES
900 W. Olympic Blvd.
Los Angeles, CA 90015
ritzcarlton.com

CALIFORNIA
LOS ANGELES

SLS Beverly Hills Hotel

SLS Hotel at Beverly Hills is a new creation for the Luxury Collection of Starwood. The first in this latest extension of the brand, it's funky, fun, and fashionable. Young, fresh, unique…SLS promises to knock your socks off with its wonderfully wacky, slightly Alice in Wonderland look. One thing is for sure, this place isn't your typical Luxury Collection hotel.

The initials don't stand for anything in particular, but that first "S" could be surprise. That's because this Los Angeles hotel surprises you at every turn with its unique accents, touches, and stand-out furnishings.

The "L" in SLS might as well stand for location, since this hotel is ideally located in Los Angeles' Restaurant Row. A block from the Beverly Center, a short distance from Rodeo Drive, not far from the Getty Center and the Los Angeles County Museum of Art, SLS puts Los Angeles at your feet.

The 236 rooms and 61 suites are marvelously modern. Philippe Starck has put his signature imprint on these luxurious rooms which share a bit of a downtown New York flair mixed with LA verve.

The "S" in SLS certainly stands for style. Take one look at the sixth-floor altitude pool deck. Two pools, one a plunge pool for dipping and the other a reflecting pool for sunbathing, surrounded by chaises and private cabanas, create a chic outdoor living room. Outdoor sculptures (love the pig!) create a gallery-like vibe.

Start off with a blank slate at the white-on-white Ciel Spa, where custom blended aromatherapy begins your treatment.

Chef José Andrés shows off his considerable talents at perpetually packed Bazaar and Trés restaurants.

SLS HOTEL AT BEVERLY HILLS, A LUXURY COLLECTION HOTEL
465 South La Cienega Boulevard
Los Angeles, CA 90048
luxurycollection.com/slsbeverlyhills

273

CALIFORNIA
MENLO PARK

Rosewood Sand Hill

Yahoo! Rosewood Sand Hill is proof positive that business trips to Silicon Valley don't have to be boring.

Just 35 miles south of San Francisco and 14 miles north of San Jose, Rosewood Sand Hill's scenic Bay Area location at the foothills of the Santa Cruz Mountains is steps away from Stanford University and the gateway to Silicon Valley and its world-renowned companies. Leave the office parks behind when you stay at Rosewood Sand Hill. This attractive hotel is nestled on 16 acres of blooming and fragrant gardens. Its unparalleled views of the Santa Cruz Mountains just might convince you that you're in a resort town.

Rosewood Sand Hill is a triumph of traditional California Ranch architecture set around lush courtyard gardens. The 121 rooms and suites are havens of luxury. Soft, soothing color palettes, contemporary art by Californian artists, and state-of-the-art technology all combine to create sophisticated comforts.

The business center and conference facilities are superior, but it's not all work and no play at Rosewood Sand Hill. Instead, you can unwind in the warm sun at the outdoor pool or head to the fabulously comprehensive Sense Spa, where 13 treatment rooms, a fully equipped fitness center, and highly trained therapists ensure your well being.

When you're in need of bites (not bytes), look no further than the hotel's own restaurant, Madera. This Michelin starred establishment wows with its stylish interiors and its award-winning cuisine. The artisan wood-burning kitchen serves American cuisine with proud Western influences. Not surprisingly given both the proximity to the wine country and the restaurant's dedication to excellence, the wine list is expertly curated.

ROSEWOOD SAND HILL
2825 Sand Hill Road
Menlo Park, CA 94025
rosewoodhotels.com

CALIFORNIA
NAPA

Auberge du Soleil

Is it an inn with fine dining or a restaurant with guest rooms? At Auberge du Soleil, it's both. This exceptional resort began life 30 years ago as an award-winning restaurant that drew city slickers simply for a taste of its fine French inspired cuisine. As the guests continued to linger with a glass of wine in hand, the idea for expansion into an inn quickly blossomed, and voila! Auberge du Soleil was born. Napa Valley has never been the same since.

Auberge du Soleil is appropriately named, since the sun truly does shine on this fabulous retreat which feels like a bit of Provence in California wine country. Nestled on 33 acres of rolling hills dotted with olive trees and the Mayacamas Mountains in the distance, Auberge du Soleil is blessed with an unparalleled intimacy in the world-renowned Napa Valley winemaking region.

The 30 rooms, 19 suites, and 2 cottages marry the sunny spirit of Provence with the laid-back luxe of California. Wood floors, unique accents, and distinctive furnishings lend a residential air, while the dreamy views of the hillsides and surrounding valley make it a peaceful haven.

Auberge du Soleil pampers with a delightful country spa. Indulge in a therapy that uses ingredients sourced right here on the property or nearby. Certainly, one of the best ways to soak up the beauty of this spectacular setting is lounging by the pool, especially while snoozing on a day bed under the gauzy canopy.

And then there is the food…it's legendary. Served in the Michelin starred Restaurant or the Bistro & Bar, it is the very definition of Mediterranean-influenced California cuisine, then add Napa Valley wines and everything is sunny at Auberge du Soleil.

AUBERGE DU SOLEIL
180 Rutherford Hill Road
Rutherford, CA 94573
aubergeresorts.com

CALIFORNIA
NEWPORT BEACH

Pelican Hill Resort

The glittering Newport Coast is the embodiment of California's good life and there is no better place to enjoy the splendor than at Pelican Hill Resort.

Pelican Hill is perched on 504 acres overlooking the Pacific Ocean midway between Newport Beach and Laguna Beach. Designed to replicate a Tuscan village, the resort's 204 bungalows and 128 villas are the last word in seaside elegance. Fireplaces, wood-beamed ceilings, and country-style furnishings create luxurious havens where tranquility reigns.

This Mediterranean-style resort takes the cake for being the ultimate resort for the entire family in Southern California. Its setting is unmatched, with views of the crashing Pacific Ocean that will linger in your memory, and then there are the amenities. Where to begin?! You can swing your clubs on the two championship oceanfront Tom Fazio-designed golf courses or sit pretty at the sensational spa, where men and women are treated to a medley of rejuvenating treatments. Spend time by the Coliseum pool, the social center of the resort, or if you're a Villa guest, retreat to your private pool. Pelican Hill pays special attention to its smallest guests with the Pelican Club, where a private clubhouse, pool, bubble jet fountain, among other facilities will have them grinning from ear to ear.

Are we in Naples or Newport Beach? As you twirl your fork around the tender pasta made in-house, you might just think you've flown to Italy. Pelican Hill's five restaurants showcase the flavors of Italy and California in a number of settings. Nothing matches the allure of al fresco dining as the resort's graceful arches frame views of the cerulean Pacific. Ciao Bella!

PELICAN HILL RESORT
22701 Pelican Hill Road South
Newport Coast, CA 92657
pelicanhill.com

CALIFORNIA
SAN DIEGO

The Grand Del Mar

Grand, indeed. This San Diego showstopper has it all with a sunny locale, elegant style, and five-star amenities.

The 218 rooms and 31 suites are traditional with a definitive European influence. Far from fussy, these sophisticated accommodations are the perfect place to rest your weary head after a long day of fun in the sun.

If golf is your game, The Grand Del Mar is definitely for you. This resort is a golfer's dream…the scenic Tom Fazio-designed course is unbelievable.

The Spa, just one of 20 spas in the country to win five stars, is truly a destination unto itself. Its elegant Mediterranean ambience is just right for the indulgent pampering you'll experience.

The Grand Del Mar may be a premier golf and spa resort, but that doesn't mean you have to putt and primp your entire stay. Take advantage of the resort's plentiful activities. There are 37 miles of canyon trails for hiking, cooking classes to bring out your inner chef, and four pools offering everything from underwater music to private cabanas. The Equestrian Center features pony rides for the kids and professional instruction. Speaking of kids, they'll think that this resort was created just for them after spending time at the Explorer's Club. From Legoland and SeaWorld to the San Diego Zoo all nearby, it really is a place for adults and kids to have fun.

At The Grand Del Mar, you can dine with the family one night and then have a special, romantic date night the next. While all deliver terrific food with casually elegant settings, the one to savor is Addison for its award-winning cuisine.

THE GRAND DEL MAR
5300 Grand Del Mar Court
San Diego, CA 92130
thegranddelmar.com

CALIFORNIA
SAN DIEGO

The Lodge at Torrey Pines

Play a round of golf on a legendary Southern California golf course and when finished, find yourself in a luxurious resort. You have arrived at one of California's most cherished resorts, The Lodge at Torrey Pines.

Snuggled on the 18th fairway of the famous Torrey Pines golf course, The Lodge at Torrey Pines could stop right there, but it doesn't. Throw in its location, perched above the glorious Torrey Pines State Beach and the Pacific Ocean and you'll see why this resort is a favorite.

The Lodge's architecture pays tribute to California's proud heritage of Arts and Crafts design. The 161 rooms and 9 specialty suites echo that spirit with Craftsman furnishings and stone fireplaces.

Walk in the golf shoes of giants at Torrey Pines Golf Course. This course has hosted a PGA tournament annually since 1952. Only the Lodge, nestled at the 18th hole, puts you front and center to this majestic course and guaranteed tee times are an added plus.

After a competitive round of golf, visit the Spa to work out the kinks. Set within the native pine forest, the Spa captures the spirit of this sea and forest setting.

Grab a bite at the Grill & Bar, conveniently located near the practice putting green. When you want to regale your companions with stories from the course or spend a romantic evening with a special someone, visit A.R. Valentien, the Lodge's premier restaurant with a strong farm-to-table focus. Named for the California Arts and Crafts artist from the 1900s, the dining room showcases an impressive collection of his paintings and ceramics.

**THE LODGE
AT TORREY PINES**
11480 North Torrey Pines Road
La Jolla, CA 92037
lodgetorreypines.com

CALIFORNIA
SAN FRANCISCO

Mandarin Oriental, San Francisco

From Spanish colonists to the 1849 Gold Rush, San Francisco has a fascinating history. Home to the oldest and largest Chinatown outside Asia, this city by the Bay is packed with culture, cuisine, and cable cars!

"Sky-high views of the Golden Gate Bridge and the city of San Francisco sound good to you? If so, look no further than the Mandarin Oriental, San Francisco." This stylish downtown hotel occupies the top eleven floors of the city's third-tallest building, so those jaw-dropping views? They are standard here.

Centrally located in the Financial District, Mandarin Oriental puts you within walking distance of major attractions by the bay. "A wonderfully convenient location for both business and leisure stays…amble down to Fisherman's Wharf or over to Chinatown."

The 144 rooms and 7 suites give you a bird's eye view of the city, but it's not just the outside that counts at Mandarin Oriental (though definitely pack your camera, as you'll want to snap photos from your room). Inside, the accommodations excite the senses with tantalizing colors like mandarin orange and Imperial yellow. They have a chic and cosmopolitan outlook interspersed with intriguing Asian accents.

"When is the last time you soaked in a bubble bath while gazing out at the Golden Gate Bridge? At Mandarin Oriental, it's all in a day's stay."

Silks, the restaurant located on the second floor, takes local ingredients and jazzes them up with Asian flavors. MO Bar, just off the lobby, is a happening spot all day long, whether for traditional Mandarin tea or cocktails with small plates like Dungeness crab club sandwiches and Kobe beef sliders.

MANDARIN ORIENTAL, SAN FRANCISCO
222 Sansome Street
San Francisco, CA 94104
mandarinoriental.com

CALIFORNIA
SAN FRANCISCO

The Ritz-Carlton, San Francisco

The Ritz-Carlton, San Francisco takes the old world and makes it glamorous again.

This impressive neo-classical building was once the home of Metropolitan Life Insurance. When it opened in 1909, it stirred a major controversy for not being in the heart of the Financial District. It sat in ruins for years until Ritz-Carlton came along and breathed new life into this majestic building.

"Opened in 1991 as The Ritz-Carlton, San Francisco, the hotel's exquisite atmosphere and impeccable service quickly made it a top spot. Its distinguished ambience is evident everywhere…take a look at the museum-quality collection of European and American art and antiques. Aubusson tapestries, 19th century Waterford crystal chandeliers, Persian carpets, Georgian and Regency antiques…it is all so aristocratic and so gorgeous."

The 294 rooms and 42 suites are elegantly appointed with traditional, English-style decor while the furnishings are comfy just like at home. Obviously, no modern amenities are missing.

From mango and passion fruit body treatments to green coffee therapies, the Spa de Vie at The Ritz-Carlton promises a delicious array of selections. A fully equipped fitness center keeps exercise enthusiasts at the top of their game.

The Lobby Lounge now is the go to spot for breakfast, lunch, dinner, and cocktails too!

"A year ago, I dined at The Ritz-Carlton Dining Room on Ron Siegal's exquisite cuisine and marveled at the flawless service. Little did I know that this week this award-winning restaurant would close for a total revamp, style change, food change, even name change, but fortunately Ron Siegal remains. I look forward to being at the opening of this new creation."

THE RITZ-CARLTON, SAN FRANCISCO
600 Stockton Street at California Street
San Francisco, CA 94108
ritzcarlton.com

CALIFORNIA
SAN FRANCISCO

The St. Regis San Francisco

Nobody ever said that artistic flair only comes to those with little pockets. Take The St. Regis San Francisco, for instance. This hotel breaks all of those "starving artist" clichés. Creative and eye-catching, The St. Regis is proof that luxury can be modern and artistic too.

The St. Regis San Francisco makes a break from the brand's tradition and instead of standing on its own, it coexists with a powerful result. Take the historic Williams Building, then add a 40-story tower, and incorporate the Museum of African Diaspora, roll it into one; it makes for an unusual combination. Plus, its location adjoining the Museum of Modern Art isn't too bad, either. "If you enjoy Asian art, like I do, after breakfast take a short walk to the Asian Art Museum."

"Enjoy stylish, contemporary furnishings and dazzling pieces of art in the 260 guest rooms and 46 suites. A residential feeling permeates these handsome accommodations, where terrific city views leave you breathless."

The surrounding SoMa (South of Market) neighborhood is bustling with creative energy, but inside The St. Regis' 9,000 square foot Remède Spa, you will feel sheltered from the world. The indoor infinity pool is bathed in glorious sunlight and is a tranquil spot for reflection.

Breakfast or lunch on the Yerba Buena terrace or inside the bright and airy dining room at Vitrine; they are delightful. The hotel's flagship restaurant is the much buzzed about Ame, situated in the lobby in the historic Williams Building section. Gourmands can't get enough of the culinary talents of Hiro Sone and Lissa Doumani, who have done it again with their New American cuisine.

THE ST. REGIS SAN FRANCISCO
125 3rd Street
San Francisco, CA 94103
stregis.com/sanfrancisco

CALIFORNIA
SANTA BARBARA

Four Seasons Resort Santa Barbara

Santa Barbara, snuggled between the Santa Ynez Mountains and the Pacific Ocean, is often referred to as "America's Riviera." Its temperate climate, beautiful beaches, and celebrity-studded neighborhoods make this California town one of the most scenic in the state.

The Four Seasons Resort Santa Barbara has long been this town's finest resort. Originally known as The Biltmore, it first opened in 1927 and quickly became legendary as an exclusive enclave of the rich and famous.

The Four Seasons Resort enjoys a stunning setting on 20 acres overlooking the Pacific Ocean. The landscaped grounds are blessed with bountiful flowers, trees, and plants, creating a veritable Utopia for guests.

The Four Seasons shares the region's adoration of Spanish Colonial architecture in its hacienda-style main building and 12 cottage buildings. Located in the main building and throughout the cottages, the 181 guest rooms and 26 suites establish a sense of place with traditional colonial style while incorporating international influences.

"I love lounging by the pool in the historic center of the resort. The oasis setting, surrounded by Kentia palms and Australian tree ferns, creates a wonderfully calming effect."

Prefer to go to the beach? Their exclusive beach club with Olympic-size pool is at your service with 31 private cabanas.

Bella Vista showcases organic, Italian-inspired California coastal cuisine in a sophisticated setting complete with fireplaces, a hand-carved wine wall, rich mahogany, and rare marble. Tydes overlooks Butterfly Beach and has unparalleled panoramic views of the Pacific Ocean, Channel Islands, and the Santa Barbara coastline.

"You may not be Esther Williams, but the Four Seasons Resort Santa Barbara is sure to make you feel like a star."

FOUR SEASONS RESORT SANTA BARBARA
1260 Channel Drive
Santa Barbara, CA 93108
fourseasons.com

COLORADO
ASPEN

The St. Regis Aspen Resort

Aspen is America's St. Moritz. Pack your fur, don your diamonds…just because you're skiing doesn't mean you shouldn't look fabulous. This celebrity-studded town in the Rocky Mountains looks great whether snow-capped or green.

"When you're visiting the best, you have to stay at the best, and in Aspen, it's the St. Regis. This resort is the hub of everything haute at the base of Aspen Mountain. Terrific views? Of course. Five-star service? You bet. Access to Aspen's best entertainment and shopping? Why, certainly!"

The St. Regis takes the classic ski chalet look and dresses it up. "Curved wooden headboards and country-style furnishings may look straight out of Austria, but when juxtaposed with dynamic stripes and contemporary accents, this look is defiantly chic. Having just spent $30 million on room renovations, The St. Regis spoils guests with its new finery."

Don't bother thinking, since The St. Regis has already done it all for you. The service is highly intuitive, with offerings like ski butlers and 24-hour in room butler service. With access to four renowned mountains, Aspen is a natural choice for skiers, but this resort is glorious year-round and is a delight for mountain bikers, hikers, anglers, golfers, and spa-goers, who will adore the Remède Spa.

Wind down the day with a warm beverage or cocktail in front of the fire at the Shadow Mountain Lodge or in summertime on the terrace. But be sure to save room for the scrumptious dishes at The Restaurant. From poached Lobster Cobb to goat cheese macaroni and cheese to braised short ribs, The St. Regis Aspen Resort does comfort food like nobody can.

THE ST REGIS ASPEN RESORT
315 East Dean Street
Aspen, CO 81611
stregis.com/aspen

COLORADO
AVON

The Ritz-Carlton, Bachelor Gulch

Stay at the incomparable Ritz-Carlton, Bachelor Gulch. Tucked away on a quiet mountainside in Vail between Beaver Creek and Arrowhead, the village of Bachelor Gulch (originally settled by, you guessed it, bachelors) offers unmatched charm.

"No other resort gives you access to this renowned destination like The Ritz-Carlton does. There's unparalleled ski-in/ski-out access, for one. Next up is the exclusive partnership with the area's best golf courses. How about a world-class spa for some world-class relaxation? Oh, and did I mention fine dining at Wolfgang Puck's renowned Spago? All this and more…you will never want to leave."

The 140 rooms and 40 suites are refined Rocky Mountain retreats. Stone fireplaces, country furnishings, and charming fabrics lend a luxurious lodge feel to the accommodations.

The question at The Ritz-Carlton isn't what is there to do – it's what isn't there to do?! This resort is perfect for families who want to spend time together bonding over chats by the fire pit or carving fresh tracks on perfectly groomed trails in winter or swimming in the outdoor pool and golfing, hiking, or biking in summer. Save time for the stunning spa any time of the year.

"Whether you've sidled up to the Buffalo Bar, grabbing a snack at 7, or tucking into a steak at the Mountainside Terrace, The Ritz-Carlton, Bachelor Gulch captures the spirit of the West with a refined twist." Nothing matches the cosmopolitan cooking at Spago, an outpost of the renowned California restaurant from celebrity chef Wolfgang Puck. Its cow-printed chairs and wooden beams speak of the Wild West, while the kitchen beckons with its Asia-meets-West Coast flavor.

THE RITZ-CARLTON, BACHELOR GULCH
0130 Daybreak Ridge
Avon, CO 81620
ritzcarlton.com

COLORADO
VAIL

Four Seasons Resort Vail

You work hard so you deserve to get away to a place that takes your downtime very seriously. You want a resort that understands your sensibilities and needs and delivers them seamlessly. In Vail, that place is the Four Seasons Resort.

Vail is a veritable playground. No matter the season, this Colorado resort town is brimming with possibility. From terrific skiing and alpine adventures to majestic scenery and world-class culture, Vail nails it. Situated at the gateway to Vail Village, the Four Seasons places you within walking distance of shopping, dining, and entertainment.

In true Four Seasons style, the resort stands out on its own with a sophisticated blend of cozy rustic details and elegant contemporary styling. The 97 rooms and 24 suites offer the utmost luxury with gas-burning fireplaces, furnished balconies, and limitless views.

You can swim year-round in the outdoor pool with views of Vail Mountain. Swim while it snows and upon exiting the pool, you will be wrapped in a heated robe and handed a hot chocolate. Walk along the heated pathway to the Ski Concierge at the base of the chairlift to be fitted and fashioned without fretting. If you've come during the warmer months, the Four Seasons will see to it that you are taken care of no matter which adventure you may choose. If your taste for adventure leans more toward body scrubs, visit the premier alpine-influenced spa.

Classic American cooking is the focus at the three Four Seasons Resort Vail dining venues. Enjoy the poolside setting or retreat indoors to the Fireside Lounge and Flame Restaurant, which both share warm and inviting settings…and delicious dining.

FOUR SEASONS RESORT VAIL
One Vail Road
Vail, CO 81657
fourseasons.com

DISTRICT OF COLUMBIA
WASHINGTON, D.C.

Four Seasons Hotel Washington, D.C.

Washington's prestigious and exclusive Georgetown neighborhood is home to members of Congress, senators, and the tony Four Seasons Hotel. Close to the business of the nation's capital, the Four Seasons introduces you to the quiet charms of the city's first residential neighborhood.

The 173 rooms and 59 suites are divided among two wings connected by a glass-enclosed garden walkway. The elegant and tasteful accommodations in the east wing sport contemporary Parisian styling by renowned designer Pierre-Yves Rochon, while the west wing is styled with contemporary furnishings and modern artwork. "The totally renovated Four Seasons Washington has a fabulous new look but the same outstanding hospitality."

The Four Seasons offers a comprehensive fitness and spa facility. You can even reserve a lane to swim laps in the indoor pool. Forgot to pack your fitness gear? You can fit in a workout without the worry, since the hotel can provide guests with exercise clothing. The luxurious spa lures stressed-out Georgetown residents and hotel guests seeking a respite from their hectic pace.

Stop by before or after dinner to the Lounge at Bourbon Steak, which overlooks the historic C&O Canal. Power breakfasts and Sunday brunch are among the highlights at Seasons.

"The nation's capital may be known for its 'pork,' but if you're looking to tuck into a juicy piece of meat, look no further than Bourbon Steak. Created by celebrity chef Michael Mina and designed by renowned architect David Rockwell, this restaurant is not to be missed. This is traditional American steakhouse at its best."

"Let the grace of Georgetown and the Four Seasons Hotel Washington, D.C. be your home in the capital."

FOUR SEASONS HOTEL WASHINGTON, D.C.
2800 Pennsylvania Avenue N.W.
Washington, D.C. 20007
fourseasons.com

DISTRICT OF COLUMBIA
WASHINGTON, D.C.

The Jefferson

Washington, D.C. is often known for its bravado, but sometimes it's the little things that shine the brightest. It's certainly true of The Jefferson. This elegant hotel is unassuming with less than 100 accommodations, but what it may lack in size, it makes up for in sensational, sophisticated style.

"The Jefferson has deep roots in the capital. It first opened in 1923, but after a two-year transformation and reintroduction in late 2009, it is polished to perfection."

Indeed, the oh-so-elegant Jefferson would make its namesake very proud. Designed to blend Parisian and European elements with an undecidedly American flair, The Jefferson seduces guests with its stately, yet comfortable, décor. The 79 rooms and 20 suites are a lovely reflection of the hotel's dedication to details with a Jeffersonian feeling. From parquet floors and crystal chandeliers to silk-covered walls and architectural impressions, the refinements are superb.

If the Capital's bickering has you at your wit's end, march straight for the Jefferson's Spa. This luxurious urban oasis will transport you away from the everyday and into a world of serene sophistication.

As if polished interiors and first-rate service were not enough, The Jefferson boasts one of the Beltway's best restaurants. Plume is the feather in the hotel's cap. "The book room, bar, and dining room simply sparkle, add murals of Monticello, and throw in award-winning cuisine, and you have Thomas Jefferson's joie de vivre." Inspired by the harvest at Monticello, the chef expertly crafts astonishing seasonal menus.

"In The Jefferson, I trust. That's because I always know this elegant hotel will exceed expectations with its distinguished design, premier address, and white-glove service."

THE JEFFERSON
1200 16th Street, N.W.
Washington, D.C. 20036
jeffersondc.com

DISTRICT OF COLUMBIA
WASHINGTON, D.C.

Mandarin Oriental, Washington, D.C.

The Mandarin Oriental, Washington, D.C. shows the softer, gentler side of this world capital city. Set within gardens along the Potomac, there's no debating that the Mandarin Oriental offers a refreshingly quiet pace, but don't mistake tranquility for inaccessibility. Walk just steps and you're at the Washington Monument and the National Mall. Just two blocks away are 10 of the 14 Smithsonian Museums. It's all within reach from the Mandarin Oriental.

"Drawing from its Asian roots, the Mandarin Oriental's classically styled 347 rooms and 53 suites embody the principles of feng shui for a pleasing environment." Attractive blends of American and Asian accents create a sense of serenity, while striking views are decidedly D.C. Gaze out at the Potomac Tidal Basin, Arlington National Cemetery, the Pentagon, or the splendid Jefferson Memorial from your room or suite.

The treasures of the world-renowned museums are just steps away, but the Mandarin Oriental showcases its own collection of artwork in a special arrangement with the Smithsonian. Enjoy nature's art outdoors at the heated pool or enjoy the view from the waterfront fitness center. Celebrate the art of relaxation at the Mandarin Oriental's Eastern-influenced, Zen-like spa.

Drop in for drinks or settle in for afternoon tea at the elegant Empress Lounge. "Sou'Wester whips things up with a river view and a mouthwatering selection of American classics, but it is without a doubt CityZen that gets all the talking heads buzzing. Eric Ziebold dazzles diners with his artistic culinary creations. Who ever said Washington was stiff and staid clearly hasn't been to this white-hot restaurant."

"For business or pleasure, seek refuge at the Mandarin Oriental, Washington, D.C."

MANDARIN ORIENTAL, WASHINGTON, D.C.
1330 Maryland Avenue, S.W.
Washington, D.C. 20024
mandarinoriental.com

DISTRICT OF COLUMBIA
WASHINGTON, D.C.

The St. Regis Washington, D.C.

Opened in 1920 with President Calvin Coolidge cutting the ceremonial ribbon, The St. Regis was originally known as The Carlton. Designed by Turkish architect Mihran Mesrobian to resemble an Italian palazzo, this grand hotel is a Washington, D.C. landmark and a National Historic Place. Throughout the years, the hotel has hosted many of the world's luminaries.

"During White House renovations (it is just two blocks away), President Truman did most of the official entertaining here, and it was the one and only choice for Queen Elizabeth's private reception during her visit to the United States. Charlie Chaplin, Princess Grace, and The Duke of Windsor all chose the hotel as their home in Washington, D.C. Think of the secrets shared if only the walls could talk."

"After being reimagined as a St. Regis in 1999, the hotel once again sparkles. The original gilded lobby and coffered ceiling gleam as if new. Marvel at the Louis XVI chandeliers and relax to the gentle strains of a harp as you enjoy traditional afternoon tea."

Original Palladian windows, Italian Renaissance, and Louis XVI chandeliers are equally at home with contemporary touches, custom-designed furnishings, and modern amenities in the 157 rooms and 25 suites. At once classic and cutting edge, the accommodations are comfortably chic.

"The St. Regis Bar is well known for 'power' drinks. Plush purple velvet furnishings and black Kenyan marble…it's dark and decadent with so much power." The hotel's crowning glory is Adour Alain Ducasse. Following his success in New York, Ducasse has taken his show on the road to The St. Regis Washington, D.C. It is a celebration of American cuisine.

THE ST. REGIS WASHINGTON, D.C.
923 16th and K Streets, N.W.
Washington, D.C. 20006
stregis.com/washingtondc

FLORIDA
AMELIA ISLAND

The Ritz-Carlton, Amelia Island

Amelia Island is the southernmost barrier island off the northeast coast of Florida. Its protected harbor and high bluffs made it a favorite of various armies, and the island has been under the rule of eight different flags throughout its history.

Stay at the island's premier resort, The Ritz-Carlton, Amelia Island. Nestled in the wild dunes along the Atlantic Ocean, the resort has 400 rooms and 45 suites with private balconies for breezy coastal views, traditional décor, and uplifting, tropical island patterns. The service, which blends Southern hospitality with Ritz-Carlton standards, is unbeatable.

The resort's location along 13 miles of pristine coastline makes it a natural choice for beach-loving families. Whether you're seeking shells, the sun, or the surf, this white sand beach is perfect. The pool, with dedicated play area, is also ideal for family fun.

The Ritz-Carlton entices golfers with a beautiful 18-hole championship golf course, the renowned Anne Cain golf academy, oceanfront tennis courts, and an exceptional spa and fitness facility. The Ritz Kids Program goes above and beyond and offers everything from pirate bedtime tuck-ins, tennis camps, arts and crafts, and fun marine life educational programs.

Be worth your salt in the kitchen and take a cooking class with the chef de cuisine at the acclaimed Salt Restaurant. You will learn French, American BBQ, and even the worrisome holiday meal, or just leave it to the pros and feast on delectable seafood, burgers, Italian, and sophisticated snacks at five restaurants.

"The Ritz-Carlton, Amelia Island is perfect for a family reunion, as the activities are plentiful for those ages 1 to 100!"

THE RITZ-CARLTON, AMELIA ISLAND
4750 Amelia Island Parkway
Amelia Island, FL 32034
ritzcarlton.com

FLORIDA
KEY BISCAYNE

The Ritz-Carlton, Key Biscayne

The Ritz-Carlton, Key Biscayne gives you the best of both worlds in south Florida. "This family friendly resort is nestled on a perfect beach, and that's not just my opinion. Dr. Stephen Leatherman, aka Dr. Beach, has selected this sand as one of America's Best Beaches." The energy and vibrancy of South Beach may be just a short ride away, but once you drive across the bridge to this restful resort, you will leave it all behind.

The Ritz-Carlton might have you feeling like you're enjoying an island getaway, but getting here is hassle free. Unwind in one of the 337 rooms or 113 suites. Contemporary furnishings and accessories blend with an upscale mood giving these stylish accommodations a city-meets-the-beach atmosphere.

Key Biscayne's quiet village appeals to shoppers and diners, but you could easily hole up at The Ritz-Carlton, where everything is at your disposal. The resort's Cliff Drysdale Tennis Center is renowned as one of the largest of any Ritz-Carlton. If golf is your game, the Crandon Golf Course, considered one of Florida's most beautiful, is just minutes away. Swimming is a must, whether you choose the ocean or pool. Ritz Kids keeps the little ones smiling.

You could spend your entire visit taking advantage of the award-winning and exclusive spa, where 21 treatment rooms are just the beginning. "Pamper yourself with a coastal inspired therapy that will have you wishing you were a mermaid."

The resort impresses with its astonishing array of restaurants and bars with distinctive specialties and settings. "Imaginative Italian, juicy burgers, or creative Cuban cuisine… The Ritz-Carlton, Key Biscayne is the key to a perfect holiday."

THE RITZ-CARLTON, KEY BISCAYNE
455 Grand Bay Drive
Key Biscayne, FL 33149
ritzcarlton.com

FLORIDA
MIAMI

Canyon Ranch Hotel & Spa

You don't still think that South Beach is just for night owls who dance until the wee hours, do you? Canyon Ranch Hotel & Spa shows you the softer side of Miami Beach.

This unique resort marries the conveniences of a luxury hotel with the renowned lifestyle programs of the Canyon Ranch destination spas. Maybe you don't have the time to dedicate a week to changing your life, but want to get away and incorporate a little renewal? Canyon Ranch Hotel & Spa is for you.

Stay in one of the 150 suites inside the beachfront historic Carillon building. This 1950s-era hotel, once on the cutting edge of Miami's modern architecture movement, has been infused with a new life, thanks to Canyon Ranch. Enjoy beach views from the chic and contemporary accommodations designed by David Rockwell.

"Like to spa? How does 70,000 square feet of pure indulgence sound? It's the largest spa in Florida, and you can do everything from swim laps, work out, and climb an indoor rock wall to vegging out with luxurious treatments. Anything and everything is available for good health and wellness."

Fit in some time to reassess your goals with a top-notch physician or listen and learn at a number of daily presentations and classes. You can jump head-first into the programs or just spend time soaking up the south Florida sun at the rooftop pool.

Drink and eat to your health's content at the sophisticated restaurants, where organic wines and spirits are served alongside delicious cuisine.

"Spa or not to spa. It's up to you at Canyon Ranch Hotel & Spa in Miami."

CANYON RANCH HOTEL & SPA
6801 Collins Avenue
Miami Beach, FL 33141
canyonranch.com

FLORIDA
MIAMI

Mandarin Oriental, Miami

The Mandarin Oriental, Miami is a dramatically styled hotel tucked away on Brickell Key, a 44 acre residential community on Biscayne Bay. Close to South Beach, Coconut Grove, and the financial district, you are within reach of all things Miami while enjoying a laid back atmosphere right on the waterfront.

"Mandarin Oriental's company logo is a fan, so it may not come as a huge surprise that the hotel is shaped like one. The stunning modern building is 20 stories of glass, so fantastic views of the bay and city are incomparable."

Miami is a hot bed of Art Deco design and the hotel pays homage to that heritage with bright colors while incorporating Asian elements for a uniquely Mandarin Oriental design. The lobby is striking and sensational. Its floor-to-ceiling windows look out over the bay, while its eclectic furnishings are dazzling. The 295 rooms and 31 suites are bathed in glorious sunshine. Asian accents and vibrant colors create a soothing sophistication, while balconies and terraces invite you to enjoy the outdoors.

"The Spa at Mandarin Oriental, Miami stands on its own two feet as one of the city's top spas. It's hard to say which is better – the floor-to-ceiling views or the Asian-influenced treatments."

The dining is dynamic. Café Sambal has a casual feel overlooking the infinity edge pool, while M Bar is the hip spot for cocktails, but there is no doubt that Azul will stop you in your tracks. This fashionable place turns up the heat in Miami with its Latin food mixed with Caribbean, Asian, and French influences.

"The Mandarin Oriental, Miami makes a big splash."

MANDARIN ORIENTAL, MIAMI
500 Brickell Key Drive
Miami, FL 33131
mandarinoriental.com

FLORIDA
MIAMI

The Ritz-Carlton, South Beach

Beautiful beaches lined with even more beautiful people, thrilling dance until dawn nightlife, and bright Art Deco architecture define South Beach. Fashion forward and fun, this Miami resort has long lured travelers, but for years the town lacked a grown-up resort. Not so anymore. The Ritz-Carlton puts the SO-phistication back in South Beach.

It turns out that it is true, you can improve on a legend – at least if Ritz-Carlton is behind it. They took a down-on-her-luck landmark 1953 Morris Lapidus Art Deco masterpiece and brought back its polish. This girl is back thanks to Ritz-Carlton and she's the most gorgeous on the block. The hotel has a prime location – go from flip-flops at the beach to stilettos at Lincoln Square in just a few steps.

The 375 rooms and suites are a wondrous mix of cherry wood furnishings and natty nautical-inspired striped accents. Enjoy views of the pool, Atlantic Ocean, and South Beach.

The spa's La Maison de Beauté Carita treatments are a luxurious treat, but nothing beats the Rhythm Massage, set to the tunes of Latin music. Only in South Beach!

Traipse over to DiLido Beach Club, an elegant enclave with breezy views and sunny Mediterranean fare. "You can't be in South Beach without a cocktail in hand, so order one at the Lobby Lounge or the Lapidus Lounge, where Sunday Brunch is a major hit." Bistro One LR has sensational American bistro-style food with a South Beach sizzle.

"The glorious beach awaits, but I prefer the inviting pool. Sit back, relax, have a cool concoction, and enjoy the style of The Ritz-Carlton, South Beach."

THE RITZ-CARLTON, SOUTH BEACH
One Lincoln Road
Miami Beach, FL 33139
ritzcarlton.com

FLORIDA
ORLANDO

The Ritz-Carlton Orlando, Grande Lakes

What Las Vegas is to adults, Orlando is to kids and families. This fun-filled city really knows how to put on a show and a smile on the faces of its visitors of any age. There is just one place in the world where you can breakfast with Mickey Mouse, watch whales do aquatic acrobatics, visit half a dozen countries on your own two feet, and even act as a star in your favorite movie. In this exuberant destination there is just one place that serves up Orlando on a silver platter, The Ritz-Carlton Orlando, Grande Lakes.

The palazzo-style Ritz-Carlton is a gracious world unto itself in the Grande Lakes community. Everything is a skip away, but the resort enjoys the away-from-it-all wondrousness. The 519 rooms and 63 suites are elegant enough for Mom and Dad, but relaxed and comfortable for the kids. Garden, lake, and golf course views create a peaceful mood.

The theme parks and attractions are just a complimentary shuttle ride away, but Mickey might have to wait once you lay your eyes on that beautiful Greg Norman designed golf course. The kids can even tag along for free. The Ritz-Carlton Spa is a major relaxation destination – there are 40 treatment rooms! Nothing spells happiness quite like a massage after a long day communing with cartoon characters.

There are nine restaurants at The Ritz-Carlton, Orlando, where you dress up or down. Enjoy family time at a number of spots with casual food and mood, or bring back the romance and have a date night at one of the electrifying and sophisticated spots.

"The Ritz-Carlton Orlando, Grande Lakes is the perfect choice."

THE RITZ-CARLTON ORLANDO, GRANDE LAKES
4012 Central Florida Parkway
Orlando, FL 32837
ritzcarlton.com

FLORIDA
PALM BEACH

The Breakers

Grand traditions are alive and well at The Breakers. This timeless resort reflects America's gilded age.

Built by Henry Morrison Flagler, who amassed a large fortune as John D. Rockefeller's partner in Standard Oil, The Breakers first opened in 1896 and has been a part of Palm Beach's legacy and history ever since. It was originally named the Palm Beach Inn and was renamed after guests repeatedly asked for rooms "down by the breakers." The grand Italian Renaissance exterior is equally resplendent inside, with Venetian chandeliers, oil paintings, and gold leaf, handpainted ceilings crafted by Florentine artists.

"Despite its grandeur, The Breakers is as welcoming to children as it is to adults." They even have a Kids Advisory Board, comprised of members aged 5-12, that meets once a month to discuss new programs and activities. Kids camps are offered year round.

The 472 rooms and 68 suites exude the elegance of a seaside home. Pastel colors, ocean-themed artwork, and casually sophisticated furnishings make these rooms inviting and relaxing. Of course, the views of the resort's 140 oceanfront acres certainly add to the unrestrained and breezy ambience, too!

"Playtime is so easy at The Breakers. Build castles on the beach or swim in the large pools. Play tennis on one of 10 Har-Tru courts, golf on one of two championship 18-hole golf courses, or splash in one of four sensational beachfront pools. Nourish your body and soul at the spectacular spa."

Steaks and seafood and snacks, oh my! The Breakers never ceases to impress with nine restaurants and bars. From casual atmospheres to more formal dining, The Breakers has it all.

THE BREAKERS
One South County Road
Palm Beach, FL 33480
thebreakers.com

FLORIDA
PALM BEACH

Four Seasons Resort Palm Beach

The Four Seasons Resort Palm Beach is an elegant choice in Palm Beach that the entire family will enjoy.

The hotel's dramatic architecture and manicured grounds invite you to unwind in the lap of luxury. Calling a gorgeous stretch of beach its own, the Four Seasons overlooks the Atlantic Ocean while remaining minutes away from Palm Beach's glittering boutiques and restaurants of Worth Avenue.

Recently renovated, the 197 rooms and 13 suites with a predominantly white palette are a breath of fresh air. Tufted headboards and unique accents lend a bit of an Art Deco flair, while coastal-themed artwork plants you firmly in Palm Beach. "It goes without saying that the private terraces and balconies with ocean views are a highlight."

The oceanfront swimming pool is the heart of the resort shaded by palms and just steps from the sand. The pool terrace is a wonderful spot for basking in the glory of the Florida sun. The tennis courts are an athletic diversion, and the pro will help you perfect your serve. The kids are tickled pink by the Kids for All Seasons program with its host of activities. The sophisticated spa captures the elegance of Palm Beach and provides a wide variety of indulgent therapies.

Dine with a view of the pool at the Ocean Bistro or sip a tropical drink on the oceanfront patio at Atlantic Bar & Grill. "Linger just a few minutes longer at their signature Restaurant, with its refined setting and gourmet food, or for a special treat, arrange for a candlelight dinner for two in a beach cabana at the Four Seasons Resort Palm Beach."

FOUR SEASONS RESORT PALM BEACH
2800 South Ocean Boulevard
Palm Beach, FL 33480
fourseasons.com

FLORIDA
PALM BEACH

The Ritz-Carlton, Palm Beach

Have a memorable vacation in a perfect setting at the glorious Ritz-Carlton, Palm Beach. The resort snuggles on more than seven acres of prime oceanfront property in exclusive Manalapan. Close to Palm Beach's legendary shopping and dining, guests will feel tucked away in a special part of the world. This refined resort has reigned for almost 20 years, while the recent $130 million transformation is remarkable.

The 215 rooms and 36 suites welcome guests to a privileged world with private balconies, beautiful furnishings, and modern enhancements. Rich woods are set against soft greens and salmons for an elegant interpretation of traditional Floridian flair.

Perhaps one of the best reasons to stay at The Ritz-Carlton is its bevy of leisure pursuits. Relax in a private cabana on the golden beach or luxuriate in one of the two oceanfront pools (one for adults only). Water sports ranging from waverunners and Hobie cats to scuba diving and snorkeling, are all available at the water sports center. Play tennis on the resort's top notch courts or play golf at area courses. Kids will go nuts for the fantastically fun programs, while teens will love their own cool club.

"You deserve a break and there is no better place to unwind than at the fabulous Eau Spa. Every detail, from the wish pond on arrival to the wicker chairs suspended over water in the relaxation lounge, will entice you. Come alone, with treasured friends, or spend quality mother-daughter time at this palace of pampering."

From casual to chic, the restaurants at The Ritz-Carlton, Palm Beach are dressed to impress with gorgeous settings and gourmet dining.

THE RITZ-CARLTON, PALM BEACH
100 South Ocean Boulevard
Manalapan, FL 33462
ritzcarlton.com

GEORGIA
ATLANTA

The Ritz-Carlton, Buckhead

The Ritz-Carlton, Buckhead is a 'peach' of a hotel in Atlanta's fashionable and exclusive Buckhead. Atlanta's best shopping is within walking distance and you can take your pick from exceptional restaurants when you make this hotel your home.

It enjoys a residential ambience. The 454 rooms and 56 suites are individually appointed with a beautiful, traditional European influenced elegance. Soft pastel colors (peach, of course!) lend a soothing tone to these urban havens.

Fitness enthusiasts can stick to their routine at the well-equipped fitness center with junior Olympic size indoor pool. Lounge on the deck for a post-workout snooze.

After a busy day at the world-famous aquarium, impressive art museum, or after hunting for treasures in the many shops, spend some time at the luxurious spa. From sweet magnolia pedicures and Georgia clay body treatments to sweet tea body buffs, the spa celebrates the many traditions of the South on its extensive treatment menu.

Prefer your Southern comforts to be more edible? Look no further than the Ritz-Carlton's Lobby Lounge and Café. Participate in the afternoon tea that has become an Atlanta tradition or sway to the beats of live jazz. The Café brings together the culinary spirit of the South with its refined regional cooking, but don't miss the Sunday Brunch. Take your pick from 50 different brunch specialties at this local's favorite.

"It was over 20 years ago that I first visited the lovely Ritz-Carlton, Buckhead and I have been back ever since for its gracious Southern hospitality. I love that it has maintained a classic Ritz-Carlton traditional décor…and adore the Lobby Lounge for tea and jazz with cocktails!"

THE RITZ-CARLTON, BUCKHEAD
3434 Peachtree Road, N.E.
Atlanta, GA 30326
ritzcarlton.com

GEORGIA
ATLANTA

The St. Regis Atlanta

Meet The St. Regis Atlanta. She is polished and oh so pretty. In fact, if *Gone with the Wind* were set in the 21st century, it would likely take place at this glorious hotel. Take one look at that sweeping staircase with glittering crystal chandelier and you'll be conjuring up your best Scarlett O'Hara in no time.

Enjoy the privileged setting in prestigious Buckhead, just a few miles from downtown Atlanta. Everything about The St. Regis sparkles. Take the traditions of the old world, the sexy styling of Art Deco, and the sleek lines of contemporary décor and you have the sensibility behind this Southern charmer. The 120 rooms and 31 suites are enclaves of glamour and fitted with luxurious creature comforts. Butler service, of course!

The St. Regis Atlanta spoils its guests with white-glove services and first-rate amenities. Retreat to the sumptuous Remède Spa for sheer rejuvenation or linger around the impressive Pool Piazza. This elegant and welcoming place encourages you to relax in refinement… soothe tired muscles in the jacuzzi, enjoy the outdoor fireplace and cascading waterfall, or unwind at the Poolside Café & Bar.

"The King Cole Bar at The St. Regis New York introduced the Bloody Mary, so order a signature West Paces Mary at The St. Regis Bar Atlanta." The Long Gallery is certainly long on looks so sip tea and sample delicate pastries in this sophisticated space. Paces 88 American Bistro is the hotel's shining star and this restaurant is perfect for breakfast, lunch, and dinner. Take in the views of the landscaped gardens from this restaurant, where American fine dining is a revelation.

THE ST. REGIS ATLANTA
88 West Paces Ferry Road
Atlanta, GA 30305
stregis.com/atlanta

HAWAII
HONOLULU

Halekulani

Halekulani has been saying 'aloha' to guests for over 100 years. Halekulani, which means "house befitting heaven," is inextricably linked to the history of Oahu. Preservation and transformation has kept this Hawaiian hotel on the radar of savvy travelers for over a century.

The resort rests on five prime oceanfront acres on Waikiki Beach. The resort's five buildings are surrounded by open courtyards and lush gardens. The 409 rooms and 44 suites show off tasteful traditional Hawaiian and tropical décor with rattan furnishings, upbeat colors, and sensational views since 90% of the rooms face the beach and ocean.

"Halekulani's heated freshwater pool overlooking Waikiki

Beach is mesmerizing. Named the orchid pool because of its stunning mosaic of a Cattleya orchid and comprised of 1.2 million pieces of imported South African glass tiles, this pool is a true work of art." Sit in the sun on the spacious sun deck or head for the soft sand of world-famous Waikiki Beach.

Let the spirit of the Polynesian Islands wash over you at the tranquil Spa Halekulani. From couples treatments to alone time to treatments designed specifically for tweens and teens, this Spa offers it all in a peaceful setting. If retail therapy is more your bag, the six intriguing shops at Halekulani will have something for you to take home and treasure.

"Halekulani's casual dining spot, House without a Key, has sunny views and a Hawaiian spirit, but I enjoy it most at sunset with a Mai Tai in hand. Orchids has an elegant oceanfront island ambience with scrumptious Pacific Rim cuisine. For award-winning dining in a romantic setting, select La Mer."

HALEKULANI
2199 Kalia Road
Honolulu, HI 96815
halekulani.com

HAWAII
HONOLULU

The Royal Hawaiian

Known as the "pink palace of the Pacific," The Royal Hawaiian is a legendary beach resort. This Luxury Collection property opened in 1927 and has been providing guests with an idyllic Hawaiian island experience ever since.

Resting right on Waikiki Beach, The Royal Hawaiian is in the heart of Waikiki and is a perfect base for exploring the many exciting adventures in store for you in Honolulu.

Take the pinks and pastels of classic Hawaiian décor and give them a modern flair and you have the inimitable style of the Royal Hawaiian's 494 rooms and 34 suites. Mink boudoir pillows, raffia headboards, and tropical art add a slightly whimsical touch to these comfortable accommodations.

The accommodations are fantastic, but there is no doubt that the place to be at this resort is on the beach. Waikiki Beach with its famous views of Diamond Head is a sand and sun seeker's dream, but throw in the billowing canopies of the exclusive beach cabanas and you have discovered Eden. Play at the beach… but don't miss the dolphin connection, a unique program that will let you get nose-to-bottlenose with a dolphin. "Here is a perfect Royal Hawaiian day: nap on the beach, linger at the pool, then unwind at the Abhasa Spa, adjacent to the lush, historic gardens."

As the sun rises, traipse to Surf Lanai for a beachside breakfast. At sunset or day's end, listen to live music with a cocktail at the Mai Tai Bar, but remember to enjoy seafood by award-winning chef Jon Matsubara at Azure.

"I am always tickled pink at The Royal Hawaiian and you will be too."

THE ROYAL HAWAIIAN
2259 Kalakaua Avenue
Honolulu, HI 96815
luxurycollection.com/royalhawaiian

HAWAII
KAUAI

The St. Regis Princeville Resort

Welcome to a world of sophistication at The St. Regis Princeville Resort. This elegant resort, located on the emerald green northern coast of Kauai, rests atop a bluff with unsurpassed views of the crashing sea.

The 200 rooms and 51 suites represent the best of contemporary coastal beach design. Pleasing colors, warm woods, ocean views, five star amenities…it doesn't get much better. Oh, but wait, it does…

It all begins with the resort's gorgeous private Pu'u Po'a Beach… you might never leave. Sun by the spectacular infinity swimming pool, edged in lava rock and surrounded by lush tropical landscaping overlooking the beach and bay.

Spend quality time with the entire family at this luxurious haven overlooking sparkling Hanalei Bay. Learn to surf the waves, explore the kaleidoscope of colors under the sea on a snorkeling adventure, ride horseback along the majestic Na Molokama mountain range, hike Napali, or kayak on the Hanalei River. Play golf nearby on the courses, including one rated the best in all of Hawaii, the Prince Golf Course. You can do all of this and so much more when you make The St. Regis Princeville your Hawaiian home.

The resort's young voyagers program opens kids' eyes up to a world of fun Hawaiian island-style. Seek seclusion from the sun in the serene Halele'a (House of Joy) Spa. And, yes, it does live up to its name.

Whether at Nalu Kai, Makana Terrace, Napala Café, or The St. Regis Bar, casual sophistication is the order of the day. But leave it to The St. Regis Princeville Resort to bring award-winning chef Jean Georges Vongerichten to Hawaii. His Kaua'i Grill is a showstopper!

THE ST. REGIS PRINCEVILLE RESORT
5520 Ka Haku Road, Princeville
Kauai, HI 96722
stregis.com/princeville

HAWAII
KONA

Four Seasons Resort Hualalai

The Four Seasons Resort Hualalai is located on the north Kona coast of Hawaii's big island. This destination is astonishingly beautiful with 4,000 square miles of rain forest, tropical orchards, and rugged coastline. Carved from landscape formed by 19th century eruptions of the Hualalai volcano, the resort seamlessly blends with its surroundings.

"Exotic flora and rare birds are at home on the resort's lush grounds, where remnants of ancient lava flows can be discovered. The torch lighting ceremony held each evening is a lovely memory."

The Four Seasons' bungalow-style 192 rooms and 51 suites are set around shimmering pools and connected by landscaped walkways. The lanais or porches are ideal for enjoying the ocean views. The spacious luxury accommodations, peppered with an extensive art and artifact collection, are a throwback to Hawaii's heritage.

In addition to seven different pools (including a children's pool), there is a one-of-a-kind pond sculpted out of lava rock. This unique King's Pond is home to over 3,000 tropical fish, including green parrotfish and white puffers. Snorkelers and scuba divers will love this alternative to the Pacific Ocean.

"Share in the healing traditions of Hawaii at the Spa, play tennis on one of the eight courts, or play golf on the Jack Nicklaus course sculpted out of rugged terrain and black lava."

Beach barbecues, Asian-Pacific cuisine, even Italian food are all available at the five restaurants and bars. Go barefoot and have dinner in a poolside cabana or have an upscale oceanfront picnic for an extra touch of romance.

"My first choice of all the resorts on the Kona Coast is Four Seasons Resort Hualalai."

FOUR SEASONS RESORT HUALALAI
72-100 Ka`upulehu Drive
Kailua-Kona, HI 96740
fourseasons.com

HAWAII
LANA'I

Four Seasons Resort Lana'i at Manele Bay

A few miles off Maui discover the tiny island of Lāna'i (only 13 miles x 18 miles in size). This island is old Hawaii. Imagine mist-shrouded mountains and lush green forests set against white sand beaches, rugged lava cliffs, and crystalline waters. For a century, it was nicknamed "pineapple island" because of its pineapple plantations. In the American South, the pineapple is celebrated as a symbol of hospitality, so it's not just a coincidence that the Four Seasons Resort Lāna'i at Manele Bay selected this special place.

The resort's 215 guest rooms and 21 suites feature a classic tropical spirit with warm golden tones, rich cherry wood, wicker furniture, botanical artwork, and many beautiful East Asian accents. Bring a page turner and stretch out on the daybed on your private lanai, though you might not get much reading done with the lovely views of the landscaped gardens, Hulopo'e Bay, or the Pacific Ocean.

This oceanfront resort borders a marine preserve home to tropical fish and protected green turtles and spinner dolphins. Enjoy the sunny outdoors at the stunning beach or laze by the shimmering pool. The Jack Nicklaus-designed golf course, The Challenge at Manele, is certainly that…high above the crashing surf and built on lava outcroppings, the course knocks your socks off.

Dine outdoors in a variety of casually sophisticated settings or sit indoors in the Dining Room for a grand plantation estate atmosphere.

"When I first visited Hawaii in 1968, from Maui, all you could see were the pineapple fields of Lāna'i. Now, this tranquil place, home to Four Seasons Resort Lāna'i at Manele Bay, is my favorite Hawaiian resort."

FOUR SEASONS RESORT LANA'I AT MANELE BAY
One Manele Bay Road
Lana'i City, HI 96763
fourseasons.com

HAWAII
MAUI

Four Seasons Resort Maui at Wailea

Formed by two volcanoes that erupted long ago, Maui is Hawaii's most well-known island. Great beaches, luxurious resorts, and outstanding golf courses comprise this island destination.

Four Seasons Resort Maui at Wailea occupies 15 oceanfront acres and is a marvelous mosaic of pools, terraces, and gardens set against a white sand beach. The resort retains an intimate atmosphere in busy Wailea. Open air spaces, showcasing the dramatic views and inviting the fragrant breezes to waft through, are a sensational element of design at this resort. Reproductions of early Hawaiian furniture, paintings, sculptures, and crafts displayed throughout the resort capture the essence of Maui.

The 305 rooms and 75 suites are decorated in soft pastels indicative of the tropical locale. A carefree elegance is established with rattan and wicker furnishings with overstuffed cushions. Thanks to the resort's u-shaped architecture, almost all of the accommodations show off ocean views.

Topped off by a tall fountain in the center and a whirlpool at each end, the swimming pool is the heart of the resort. There is even a separate free form pool and a children's pool with slide.

The Spa at Four Seasons Resort Maui is the perfect tropical escape with 13 treatment rooms and three ocean-side hales.

Hawaii's fresh and abundant fish and produce are on the menus at the restaurants. "Ferraro's at Seaside is a must for sensational sunsets and yummy Italian cooking." Spago from celebrity chef Wolfgang Puck is a California meets Hawaii superstar, while DUO spotlights Pacific Rim cuisine.

"Whether here with family or on a romantic getaway, erupt with joyfulness at the Four Seasons Resort Maui at Wailea."

FOUR SEASONS RESORT MAUI AT WAILEA
3900 Wailea Alanui Drive
Wailea, Maui, HI 96753
fourseasons.com

HAWAII
MAUI

The Ritz-Carlton, Kapalua

Nourish your body and soul at The Ritz-Carlton, Kapalua. This elegant resort shares the treasures of Maui with you.

Set amidst a 23,000 acre pineapple plantation, the resort enjoys a prime location in an unspoiled region of Maui. Just ten miles north of Lahaine, a century-old whaling village, The Ritz-Carlton enjoys a rugged, natural setting overlooking the island of Moloka'i.

The plantation-style building is comprised of two six-story buildings that are contoured to the rolling terrain. Original paintings and ceramics by local Maui artists blend with furnishings that resemble a traditional Hawaiian plantation estate. All 356 guest rooms and 107 suites feature informal fabrics and tropical botanical artwork.

"The Ritz-Carlton is a golf and tennis paradise. Kapalua's Plantation Course and Bay Course offer two 18-hole golf experiences, each with distinct character, challenges and incredible views. Kapalua's Plantation Course was rated #1 in Hawaii by *Golf Digest*, while the Bay Course is an Arnold Palmer and Francis Duane collaboration." As the resort is certified as an Audubon Heritage resort, the golf course limits pesticide use and conserves water to protect area wildlife. Poised above the beach, the tennis courts are widely considered the finest in Hawaii. After a competitive game, escape to the three-tiered cascading swimming pool or walk the unspoiled beach.

Savor the flavors of the islands at one of the six restaurants and bars, where Hawaii's abundant fresh harvest and local catches are celebrated. Hankering for sushi? Dine at the new Kai Sushi for fresh sushi and Japanese dishes.

"Scenic views, comfortably chic settings, fabulous activities for young and old, and Hawaiian hospitality make The Ritz-Carlton, Kapalua unforgettable."

THE RITZ-CARLTON, KAPALUA
One Ritz-Carlton Drive
Kapalua, HI 96761
ritzcarlton.com

ILLINOIS
CHICAGO

Four Seasons Hotel Chicago

The capital of America's Midwest, Chicago is internationally recognized for its innovative architecture, thriving businesses, and creative arts scene. "My first trip to a major city was Chicago as a teenage Girl Scout. I fell in love with the energy and excitement and knew then that I would leave small town life behind for big city living."

The Four Seasons Hotel Chicago enjoys close proximity to Chicago's business and financial centers with a skytop location overlooking glittering Michigan Avenue. The hotel features unrivaled city views with Lake Michigan in the background, and is just steps from stylish shopping, or a short ride for family fun at Navy Pier.

"I never miss a visit to the acclaimed Art Institute of Chicago for its collection of Impressionists. The 68 Thorne Miniature rooms are an interesting display of European interior design."

Exuding refinement, the hotel's 160 rooms and 185 suites are an elegant place to call home while visiting the Windy City. Spectacular views of Lake Michigan or the Chicago skyline are a given from these accommodations located on floors 30 through 46, but don't overlook the interiors' chic contemporary décor fusing modern American with subtle French undertones. Completely renovated, their new look has been refashioned by renowned designer Pierre-Yves Rochon.

The Four Seasons offers a delightful refuge at the luxurious spa. The indoor pool, complete with a domed ceiling and Roman columns, is a classic retreat. The new chic restaurant featuring contemporary American Cuisine is the hottest thing in town.

"Go big at the Four Seasons Hotel Chicago – this hotel has more spacious suites than anyone in town."

FOUR SEASONS HOTEL CHICAGO
120 East Delaware Place
Chicago, IL 60611
fourseasons.com

ILLINOIS
CHICAGO

Park Hyatt Chicago

Michigan Avenue is the center of Chicago's world so make your world revolve around the perfectly sited Park Hyatt Chicago. You will be in the heart of the Gold Coast, where the Magnificent Mile tempts with hundreds of shops and award-winning restaurants.

The Park Hyatt Chicago, part of the 67-story Park Tower comprised of luxury boutiques, residences, and restaurants, is a stunner. Walk into the lobby - this handsome, sexy space crafted of rich, dark colors and contemporary élan makes a stunning first impression. The 185 rooms and 13 suites are elegant aeries with spectacular views of Lake Michigan or historic Water Tower Place. These spacious rooms are the picture of modern chic, while roomy terraces are a welcome addition despite Chicago's windy city reputation!

It is so easy to fit in a workout at the Park Hyatt Chicago. The fitness center is open 24 hours a day and with views of the city, you'll be energized to go that extra mile. You can get a wet workout in the lap pool located on the seventh floor of the hotel. A neat way to exercise is by borrowing one of the hotel's bikes and cycling through the city streets.

It's a good thing that exercise is so enjoyable at the Park Hyatt, since you might need it after a meal at NoMI. You can taste the creations at NoMI restaurant, lounge, or during the summer months, at the seventh-floor NoMI garden. NoMI is one of Chicago's top spots with modern European flavors and fantastic interior design.

Chicago is a city of masterful architecture, and the Park Hyatt Chicago is no exception.

PARK HYATT CHICAGO
800 N. Michigan Avenue
Chicago, IL 60611
parkhyatt.com

ILLINOIS
CHICAGO

The Peninsula Chicago

East meets Midwest at The Peninsula Chicago. This hotel exudes the graciousness of the Far East while imparting a modern Midwestern approach to hospitality. Elegant and affable, The Peninsula is a triumph in the heart of the Gold Coast.

Overlooking North Michigan Avenue, otherwise known as the Magnificent Mile, The Peninsula makes it easy to shop until you drop (the bags off, that is). In fact, the 20-story tower hotel rests right above the glittering jewels of Tiffany & Co. and that heaven for little girls – American Girl Place. Saks Fifth Avenue and Neiman Marcus are just across the street, but high style isn't limited to the shops, since this hotel shines everywhere from its glorious public spaces to its 256 rooms and 83 suites. Gentle gold tones create unimaginable warmth in the guest rooms. Enjoy the views of the city skyline and the bustling streets or Lake Michigan.

Peninsula Hotels are known the world over for their dedication to wellness. The Chicago property proudly continues that tradition with an over-the-top ESPA Spa. Located on the hotel's top floor, you can tame your tension with a series of treatments in this sophisticated space.

Afternoon tea is unbeatable in the Lobby Lounge, where you can even treat yourself to a chocolate buffet and regular fashion shows. Pierrot Gourmet captures the spirit of a casual French café. Is there anything better than warming up with a steaming beverage and a pastry on a cold winter's day? Shanghai Terrace delivers a taste of Asia, but Avenues is the hotel's golden child with top awards.

"Elegant sophistication with an Asian flair makes The Peninsula Chicago one of the city's greatest hotels."

THE PENINSULA CHICAGO
108 East Superior Street
Chicago, IL 60611
peninsula.com

ILLINOIS
CHICAGO

The Ritz-Carlton Chicago, A Four Seasons Hotel

Chicago is known as the windy city. "I always thought it was from the wind coming off the lake…to be told when I visited as a salesperson in the mid-1960s that it was attributed to all the 'hot air' from the traveling salesmen (me included)!"

The Ritz-Carlton Chicago, a Four Seasons Hotel, reigns over Chicago from its lofty position atop Water Tower Place. It is just two blocks from Lake Michigan and five minutes from the financial center, but shoppers adore its location adjacent to Michigan Avenue. The hotel is the crowning glory of the city's Water Tower, a vertical shopping mall filled with fine stores.

Tasteful, contemporary style defines The Ritz-Carlton Chicago. Soft gray and cream tones set a refined mood in the hotel's 344 rooms and 90 suites. Located on floors 15 through 30, the views are sparkling, whether you look out over Michigan Avenue, the city skyline, or even toward Lake Michigan. The corner Anniversary Suites have large bathtubs that let you soak away the troubles of the day while soaking up the marvelous floor-to-ceiling views.

The Spa at The Carlton Club is a temple of well-being with a well-equipped fitness center, indoor pool, and tranquil spa. Treat yourself to a restorative massage, body treatment, or facial in this urban retreat.

"Named for its 2010 debut, Deca Restaurant + Bar is the 'in' spot in downtown Chicago. Order light bites and drinks at the Bar, but when it comes time to dine, look no further." Perfect morning, noon, and night, this brasserie is terrific. Deca delivers the classics with a modern edge in a casually elegant setting.

THE RITZ-CARLTON CHICAGO, A FOUR SEASONS HOTEL
160 East Pearson Street at Water Tower Place
Chicago, IL 60611
fourseasons.com

MARYLAND
ST. MICHAELS

The Inn at Perry Cabin

Does your busy life have you feeling crabby? Banish that bad mood and head straight for Maryland's scenic Eastern Shore. This beautiful coastline will wash away all your worries.

The Inn at Perry Cabin, an Orient-Express hotel, is the embodiment of an elegant Chesapeake Bay getaway. The original American colonial era house was built in 1816 by a former naval aide-de-camp of Commodore Perry. Today this charming manor house with three period looking buildings rests in magnificent gardens that stretch out to the gently lapping waters.

The 78 rooms and suites are characterized by country charm with a refined blend of nautical and colonial influences. "All are soft and airy, but my favorites are the Water View Master Suites." Walk into Victorian St. Michaels to explore boutiques and ice cream parlors, but return to take in the fresh air, admire the gardens, and swim in the sparkling pool. Named for the delicate trees that line the Inn's entrance, the nature-based Linden Spa is ideal for reflection, relaxation, and rejuvenation.

If The Inn at Perry Cabin looks familiar, it was the site of the wedding reception in the film *The Wedding Crashers*.

The Inn at Perry Cabin's restaurants and culinary traditions are superb. Treat yourself to afternoon tea. Purser's Pub, with a roaring fireplace, is a classic nautical pub and perfect for delicious snacks and meals. For a gourmet dining experience with views of the water that look like they were lifted from an oil painting, Sherwood's Landing is just right. "The delicious cuisine features local seafood with homegrown garden herbs. You can't beat any of their crab delicacies."

THE INN AT PERRY CABIN
308 Watkins Lane
St. Michaels, MD 21663
perrycabin.com or
orient-express.com

MASSACHUSETTS
BOSTON

Four Seasons Hotel Boston

Oh boy, Boston is such a charmer. This colonial city has a classic New England spirit. Packed with universities, Boston has a young and vibrant energy, but it never forgets where it came from. Walk its streets and you will encounter history at every corner – this city really celebrates its roots.

"Make the Four Seasons Hotel Boston your Beacon Hill residence. Overlooking the peacefully beautiful Public Garden, the Four Seasons is a relaxed, yet elegant, environment for business or pleasure." You are within steps of the city's top cultural, entertainment, and outdoor attractions. The hotel exudes comfort from the moment you check in to the time of your departure. The superlative service will have you feeling right at home (or better!).

The exceedingly inviting 196 rooms and 77 suites offer a contemporary twist on New England décor. Soft colors, colonial style furnishings…it's all so Boston, but even better. Many accommodations offer views of the Public Garden, Beacon Hill, and the gilded dome of the State House, while others overlook a landscaped plaza and city streets.

Swim laps in the indoor pool or unwind in the whirlpool. Windows from floor-to-ceiling truly bring Boston indoors. The fitness center is a boon for athletic-minded guests, and in-room spa services are a welcome treat after a long day of meetings or sightseeing.

Watch "Beantown's" business brokered over breakfast and lunch in The Bristol Lounge at the Four Seasons Hotel Boston. City dwellers and business people flock to this see-and-be-seen scene. At night, its farm-to-table American food is equally popular with guests and locals alike.

"Take pride in the Four Seasons Hotel Boston."

FOUR SEASONS HOTEL BOSTON
200 Boylston Street
Boston, MA 02116
fourseasons.com

MASSACHUSETTS
BOSTON

The Liberty

You won't need to don regulation stripes for a stay at this big house, at least anymore. The Liberty Hotel has been liberated from its former life as a prison, and you will feel far from caged inside this unique Luxury Collection hotel.

Resting at the foot of Beacon Hill, The Liberty is centrally located just steps away from shopping, dining, and Boston Common. With direct access to the Charles River Esplanade, it is ideal for running and biking, or sailing and kayaking in warm weather. You are free to roam as you please.

The 288 rooms and 10 suites are airy and bright. With many connecting rooms, why not bring the family? Cool, contemporary furnishings and sleek design make these accommodations comfortably cutting edge…being granted a life sentence in these rooms would be perfectly fine.

"The multi-tiered and striking lobby with exposed brick walls is the heart of the hotel. Its dramatic patchwork design is slick and sophisticated. Just let your mind wander as you sit in a chair and listen to live piano."

The intriguing restaurants and bars pay homage to the hotel's former incarnation. From casual patio dining at The Yard to drinks at The Liberty Bar or Catwalk, open to hotel guests only, this hotel knows how to entertain. Be let out on good behavior and you can enjoy the sensational restaurants. Scampo is Italian to the core, Alibi is sexy and seductive, and Clink is all American with a twist… when is the last time you dined (on gourmet food, nonetheless) in an original jail cell?

"Give me solitary confinement at The Liberty any day!"

**THE LIBERTY HOTEL,
A LUXURY COLLECTION HOTEL**
215 Charles Street
Boston, MA 02114
luxurycollection.com/libertyhotel

MASSACHUSETTS
BOSTON

Mandarin Oriental, Boston

Just because Boston has strong Yankee roots doesn't mean this city lacks international flavor and flair. Just look at the elegant Mandarin Oriental, Boston for proof!

The Mandarin Oriental promises an exceptional stay in Boston. With direct access to the famed Prudential Center's businesses and shops, the hotel's Back Bay location is terrific. Situated on Boylston Street, the charms and delights of Newbury Street are just steps away.

Mandarin Oriental sprinkles a bit of the Far East in this sophisticated East Coast hotel, where 136 rooms and 12 suites are among the most spacious in the city. Snuggle in to these havens of luxurious comfort and enjoy a stylish décor with overtones of contemporary international flair with soothing colors. Asian hints include silks, fabrics, and accent pieces.

"The Spa at Mandarin Oriental, Boston is a world of serenity. This 16,000 square foot spa and fitness center is the ultimate urban oasis. From quartz crystal steam rooms, vitality pools, experience showers, and ice fountains, you'll be relaxed before you have even entered the treatment room!" Be sure to book a signature spa therapy like the transporting four-hand massage – pure heaven! Afterwards, nurture your body with a fresh meal at the spa café.

Take a seat overlooking bustling Boylston Street at Asana. Inside, hand-carved limestone block walls, rich exotic wood floors, and banquette seating create an elegant modern Asian ambience. The food takes New England traditions and updates them with scrumptious results. Wagyu beef burgers, Jonah crab and watermelon soup, apricot chiboust brulée…are you booking a table yet?

"Back Bay is so Boston, and the Mandarin Oriental is a wonderful sleek new addition."

MANDARIN ORIENTAL, BOSTON
776 Boylston Street
Boston, MA 02199
mandarinoriental.com

MASSACHUSETTS
BOSTON

The Ritz-Carlton, Boston Common

The Ritz-Carlton, Boston Common is anything but common. Instead, this hotel is a place of five-star comforts and luxuries.

Located in the heart of downtown, it is a short walk to the historic Freedom Trail and Faneuil Hall Marketplace, and just steps from picturesque Boston Common. Did you know that it is the oldest public city park in the United States? You can take in Boston's beauty and culture from this prestigious location.

The 150 rooms and 43 suites are the height of elegance. Traditional blues and yellows and gleaming cherry wood furnishings with classic lines hint at Boston's colonial past, while city views plant you firmly in the present day. Ritz-Carlton pampers guests with white-glove services, but for an added level of luxury, book a room on the Club level, which offers the ambience of a hotel within a hotel with a dedicated concierge, lounge, and numerous delightful food presentations every day.

While staying at The Ritz-Carlton, Boston Common, guests are invited to attend classes, swim in the pool, or work out at the Sports Club/LA Boston. Afterwards, pop over to the Spa & Salon Marc Harris to look as good as you feel.

Have a cocktail at the impossibly chic Avery Lounge. Its mid-century mod mood is sleek and sophisticated and you can even channel your best *Mad Men* impression with one of ten signature martinis. Artisan Bistro is the newest addition to the hotel and impresses with its spirited décor complete with a zinc-top bar. The place buzzes with a contagious high energy, but the food is as attention grabbing.

"The Ritz-Carlton, Boston Common is uncommonly fantastic."

THE RITZ-CARLTON, BOSTON COMMON
10 Avery Street
Boston, MA 02111
ritzcarlton.com

MASSACHUSETTS
BOSTON

Taj Boston

In a city of landmarks, the Taj Boston is an aristocratic landmark of its own.

The Taj occupies a premier address at Arlington and Newbury Streets and overlooks Boston Public Garden and Boston Common. Watch ice-skating at Boston Common's Frog Pond in the winter or the dreamy swan boat rides at the Public Garden in warmer months.

The hotel first opened in 1927, this iconic building was completely restored in 2002 to celebrate its 75th anniversary. Its museum quality collection of art and antiques is on display throughout the hotel. There is a strong artistic and literary tradition at the hotel, as well. Tennessee Williams wrote part of *A Streetcar Named Desire* here, and Oscar Hammerstein composed the lyrics to "Edelweiss" in his room's shower. Richard Rodgers composed "Ten Cents a Dance" on a piano in his suite at this hotel.

It is easy to see why so many were inspired once you are ensconced in the hotel's 227 rooms and 45 suites. Traditional furnishings and rich fabrics lend a historic edge to the elegant accommodations... some even have fireplaces.

The hotel's tradition of excellence for guests and Bostonians is evident throughout, from the clubby Bar well known since 1930s, to international dining in the informal Café, to the perfect afternoon tea (scones, silver and all) in the French Room.

"During my college years in Boston, this hotel was known as The Ritz-Carlton and was my first encounter with a luxury hotel. It was a special treat to meet someone there for drinks, dinner, or a tea dance."

"Boston's grand heritage is alive and well at the Taj Boston."

TAJ BOSTON
15 Arlington Street
Boston, MA 02117
tajhotels.com

MASSACHUSETTS
LENOX

Blantyre

Set in the foothills of the Berkshires, stately Blantyre brings a bit of Britain to the Massachusetts countryside.

Built at the turn of the century by wealthy businessman Robert Patterson, Blantyre was modeled after his wife's ancestral castle in Scotland. "No matter the season, this 100 acre estate is glorious. The deliciously rich colors of autumn appear like spun gold, a light dusting of snow is like a winter wonderland, while luxuriant greenery harkens spring's arrival. However, it is summer that brings music to your ears with nearby Tanglewood and the Berkshire Theatre Festival."

Blantyre is the sort of place where Edith Wharton would feel right at home, and indeed she was a guest here in the early 1900s for a lavish garden party. This baronial estate's formal gardens and croquet lawns make it easy to imagine the scene.

Four-poster beds, charming fabrics, floral wall coverings, and period antiques set a romantic tone in the accommodations. The Tudor-style main house has 8 rooms, many with fireplaces, while the nearby Carriage House welcomes guests to 12 cozy rooms. Four private cottages also reflect Blantyre's illustrious heritage with elegant country décor.

Rise early for scrumptious breakfasts and go into the countryside toting one of the chef's special picnic baskets. Dining at Blantyre is rather like an intimate dinner party. Chef Arnaud Cotar turns out splendid dishes with European inspiration. These elegant feasts are served grandly on tables laid with damask and set with delicate bone china and antique crystal.

"I love to stay at Blantyre to relive a more genteel time. The manor is exquisitely beautiful and the dining is divine."

BLANTYRE
16 Blantyre Road
Lenox, MA 01240
blantyre.com

MASSACHUSETTS
LENOX

Canyon Ranch Hotel & Spa

You don't need to go to Arizona to find the ultimate spa destination. Simply head to Massachusetts and the lovely Berkshire Mountains. In the tiny town of Lenox, Canyon Ranch Hotel & Spa entices guests to slow down and rejuvenate in picturesque and beautiful New England.

Lenox is a short drive from Boston, but this all-inclusive restorative resort is as far from the rat race as you can get. Learn more about health, nutrition, and exercising, but spend your free time surrendering stress at the spa. You'll leave with more than a memento; take home a new healthy outlook on living.

Canyon Ranch is tucked inside the elegant Bellefontaine Mansion, where 102 rooms and 24 suites share a classic New England spirit and are filled with creature comforts like feather beds topped with luxurious Italian linens. After busy days packed with everything from biking down country lanes, hiking the area's mountains, and group fitness classes to cooking classes and informative presentations, you'll be glad to tuck yourself in!

Lace up your sneakers and experience a new world of exercise opportunities. In addition, Canyon Ranch offers a unique health and wellness program with a team of top doctors that focuses on whole body wellness.

It's not just about working up a sweat at Canyon Ranch, because the huge spa complex is the end all and be all of spa facilities. You can chill out with a Canyon Stone massage or unwind with a candlelit Euphoria body treatment. Every muscle in your body will be relaxed using ancient, traditional, and modern therapies for restoration and renewal at Canyon Ranch Hotel & Spa.

CANYON RANCH HOTEL & SPA
165 Kemble Street
Lenox, MA 01240
canyonranch.com

NEVADA
LAS VEGAS

Four Seasons Hotel Las Vegas

Las Vegas is over the top. This eye-popping destination never goes to sleep and its glittering lights and endless energy are equal parts exhilarating and exhausting. Founded by gold miners, Las Vegas continues to attract modern-day treasure hunters looking to strike it rich at the tables.

There are times when the crowds and exuberance proves too much…for those times, stay at the Four Seasons Hotel Las Vegas. "This hotel bucks the city's trend of over-indulgence and instead offers a respite from the glitz. It is luxuriously serene and soothing." As a non-gaming hotel on the famous Las Vegas Strip, the Four Seasons offers a refined change of pace. Should you feel the urge to roll the dice, Four Seasons is connected to the Mandalay Bay Resort and Casino.

Set on the 35th to 39th floors of the Mandalay Bay tower and accessed exclusively by Four Seasons express elevators, the 336 guest rooms and 86 suites have neon views of the famed Strip, mountains, or desert.

Relax at the Spa, where you will be pampered in style. Try the tropical escape – a therapeutic massage, foot, and body scrub that transports you to the islands.

"Cool off from the scorching heat at the swimming pool, a true oasis. Its lushly landscaped pool deck makes a perfect afternoon escape."

Guests have privileges at Mandalay Bay's 22 restaurants, but with Verandah and Charlie Palmer Steak right here, why leave?

"Have your cake and eat it too at the Four Seasons Hotel Las Vegas, where you can enjoy the many exciting shows and outstanding dining of Las Vegas but with a genteel touch."

FOUR SEASONS HOTEL LAS VEGAS
3960 Las Vegas Boulevard South
Las Vegas, NV 89119
fourseasons.com

NEVADA
LAS VEGAS

Mandarin Oriental, Las Vegas

It's sinfully sophisticated at Mandarin Oriental, Las Vegas. This trendsetting hotel could make others green with envy, thanks to its forward-thinking LEED certification. "It might be environmentally friendly, but it's also fashion forward."

Take it all in from the 23rd floor lobby, a sanctuary with picture windows overlooking the bright lights of Las Vegas, then retreat to one of the sleek and sophisticated 334 rooms and 58 suites. The accommodations blend subtle Asian accents with international influences. Throw in mesmerizing views and you have the unique appeal of the Mandarin Oriental.

"Mandarin Oriental, Las Vegas is a non-gaming hotel, making it an oasis of serenity." Nobody ever said you couldn't relax in Vegas and the Spa is a temple of Asian-influenced wellness. The look is exotic 1930s Shanghai and the feel is sublime. It's one of only 20 spas in the United States awarded five stars by *Forbes Travel Guide*. Two cascading pools, two plunge pools, and poolside cabanas are proof that you can never be too far from the water's edge, even in the desert.

Mandarin Oriental pulls out all the stops in its restaurants. Spice things up with Indian, Thai, or sushi at Mozen Bistro or live it up at the Mandarin Oriental Bar. The crowning achievement is Twist by Pierre Gagnaire. This three Michelin starred chef selected the Mandarin Oriental as his only American location, so book ahead!

"The Mandarin Oriental Hotel Company general managers and sales managers recently honored Valerie Wilson Travel's consultants for a Chinese tea at the Mandarin Oriental, Las Vegas. It was a special way to begin the annual Virtuoso Travel Mart."

MANDARIN ORIENTAL, LAS VEGAS
3752 Las Vegas Blvd. South
Las Vegas, NV 89158
mandarinoriental.com

NEW MEXICO
SANTA FE

Encantado

Spiritual and artistic, Santa Fe dances to the beat of its own drum. This place has sparked the imagination of hundreds of artists, including Georgia O'Keefe, who moved here for its glorious light. Of course, even if you can't draw a perfect circle, you can still enjoy the mysticism and magic of this special place, especially if you are at Encantado.

This Auberge Resort is nestled on 57 acres set against the foothills of the Sangre de Cristo Mountains. Blissfully quiet, the views of the Jemez Mountains and Rio Grande River and Valley are simply unparalleled. Santa Fe's unique character can easily be explored from this location, but if you choose to secret yourself away in this retreat, that's perfectly fine too!

The spirit of the Southwest is carried over to the 65 casitas, where native designs and architectural styles are enhanced by traditional furnishings and accents. Burnt sienna hues are dramatic against the largely white palettes, while fireplaces add a welcoming element to these already inviting accommodations.

Santa Fe has long been known as a mecca of healers. Encantado's luxury spa oozes understated sophistication. Treatments look to all parts of the world…here you will find traditional Eastern medicine, Ayurvedic therapies, and regionally-focused Native American treatments. There is a little bit of something for everyone.

Auberge Resorts made a name for itself at Auberge du Soleil with its gourmet restaurant, so it's not surprising that Terra, Encantado's signature dining room, is one of Santa Fe's top spots. Its strong focus on organic and local products combined with a patriotic dedication to American flavors makes it a special treat.

ENCANTADO
198 State Road 592
Santa Fe, NM 87506
aubergeresorts.com

NEW YORK
NEW YORK

The Carlyle, A Rosewood Hotel

The Carlyle, a Rosewood Hotel, is an intimate hotel on a grand scale. Since 1930, The Carlyle has held a special place in the hearts of many world travelers.

Inviting you to escape to its genteel world, The Carlyle is positioned uptown on Madison Avenue, lined with chic boutiques and elegant residences. The hotel's original character remains intact, and unique touches can be found throughout this dramatic and seductive hotel. Just off the main lobby, an intricately carved fireplace stands guard and a beautiful postal box reminds you of the days when letter writing was an art.

The Carlyle's 123 rooms and 64 suites share in the hotel's grand history. Dorothy Draper and Mark Hampton once lent their creative genius to these accommodations, while present-day stars Thierry Despont and Alexandra Champalimaud have infused the rooms with contemporary panache. Walls are decorated with Audubon prints, English countryside scenes by Kips, and architectural renderings by Piranesi.

My, what stories The Carlyle could share! Blue bloods, queens of the silver screen, and leaders of nations have all made this hotel their hideaway. It is said John F. Kennedy rendezvoused with Marilyn Monroe here.

No visit to this landmark is complete without a night at Café Carlyle. And then there's fun Bemelmans Bar… famed for its *Madeline* murals. The Carlyle Restaurant is adored by Upper East Side socialites and hotel guests who dine here regularly on Dover sole and lobster thermidor.

"The Café Carlyle has been my favorite Upper East Side haunt for almost five decades. I may not have rendezvoused with JFK, but I did sit not too far away from him at his preferred back corner banquette."

THE CARLYLE, A ROSEWOOD HOTEL
35 East 76th Street
New York, NY 10021
rosewoodhotels.com

NEW YORK
NEW YORK

Four Seasons Hotel New York

Bustling 57th street could very well be the center of the universe – at least in New York. This nerve center of energy has it all, with major offices, international flagship stores, and honking taxis, so it may seem surprising that a peaceful haven could be smack dab in the middle of Manhattan. Oh, but it is…at the Four Seasons Hotel New York.

World-renowned I. M. Pei designed the Four Seasons to be a temple of tranquility. Glide past the doors into the cool and calming marble lobby. "French limestone columns draw the eye upwards – take a seat, sip a cool drink, and enjoy the view for a bit."

The 305 rooms and 63 suites have unparalleled Big Apple views. Triple paned windows ensure that only the sights, and not the sounds, fill your room. The décor is sleek and contemporary. Simple lines, soothing honey tones of English sycamore wood, fine buttery leathers…it's all so sophisticated.

The spa takes its Big Apple location very seriously. Book the big apple treatment to enjoy a brown sugar and apple body scrub.

The Four Seasons is well known for its power meals and its two restaurants have some of the hottest names in Manhattan. The Garden restaurant, with its four 20-foot African acacia trees, is a lovely oasis in midtown, but do not miss legendary chef Joël Robuchon working his magic at L'Atelier de Joël Robuchon. The open kitchen allows a sneak peek at this true artist at work.

"The striking architectural wonder that is the Four Seasons Hotel New York is even more spectacular today than it was 20 years ago on opening night."

FOUR SEASONS HOTEL NEW YORK
57 East 57th Street
New York, NY 10021
fourseasons.com

NEW YORK
NEW YORK

Mandarin Oriental, New York

Mandarin Oriental, New York towers above Columbus Circle from its prestigious location atop the Time Warner Center. This is Manhattan like it was meant to be seen…sky-high views, sleek mod style, and fine dining and shopping just an elevator's ride away.

Go big or go home might as well be the mantra at Mandarin Oriental. This hotel does everything top-notch and in the most glamorous way. "First up, the impressive sky lobby – it will take your breath away."

Save some oohs and aahs for the sumptuous 202 guest rooms and 46 suites. With floor to ceiling views of Central Park or Hudson River, the Manhattan skyline will definitely make you feel like a master – or mistress – of the universe. The interiors are va-va-voom, with shimmering silks and other Asian accents blending seductively with contemporary furnishings.

The spa really wows with its gorgeous Asian design and ambience. Bamboo, stone, and gold leaf set a luxurious mood in this spectacular urban retreat where your wellness journey is inspired by the Far East. The indoor lap pool is flooded with sunlight and boasts river views.

"The Lobby Lounge personifies *Sex in the City* for a bite any hour of the day, while MOBar is a cool and chic spot for cocktails and chatter. Mandarin Oriental's showpiece is certainly the alluring Asiate, which elevates your senses with its American-Asian fusion cuisine. Floor-to-ceiling windows frame views of Central Park, while the über-hip ambience crafted by renowned designer Tony Chi is sensational. A glittering tree branch sculpture is suspended from the ceiling…a dramatic wall of wine houses over 1,300 bottles…it's all so marvelous at the Mandarin Oriental, New York."

MANDARIN ORIENTAL, NEW YORK
80 Columbus Circle at 60th Street
New York, NY 10023
mandarinoriental.com

NEW YORK
NEW YORK

The Peninsula New York

The Peninsula is housed in a stunning Beaux Arts building on the corner of 55th Street and celebrated Fifth Avenue.

The façade of The Peninsula New York is glorious with Doric columns and limestone carvings. Completed in 1905, the building was designed to complement the neighboring University Club. The grand world of Fifth Avenue, with its glittering and world-famous stores, is just outside the front door.

The 185 rooms and 54 suites are handsomely appointed with polished woods, contemporary furnishings, and some Art Nouveau period pieces. Known worldwide for its fabulous technological innovations, The Peninsula does not disappoint. Adjust the lighting, temperature, and in-room entertainment with the touch of a finger. My favorite rooms look down Fifth Avenue, while upper level rooms enjoy views of Central Park in the distance.

Shake up your fitness routine at The Peninsula's fitness center and pool. Its sky-reaching views, along with the indoor pool's panoramic vistas, are simply unparalleled in New York. The Peninsula Spa by ESPA is a contemporary Asian sanctuary in the heart of Manhattan.

"Experience a quintessential New York ambience at The Peninsula, where you can take your pick from three decidedly different venues for a cocktail before dinner or for a night cap after the theater. The Bar at Fives is contemporary with piano music, the elegant Gotham Lounge lives up to its name, whether for tea or a favorite watering hole, but nothing tops the view and 1930s Shanghai ambience of the Salon de Ning rooftop bar at The Peninsula New York."

From The Peninsula capped bellman's greeting to your sumptuous surroundings, The Peninsula New York is tops.

THE PENINSULA NEW YORK
700 Fifth Avenue at 55th Street
New York, NY 10019
peninsula.com

NEW YORK
NEW YORK

The Pierre

New York is constantly moving and changing. Overnight sensations wake up to discover they are yesterday's news. Something new emerges before you've had a chance to remember what was there! Luckily, some things remain the same. The Pierre has always been one of the city's grandest hotels. Reopened in 2009 after a $100 million transformation by Taj Hotels, it continues as one of the city's shining stars.

This landmark has one of the most envied locations in Manhattan, resting right on tony Fifth Avenue and overlooking leafy Central Park. This dignified hotel opened to great fanfare in 1930. Inspired by a French château, the beautiful 41 story building soon became the preferred choice among the crème de la crème of society. The Pierre has always hosted glamorous balls and weddings.

The resplendent lobby is large, yet maintains an intimacy. The 140 stunning guest rooms and 49 magnificent suites are dressed to the nines. Many showcase views of Central Park, while others share the city's charms.

The Jiva Spa is a recent addition after The Pierre's acquisition by Taj Hotels. In keeping with the hotel's Indian ownership, this refuge of serenity shares Indian traditions and therapies.

"Some of the city's greatest traditions are at The Pierrre. Enjoy afternoon tea in the beautiful rotunda with its dreamy murals and majestic staircase. What an honor it was for me to cut the 'peach' ribbon to officially open the new sleek and stylish 2 E Bar." For a little bit of London in New York, dine at Le Caprice.

"I selected The Pierre for a gala to say thank you to everyone from Valerie Wilson Travel and our preferred travel partners for our 30th anniversary. What a splendid evening was had by all."

THE PIERRE, A TAJ HOTEL
2 East 61st Street
New York, NY 10021
tajhotels.com

NEW YORK
NEW YORK

The Plaza

The Plaza and New York City are synonymous. This legendary hotel has long been a city landmark. It has appeared in countless films and even inspired the children's character Eloise. "Ask any New Yorker for their favorite memory of The Plaza and you'll likely get a different story. From the Palm Court, where taking tea has been a rite of passage for generations, to the Oak Bar, where you can feel the history in the walls, The Plaza brings you Manhattan."

First opened in 1907, The Plaza's grand baronial architecture is an iconic image rising above Central Park from a prestigious Fifth Avenue address. This landmark hotel recently underwent a $450 million transformation to bring back its glamour. "It dazzles like a brilliant diamond."

The 180 rooms and 102 suites are richly decorated with Louis XV-style furnishings and a regal air, but King Louis didn't order room service from an iPad, did he? The Plaza marries the old world and the new with fabulous results.

The Plaza is a top destination for beauty as the home of the renowned Warren-Tricomi Salon and the tantalizing Caudalie Spa, but nothing captures the timeless spirit of this grand dame better than the legendary Palm Court. Long a part of the Plaza tradition, the romantic Palm Court has served as a setting for scenes in many popular novels and films, most notably, F. Scott Fitzgerald's *The Great Gatsby*.

Shop til you drop at The Plaza's wonderful array of stores. You can pick up everything from a bauble to a bag to a burger here.

Meet me at The Plaza in a New York minute.

**THE PLAZA,
A FAIRMONT MANAGED HOTEL**
Fifth Avenue at Central Park South
New York, NY 10019
fairmont.com

NEW YORK
NEW YORK

Hôtel Plaza Athénée

Hôtel Plaza Athénée, located on a pretty tree-lined residential street on New York's prominent Upper East Side, is one of the city's gems. "I knew the neighborhood well, as I lived on East 64th Street in the early 1960s."

"This enchanting hotel is blessed with the services and conveniences of a large hotel, yet its decidedly private manner makes it a favorite of visitors seeking a residential atmosphere." Indeed, with Central Park, the alluring stores of Madison and Fifth Avenues just a few blocks away, and the palatial residences of Park Avenue just a few doors down, you will feel like a native New Yorker.

Even the lobby feels like a private residence. Walk past the brass doors to this intimate space with gleaming marble, murals, and French antiques. Personalized service is a hallmark.

The 117 rooms and 25 luxurious suites are refined retreats. The hushed interiors inspire you to enjoy the finer things in life. Rich Asian fabrics and classic furnishings reflect the hotel's individualized style. Some suites feature dining rooms or solarium terraces with charming views of the city.

Locals often pop in for drinks at Bar Seine, where animal print fabrics, and golden lighting create a seriously sophisticated cocktail lounge. Arabelle's warm atmosphere with gold domed ceiling and murals of pagodas perfectly complements the delectable and inventive French cuisine with an Asian twist. "I recently was here for a meeting and it really is the uptown spot for a New York City power breakfast."

For a bit of Paris in the heart of New York, stay at the incomparably elegant Hôtel Plaza Athénée.

HÔTEL PLAZA ATHÉNÉE
37 East 64th Street
New York, NY 10021
plaza-athenee.com

NEW YORK
NEW YORK

The Ritz-Carlton New York, Battery Park

If you have ever felt yourself repeating the words, "give me liberty," The Ritz-Carlton New York, Battery Park is for you. This hotel gives you liberty alright…Lady Liberty, that is. From its Battery Park location, this sleek and modern hotel gives you unparalleled views of the iconic Statue of Liberty.

The adage is true – no man is an island – though Manhattan is. It's easy to forget that when you're sandwiched among skyscrapers, but when you stay at the southernmost tip of Manhattan at the Ritz-Carlton, views of the New York Harbor are everywhere.

The hotel features 259 spacious guest rooms and 39 beautiful suites with a modern Manhattan apartment sleekness. "Obviously, I prefer the accommodations facing the Hudson River. Peer through the telescope across to Ellis Island and the Statue of Liberty and enjoy the expansive views."

Wall Street is just steps away but if you prefer to take stock in your well-being, visit the spa or trade your wingtips for sneakers and hit the fitness center. Jog, walk, or bike along the promenade fronting Battery Park flanking the river for a scenic outdoor workout.

Feast on everything from lobster bisque to Alaskan halibut at 2 West, a modern American bistro where comfort food with a gourmet slant is bullish. Indoors, it perfectly captures the cool atmosphere of downtown Manhattan with floor-to-ceiling windows.

"Although it was a sad and difficult time, I was so proud to be part of the opening festivities of this hotel, which delayed opening from September 2001 to early 2002."

"There are a battery of reasons to stay at the incomparable Ritz-Carlton New York, Battery Park."

**THE RITZ-CARLTON
NEW YORK, BATTERY PARK**
Two West Street
New York, NY 10004
ritzcarlton.com

NEW YORK
NEW YORK

The Ritz-Carlton New York, Central Park

Central Park inspires and invigorates…from concert hall to grand theater, even outdoor living room. For many New Yorkers, nothing says success like a residence overlooking Central Park, but don't go looking for a real estate agent…just check in to the Ritz-Carlton New York, Central Park.

Standing sentry over Central Park. The Ritz-Carlton calls to mind the elegance of New York…horse-drawn carriages are outside…while white-gloved doormen await your arrival. You will immediately feel like you are being welcomed home as you step inside the exquisite Ritz-Carlton.

The 212 rooms and 47 suites define classic elegance. Lemon-colored furnishings, beds piled high with crisp white linens, and gleaming wood furnishings – fantastic! You will be bowled over by the views looking out over the city and Park.

Visit the La Prairie Spa for a decadent indulgence. This spa has the Midas touch and everything feels glamorously good here, including skin caviar facials and other princely pampering.

The grandness is felt everywhere, but especially in the sumptuously seductive Star Lounge. Dark woods, old-world furnishings..it's so rich. BLT Market is the wildly popular restaurant run by Laurent Touroundel who dishes out inventive and modern cuisine.

"Five years ago I thought my family Christmas dinner would be spoiled when I discovered my turkey had turned. No grocery stores were open; I couldn't even get enough duck from a Chinese restaurant! I was frantic. I decided to call The Ritz-Carlton, Central Park. The duty manager called back within an hour and much to my delight and pleasure had found a fully cooked turkey for me. Ritz-Carlton saved my holiday…now that's what I call unbelievable service!"

**THE RITZ-CARLTON
NEW YORK, CENTRAL PARK**
50 Central Park South
New York, NY 10019
ritzcarlton.com

NEW YORK
NEW YORK

The Setai Fifth Avenue

Are you an uptown girl or a downtown dude? It used to be that you had to make that choice. Not anymore! Meet me in the middle at The Setai. This sleek temple of style, managed by Capella Hotels, soars 60 stories above Fifth Avenue between 36th and 37th Streets. It's a perfect middle ground - literally and figuratively. Now you can have downtown edginess with uptown prestige all under one crowned roof at The Setai.

The 157 rooms and 57 suites are quite simply the last word in modern luxury. Black oak, limestone floors, and gleaming onyx make these stellar accommodations seductively handsome. Spacious and airy, they are among the largest in the city. Creature comforts are exceedingly plush; think closets lined with Hermes-quality beige leather, Pratesi linens, and Duxiana custom mattresses.

Auriga Spa is at once dazzling and serene. Dominated by the clean lines and simple sophistication of Asian design, this extensive spa is sleek and sexy.

The contemporary look continues at Bar on Fifth for drinks and dishes all day. This fashionable spot nails that hip New York feel with a trendsetting scene. "In the evening, this bar is one of the coolest in town." Climb the lobby's sweeping staircase and step out in sophisticated style at Ai Fiori, The Setai's fine dining restaurant. The focus is on French and Italian dishes with a modern and urbane twist, but the mood is most certainly Manhattan.

"I watched the city skyline change from my office windows as The Setai reached skyward. The lighted crown appears like a constellation on the Manhattan skyline. How appropriate for this shining star!"

THE SETAI FIFTH AVENUE
400 Fifth Avenue
New York, NY 10018
capellahotels.com

NEW YORK
NEW YORK

The St. Regis New York

When it was built in 1904, The St. Regis New York on 55th Street was New York's tallest building. It has long been surpassed in height, but it retains its impressive stature.

The polished revolving doors bring you into a rarefied world. Seeking a princely home for his wealthy friends, The St. Regis was commissioned by John Jacob Astor, who spared no expense in its construction. Gleaming marble floors, 22 karat gold leaf, glittering chandeliers, and Louis XVI furniture complete the elegant European décor.

Although Astor was on board the Titanic on April 15, 1912, the legacy he created lives on at The St. Regis over a century later.

The 164 guest rooms and 65 suites are pure luxury. Gilded mirrors, exquisite antiques, and silk wall coverings are just some of the sumptuous details in these palatial accommodations, where St. Regis butlers are on call 24 hours a day.

The King Cole Bar is a New York institution. Dominated by the massive Maxfield Parrish painting of King Cole, this bar has that wonderful old New York atmosphere. The Bloody Mary was introduced here in 1934. The St. Regis is a mecca of fine dining. The Astor Court is a lovely spot for afternoon tea, but Adour by Alain Ducasse is a gourmand's heaven with Michelin-starred French dining.

"I have so many fond memories of The St. Regis New York I can't count them all, but the most memorable was in late June 2010. I had the pleasure of dining at a table for ten with Prince Harry. He is so handsome, charming, and adorable that I wanted to adopt him!"

THE ST. REGIS NEW YORK
Two East 55th Street at Fifth Avenue
New York, NY 10022
stregis.com/newyork

NEW YORK
SARANAC LAKE

The Point

There are no signs that lead you to The Point, but you will most certainly know when you have arrived at this rustic Eden.

The Point rekindles the spirit of the grand Adirondack camps of the early 19th century when the Vanderbilts and Posts came to the Adirondacks to live out their sylvan fantasies. The original country home of William Avery Rockefeller, The Point is gloriously situated on a ten acre peninsula on Upper Saranac Lake.

Do not let the native materials used in the exteriors fool you; The Point is rustic refinement at its best. Its stylish guest suites will delight discerning travelers. Eleven guest accommodations, spread throughout four buildings, are uniquely decorated with distinctive themes.

Massive stone fireplaces and custom-made beds with hand sewn mattresses add comforting touches, while antiques and Adirondack furniture provide a sense of place. Set away from the Main Lodge on the lake, the Boathouse resembles a houseboat and is a one of a kind suite.

The Point's grand style extends to its fine dining. Reviving the formal traditions of the Rockefellers, The Point encourages dressing up for dinner. The tantalizing flavors of the kitchen are enhanced by the lively conversations you will have with fellow guests in this grand dinner party atmosphere.

As the seasons change, so does The Point. Fishing, boating, and hiking are favorite pastimes in the spring, summer, and fall, while the winter brings cross-country skiing and ice skating on the lake. Or, just enjoy the great outdoors from your Adirondack chair with a terrific page turner in your hands.

Sit back and relax. After all, it is The Point.

THE POINT
222 Beaverwood Road
Saranac Lake, NY 12983
thepointresort.com

PENNSYLVANIA
PHILADELPHIA

Four Seasons Hotel Philadelphia

Philadelphia has so much to offer. From its impressive art museum (remember that famous scene in Rocky where he ran up the steps?) to its American heritage, history and culture abounds.

Close to everything, the Four Seasons Hotel Philadelphia is superbly situated at Logan Square in the center of the city. "Nearby, businesses and cultural attractions await, but inside the Four Seasons, you will be welcomed to a gracious world filled with elegance and superior service."

The 268 rooms and 96 suites are stylishly decorated with beautiful fabrics, colonial colors, and reproduction furnishings. American heritage and Philadelphia's strong sense of tradition are honored in the rooms. Many have balconies overlooking Logan Square, while others face the hotel's courtyard garden with cascading waterfall.

Get your fill at the lovely Spa, with a classic European feel and a large variety of refreshing therapies. The fitness center and indoor swimming pool are ideal for keeping in shape or relaxing after a busy day of sightseeing. Take a break and relax on the pool deck landscaped with tropical plants.

Fine dining is synonymous with Four Seasons hotels, but the Philadelphia hotel really shines. The Swann Lounge's baby grand piano and fireplace invite you to a welcoming spot. "The Fountain Restaurant is an elegant dining room handsomely furnished with rich wood and subdued lighting. A consistent winner of awards, it is favored by Philadelphians for business deals and special occasions. Be sure to ask for a table with a view of the Swann Fountain!"

"Benjamin Franklin would be impressed, and I know you will love the Four Seasons Hotel Philadelphia… in the city of brotherly love."

FOUR SEASONS HOTEL PHILADELPHIA
One Logan Square
Philadelphia, PA 19103
fourseasons.com

RHODE ISLAND
WATCH HILL

Ocean House

Set on a bluff overlooking the Atlantic Ocean, the Victorian-style Ocean House is the epitome of a classic New England resort. This grand seaside resort seems like it was crafted straight from the pages of *The Great Gatsby*. Pull up to the circular driveway at this resort and you just might find a championship croquet match taking place. Ocean House begs you to don your whites and embrace New England's preppiness and prestige at its best.

This classy coastal resort has been welcoming guests since 1868. While it treasures its rich history, Ocean House is a breath of fresh air with a modern flair. Everything is straight off the pages of a home décor magazine with its gorgeous summer home design, complete with comfortable furnishings, a massive stone fireplace, and that natty New England know-how.

Let the sea breezes wash over you in the sun-drenched 49 rooms and suites. Soft colors and wood furnishings lend a Yankee feel in the delightful accommodations. Sea views, best enjoyed from the terraces, make mornings particularly enjoyable.

The OH! Spa is a tranquil space for relaxation and reflection. Inspired in large part by its seaside setting, the spa uses marine-base ingredients in many of its treatments. The indoor-outdoor lap pool is a beautiful place to take a dip or lounge in a chaise.

Ocean House charms diners with its wide array of selections ranging from raw bar on the porch to elegant indoor dining in the restaurant. Sunday brunch is packed with locals who come for the bountiful buffet of scrumptious sweet and savory treats.

Ocean House is still the one to watch in Rhode Island.

OCEAN HOUSE
1 Bluff Avenue
Watch Hill, RI 02891
oceanhouseri.com

SOUTH CAROLINA
BLUFFTON

The Inn at Palmetto Bluff

Get away to the luscious Low Country of South Carolina at the incomparable Inn at Palmetto Bluff.

Set along the beautiful May River, this Auberge Resort is the centerpiece of an exclusive 22,000 acre riverfront community, nature preserve, and world-class golf destination.

The Inn at Palmetto Bluff is a Southern charmer. This delightful country getaway is perfect for golfers, spa-goers, families, and couples. You can also visit the garden of good and evil (at midnight or otherwise) in Savannah, just a quick drive away.

The Inn's 50 cottages and cottage suites are beautifully appointed with a classic Southern style. Vaulted ceilings, cozy fireplaces, decadent bathtubs, even verandas and screened-in porches with dramatic views that simply beg for a sweet tea and a rocking chair…it's all yours while staying at The Inn at Palmetto Bluff.

The Spa is a wondrous place of Low County living at its best. Signature therapies include the Southern Comfort treatment, the May River revival, and cypress and juniper baths. For a real treat, bathe to the sounds of nature on your private outdoor veranda overlooking the maritime forests and rivers.

Activities abound. The 18-hole Jack Nicklaus-designed course snakes along the May River and is studded with centuries old live oaks for a scenic, and oh-so-Southern, challenge.

Those 12 and under have lots of exciting adventures as a PB Explorer…camping, crabbing, fishing…it's limitless. Tweens and teens even have their own island, Page Island, for day and evening activities.

Exceptional dining is a hallmark of the Inn; four restaurants dazzle and delight.

Inn at Palmetto Bluff, you can call my bluff anytime!

THE INN AT PALMETTO BLUFF
475 Mount Pelia Road
Bluffton, SC 29910
aubergeresorts.com

TEXAS
DALLAS

The Joule

The name does say it all. The Joule, a Luxury Collection Hotel, sparkles like a jewel.

The Joule puts the dazzle in Dallas. Tucked inside a 1920s Neo-Gothic building, the Joule bridges past and present with exuberance and energy. While the exteriors were carefully restored and returned to their former glory, the intimate interiors are mystifyingly modern.

Famed interior designer Adam Tihany has once again performed his alchemy on the lobby and the 129 rooms. These interiors really pop. Unusual elements include round beds, red leather headboards, zebra print carpets, and lots and lots of stripes. It may sound haphazard, but it all works in a wonderfully creative way.

The hotel's museum-worthy art collection includes works by Richard Phillips, Andy Warhol, John Holt Smith, and Joseph Stashkevetch and gives the hotel a gallery-like vibe. From the rotating gear installations in the striking lobby to the original artwork in the accommodations, art is a part of life at The Joule.

The Joule really shines with exceptional features. A spa suite offers spa services 24/7…book a midnight massage! The cantilevered heated rooftop pool is like nothing else you have seen. Suspended beyond the building's edge, it seduces guests with sweeping views of downtown Dallas. Pool patio dining with light bites by Charlie Palmer expands your horizons.

PM Nightlife Lounge is a white hot spot for cocktails and conversation with a sultry, subterranean pull. Charlie Palmer at The Joule draws carnivores and those with a taste for gourmet American cuisine in an upscale setting.

It doesn't just look cool, The Joule, a Luxury Collection Hotel, is cool.

**THE JOULE,
A LUXURY COLLECTION
HOTEL**
1530 Main Street
Dallas, TX 75201
luxurycollection.com/joule

TEXAS
DALLAS

The Ritz-Carlton, Dallas

Dallas is all yours at the unforgettable Ritz-Carlton, Dallas. This luxurious hotel embodies the glamour of Dallas from its location in the heart of Uptown. This neighborhood is a magnet for visitors, offering gourmet dining, upscale shopping, live entertainment, and lovely parks and gardens. When you stay at The Ritz-Carlton, you are enveloped by this fashionable and fun area.

The 167 spacious rooms and 51 suites feature a charming, traditional Southern style. "The interiors are awash in elegant sophistication, yet lack a stuffy, pretentious feeling." Salmons, golden tones, burled woods, and contemporary Southwestern artwork all create a classic ambience. Lounge by the hotel's guest-only outdoor pool before going to the spa. This luxurious spa will have you dancing the two step with its gracious facilities and alluring treatments. Rejuvenating and restorative Healing Waters, dry cedar saunas, and eucalyptus steam rooms are just the beginning. Go for a signature facial or body treatments, including margarita salt glow, the ageless beauty facial, and the sensational Texas eight-hand massage.

Just when you thought it couldn't possibly get any better, it does. The Ritz-Carlton is home to Fearing's, the namesake restaurant of American celebrity chef Dean Fearing. "*Zagat* named it the best hotel restaurant in the United States...it is nothing short of miraculous." Even the dining room strays from tradition with a succession of indoor and outdoor settings instead of just one venue. You can feast on Fearing's delectable cuisine while watching the chefs at work, in the intimate Wine Cellar, or even in a glass pavilion overlooking a walled garden. Fearing's is a feat of accomplishment.

"The Ritz-Carlton does it up big in Dallas."

THE RITZ-CARLTON, DALLAS
2121 McKinney Avenue
Dallas, TX 75201
ritzcarlton.com

TEXAS
DALLAS

Rosewood Mansion on Turtle Creek

Rosewood Mansion on Turtle Creek is a Dallas landmark. Blending the old world elegance of a 1920s mansion with an expertly designed hotel tower, this hotel brings you the best of both worlds in Dallas' most fashionable residential neighborhood.

The Sheppard King Mansion is a former private residence built during the 1920s by a wealthy cotton baron. Inspired by the Italian Renaissance, the mansion is gloriously decorated with intricately carved ceilings, marble fireplaces, and a 32-foot high rotunda. Today, the mansion section is home to the highly regarded restaurant, bar, and private dining rooms.

The nine-story tower, constructed in the early 1980s after the mansion was purchased by Rosewood Hotels, perfectly complements the mansion. "Rosewood Mansion on Turtle Creek set the standards for all future Rosewood Hotels."

The 127 rooms and 16 suites exude Southern charm and grace. Recently renovated in 2009, the accommodations sport a contemporary elegance with an open, airy, uncluttered atmosphere.

The outdoor swimming pool is a perfect place to while away the afternoon. Refresh with a crisp salad or cool drink at the Pool Terrace.

The Mansion Bar has a wonderfully clubby ambience. Cognac-hued leather walls hung with modern art make a stylish setting – perfect for cocktails and comfort food. Shaded by mighty oak trees, the picturesque Terrace offers seasonal al fresco fireside dining. The delicious French and American food is courtesy of the award-winning Mansion Restaurant.

The Mansion Restaurant is a landmark within a landmark. This restaurant wows diners with excellent service and inventive American dining with French overtones.

"Everything may be big in Texas, but the Rosewood Mansion on Turtle Creek is a small jewel."

ROSEWOOD MANSION ON TURTLE CREEK
2821 Turtle Creek Boulevard
Dallas, TX 75219
rosewoodhotels.com

UTAH
CANYON POINT

Amangiri

Amangiri is tucked away from it all on 600 acres in Canyon Point. This area of southern Utah is near the Arizona border, but its dramatic landscape might just have you thinking you've landed on the moon. Its sweeping views toward Escalante National Monument, otherwise known as the Grand Staircase, are truly transporting.

Built around a central swimming pool with spectacular views, the resort seamlessly blends with its natural landscape of deep canyons and towering plateaus. Amangiri, which translates to "peaceful mountain," is just that. Only the second hotel in Aman Resorts' expansion into the United States, Amangiri shares the resort's signature understated sophistication.

With only 34 suites, Amangiri amazes guests with innovative design and luxurious comforts. White stone floors, concrete walls, and furnishings crafted of rawhide and natural timbers add a rugged element to the surreal spaces. Marvel at the uninterrupted views of the valley's dunes, plateaus, and mountain ridges. Views of the mesas at sunset are simply spectacular. Pool suites feature private plunge pools and wonderful sky terraces, ideal for sunning or star-gazing.

Like its sister Aman properties, Amangiri's spa is a masterpiece of relaxation. The design is dreamy…the entrance is reminiscent of nearby slot canyons, while the lounge area features a glass tiled, sky-lit reflection pool and a central fireplace. Navajo culture and traditions are behind the comprehensive treatment menu. Restore your "hozho," meaning "beauty, harmony, balance, and health" at this serene spa. Yoga, flotation pools…stress has definitely met its match in the middle of the Utah desert.

If you want to get away from it all, Amangiri is definitely for you.

AMANGIRI
1 Kayenta Road
Canyon Point, UT 84741
amanresorts.com

UTAH
PARK CITY

Montage Deer Valley

Fly into a major airport and in less than an hour you can be on the slopes of North America's top ski destination. Are you dreaming? No, you're in Park City.

Opened in December 2010, Montage Deer Valley harkens back to the era of the great mountain lodges of the West with its Craftsman architecture. Nestled mid mountain near the top of Deer Valley Resort, the location is unbeatable.

The 154 deluxe guestrooms and more than 66 suites and residences offer spacious accommodations with breathtaking alpine views. Gas fireplaces, elegant furnishings, custom bedding and linens…the living is very easy at Montage.

When staying at Montage, guests enjoy a coveted location atop Empire Pass with true ski-in and ski-out access to the number one ski mountain (*SKI Magazine* 2008-2011), but you don't need snow to enjoy this mountain getaway.

Year-round activities include hiking, biking, golf, and fly-fishing, and with Park City's historic Main Street just minutes away, you can dine, shop, and take in a few films (Sundance is held here annually). Don't forget to unwind at the beautiful alpine spa.

From your initial greeting by the valet to the ski and bike concierge staff, who store and prepare equipment, warm boots, and arrange lift tickets and lessons, the staff at Montage Deer Valley goes above and beyond.

Nature photography, guided hikes, mountain bike treks, and fly fishing…sound good? That's just for the kids, all available at the Paintbox children's program.

Be warmed by the luxurious comforts at Montage Deer Valley.

MONTAGE DEER VALLEY
9100 Marsac Avenue
Park City, UT 84060
montageresorts.com

UTAH
PARK CITY

The St. Regis Deer Valley

Nobody ever said that life in the mountains had to be rough and tumble. Move over rustic. The St. Regis is in town.

Nobody delivers luxury like The St. Regis Deer Valley. Here, you can have your mountain and your massage too. This hotel packs a serious punch when it comes to amenities. Ski-in and ski-out access to Deer Valley's impeccably groomed, award winning slopes? Naturally. How about a private "ski beach," complete with a split-level infinity swimming pool and adjacent hot tubs? Of course! What about a leading Remède Spa for complete pampering? The St. Regis has all this and so much more, including 24-hour butler service and ski valets.

Ideally situated in lower Deer Valley within the exclusive and private Deer Crest community, The St. Regis Deer Valley spoils guests with a glorious mountain setting. The 114 rooms and 67 suites are styled with a residential, country-contemporary ambience. Comfort may be king at The St. Regis, but style is certainly the queen. Picture-perfect views of the Wasatch Mountains are an added bonus.

Warm up with a hot beverage or cocktail in the Library or St. Regis Bar, while wine lovers will go straight for the Wine Vault. Take a break between ski runs and stop in for a snack at the Terrace Café… only The St. Regis would bring ski lodge snacks from Jean Georges Vongerichten! Overlooking both Deer Hollow Run and Deer Valley, the mountain terrace isn't bad either. For more of Vongerichten's talents, return for a memorable meal at his signature restaurant, J&G Grill.

The St. Regis Deer Valley is the perfect choice in this modern mountain resort.

THE ST. REGIS DEER VALLEY
2300 Deer Valley Drive East
Park City, UT 84060
stregis.com/deervalley

VERMONT
BARNARD

Twin Farms

Run for the hills…and straight for Twin Farms. Tucked away on 300 acres of rolling meadows blanketed in wildflowers, ancient gardens, and private ponds, Twin Farms is the ultimate country getaway in picturesque Vermont.

Twin Farms isn't just adorable; this getaway has a serious provenance. The original farmhouse, which dates back to 1795, was once the country home of Sinclair Lewis and his wife Dorothy Thompson. Lewis was the first to receive the Nobel Prize in literature, while Thompson gave Eleanor Roosevelt a run for her money in popular opinion.

The intimate 20 accommodations of Twin Farms are comprised of 10 suites in The Main House, Lodge, or The Farmhouse, as well as 10 individual cottages sprinkled amidst the property. Exteriors crafted of stone, pine, maple, and brick are the embodiment of the classic Vermont Cape-style farmhouse. But wait! It's not just New England niceties. Come inside for a look…you will find everything from marvelous Moroccan to artsy and modern. It's up to you.

At Twin Farms, you can do everything or nothing. Fly fishing, biking, and hiking. Each of the seasons brings a new way to enjoy the resort and the Vermont countryside. Come in from the outdoors to the Out of the Woods Spa, an award-winning retreat.

Whether you sip Pimms in the garden or mulled cider in the Pub, nothing says "good evening" like cocktail hour, but the food is something else. City chic with fresh country ingredients…you will look forward to each new meal with baited breath.

"Twin Farms is a romantic retreat in beautiful Vermont, but oh so special as a foodie heaven."

TWIN FARMS
P.O. Box 115
Barnard, VT 05031
twinfarms.com

WASHINGTON
SEATTLE

Four Seasons Hotel Seattle

Seattle has its own brand of urban sophistication. Defined by its rivers, lakes, and canals, Seattle is an incredibly cultured city with a thriving arts and entertainment scene.

Sharing the city's affection for the arts, the Four Seasons Hotel Seattle is the most deluxe hotel here. This Renaissance Revival masterpiece took the world by storm when it opened in the early 1920s as the Olympic Hotel. Its grand architecture and interior design were unprecedented in the West at that time. Terrazzo marble floors, antique mirrors, and Italian or Spanish statuary set a refined, formal tone that lingers today.

The Four Seasons is perfectly situated in downtown Seattle's Rainier neighborhood. Located near the financial and retail districts, the Four Seasons is within walking distance of the waterfront, Pike Place Market, and museums.

The 134 rooms and 13 suites offer a clean, contemporary look with soft, natural hues. The interior design is further enhanced by a selection of works by Northwest artists, all reproduced from the collection of the Seattle Art Museum.

From coastal Puget Sound to the evergreen rainforests, the spa's treatment menu is like a love letter to Seattle and the state of Washington.

Stay in shape with a swim in the outdoor pool.

Seattle has always been on the cutting edge of culinary movements, and the Art Restaurant & Lounge at the Four Seasons spotlights fresh fish and delicacies from the Pacific Northwest with an artistic flair.

"I select my Alaska family cruises so we can begin and end at the Four Seasons Hotel Seattle. I always take a room with a view…of Elliot Bay and Puget Sound."

FOUR SEASONS HOTEL SEATTLE
99 Union Street
Seattle, WA 98101
fourseasons.com

WYOMING
JACKSON HOLE

Amangani

Go West young man 'or woman' and see the majestically beautiful Jackson Hole. The snow capped Teton Mountains, the Snake River Valley, even the meadows…it all speaks to your soul and is the very definition of the ruggedly scenic American West. Even better, Jackson Hole is the southern gateway to Grand Teton National Park and Yellowstone National Park.

It is fitting that in the middle of this wonderful wilderness Aman Resorts chose to open its first U.S. resort. Amangani means "peaceful home," and is indeed that. Resting atop the crest of East Gros Ventre Butte, guests will be treated to an unspoiled landscape with magnificent views of the Grand Tetons and Snake River Valley.

Amangani offers 40 luxurious suites. The interiors pay homage to the rustic setting with woven cowhide chairs and faux wolf throws. Simplistic design with a true East meets Wild West is the mantra here.

Amangani's unique location offers panoramic views of the snow-capped peaks around Grand Teton National Park. The resort's private ski lounge at Teton Village is perfect…*Condé Nast Traveler* voted Amangani a top ski hotel. No matter the season, there's something to do in these great outdoors. Take a horse-drawn sleigh ride into the National Elk Refuge, and of course, white-water river rafting on the Snake River and excursions to Yellowstone and Old Faithful simply can't be missed.

One of the best ways to absorb Amangani is by doing nothing at all but resting by the misty pool or stretching out at the spa. Sit on your private porch and take in the view.

Be inspired to do nothing… it's the very essence of Amangani.

AMANGANI
1535 North East Butte Road
Jackson, WY 83002
amanresorts.com

WYOMING
JACKSON HOLE

Four Seasons Hotel Jackson Hole

Looking for a Rocky Mountain high? Look no further than the paradisiacal Four Seasons Resort Jackson Hole. Set high in the Rockies with easy access to Grand Teton and Yellowstone National Parks, the Four Seasons is a perfect year-round resort. Breathe in that fresh air, spot an amazing array of wildlife, and star gaze on perfectly clear nights. Just when you thought places like this didn't exist anymore, along comes the Four Seasons.

In a lodge-style building, the Four Seasons puts a polish on the rugged spirit of the Wild West. The 106 guest rooms and 18 suites are the embodiment of rustic refinement and cowboy chic with dark woods, abundant use of stone, and leather accents. Native American throw rugs and accents add to the local flavor of these inviting accommodations.

Let the tranquil beauty of the surroundings move you - to the spa, that is. Inspired by the serenity of the tranquil streams and expansive valleys of the mountain wilderness, the alpine spa is a mountain masterpiece.

Snuggled on the slopes of Jackson Hole Mountain Resort, the Four Seasons Resort is steps away from the Bridger Gondola, Eagle's Rest, and Teewinot chairlifts and overlooks over 5,000 acres of awe-inspiring skiable terrain, so it is a skier's dream come true, but there are endless year-round pursuits from this exceptional resort.

Savor the flavors of the American West with a focus on grilled meat, game, and fish in the cozy interiors of the restaurants. Warm your hands by a fireplace or sit outdoors around the fire pits on the terraces.

Hole up at this fabulous Four Seasons Resort.

FOUR SEASONS HOTEL JACKSON HOLE
7680 Granite Loop Road
Teton Village, WY 83025
fourseasons.com

MEXICO
CABO SAN LUCAS

Capella Pedregal

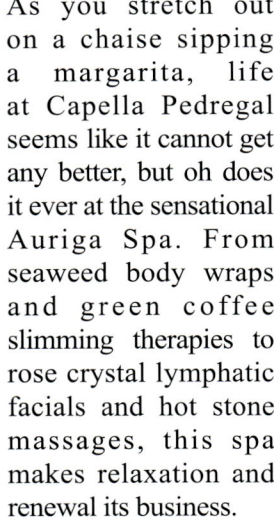

Capella Pedregal quite literally bridges two worlds, or oceans, since it sits right where the Pacific Ocean meets the Sea of Cortez. Like the Faraglioni is to Capri, the legendary rock formations of Land's End are to Cabo, and Capella offers a front row seat.

This luxury resort and spa seduces guests with its alluring views and sophisticated design. While you may feel tucked away from it all, you can easily walk to the village of Cabo San Lucas to experience the local culture, dine at area restaurants, and pick up a few souvenirs for friends and family. The 52 rooms and 29 suites all boast ocean views, private terraces with plunge pools, and unique Mexican handcrafted furnishings. Casitas and villas offer even more space and range from one to four bedrooms.

Seafood shack-style dining and elegant old world Mexican combine to offer gourmet cuisine in luscious settings that take advantage of the resort's cliffside locale.

As you stretch out on a chaise sipping a margarita, life at Capella Pedregal seems like it cannot get any better, but oh does it ever at the sensational Auriga Spa. From seaweed body wraps and green coffee slimming therapies to rose crystal lymphatic facials and hot stone massages, this spa makes relaxation and renewal its business.

CAPELLA PEDREGAL
Camino del Mar – 1
Cabos San Lucas 23455 Mexico
capellahotels.com

Pampering is Capella Pedregal's first, last, and middle name. The stunning infinity pool is the heart of the resort and the place to be morning, noon, and night. Poolside service includes everything from rose champagne to lobster tacos, but it is the lovely views stretching out to the Pacific that make this place feel worlds away from the everyday.

MEXICO
CABO SAN LUCAS

Esperanza

Think Cabo is just a Mexican version of Las Vegas with tequila-infused wild parties and Spring Break-style hoopla? Think again Esperanza, part of the exclusive Auberge collection of one-of-a-kind resorts, bucks the trend with its quiet luxury and unique charm.

Esperanza seamlessly blends the ambience and character of an inn with the superior amenities and services expected of a full-service resort. A darling of the media (and selected as Mexico's #1 resort in 2010 by *Travel + Leisure*), Esperanza deserves every word of its good press.

The gorgeous setting above the crashing surf is just the beginning. Its distinctive design, which can best be described as laid-back luxe, is a stand-out, but when blended with a private beach, gourmet dining, and a world-class spa, the results are unforgettable.

All 42 rooms and 15 suites have ocean views, and you will certainly remember relaxing in your own infinity-edge hot tub from your suite or casita, as you spot whales and dolphins frolicking in the distance.

The Spa at Esperanza is a temple of serenity and an integral part of the experience at the resort. With 14 treatment rooms, soaking pool, outdoor shower, and private sunbathing area, it is a comprehensive facility. Soothing aloe glaze body wraps, sea salt body polish treatments, and desert clay purification therapies are among the spa's signatures.

The circular palapa-roofed El Restaurante is carved into the bluffs overlooking the Sea of Cortez and is a romantic setting on three levels with Cocina del Sol "sun-filled" Mediterranean cuisine. Or, enjoy casual dining for lunch daily or dinner on weekends at La Palapa, with a swim-up bar and exhibition kitchen.

Hopes and wishes become reality at Esperanza.

**ESPERANZA
AN AUBERGE RESORT**
Carretera Transpeninsular KM 7
Manzana 10, Punta Ballena
Cabo San Lucas, Mexico 23410
aubergeresorts.com

MEXICO
CABO SAN LUCAS

Las Ventanas al Paraíso, A Rosewood Resort

Mexico's Baja peninsula is a stunning desert landscape dotted with flowering acacia and saguaro cacti. The warm waters of the Sea of Cortez and the wild waves of the Pacific Ocean meet here with a dazzling result. It is a playground for a wide variety of marine life, including dolphins, turtles, and whales.

Las Ventanas al Paraíso, or "windows to Paradise," is one of the region's most glorious resorts. Hugging the coastline above the sapphire ocean, Las Ventanas is a desert beach resort with a blend of Mediterranean and Mexican architecture. Grand hacienda-style buildings house 71 stylish and spacious guest suites. The resort's dedication to Mexican handicraft is noticeable throughout, with colorful native paintings, intricately carved furnishings, and traditional Conchuela limestone floors. Adobe or terracotta wood-burning fireplaces add a comforting touch. All suites feature telescopes, excellent for stargazing or observing whales in the distance.

The dramatic setting and graceful curves of the infinity-edge pools are the resort's signature and are the place to be and be seen at this posh hideaway. From tennis courts and a locally influenced spa to the Rose Buds children's program, the resort welcomes guests of all ages with its superior amenities.

A swim-up bar with in-water stools completes the buoyant mood. As might be expected, seafood and fresh ingredients from the 1,000-mile Baja Peninsula are a focus of the Restaurant and poolside Sea Grill. The tequila, ceviche, and sushi bar is just the spot for a snack or sip with an intoxicating atmosphere. "For a truly romantic evening have a private dinner on the beach."

Open the windows of your soul to paradise at Las Ventanas.

**LAS VENTANAS AL PARAÍSO
A ROSEWOOD RESORT**
Km. 19.5, Carretera Transpeninsular
San Jose del Cabo 23400 Mexico
lasventanas.com or
rosewoodhotels.com

MEXICO
CABO SAN LUCAS

One&Only Palmilla

There really is just one Palmilla. It is rare to find a hotel that has maintained its allure for so many years, but One&Only Palmilla stands alone as one of Cabo's most distinguished properties. It all began in 1956, when the son of the President of Mexico constructed a 15-room resort that immediately attracted the likes of John Wayne and Bing Crosby. They came for the sun, the deep-sea fishing, and the "forget all of your troubles" serene setting. What was hip then has been renewed decades later. One&Only, known for their standard-setting service, has expanded on Palmilla's legend and transformed this historic hideaway into one of the region's poshest getaways. Hollywood celebrities still seek the seclusion and hide out at this resort.

Today there are 61 rooms and 112 suites, but One&Only Palmilla's accommodations retain their intimate ambience with soothing Pacific or Sea of Cortez views and sun-splashed interiors enhanced with Mexican details. "For the ultimate in luxury, private jet to One&Only Palmilla's 10,000-square-foot incredible hacienda-style Villa Cortez."

One&Only Palmilla is well known for its award-winning Jack Nicklaus-designed golf course. This par-72 golf course has 27 holes with stunning views of desert landscapes set against the crashing sea. Take an excursion or charter the resort's private yacht, play tennis, or indulge in a soothing treatment at the spa, all while letting the kids have some fun of their own while making piñatas, playing tug-of-war, or practicing downward dog at the complimentary KidsOnly Club. After a busy day, find yourself at one of five restaurants or bars with an enticing array of food and drink.

The legend lives on at One&Only Palmilla.

ONE&ONLY PALMILLA
Km 7.5 Carretera Transpeninsular
San Jose Del Cabo, BCS, CP 23400
Mexico
oneandonlyresorts.com

MEXICO
IXTAPA

Capella Ixtapa, Resort & Spa

Carved into the craggy cliffs overlooking the Pacific Ocean, Capella Ixtapa invites you to slow down and enjoy the view.

This exceptional beach resort whispers of seduction and luxury from its unique vantage point in this quiet stretch of Mexico, where white sand beaches and quaint fishing villages urge you to stop and unwind from today's busy schedules.

With just 59 suites, this rarefied world is open to a limited number of visitors. "Each boasts an infinity-edge plunge pool for maximum enjoyment of the Pacific Ocean view… just imagine the sunsets!"

From the moment your room is booked to the time of your departure, Capella's renowned service and signature personal assistants attend to your every need. Capella's philosophy, like the double celestial star for which it is named, sets an exceptional standard of service between the hotel and its guests.

Everything about this resort has been designed to live harmoniously with its setting. From the open-air lobby to the traditional Mexican design mixed with modern elements, Capella Ixtapa is fresh and fantastic. Whether you are drinking in the view while sipping a cocktail at the poolside bar, surrendering to a massage in one of the outdoor treatment "rooms" at the 6,000-square-foot spa, or soaking in your plunge pool on your private terrace, it is about enjoyment of the outdoors. If you prefer to unwind by revving things up, your personal assistant is on hand to arrange everything from tee times at area golf courses to deep-sea fishing excursions.

Enjoy the peace and quiet of Capella Ixtapa.

CAPELLA IXTAPA, RESORT & SPA
Paseo Playa Linda
Ixtapa, Guerrero 40880 Mexico
capellaresorts.com

MEXICO
MEXICO CITY

Four Seasons Hotel México

Mexico City, the oldest capital city in the Western Hemisphere, is the cultural, political, and economical capital of Mexico. Its wide, tree lined boulevards are home to modern glass structures and low-rise colonial buildings. Like most cities, Mexico City pulsates with a frenetic pace.

Away from the whirlwind of activity, the Four Seasons Hotel is an oasis. Since 1994, this hotel has been considered one of the city's best. Its prime location on the Paseo de la Reforma places it near the major corporate, retail, and residential districts. The National Museum of Anthropology and History, one of the world's most notable museums, is within ten minutes of the hotel, and Chapultepec Park is just a five-minute walk. You can get almost anywhere from this hotel, but you may choose to simply relax within this sanctuary.

The eight-story city hotel celebrates colonial architecture while adding a European twist. The building surrounds a traditional Mexican courtyard with a trickling fountain. Most of the 240 guest rooms and suites overlook this tranquil setting. The accommodations tastefully blend European antiques and contemporary furniture with Mexican decorative objects.

From in-room spa treatments to knowledgeable concierge services, thoughtful service is evident throughout the hotel.

Fine dining Italian-style is available at Reforma 500, which overlooks the tranquil courtyard, while the library style El Bar is ideal for lunch. A swim in the rooftop pool is a great way to work off a decadent meal, especially if you dined on the chef's signature short ribs with hoja santa and guajillo scented asparagus risotto.

The Four Seasons Hotel México is a dynamic hotel in a vibrant city for business and leisure travel.

FOUR SEASONS HOTEL MÉXICO, D.F.
Reforma 500, Colonia Juárez
México, D.F. 1195 México
fourseasons.com

MEXICO
MEXICO CITY

The St. Regis Mexico City

The St. Regis is a modern architectural icon in Mexico City.

This bustling city is renowned for its architecture, but the Cesar Pelli-designed Torre Libertad, home to the St. Regis Hotel, is 31 stories of sleek modern design. Even in a city synonymous with architectural treasures, this sky-reaching tower stands out among the crowd on the Paseo de la Reforma.

As would be expected, the 153 rooms and 36 suites feature awe-inspiring city views, but the comfortably chic interiors also command your attention. Celadon, soft beiges, and rich plum colors set a serene and refined tone, while creature comforts and plush amenities, like 24-hour butler service, cosset guests.

Whether requesting secretarial services in the business center, seeking directions to a local attraction, or requiring assistance in the fitness center, attentive personal service is found throughout the hotel.

The St. Regis Mexico City brings a bit of its Manhattan flagship to Mexico with the King Cole Bar, inspired by the New York original, honoring the St. Regis tradition with its own signature Bloody Mary, the Sangrita Maria. J&G Steakhouse, by leading chef Jean-Georges Vongerichten, has been one of the city's hot spots since it opened in late 2011, but for upscale Mexican cuisine, head to Diana Restaurant.

THE ST. REGIS MEXICO CITY
Paseo de la Reforma 439
Colonia Cuauhtemoc
Mexico City, Federal District 06500 Mexico
stregis.com/mexicocity

The well-equipped fitness center brings new meaning to the term "runner's high" with its far-reaching views from your exercise machine. Take a relaxing dip in the indoor pool before or after a customized spa experience at the Remède Spa, or simply relax while gazing at the magnificent city view.

MEXICO
PUNTA MITA

Four Seasons Resort Punta Mita

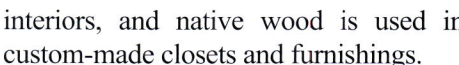

The Four Seasons Resort Punta Mita is a slice of paradise on Mexico's western coast overlooking the Pacific Ocean.

Punta Mita, northwest of Puerto Vallarta, is an enviable stretch of unspoiled landscape that is on the northern tip of Bahia de Banderas, one of the world's largest bays. Offering distant views of the rugged Sierra Madre Mountains, Punta Mita has abundant marine life and some of the finest beaches in Mexico. Each winter, the gray whales come to Banderas Bay to raise their young.

Designed to live in harmony with the spectacular setting, the Four Seasons Resort resembles a small village. The main building is open-sided and features a palapa roof, handwoven from palm fronds. The building overlooks the breathtaking infinity-edge pool that curves along a hill above the beach. It is indistinguishable where the pool ends and the ocean begins.

Traditional tile-roofed casitas house 141 guest rooms and 32 suites. Accommodations open out to terraces facing the garden or ocean, and all suites feature private plunge pools. Textiles hand embroidered by native Huichol Indians complement the serene interiors, and native wood is used in custom-made closets and furnishings.

Walk the beach, learn scuba diving, or snorkel the pristine waters. The 18-hole Jack Nicklaus-designed Pacifico golf course features the only natural island hole in the world, known as "the tail of the whale," and 199 yards out into the ocean! The Nicklaus-designed Bahia course is a putter's challenge. After a round, hit the spa for the Punta Mita massage, featuring sage oil and tequila.

"The Four Seasons Resort Punta Mita brings you Mexico like you have never seen it before."

FOUR SEASONS RESORT PUNTA MITA
Bahía de Banderas
Nayarit, Mexico 63734
fourseasons.com

MEXICO
PUNTA MITA

The St. Regis Punta Mita Resort

The St. Regis really outdoes itself. Not just a pretty face, this resort offers so many ways to play in the sun, shade, and sea.

Tennis players delight in the lessons and facilities at the Peter Burwash International-run tennis center. Golfers are treated to preferential tee times at two area Jack Nicklaus designed courses. Sun seekers take their pick from a stretch of sandy beach or three shimmering swimming pools. Take a deep breath and unwind at the Remède Spa, brush up on your Spanish, learn to mix Mexican cocktails like a pro, or sway to the beats in a salsa dance class. It is all part of the comprehensive experience. The kids can get in on all of the action at La Tortuga Children's Club, designed for children aged 5-12.

The multitude of activities may have your head spinning, but step inside the calming 89 guest rooms and 31 suites and you will find a decidedly elegant oasis. The spacious accommodations honor Mexican design heritage with tile floors and handwoven throws while incorporating sophisticated elements, such as the sensual outdoor showers.

Each of the four restaurants and bars has a unique setting, but all are guided by The St. Regis' dedication to service. Regional Mexican specialties are on the menu at Las Marietas Restaurant & Bar, while seafood is the focus at Sea Breeze and the well-regarded Carolina.

Whether for a honeymoon, a weekend getaway, or a family vacation, The St. Regis Punta Mita is right on point.

"Enjoy a luxurious Mexican holiday at The St. Regis Punta Mita, surrounded by lush gardens, water features, and the Pacific Ocean."

THE ST. REGIS PUNTA MITA RESORT
Lote H-4
Carretera Federal 200, km 19.5
Punta de Mita, Nayarit 63734 Mexico
stregis.com/puntamita

MEXICO
RIVIERA MAYA

Maroma Resort and Spa

Occupying 25 beachfront acres of a 500-acre coconut plantation, Maroma is at once lush jungle and silky soft beach. Bordered by the second largest barrier reef in the world, the area is a magnet for underwater explorers but with romantic accommodations and top-notch services, even landlubbers fall for this enchanting spot.

Mexico's Riviera Maya draws everyone from beach lovers to culture vultures who come to this region seeking everything from powdery beaches and pristine water teeming with marine life to fascinating ancient Mayan ruins.

Maroma's white stucco buildings with thatched roofs perfectly capture the essence of the tropics. Built by hand by a family of local Mayan Masons, this resort is part of the prestigious Orient-Express collection. There are just 65 accommodations at this retreat. Details like hand-loomed bed linens and rugs, original artwork, and handmade Mexican-tiled bathtubs (no two are alike!) proudly display local pride.

Dining at Maroma is a special treat, with three restaurants from traditional Mexican classics to Caribbean seafood specialties. Be sure to stop by Freddy's Tequila and Ceviche Bar, where Freddy will give you an entertaining lesson on the finer points of tequila drinking.

Get in touch with your inner goddess at Kinan Spa, where each treatment room is named for a different Mayan deity. Relax by one of three swimming pools or dig your toes in the powdery sand and enjoy the beachfront services, which include a variety of watersports.

Find your place in the sun at Maroma Resort and Spa.

"Maroma enjoys a close-to-perfect tropical garden and beach setting on the Yucatan Peninsula in the heart of the Rivera Maya."

MAROMA RESORT AND SPA
Highway 307, Km. 51
Riviera Maya, Quintana Roo,
77710 Mexico
maromahotel.com or
orient-express.com

MEXICO
RIVERA MAYA

Rosewood Mayakobá

Can you honor history while turning it on its head? You can if you are Rosewood Mayakobá. This resort's striking architecture hints at the region's famous ancient ruins while creating an entirely new look.

Everything about Rosewood Mayakobá is different than your average beach resort. Set on 1,600 acres carved out of the jungle and fronting the Caribbean Sea, the resort is designed to offer guests the ultimate luxury of complete privacy.

The 128 suites are nestled within the lagoons (actually cenotes which spring from subterranean rivers), and some suites are scattered along the beach. "There is nothing quite like the first impression you get when arriving by electric launch to your suite." Resembling a jungle treehouse with its contemporary angles and organic materials, the spacious suites are designed to maximize outdoor living. Many come with private plunge pools and outdoor rain showers.

Life at Rosewood Mayakobá could easily be enjoyed within the confines of these unique contemporary suites, but with so many first-rate offerings, it would be a shame to stay in. Laze away the day on the beach or by the curvy infinity edge swimming pool, or pop over to Sense Spa for a relaxing spa journey…even children are fascinated by this eco-friendly resort. Watersports abound in these marine life-rich waters or play golf at the nearby Greg Norman 18-hole course, as it snakes through Mayakobá. Visit Agave Azul or the Bar before indulging your appetite at Casa del Lago or Punta del Bonita.

"I describe the architecture of Rosewood Mayakobá as modern Mayan with beach elegance – perfect for a romantic getaway or a family vacation."

ROSEWOOD MAYAKOBÁ
Ctra. Federal Cancún-Playa del Carmen KM 298
Solidaridad, Quintana Roo, CP 77710 Mexico
rosewoodhotels.com

MEXICO
SAN MIGUEL DE ALLENDE

Casa de Sierra Nevada

If you think Mexico is limited to beach vacations with tropical drinks, you obviously have not been to San Miguel de Allende. This colonial Mexican city has nearly a 500-year-old history and has long been a favorite haunt of artists. Unique architecture and a funky vibe have contributed to this creative capital's status as a UNESCO World Heritage Site, as well as one of the most vibrant destinations in Mexico.

Stay in the heart of it all while at the Orient-Express Casa de Sierra Nevada. This one-of-a-kind hotel occupies a cluster of five buildings, including four colonial mansions, and is in the center of the city. Step outside and the sights and sounds are within your grasp. Of course, if those same sounds and sights prove a bit too much, retreat to the lovely Laja Spa.

This hotel offers the ultimate in intimacy, with just 15 rooms spread across the five historic buildings. The buildings have been painstakingly preserved but creature comforts abound. No two rooms are alike, yet all have perfectly captured the flourish and spirit of this energetic city.

Fine dining is an integral part of the experience, and Casa del Parque and Andanza are favored by guests and locals alike for their delicious regional cooking and pleasant atmospheres.

Take home a cherished memory instead of just a souvenir and sign up for the Sazon Culinary Experience, where you will tag alongside a chef on a market tour and then return for a class. You will certainly wow your guests at your next dinner party after learning a few secrets!

Savor the secrets of Casa de Sierra Nevada.

CASA DE SIERRA NEVADA
Hospicio 42
San Miguel de Allende, Guanajuato,
37700 Mexico
casadesierranevada.com or
orient-express.com

MEXICO
SAN MIGUEL DE ALLENDE

Rosewood San Miguel de Allende

San Miguel de Allende may have 500 years of history, but this alluring city doesn't rest on its laurels. Its vibrant personality can be seen in the spirit of its people and in the shops that line the cobblestone streets, but perhaps the best example of this constantly evolving city is the new Rosewood San Miguel de Allende resort. Quite simply, it is the hottest thing to hit Mexico since the silver rush.

Echoing the romantic colonial architecture of the city, the Rosewood resort is a sensational blend of arches, courtyards, and lush gardens, but the interiors are where Rosewood really shows off. From the lobby and restaurants to the 67 rooms, the décor showcases a striking and dramatic design which blends Mexican handicraft objects with a more modern approach. The accommodations, most with fireplaces, patios, and terraces, are inviting oases in this pulsating city.

The mix of old and new is found throughout Rosewood, especially at the 1826 Restaurant & Bar, where guests will find the classics alongside innovative dishes. Luna Rooftop Tapas Bar, populated with well-dressed locals and hotel guests, is the see-and-be-seen "it" spot in town.

Enjoy a swim in the sleek outdoor pool, relax in the gardens, or spend time in the top-floor Sense Spa. The joys of San Miguel de Allende aren't limited to adults at Rosewood, where the Rose Buds program entices younger guests with art workshops and Spanish language classes.

Everything is within a hop, skip, and a jump from here. Don't miss a chance to peruse the many charming boutiques – an interior designer's dream with fantastic furnishings and decorative objects!

**ROSEWOOD
SAN MIGUEL DE ALLENDE**
Nemesio Diez 11, Colonia Centro
San Miguel de Allende, 37700 Mexico
rosewoodhotels.com

CENTRAL AMERICA
COSTA RICA

Four Seasons Resort Costa Rica

From brightly colored birds and macaws to fragrant blooms, Costa Rica offers a kaleidoscope of color. This Central American country has long attracted nature lovers who trek here for its amazing bio-diversity and to revel in the beauty of a rugged landscape defined by golden beaches and lush rain forests.

The Four Seasons Resort Costa Rica at Peninsula Papagayo puts the elegance in eco-travel. Positioned on Costa Rica's northwest Pacific coast, it has a tropical setting. Terraced on a hillside down to an isthmus, this resort hideaway has not just one, but two, perfect white sand beaches.

The 60 guest rooms and 25 suites capture the essence of Costa Rica with comfortable rattan and bamboo furnishings, local artwork, and indigenous wood and stone. "My favorites are the canopy suites, which sit tree house-like on the hillside and offer exotic views through the forest canopy down to the water."

Golf is award-winning. Designed by Arnold Palmer, the 18-hole golf course is a stunner and is ranked among the "Best 100 Courses outside the United States" by *Golf Digest*.

Five restaurants and lounges exude a jazzy island spirit with terrific Latin and fusion food.

"The Four Seasons Resort Costa Rica is rich with delights."

FOUR SEASONS RESORT COSTA RICA
Peninsula Papagayo
Guanacaste, Costa Rica
fourseasons.com

It's not just about the beach, though they are fantastic… it's about the pools too! Set between the two beaches, three swimming pools surrounded by lush landscaping await swimmers and sunbathers. The chic spa uses mineral-rich muds and other local ingredients to heal your body and soul.

"It is worth the effort to go off property to zipline over the treetops of the fascinating rainforest!"

ARGENTINA
BUENOS AIRES

Alvear Palace Hotel

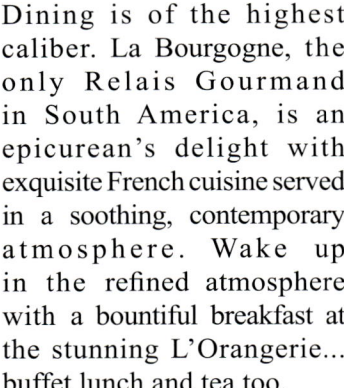

The very wide boulevards and French-influenced architecture prompt many to call Buenos Aires the "Paris of South America." The city's distinctly European flavor is due in large part to its residents, or porteños, as they are known, who often hail from abroad. Its unique blend of European grandeur and Latin sizzle makes Buenos Aires an exciting and sophisticated city.

The Recoleta district glitters with palatial mansions, chic cafés, and exclusive shopping. One of the city's grandest hotels, The Alvear Palace, shares a classic old-world elegance with guests. Step through the revolving doors to the rarefied world of the Alvear Palace, where the intimate lobby with rich furnishings and gleaming brass is reminiscent of Paris. Afternoon tea at the Alvear has become a local tradition, and the city's most fashionable women don their very best jewels and fashions to see and be seen.

The Alvear Palace's 97 rooms and 100 suites are classically European, with Louis XV and Empire furnishings. Objets d'art and fresh floral arrangements add a personal touch to the elegant rooms, and 24-hour personal butler service guarantees contentment. The hotel's personal shopping services are a boon to those with little time. Travelers who want to stay in shape or unwind will find a delightful fitness center, indoor swimming pool, and La Prairie Spa.

Dining is of the highest caliber. La Bourgogne, the only Relais Gourmand in South America, is an epicurean's delight with exquisite French cuisine served in a soothing, contemporary atmosphere. Wake up in the refined atmosphere with a bountiful breakfast at the stunning L'Orangerie... buffet lunch and tea too.

"The Alvear Palace Hotel proves that traditional elegance and first-rate service never go out of style."

ALVEAR PALACE HOTEL
Avenida Alvear 1891
1129 Buenos Aires, Argentina
alvearpalace.com

ARGENTINA
BUENOS AIRES

Four Seasons Hotel Buenos Aires

It is not often that you can find history and haute design in one setting, but leave it to the Four Seasons Buenos Aires to deliver the perfect blend of old and new.

How does the Four Seasons do it? By marrying a sleek, contemporary tower with a one-of-a-kind Belle Epoque mansion. Almost all of the 116 rooms and 49 suites are secreted away in the tower and offer a world of serenity within this bustling city. The accommodations feature a contemporary design and are packed with amenities. La Mansión is certainly the pièce de résistance at the Four Seasons and those with a penchant for historical details will fall head-over-heels for the seven special suites. Outfitted with an eye for classic French design, these suites have an unmatched personality.

Set within the Recoleta district, the Four Seasons Hotel Buenos Aires puts the city at your feet. Steps from the finest shops, hottest restaurants, and buzzing businesses, guests who call the Four Seasons their home have it all within their reach. Of course, with a state-of-the-art fitness center and luxurious spa that caters to your well being, a delicious Mediterranean restaurant, and one of the city's favorite brunches served in the lovely Mansión, there might not be a reason to ever leave. Looking for the best way to soak up this elegant hotel's ambience? Snag a chaise at the Roman style pool nestled within La Mansión's gardens.

"Take a tango lesson, wander through this eclectic city, and don't forget to shop for wonderful leather goods, but return to the Four Seasons Hotel Buenos Aires – your home away from home."

FOUR SEASONS HOTEL BUENOS AIRES
Posadas 1086/88
1011 Buenos Aires, Argentina
fourseasons.com

ARGENTINA
BUENOS AIRES

Palacio Duhau, Park Hyatt Buenos Aires

A premier location, stunning gardens, six venues for wining and dining, a fitness center with spa, and elegant accommodations…Palacio Duhau – Park Hyatt Buenos Aires certainly does not miss a beat.

This refined hotel delivers a comprehensive and luxurious experience. Wander the stunning gardens, pop over to the private art gallery, or browse the area's boutiques – it's all part of a stay at this posh Park Hyatt which occupies the former French Palace Duhau dating to 1932.

It may occupy a historic palace, but make no mistake about it – the Park Hyatt mixes things up inside and delivers one of the city's hippest interiors. Historic touches, such as crown mouldings, tall ceilings, and carved mantels, are a nod to the building's past, while the design in the 126 rooms and 39 suites is marvelously modern. Cool furnishings and polished wood floors set a contemporary mood, while oversized marble bathrooms and spacious workspaces are proof that Park Hyatt knows how to treat today's travelers.

"If you can splurge, step back in time and feel like the lord and lady of the Palacio Duhau when staying in your palatial suite."

From its steaks to its red wines, Argentina is celebrated for its cuisine, and the Park Hyatt's five restaurants and bars honor that heritage. Choose from the mind-boggling 7,000 bottles of Argentine wine at La Vinoteca or feast on Argentine cuisine at Duhau Restaurante.

If the gourmet food and wine has not elevated your senses, head to the Ahin Wellness & Spa for an ah-ha moment.

**PALACIO DUHAU
PARK HYATT BUENOS AIRES**
Avenida Alvear 1661
C1014AAD Buenos Aires, Argentina
parkhyatt.com

ARGENTINA
BARILOCHE

Llao Llao Hotel & Resort, Golf-Spa

It may be just a quick two-hour flight from Buenos Aires (and sister property Alvear Palace Hotel), but Llao Llao Hotel & Resort is a world away from the hustle and bustle of the capital city.

Known for its protected wilderness and rugged mountainous scenery, it wasn't until the 1930s that Patagonia was discovered as a tourist destination. This majestic place has maintained its lack of development and is a paradise for nature and outdoor enthusiasts. Since its construction in 1934, Llao Llao has been the home for those who want to "rough it," albeit in the lap of luxury.

It all begins with a picture-perfect setting in the lower mountains of the Nahuel Huapi National Park. "Designed to resemble an exclusive hunting lodge, the hotel maximizes the inspiring views of Moreno Lake and Mount Tronador. The impressive lobby, with its beamed ceilings, antler chandeliers, and leather furnishings, is decidedly masculine, while the 173 rooms and 32 suites share a softer side, many with floral fabrics and country style furnishings."

Llao Llao challenges guests with multi-seasonal activities. The resort is a veritable playground. Enjoy water sports, such as canoeing, kayaking, fishing, and whitewater rafting. Trekking, hiking, biking, rappelling, archery… if you can dream it, you can do it here. Of course, Llao Llao is a magnet for golfers, who come to swing on the acclaimed 18-hole course. During winter months, ski at the private mountain refuge, but remember to soothe your tired muscles at the relaxing spa.

"All that oxygen-pumping activity and fresh alpine air will stir up your appetite for the varied gourmand experiences at Llao Llao."

LLAO LLAO HOTEL & RESORT, GOLF-SPA
Av. Ezequiel Bustillo Km. 25
Bariloche, Río Negro, Argentina
llaollao.com

BRAZIL
IGUASSU FALLS

Hotel das Cataratas

Some hideaways promise the gentle lapping of ocean waves or the soft sounds of trickling fountains, but how many can promise the thunderous thrill of rushing water from a gigantic waterfall? Only one – Hotel das Cataratas.

This Orient-Express hotel is the only hotel located within Brazil's Iguassu Falls National Park. The privileged position allows for unmatched access to the mighty Iguassu Falls and an unbeatable natural setting rife with flora and fauna, but this resort offers so much more than just a great location. Hotel das Cataratas enjoys a long history of welcoming nature lovers – it has been open for more than half a century.

The distinguished colonial Portuguese design continues to the 178 rooms and 15 suites, where elegance is defined by colonial furnishings, bright pops of tropical colors, and uplifting prints. Tradition continues at the two restaurants and bar, where everything from the design to the menu reflects a proud Brazilian heritage.

Let the healing powers of the Amazon wash over you at the Spa, where sustainable ingredients straight from the lush rain forest are the basis for many of the restorative therapies. Soak up the sun and the lush setting at the swimming pool or let the little ones safely splash at the children's pool, but no stay is complete without one of the heart stopping adventures in the National Park. Adrenaline junkies will get their fill with everything from rock and tree climbing to river rafting, while those who prefer gentler adventures will appreciate the guided nature walks.

Get a front row seat to the action of Iguassu Falls at Hotel das Cataratas.

HOTEL DAS CATARATAS
Iguassu Falls National Park
Paraná, Brazil
hoteldascataratas.com or
orient-express.com

BRAZIL
RIO DE JANEIRO

Copacabana Palace

Brazil's Rio de Janeiro needs no introduction. Its playful, fun-loving spirit is renowned and perhaps best expressed in the annual festival of Carnaval, where the cariocas, or residents of Rio, take to the streets to dance until the wee hours.

Rio's infectious enthusiasm is closely tied to its beautiful beaches, and Copacabana Beach stands out as one of the city's finest. Reigning over this popular spot since the early 1920s, the Copacabana Palace is a glamorous hotel that has long been the darling of Rio society and the international jet set. The pulse of the city is felt just outside its refined doors.

Designed by a French architect who was inspired by the grand architecture of the French Riviera, Copacabana Palace has 116 guest rooms and 129 suites in the classic main building or tower wing. Fine art and antiques decorate the stylish rooms, which frame views of the world famous beach or the pulsating city.

Copacabana Palace has two restaurants with two very distinct atmospheres. Hotel Cipriani Restaurant shares the Italian delicacies made famous at the Orient-Express' sister Venetian hotel, while the poolside Pérgula is a breezy, casual spot. "Once the sun sets, I always join the fashionable locals at the Bar do Copa, which lights up the night with its white-hot scene."

Whether you choose to sun on its beaches or visit Sugar Loaf Mountain, Copacabana Palace provides the ideal location for experiencing Rio, but with a spa and salon, exclusive swimming pool and beach services, and hip nightlife, you never need to leave this bastion of sophistication.

COPACABANA PALACE
Avenida Atlantica 1702
Rio de Janeiro, 22021 001 Brazil
copacabanapalace.com or
orient-express.com

COLOMBIA
CARTAGENA

Sofitel Legend Cartagena Santa Clara

Experience the history and culture of Cartagena at the Sofitel.

The Sofitel offers an unparalleled peek inside the walled city of Cartagena de Indias Bay, a UNESCO World Heritage Center. This Spanish colonial city was founded in 1533, though historians have found evidence of earlier discovery during Pre-Colombian civilization. Grand architecture and lush beauty are two of the reasons to visit this unique South American city, but the Sofitel runs a close third. Originally built as a monastery in 1621, the hotel effortlessly honors its heritage while implementing 21st century modern luxuries. The ancient walls once offered religious seclusion, where today they envelop you in luxury. The lobby's cinnamon hued walls and Colombian objets d'art are the first sign that this hotel evokes the splendor of days gone by.

This 17th-century hotel is an urban oasis complete with its own gardens. The 103 rooms and 19 suites are gracefully decorated with two design schemes. Some rooms have a more contemporary look, while others reflect a country Colombian décor. Views of the internal gardens, ancient city, or the Caribbean Sea are an added bonus.

Dine on gourmet French cuisine in the original Clarisas nuns' dining room or enjoy a martini at El Coro, the original choir. At the Sofitel, the two restaurants and bar reflect traditions while offering fresh takes.

It is not likely that the nuns got to enjoy any downtime here, but modern-day guests certainly will. From the outstanding facilities at LeSpa, which includes eight treatment rooms, a fitness center, and serene terrace to the shimmering outdoor swimming pool, relaxation is next to godliness at Sofitel Legend Cartagena Santa Clara.

SOFITEL LEGEND CARTAGENA SANTA CLARA
Calle Del Torno 39-29
Barrio San Diego
Bolivar, Cartagena, Colombia
sofitel.com

PERU
COLCA CANYON

Las Casitas del Colca

Looking for a virtually undiscovered paradise? Peru's Colca Canyon is the answer.

Hidden away in southern Peru, the Colca Canyon is an unbelievably beautiful and peaceful place. Nestled within the rugged Andean mountains are the Colca Canyon's towns and villages, most of which have been untouched for 400 years. Twice as deep as the Grand Canyon but half as well known, Colca Canyon is a place of astonishing beauty.

World-weary travelers hoping to get away from it all will find their salvation at Orient-Express' Las Casitas del Colca. This hideaway is a collection of cottages that offer a unique vantage point on Peru's Andes, but with gourmet food sourced from the resort's own farm and a first-rate spa, there's nothing backward about this remote resort.

There are just twenty private casitas sprinkled throughout the property. Brick walls and Laja tiles are among the natural materials used in construction, but their simple exteriors belie the luxurious elements found within. From heated floors and heated plunge pools to bathrooms designed with skylights for soaking with a view, these casitas boast top-notch amenities.

Wend your way through the eucalyptus grove to reach the Spa Samay, which takes its name from the ancient Incan language. From herbs grown in the greenhouse to honey from the hotel's beehives, inspiration for many therapies has sprouted from the setting.

Explore the many tastes of Peruvian cuisine and pick up a few tricks to try at home during one of the cooking classes offered at Las Casitas del Colca. If you can tear yourself away from the resort's serene setting, try horseback riding in the Canyon, trekking, or condor spotting.

LAS CASITAS DEL COLCA
Parque Curiña s/n Yanque
Arequipa, Peru
lascasitasdelcolca.com or
orient-express.com

PERU
CUSCO

Hotel Monasterio

A rare blend of museum and five-star hotel, the Hotel Monasterio occupies the converted San Antonio Abad Seminary, originally built in 1592. It offers a peek inside Peruvian culture on a corner of an idyllic square in Cusco.

The colonial city of Cusco, with its terracotta-tiled roofs and blend of Incan and Spanish architecture, is a marvelous destination. The town's main square is a short walk and cobblestone streets lead you to fascinating ruins, bustling markets with colorful crafts and traditional festivals. The mysterious ruins of Machu Picchu are only 75 miles away and can be reached from this Orient-Express property by their scenic and luxurious train, the Hiram Bingham.

Hotel Monasterio's 107 rooms and 19 suites combine colonial and modern styles and incorporate many Incan decorative objects. A unique element of this hotel is its oxygen enriched rooms for those who may have trouble acclimatizing to Cusco's high elevation. It is easy to imagine the monks who resided here when you glance out your window to the cloistered courtyard.

Whether you are in your room or enjoying the stone courtyard or gardens, a great sense of peace pervades. Hotel Monasterio's 18th century chapel is glorious with intricate carvings, frescoes, and paintings that date from the Inquisition. The hotel even has its own resident ghost; an old woman in white is said to roam the roof late at night!

El Tupay, the monastery's original refectory, serves Peruvian and international dishes, while the Illariy Café, lined with the seminary's ancient paintings, offers continental cuisine. Or, dine in the outdoor cloistered courtyard.

HOTEL MONASTERIO
Calle Palacios 136
Plazoleta Nazarenas
Cusco, Peru
monasteriohotel.com or
orient-express.com

PERU
LIMA

Miraflores Park Hotel

Peru's vibrant capital city of Lima, a city bridging colonial treasures and cool, contemporary living, is home to the gracious Miraflores Park Hotel, an Orient-Express hotel.

It is fitting that the city's top hotel is also located in its most prestigious neighborhood, but this hotel goes above and beyond with its superior location. Directly across from Miraflores Park, the view from the hotel stretches from the rainbow of colors of the gardens to the sparkling blue of the Pacific Ocean.

Miraflores Park Hotel also exceeds expectations with its 82 spacious suites. From junior suites to presidential suites, this hotel's accommodations treat guests to amenities like in-suite roman baths, Jacuzzis, and saunas, in addition to private terraces with pools.

Enjoy breakfast with a spectacular city and ocean view from the 11th floor Observatory, where each morning outdoes the next with bountiful buffets. Mesa 18, with a sleek and modern design and cutting-edge menu, has established itself as one of Lima's top restaurants. Don't forget to order Peru's signature drink, a Pisco sour, at the Dr. Jekyll and Mr. Hyde Bar. Of course, should you choose to remain in the privacy and luxury of your suite, 24-hour room service is available.

Miraflores Park Hotel attracts both business and leisure travelers with its array of services. Zest Spa awaits the arrival of weary travelers, while the rooftop swimming pool will provide a refreshing wake-up call with spectacular views. Bath butlers are on call to draw baths catering to everyone from couples to gentlemen who want to enjoy a cigar while soaking away the stresses of the day.

MIRAFLORES PARK HOTEL
Av. Malecón de la Reserva 1035
Miraflores, Lima 18 Peru
miraflorespark.com or
orient-express.com

PERU
MACHU PICCHU

Machu Picchu Sanctuary Lodge

There are few places in the world that capture the attention and captivate the imagination like the ancient ruins of Machu Picchu. This Lost City of the Incas is one of the finest examples of Incan architecture. Built in the mid-15th century, it was hidden until discovery in 1911 by American explorer Hiram Bingham. A place of magic and mystery cloaked in mist by day and clear moonlit nights.

Let all the crowds come and go, since you will have the ruins essentially to yourself while staying adjacent to the ruins at the Machu Picchu Sanctuary Lodge. A room key at this unique lodge does not just give you a bed – it offers unprecedented early-morning, late afternoon, and evening access to the ruins, unavailable to others.

Stay in the shadow of the Lost City at this eco-friendly hotel that goes above and beyond to respect the environment and its sensational setting. From its use of strictly biodegradable products to its ban on plastics to its electric kitchen, this hotel puts its best foot forward when it comes to environmentally friendly practices.

The 29 rooms and 2 suites offer all of the modern comforts expected of an Orient-Express property while showcasing unbeatable views of the surrounding area. The eco-lodge atmosphere is evident from the outside, while the comfortable accommodations are in a regional country design.

Tampu Restaurant lets you rest your tired feet as you feast on a wide variety of Peruvian specialties. Need a lunch break from all that trekking? Refuel at the lunch buffet served at the Tinkuy Buffet Restaurant.

Elevate your senses at Machu Picchu Sanctuary Lodge.

MACHU PICCHU SANCTUARY LODGE
Machu Picchu, Peru
sanctuarylodgehotel.com or
orient-express.com

PERU
SACRED VALLEY

Hotel Rio Sagrado

Incan ruins, charming Andean villages, majestic mountains, the rushing waters of the Urubamba River, and access to Machu Picchu. This is all part of a visit to Peru's Sacred Valley and its lovely Orient-Express Hotel Rio Sagrado.

Hotel Rio Sagrado occupies an enviable location set amidst towering mountains and lush green acreage on the banks of the Urubamba River. Built to mimic the nearby Andean villages, this hotel is truly one of a kind. The 10 rooms, 11 suites, and 2 villas are designed to highlight a particular pride of place with their abundant use of natural stones and woods, bright pops of magenta and orange, and traditional Peruvian embroideries. Everything, including the placement of the beds, has been designed to take advantage of the views of this picturesque riverbank setting. Even the Spa Mayu Wilka (Sacred River) has been designed to reflect the area's Incan heritage.

El Huerto Restaurant and Bar both proudly showcase Peruvian and local specialties, and much of the food is sourced from the hotel's on-site farm. Enjoy a cocktail only a few feet from the soothing waters of the Urubamba River.

The Sacred Valley is rife with recreational and cultural activities. From horseback riding and river rafting to trekking the trail of the ancient Incas, there are a variety of opportunities for outdoor exploration. Of course, no visit to this region is complete without an excursion to Machu Picchu. Located on a lower elevation than nearby Cusco, but within a short distance of the renowned mystical ruins, the Sacred Valley is an ideal gateway for travelers with trouble acclimatizing.

Retrace history while making memories at Hotel Rio Sagrado.

HOTEL RIO SAGRADO
Km. 75.8, Carretera Urubamba
Ollantaytambo, Sacred Valley, Peru
riosagrado.com or
orient-express.com

ANGUILLA

ANTIGUA

BAHAMAS

BARBADOS

BERMUDA

CAYMAN ISLANDS

JAMAICA

Bahamas • Bermuda • Caribbean

NEVIS

PUERTO RICO

SAINT-BARTHÉLEMY

ST. JOHN

ST. MARTIN

ST. THOMAS

TURKS & CAICOS

VIRGIN GORDA

ANGUILLA

Cap Juluca

Resting between the Atlantic Ocean and the Caribbean Sea, Anguilla is a small and tranquil island only 16 miles long and 3 miles wide. The most northerly of the Leeward Islands, Anguilla enjoys British influences infused with a decidedly tropical flair.

"Though it was 1972, it seems like just yesterday that I sailed into Maundays Bay on a Chinese junk. At the time, this pristine, crescent shaped beach was an undiscovered slice of paradise, and I thought to myself, what a fabulous spot for a resort! I certainly wish I had become a hotelier then."

Set on 179 secluded acres, Cap Juluca is one of the world's most exclusive resorts. It brings a little bit of Morocco to the Caribbean with its inspired whitewashed architecture of turrets, domes, and parapets. The cool interiors of the 62 guest rooms, 29 junior suites, and 6 pool villas provide a relaxing atmosphere. There is no bad view at this resort, where all accommodations are steps from the sparkling turquoise sea and white sand.

If the sugar-soft sand of the beach is not enough to capture your attention, enjoy the bevy of watersports, including the resort's own 32-foot boat. Unwind at the spa, where the island's tropical flowers, herbs, and intoxicating scents are incorporated into many of the wellness rituals.

The family-friendly beachfront bistro, Blue, is a casual spot, while Spice heats things up with its Pan-Asian menu. Pimms Restaurant specializes in dressed-up dinners, where European styles and flavors merge with Caribbean ingredients.

"Cap Juluca, with its seductive architecture, magnificent beach, and relaxing activities, is a perfect beach getaway."

CAP JULUCA
Maundays Bay
Anguilla,
2640 British West Indies
capjuluca.com

ANGUILLA

CuisinArt Golf Resort & Spa

Food lovers instantly recognize the name, but CuisinArt isn't just a top-notch kitchen accessory. It's also a fantastic Caribbean beach resort favored by travelers seeking the sun in Anguilla. Located on a perfect sandy beach, CuisinArt is a refreshing and contemporary resort.

"Its whitewashed buildings with distinctive arches are reminiscent of the seductive Greek islands." Inside the 82 suites, 11 guest rooms, and 6 private villas, it is easy, breezy, and casually Caribbean. The resort's relaxed attitude is perfect for families, who will feel very much at home here.

A philosophy of healthy living and enjoyment of the outdoors prevails at CuisinArt. Water sports are plentiful and fitness enthusiasts may enjoy everything from aquatic kickboxing to beach boot camp. The Venus Spa and the Greg Norman-designed Temenos Golf Course duel for your attention. The golf course offers breathtaking views of the island and sea with spectacular water features and challenging holes. For a more sybaritic experience, make a beeline for the Venus Spa, where you will luxuriate in a tropical paradise.

"Perhaps one of the most unique features of this resort is its hydroponic farm, the first of its kind in any resort in the world. Vegetables, fruit, edible flowers, and herbs are grown using a unique pesticide-free process that delivers spectacular results. You will quickly taste for yourself at the resort's enticing restaurants." Dine poolside at Mediterraneo, soak up the vibe at Santorini, or go for Japanese at Tokyo Bay, as fine dining is a hallmark of this resort.

Relax with the warm sun and tropical breezes at CuisinArt, a Golf, Spa and Beach Resort.

CUISINART GOLF RESORT & SPA
Rendezvous Bay
Anguilla 2640, British West Indies
cuisinartresort.com

ANGUILLA

Viceroy Anguilla

This is definitely not your grandmother's Caribbean. There is nary a tropical print in sight at the über-chic Viceroy.

This posh resort, nestled on 35 acres fronting Meads and Barnes Bays, is a hipster's haven. Its blazing white exterior hits all the right angles and serves as the perfect frame for the chic interiors styled by famed designer Kelly Wearstler. The 76 rooms, 80 suites, and 32 villas are dramatically understated in shades of white, cream, and khaki. The sleek accommodations will make any urban dweller feel instantly at home, while the A-plus amenities, like Sferra custom-designed bed linens and silver travertine outdoor showers, pamper the privileged.

The two-level oceanfront Spa has a serene setting with a dash of contemporary élan while focusing on mental, spiritual, and physical well-being. Go beyond the traditional facial or body treatment and elevate your lifestyle with a healthy cooking class or meditation session.

Two marvelous white-sand beaches and a stunning pool are the nerve center of this hotspot, though the five restaurants and bars run a close second with their sensational views, cool breezes, and captivating cuisine. Feast on Asian accented seafood at Cobà, enjoy casual all-day dining at Aleta, savor the flavors of the Caribbean at the Bamboo Grill & Bar, or slip in for a snack at the Half Shell, which is carved into the cliffs along Barnes Bay. As soon as the sun begins to set, wander over to The Sunset Lounge, with its adults-only infinity pool and a DJ spinning tunes.

"For a slice of the cosmopolitan Caribbean, visit the Viceroy Anguilla."

VICEROY ANGUILLA RESORT & RESIDENCES
P.O. 8028 West End
Anguilla, 2640 British West Indies
viceroyhotelsandresorts.com

ANTIGUA

Curtain Bluff Resort

Leave your worries (and your wallet) behind when visiting Curtain Bluff.

If love means never having to say you're sorry, then Curtain Bluff means never having to say "no." This exclusive resort includes everything, so you can snorkel, sail, sip, and sup to your heart's content. Curtain Bluff has been inviting guests to its gracious home for over 50 years – just one of the reasons this place has so many repeat guests.

"Within an hour, I found myself 'on island time' relaxing at Curtain Bluff." The 72 rooms and suites rest along the beach and bluff. All accommodations are comfortable and cheery with tropical motifs and rattan furnishings. With features like pull-out beds and oversized space, it is clear that Curtain Bluff was designed with families in mind. Water skis and Hobie cats and tennis courts, oh my! The recreational opportunities are truly limitless. Rather like an upscale version of the summer camp you once loved, Curtain Bluff lets you fill your days with athletic and relaxing pursuits. "Sip a cup of lemongrass ginger tea (grown in the hotel's own garden) at the 5,000 square-foot spa before you surrender to a detoxifying Caribbean green coffee body wrap. Spa treatments are not included in the price, but worth the extra charge."

Meals are prepared by French-born chef, Christophe Blatz, who trained under the likes of Alain Ducasse and spent time manning the stoves at several Michelin starred restaurants in France before decamping to Antigua and Curtain Bluff.

CURTAIN BLUFF RESORT
St. John's
Antigua, West Indies
curtainbluff.com

ANTIGUA

Jumby Bay, A Rosewood Resort

Escape to Jumby Bay, a private 300 acre island set two miles off the coast of Antigua.

First discovered by Christopher Columbus, this former sugar plantation has been on the map for savvy travelers since its opening in 1983. Accessible from the mainland by private boat service, Jumby Bay is a sophisticated resort.

With 40 rooms, suites, and villas spread throughout the island and connected by charming stone paths, Jumby Bay offers an exclusive world with extreme privacy. All accommodations are near the beach and feature ocean views. The décor is a chic blend of West-Indian influences and English plantation manor style, with louvered doors, mahogany furniture, and four-poster beds. "I fell in love with the new beach suites, each with magnificent vaulted ceilings, a living room area opening to the beautiful bedroom, and huge dressing room and bath, but the pièce de résistance is the outdoor garden courtyard with shower and soaking tub. The only thing better is having this suite with a private pool!"

Jumby Bay is a naturalist's haven. Pasture Bay Beach, one of the island's three powdery, white-sand beaches, is home to the endangered Hawksbill turtle. A variety of rare birds and even sheep, whose ancestors were brought here over 300 years ago, also share this lovely spot.

Windsurfing, snorkeling, and other watersports are among the many services included with a stay at Jumby Bay. The living is easy here, where you can drop the kids off at Rose Buds and retreat to Sense Spa or bliss out by the infinity-edge oceanfront pool.

Jumby means "friendly spirit" in Arawak, and the resort takes its name seriously with a caring staff and pleasant attitude. Jumby Bay offers relaxed dining in four different settings.

Indulge your fantasies of a private tropical island at Jumby Bay.

**JUMBY BAY
A ROSEWOOD RESORT**
St. John's
Antigua, West Indies
rosewoodhotels.com

BAHAMAS

The Cove Atlantis

Take a little bit of Las Vegas' penchant for big impressions and mix in glorious Bahamian sunshine, and you have Atlantis. This over-the-top resort is mind-boggling. If they don't have it here, you don't want it. Casinos, aquariums, pools, restaurants, spa, water park, dolphin encounter, live entertainment, even a speedway – it's all here. So how do you take what you want and leave the rest behind? Book a stay at the exclusive Cove Atlantis and you will get the best of both worlds.

The Cove is the jewel-in-the-crown of Atlantis. Designed for adults only, this upscale all-suite property has an unmatched intimacy and luxury. All suites sport stunning ocean views and a contemporary décor. Club level suites come with the added bonus of a private lounge and dedicated concierge – a serious boon for guests trying to sort out this resort's dizzying array of recreational pursuits.

From its seductive shimmering pool with private cabanas to its outdoor gaming opportunities to its dining, Cain at The Cove is definitely the place to be, and it is available exclusively to Cove guests. Of course, an entire world of dolphin encounters, golf, spa, dining, and shopping awaits within the larger Atlantis complex.

From steak and sushi to sandwiches and snapper, you can certainly take your pick from a world of culinary destinations at Atlantis, but right here at The Cove you can dig in to celebrity chef Bobby Flay's outpost of New York's Mesa Grill.

Having your cake and eating it too is easy at The Cove Atlantis, where you can drink it all in and then retreat to a private and luxurious world.

THE COVE ATLANTIS
Paradise Island, Bahamas
atlantis.com

BAHAMAS

One&Only Ocean Club

It is called Paradise Island for a reason, and the island's One&Only Ocean Club is a tropical nirvana.

Once a grand private estate, One&Only Ocean Club is a stylish resort with delightful accommodations, spectacular gardens, and impeccable service. The landscaped gardens are unlike any in the Caribbean. Based on Versailles, the gardens have seven terraced levels. Each plateau features rock ridges and stone steps, and magnificent European marble and bronze statues can be found within the grounds. The majestic gardens are topped off with a 12th century stone Augustinian cloister.

The 86 rooms, 14 suites, and 5 villas are decorated in a blended contemporary, tropical décor and a classic British Colonial style, and all rooms have balconies or terraces. "The British traditional twist with contemporary splash is refreshingly fun." Villas are the perfect choice for families seeking a bit more space.

One&Only Ocean Club provides a nice selection of dining, including renowned chef Jean-Georges Vongerichten's Dune. The Courtyard Terrace is an elegant setting, with a sparkling fountain, candle-lit reflecting pool, and overhanging palms, or hop over to sister property Atlantis for a world of choices.

"Wind up or wind down at this resort where the One&Only Spa is a tranquil setting for relaxation." Balinese-style treatment villas set a seductive tone and all treatments conclude with a lovely Japanese tea ceremony. The highly respected 18-hole Tom Weiskopf-designed golf course thrills and delights golfers. Water sports, tennis, local excursions, and a terrific children's program are among the other pursuits.

ONE&ONLY OCEAN CLUB
Nassau, Bahamas
oneandonlyresorts.com

BARBADOS

Sandy Lane

Barbados has a warm, friendly spirit blended with the elegant traditions of Britain. The glittering turquoise Caribbean Sea, gentle hills, and perfect beaches make for a glorious tropical setting.

The west coast of Barbados has been nicknamed "the platinum coast" because of its stunning setting and exclusive resorts. It is Sandy Lane that stands out among the crowd and is revered as one of the world's best. Committed to providing the highest levels of service in the most luxurious setting, Sandy Lane is where the elite head when they need to get away from it all.

Understated elegance defines the 96 rooms, 16 suites, and 1 villa at Sandy Lane. Designed to mimic the refinement of a palatial home, these accommodations are sophisticated, yet inviting.

Sandy Lane draws sun seekers who want nothing more than to dig their toes in the luscious sand, but it is equally well known for its fantastic golf. Three courses await players, including the renowned Green Monkey course, designed by Tom Fazio and carved out of a stone quarry. Challenging and scenic, this course is available exclusively to Sandy Lane guests.

"While some resorts cater to couples or families, Sandy Lane is well suited for both. It can be restful and romantic or fun and full of activities." Nine tennis courts, the exceptional Treehouse children's program, and a knock-your-socks-off Spa are among the highlights.

From the fine dining at L'Acajou to the casual, lighter dining at Bajan Blue, the Spa Café, and the Clubhouse Restaurant, there is something for everyone. Take home more than just a souvenir when you take part in a lecture or class at the Culinary School.

"I wish I could live the good life at the alluring Sandy Lane forever!"

SANDY LANE
St. James
Barbados, West Indies BB24024
sandylane.com

BERMUDA

Cambridge Beaches Resort & Spa

Bermuda is an enchanted island with pastel houses, manicured lawns, and pink beaches. One of the wealthiest countries in the world, Bermuda honors its British history while incorporating an island feel.

"When I think of Bermuda, I think of Cambridge Beaches, Bermuda's finest resort." Situated on a 30-acre private peninsula on the western tip of the island in Somerset, it is nearly surrounded by ocean and bay waters. Opened in 1928, Cambridge Beaches is a distinguished pink cottage colony with four private beaches and numerous coves. Impeccable service and a spectacular setting make an adult-only holiday at Cambridge Beaches unforgettably romantic.

Evoking Bermuda's seagoing heritage, several of the resort's cottages, such as Windswept and Pegem, date back over 200 years, but multi-million dollar renovations have elevated this resort to one of the world's best. All 94 rooms, suites, and cottages feature a charming, contemporary décor and with views like these, you will never want to leave.

Just in case the lapping of the ocean waves has not lulled you, the Ocean Spa, with its Aquarian baths and European-trained staff, is on hand to soothe your body and soul. The natural ocean pool and full-service marina with a wide variety of watersports, will keep water enthusiasts at bay.

"See the world through pink-colored glasses at Cambridge Beaches."

CAMBRIDGE BEACHES RESORT & SPA
30 Kings Point
Somerset MA 02 Bermuda
cambridgebeaches.com

Everything at Cambridge Beaches is designed to take advantage of the views. Restaurants are oceanview and poolside, but these spots deliver great taste in addition to stunning views. Tamarisk, Cambridge Beaches' fine dining venue, has been tapped by *Food + Wine* Magazine as a top spot with good reason.

CAYMAN ISLANDS

The Ritz-Carlton, Grand Cayman

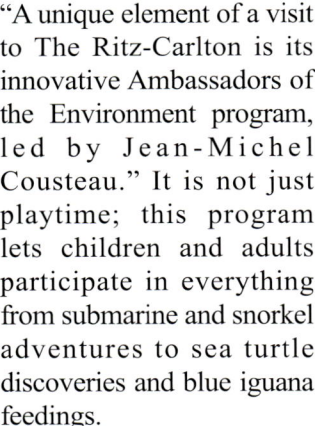

From sea to shining sea, The Ritz-Carlton, Grand Cayman really sparkles.

Stretching from the North Sound to the Caribbean Sea, The Ritz-Carlton, Grand Cayman occupies a prime 144-acre location on Seven Mile Beach. It does not get any better than this top resort, where location reigns supreme and amenities are five-star.

The Ritz-Carlton's 365 accommodations are the very definition of relaxed elegance. Generously sized, the pastel-hued rooms and suites are enhanced with cheery English country floral patterned fabrics and elegant British Colonial style furnishings.

Five restaurants are part of the well-rounded experience, but do not miss a chance to dine at Blue by Eric Ripert, of New York's famed Le Bernardin, who is world renowned for his creative takes on fish.

The Caymans are teeming with marine life and the pristine waters are a focal point at this resort. Stretch out on Seven Mile Beach, scuba or snorkel with stingrays, tropical fish, and sea turtles, or swim in the pool. Dry off and head to the water-laced nine-hole Greg Norman-designed Blue Tip golf course. Even the Silver Rain Spa is inspired by the waters with Swiss hydrotherapy and La Prairie products and treatments.

"A unique element of a visit to The Ritz-Carlton is its innovative Ambassadors of the Environment program, led by Jean-Michel Cousteau." It is not just playtime; this program lets children and adults participate in everything from submarine and snorkel adventures to sea turtle discoveries and blue iguana feedings.

"Something for everyone of every age makes a vacation at The Ritz-Carlton, Grand Cayman truly special."

THE RITZ-CARLTON, GRAND CAYMAN
Seven Mile Beach, Grand Cayman
Cayman Islands
ritzcarlton.com

JAMAICA

Jamaica Inn

Winston Churchill stayed at Jamaica Inn for the light, declaring it was the best for his watercolors, and Noel Coward, Errol Flynn, and Ian Fleming were also regular guests. It is certainly no wonder - with its lovely stretch of private beach, charming accommodations, and timeless elegance!

Just outside of Ocho Rios, Jamaica Inn is a genteel hideaway steeped in tradition. The 47 suites are decorated with traditional pieces and Jamaican antiques. "All rooms enjoy terrific views of the sea and gardens from their spacious balconies. Private beachfront verandas create an old world feel."

Grand traditions are revived at Jamaica Inn. Waiters dressed in refined red jackets serve tropical drinks on silver trays to parched sunbathers, while guests enjoy Caribbean-influenced European cuisine in the evenings. Elegant without ever being stuffy, Jamaica Inn makes guests feel as if they were at home. Indeed, this is one of many reasons the resort attracts a loyal clientele that visits annually.

Though water sports are available and golf or tennis is nearby, the favorite pastime here is utter relaxation. The thatched umbrellas that dot the pristine beach are perfect for catching up on the latest bestseller, daydreaming, or even taking a leisurely nap, but don't miss the locally influenced treatments at the oceanfront spa. Nestled on the coral cliffs of Cutlass Bay, KiYara Ocean Spa's natural setting lulls you into relaxation before your treatment even begins.

"Civilized and aristocratic, Jamaica Inn is a gem in the Caribbean. I always feel like I am returning home when I arrive here."

JAMAICA INN
Ocho Rios, St. Ann
Jamaica, West Indies
jamaicainn.com

JAMAICA

Round Hill Hotel and Villas

A former pineapple plantation, Round Hill Hotel and Villas has epitomized chic since opening in 1952.

John Pringle, a successful Jamaican businessman, envisioned Round Hill as a vacation destination for the international elite. He developed a hotel and divided the former plantation into 29 lots. Prominent Americans and Europeans soon built cottages on these lots, and Round Hill's reputation as one of the world's most exclusive resorts was sealed.

Today's visitors to Round Hill may reside in one of the 36 oceanfront rooms in the Pineapple House or in one of the 27 private villas. The cathedral ceilings and louvered windows of the rooms are reminiscent of grand plantation manors. Rich woods are complemented by splashes of color in the various prints. The fabrics are influenced by designer Ralph Lauren, owner of one of Round Hill's private villas.

The 27 villas, surrounded by 30 lush tropical acres, offer a very private way to experience Round Hill. While they are individually decorated by the owners, all reflect the relaxed elegance of this posh resort. Most have private swimming pools and all are staffed with a private housekeeper who prepares you a delicious breakfast daily.

Three settings for the main dining room include the seaside terrace, upper terrace, or Georgian room. The cuisine uses fresh, local ingredients to enhance its Jamaican and international specialties. The spa, tucked inside an 18th century plantation house, is a delightful retreat.

"Whether I am playing a set of tennis, reclining on the beach, or wandering through the gardens, I feel the magic of Round Hill."

ROUND HILL HOTEL & VILLAS
John Pringle Drive
Montego Bay
Jamaica, West Indies
roundhilljamaica.com

NEVIS

Four Seasons Resort Nevis

The luxurious Four Seasons Resort Nevis is located on a fabulous four-mile stretch of powder sand beach.

Nevis, in the West Indies archipelago of the Leeward Islands, enjoys a rich history. This verdant island of fertile volcanic soil was once a playground for wealthy sugarcane plantation owners, but is better known as the birthplace of Alexander Hamilton. Since the island enjoys little development it has retained its quiet charm.

Two-story gingerbread trimmed cottages house 179 rooms and 17 suites which blend with the tropical setting. All rooms combine Anglo-Indian mahogany furniture with contemporary style and all the conveniences of the 21st century. From your private terrace or screened veranda, enjoy views of the golf course or ocean...of course, the most prized are the 143 facing the beach. The Great House, like a West Indies plantation house, is home to the Library Bar, Coral Grill, and Neve restaurants.

The glorious Pinney's Beach is the centerpiece of this resort, while those who want to keep sand out of their toes will stretch out on a chaise by one of the three infinity swimming pools.

Activities are boundless… tennis courts, health club, relaxing spa, and an amazing array of water sports. Families appreciate the Kids for All Seasons program. The Robert Trent Jones II 18-hole golf course is one of the Caribbean's finest, with sensational views as it meanders up the hills toward Mt. Nevis and down to the glittering sea.

"Do as I do at the Four Seasons Resort Nevis. Have a family reunion or a romantic weekend, walk the beach and unwind, but do not miss their delicious Caribbean lobster club sandwich, another weakness of mine!"

FOUR SEASONS RESORT NEVIS
Pinney's Beach
Charlestown, Nevis, West Indies
fourseasons.com

PUERTO RICO

The Ritz-Carlton, San Juan Hotel, Spa & Casino

The Ritz-Carlton, San Juan brings the best of Puerto Rico together in its beachfront setting. Minutes from the historic sites of Old San Juan, the resort enjoys a lush eight acres of privacy and privilege in the exclusive area of Isla Verde.

The 406 rooms and 10 suites are decorated with a blend of tradition and tropical flair. Rattan furnishings, vibrant colors, and contemporary artwork by Puerto Rican artists show off local pride, while luxuries like Frette linens and gleaming marble bathrooms are decidedly Ritz-Carlton.

The sparkling oceanfront swimming pool and sandy beach are paramount, but the action never stops. Puerto Rico is known for its gaming, so roll the dice in style at the resort's 24-hour casino. Bliss out at the 12,000-square-foot spa, where botanicals from the nearby El Yunque rainforest are the basis of many therapeutic rituals. The ever-present rhythm of the ocean inspires renewal whether you are having a treatment, soaking in the whirlpool, steaming in the sauna, or exercising in the fitness center.

When it is time for a little culinary indulgence, The Ritz-Carlton certainly delivers with five dining options, including Mares, a café overlooking the pool, and casual beach fare at The Ocean Bar & Grill. New York's favorite Italian restaurant, Il Mulino, has opened an outpost here, as well as BLT Steak, by leading chef Laurent Touroundel.

"The Ritz-Carlton is more than family friendly and provides fabulous activities with its Ritz Kids program. Cooking classes, arts and crafts, and water sports are just some of the fun. Experience exciting San Juan at its best at The Ritz-Carlton."

THE RITZ-CARLTON, SAN JUAN HOTEL, SPA & CASINO
6961 Avenue of the Governors
Isla Verde, Puerto Rico 00979
ritzcarlton.com

PUERTO RICO

The St. Regis Bahia Beach Resort

If there is a patron saint of island getaways, he surely blessed The St. Regis Bahia Beach Resort. This Puerto Rican resort has a serious "wow" factor. From cuisine by internationally renowned chef Jean-Georges Vongerichten to the golf course designed by Robert Trent Jones, Jr. to the Remède Spa, this spot has star power.

It all begins with a glorious location. The St. Regis is snuggled on a white-sand, sugar-soft beach at the foot of the lush El Yunque rainforest. The natural beauty of the landscape is matched only by the stunning, curvaceous design of the golf course, which snakes its way along the ocean and throughout the property.

The 104 rooms and 35 suites offer a contemporary take on island design with rattan ceiling fans, custom-designed cherry furnishings, and dramatic nature photographs. The classic St. Regis butler service is just one of the many plush amenities that come "standard" at this exclusive resort.

"If the stylish surroundings and stunning scenery have not captured your heart, the plentiful activities and posh amenities certainly will." Three restaurants, with Jean-Georges' acclaimed Fern, are part of the five star experience, as is the serene spa. From the tennis center, fitness facilities, and aquatic center to the children's Iguana Club, the St. Regis leaves no stone unturned in the quest for the perfect Caribbean vacation.

THE ST. REGIS BAHIA BEACH RESORT
State Road 187, Km. 4.2
Rio Grande, Puerto Rico 00745
stregis.com/bahiabeach

ST. BARTHÉLEMY

Eden Rock

This chic island is an alluring combination of stunning Caribbean landscape coupled with French savoir-faire. Though just over eight square miles, Saint-Barthélemy, affectionately known as St. Barths, packs a stylish punch. It has a style and character all its own.

Eden Rock, St. Barths' first hotel, was established in the 1950s by adventurer and famous aviator Rémy de Haenen. Originally a private residence, Eden Rock enjoys a unique and favorable setting carved out of a rocky promontory in Baie de Saint-Jean. Surrounded by delicately soft beaches and the turquoise waters of the bay, Eden Rock is a spectacular hideaway. Its stylish setting and incredible privacy made it a favorite of stars like Robert Mitchum and Greta Garbo, who famously sought "alone" time.

Eden Rock's selection of 34 rooms, suites, cottages, and villas rests on the water's edge. The individually designed interiors are breezy and romantic, some with traditional décor and others with contemporary flair. "Become a celebrity but outsmart the paparazzi; stay in your private, secluded villa at the Eden Rock." The hotel's treasure trove of artwork is museum worthy and guests feeling inspired can take a watercolor or oil painting class with the artist-in-residence.

"St. Barths' French accent translates to seriously sophisticated cuisine, and the restaurants at Eden Rock are no exception." Enjoy breakfast or lunch on the beach at the appropriately named Sand Bar and savor a gourmet dinner at On the Rocks, where three levels of dining frame stunning bay views.

"Eden Rock lives up to its reputation as a true hideaway."

EDEN ROCK
Baie de Saint-Jean
97133 Saint-Barthélemy,
French West Indies
edenrockhotel.com

ST. BARTHÉLEMY

Hotel Guanahani & Spa

Looking for a getaway with a unique flavor? Look no further than Hotel Guanahani & Spa. This resort has its own style and personality.

All of the 30 rooms and 37 suites are housed in bougainvillea and hibiscus colored cottages nestled among the fragrant gardens. Ranging in vivid colors from yellow and purple to indigo and bright green, the cottages have a distinctive contemporary West Indian flavor. Each cottage has an individualized and vibrant personality. The accommodations have an eclectic décor, while rare woods and cotton fabrics remind you that you are in the luscious Caribbean. The suites bring the outdoors in with private terraces and gardens, and some have private pools; perfect for families, as are the Kindergarten and Junior's programs for children.

Guanahani's location at the end of Grand Cul de Sac Bay indulges your relaxation with two gorgeous beaches at your disposal. One beach faces the reef protected bay, while the other is located on the ocean side of Marigot Bay. "Whether you fancy the waves or prefer a gentle swim, you will be pleased. Two freshwater swimming pools provide scenic spots for a lazy afternoon. Snorkel or head straight for the spa - the Clarins beauty treatments are luxuriously decadent."

Three restaurants live up to the island's reputation. A tropical refreshing breakfast buffet at the Indigo Restaurant is a terrific way to begin your day, while Indigo on the Beach is just the spot for barefoot casual dining. Dinner is served at Bartolomeo, which fuses Creole and French cuisine in a lush garden setting.

"To me, Guanahani is a slice of Saint-Tropez in the Caribbean. Let the spirit of the islands wash over you here."

HOTEL GUANAHANI & SPA
Anse de Grand Cul de Sac
97133 Saint-Barthélemy,
French West Indies
leguanahani.com

ST. JOHN

Caneel Bay, A Rosewood Resort

Tucked inside the 170 acre Virgin Islands National Park, this resort was "green" long before the term became popular. First developed by environmentalist Laurance Rockefeller in the 1950s, Caneel Bay was designed to live in harmony with nature. Surrounded by nature and seven pristine beaches, Caneel Bay has a lock on peace and quiet – there are no phones or televisions in the guestrooms to distract from the serenity.

The 166 accommodations are a breath of fresh air with soft colors, handcrafted furniture, and abundant use of native stones and natural woods reflecting the resort's founding principles. All rooms feature expansive views of the fragrant gardens, island's hillsides, or the sapphire sea. Once the Rockefeller family's home, Cottage 7 is one of the most requested accommodations at Caneel Bay.

"Caneel Bay is as equally well-suited for honeymooning couples as it is for families seeking quality time together." Adults may set sail for a neighboring island, take a garden tour, or enjoy an underwater adventure, while the Rose Buds Turtle Town welcomes children 12 and under with an enticing array of indoor and outdoor activities. Five restaurants from elegant to easy-breezy ensure lively or romantic evenings.

"Experience the lush, unspoiled beauty of the Caribbean at Caneel Bay, A Rosewood Resort."

**CANEEL BAY
A ROSEWOOD RESORT**
St. John, US Virgin Islands 00831
rosewoodhotels.com

ST. MARTIN

La Samanna

St. Martin's French and Dutch heritage gives this sophisticated Caribbean island an unmistakable European panache. Its lush foliage, true-blue waters, and sugar-soft beaches attract savvy travelers from all over the globe. Originally planned as a romantic retreat, today La Samanna is the island's most luxurious destination for all ages.

Located on the French side of the island, La Samanna, an Orient-Express resort, boasts 55 acres of beachfront property perfumed with fragrant foliage, but its location on Baie Longue, the largest and most beautiful beach on St. Martin, really sets it apart. With its crescent shape and aqua waters, Baie Longue is one of the finest and most secluded beaches in the world.

Blending the amenities of a luxury beachfront resort with the intimacy and individualized service of a private villa, La Samanna exudes an informal elegance. The 80 rooms and suites, plus a few incredible private villas are tastefully decorated with pleasant colors and island atmosphere. The reception, lobby, and dining areas have spectacular views and are bathed in sunlight and fresh sea air.

Life is good here, and a day at the beach is the ultimate luxury. Balinese bamboo beach cabanas are just the spot for sun-splashed relaxation or take that relaxation to another level at the sensational spa. Everything from windsurfing, waterskiing, snorkeling, sailing, and tennis will have you breaking a sweat in style.

Two restaurants spotlight sophisticated French and Caribbean cuisine, but La Samanna is perhaps best known for its impressive wine cellar – one of the largest collections in the Caribbean.

"Although La Samanna has stretched along the beach since my first visit way back in 1972, I continue to adore this elegant Caribbean resort. It will fulfill all of your tropical dreams."

LA SAMANNA
Baie Longue
97064 St. Martin, French West Indies
lasamanna.com or
orient-express.com

ST. THOMAS

The Ritz-Carlton, St. Thomas

The Ritz-Carlton is located on a private 30-acre waterfront estate with perfumed tropical gardens where color seems to explode. The magenta of the bougainvillea seems brighter and the sapphire sea seems richer here. The Ritz-Carlton graciously resides on the eastern tip of St. Thomas in the U.S. Virgin Islands. Peach stucco walls and coppertine roofs surrounded by trickling fountains and lush landscaping is reminiscent of a Mediterranean villa. All of the 157 rooms and 23 suites open out to the sea and exude elegance with a distinctly Caribbean atmosphere complete with pleasing colors and relaxing balconies.

Relax with a blended drink by the infinity swimming pool or enjoy a sail on the Lady Lynsey, the 53-foot luxury catamaran. Tension melts away at the spa, especially in one of its seaside cabanas. Get creative; take a watercolor class or learn sushi secrets from the resort's chef. Water sports, tennis, fitness facilities – it's all here and more. This resort is particularly ideal for families, as the fun-filled Ritz Kids program includes so much, from tennis lessons and beach games, such as volleyball and sack races, to Hobie cat sails and kayak races.

Dining options are plentiful. Coconut Grove and Sails, steps from the beach and pool, offer tropical cocktails and casual dining, while Great Bay Lounge is the spot for sushi and Asian-inspired delicacies. Bleuwater, an award-winning oceanfront restaurant, features the tastes of the Caribbean.

"Classic Caribbean and warm island spirit make The Ritz-Carlton, St. Thomas the island's best resort. It serves up the very best on a silver platter."

THE RITZ-CARLTON, ST. THOMAS
6900 Great Bay
St. Thomas, US Virgin Islands 00802
ritzcarlton.com

TURKS & CAICOS

Amanyara

Do you dream of a place where the only sound you hear is the gentle lapping of the ocean waves? Dreams become reality at Amanyara, which means "peaceful place."

This exclusive resort, in the Turks and Caicos part of the renowned collection of Aman Resorts, truly lives up to its name. From its serene architecture to its pristine setting, Amanyara is the antidote for civilization.

Retreat to your own private pavilion, where the lines between indoors and out are blissfully blurred. The 40 pavilions and private villas scattered amidst tranquil ponds, the pool, or ocean, offer the ultimate in privacy and space. From the open-air design to the soothing teak interiors and white-on-white palette, sophisticated simplicity reigns

Located on a dune above the white sand beach, the Beach Club features a grill menu, afternoon tea, and evening barbeques, with multiple indoor and outdoor seating options, including a terrace and expansive timber deck. From sea breezes to air conditioned interiors, The Restaurant focuses on Asian classics and modern Mediterranean dishes. Before dining, have a cocktail and watch the sun set from the Bar.

Amanyara's beachfront setting borders Northwest Point Marine National Park, so scuba diving and snorkeling rank among the top activities. Lounge on the white-sand beach or by the oceanfront pool, work out in the state-of-the-art fitness center, or chase that fuzzy yellow ball on the tennis courts, but be sure to schedule time at the stunning spa. From luxurious treatments and holistic therapies to outdoor yoga, this spa helps you surrender your stress at the door.

Tame your tension in the island paradise of Amanyara.

AMANYARA
Providenciales
Turks & Caicos,
British West Indies
amanyara.com

TURKS & CAICOS

Gansevoort Turks + Caicos

Take a little bit of New York's modern chic, blend with a slice of South Beach sizzle, and place it firmly on what is considered one of the world's best beaches, and you have the Gansevoort Turks + Caicos resort.

If the name sounds familiar, it's because it is. Gansevoort made a name for itself in Manhattan's Meatpacking District when it was still a neighborhood better known for butchers than for buzz and the Caribbean resort is quickly making waves as one of the tropics' trendiest.

Resting right on Grace Bay beach, this boutique resort has 55 rooms, 32 suites, and 4 penthouses, and nearly all have ocean views. Inside, the look is refreshingly sleek and urban modern. From the walls to the bed linens, crisp white dominates the color scheme with dark woods providing a dramatic contrast. Suites, ideal for families, are equipped with full kitchens boasting top-notch appliances that will make any home chef green with envy.

Of course, what this resort does best is entertain. Whether your favorite form of entertainment is lounging by the 7,000-square-foot infinity pool, digging your toes in the sand, dancing to the beat at Bagatelle Bistrot, or practicing downward dog at the Exhale Spa, the Gansevoort has you covered.

Dance to a different beat at the Gansevoort Turks + Caicos.

GANSEVOORT TURKS + CAICOS
Grace Bay Beach
Turks & Caicos, British West Indies
gansevoortturksandcaicos.com

TURKS & CAICOS

Grace Bay Club

Leave the world behind at Grace Bay Club in the Turks & Caicos.

The Turks & Caicos remain relatively undiscovered despite their white-sand beaches and cerulean water. Comprised of more than 40 different islands and cays and ringed by a barrier reef, the Turks & Caicos is an underwater paradise with crystal clear waters teeming with marine life.

Located on the peaceful island of Providenciales, Grace Bay Club is an exclusive getaway. Nestled on part of a twelve-mile stretch of powdery beach, Grace Bay Club encompasses three separate areas – the adults-only, all-suite Hotel, the family-friendly Villas where oversized suites await the arrival of little feet, and the ultra-luxurious 22 Estate Residences.

Secluded and luxurious, the resort resembles a Spanish hacienda with its red-tiled roofs and trickling fountains. Rattan and wicker Caribbean furniture meets a contemporary flavor with an informal elegance throughout.

"Everyone feels special here, especially kids who are treated to the 'Very Important Kids' program. From half and full day excursions to fun and exciting events at the resort, kids of all ages are entertained." Adults will find the beach and the oceanfront pools beckon, but Grace Bay Club also entices guests to climb out of their chaises and get out on the water with a variety of water sports. If wave running doesn't float your boat, traipse over to the Anani Spa for a refreshing and rejuvenating experience. After a day in the sun and surf, visit one of the five restaurants and bars for a meal with a view.

Let the gentle trade winds of Grace Bay Club cosset you and yours.

GRACE BAY CLUB
Grace Bay Circle Road
Providenciales
Turks & Caicos Islands,
British West Indies
gracebayclub.com

TURKS & CAICOS

Parrot Cay

Parrot Cay introduces you to a world of serenity on a private island in the Turks & Caicos.

Parrot Cay is a stylish Caribbean hideaway with 1,000 acres of unspoiled landscape, a mile-long powdery, white sand beach, and crystal clear water, only accessible by private launch.

The 58-room resort reflects a modern colonial sensibility. Parrot Cay's main buildings and beachfront villas were designed to blend with the natural environment and landscape while avoiding disruption of the island's skyline.

The resort's serene décor is a study in minimalist luxury. Soft, polished woods complement romantic four-poster beds swathed in white muslin. Many rooms showcase inspiring ocean views. Private villas are available for rent through the resort and boast private plunge or swimming pools.

This enlightened resort is dedicated to relaxation and personal well-being, whether you are taking a swim in the beautiful infinity-edge pool, practicing Pilates, or sipping a fresh juice from the juice bar. The COMO Shambhala Spa is a signature at Parrot Cay. This Eastern inspired holistic spa's mind and body treatments include meditation and contemplation, Chi balancing, Thai and Chinese massage, and yoga, even on the beach. Several times throughout the year, Shambhala Spa invites guests to participate in week-long retreats designed by leading yoga and Pilates masters.

If bonefishing and scuba diving excursions by boat charters oversatiate your appetite for adventure, opt for snorkeling, sunset cruises, or a tiki hut lunch.

In keeping with its principle of promoting healthy lifestyles, the two restaurants have developed a splendid, light cuisine blended with Asian, Caribbean, and Mediterranean influences.

Parrot Cay offers peaceful seclusion in the Turks & Caicos.

PARROT CAY
Providenciales
Turks & Caicos,
British West Indies
parrotcay.com

VIRGIN GORDA

Rosewood Little Dix Bay

Rosewood Little Dix Bay, on the island's northwest corner, was developed by Laurance Rockefeller in the early 1960s. Noted for his conservation efforts, Rockefeller's dream was to create a resort where natural beauty and native vegetation coexisted with travelers. Long before Rockefeller, Christopher Columbus discovered and named Virgin Gorda on his second world voyage.

Surrounded by sea grapes and bougainvillea, the rooms and suites are not visible from the sea. The essence of nature is instilled in the 105 rooms with soothing tones and Pacific Rim furnishings. Native stones and rocks are used decoratively, while balconies and terraces spotlight splendid garden views or seascapes.

"Virgin Gorda's stunning scenery begs to be explored. For a little adventure, try seeing the island by horseback, Jeep safari, or nature hikes. Better yet, have the hotel take you by one of their Boston Whaler boats to a secluded beach for a picnic lunch."

Go native at Sense Spa, where you can partake in treatments like an Island salt scrub or a goat milk body wrap. "I always allow relaxation time before and after a treatment to soak in the spa pool or daydream while overlooking the gardens and bay below."

The entertaining Rose Buds children's program educates younger guests about the local environment. Based on Rockefeller's founding principles, the children's program is located in a mahogany preserve. From shell collecting adventures to treasure hunts, the fun is limitless.

Rosewood Little Dix Bay's intimate restaurant settings feature tastes of the Caribbean.

"It may be hard to believe there is a world outside Rosewood Little Dix Bay!"

ROSEWOOD LITTLE DIX BAY
Lee Road, The Valley
Virgin Gorda, British Virgin Islands
VG1150
rosewoodhotels.com

AGRA • AMELIA ISLAND • AMSTERDAM • ANGUILLA • ANTIG
AVON • BADEN-BADEN • BAHAMAS • BALI • BANFF • BAN
BAUX DE PROVENCE • BEIJING • BEIRUT • BERLIN • BER
BORA BORA • BORDEAUX • BOSTON • BRUSSELS • BUDAP
CANYON POINT • CAP D'ANTIBES • CAPE TOWN • CAPRI
CHIANG RAI • CHICAGO • CHOBE • COLCA CANYON • CON D
DALLAS • DAMASCUS • DEIA • DRESDEN • DUBAI • DUBLIN •
FEZ • FIESOLE • FIJI • FLORENCE • FRANKFURT • FRANSC
GURGAON-NEW DELHI • HAMPSHIRE • HANOI • HAWKE'S
HYDERABAD • IGUASSU FALLS • INTERLAKEN • ISTANBUL •
JOHANNESBURG • KAUAI • KEY BISCAYNE • KOH KOOD
LAGUNA BEACH • LAGUNA NIGUEL • LAKE COMO • LAKE LOUI

Valerie Wilson's World

LENOX • LHASA • LIMA • LISBON • LOMBOK • LONDON •
MADEIRA • MADRID • MALDIVES • MARBELLA • MARRAKECH
MEXICO CITY • MIAMI • MILAN • MONTE CARLO • MOREMI G
MYKONOS • NAPA • NEVIS • NEW DELHI • NEW MILTON • NE
ORLANDO • PALM BEACH • PARIS • PARK CITY • PHILADELPH
PUERTO RICO • PUNTA MITA • QUEENSTOWN • RABAT • R
ROME • SABI SAND GAME RESERVE • SACRED VALLEY •
SAN DIEGO • SAN FRANCISCO • SAN MIGUEL DE ALLEND
SARDINIA • SCIACCA • SCOTTSDALE • SEATTLE • SERENGETI • S
ST. JOHN • ST. MARTIN • ST. MICHAELS • ST. MORITZ • ST. P
TARANGIRE NATIONAL PARK • TAUPO • TOKYO • TORONTO • TUC
VENCE • VENICE • VIENNA • VIRGIN GORDA • WASHINGTON